The African-American Travel Guide

Wayne C. Robinson

HUNTER
PUBLISHING

Hunter Publishing, Inc.
130 Campus Drive, Edison NJ 08818
☎ 732 225 1900 or 800 255 0343; Fax 732 417 1744
E-mail: hunterpub@emi.net

In Canada:
1220 Nicholson Road, Newmarket, Ontario
Canada L3Y 7V1
☎ 800 399 6858 / fax 800 363 2665

ISBN 1-55650-797-6
© 1998 Wayne C. Robinson

For complete information about the hundreds of other travel guides
offered by Hunter Publishing, visit our Web site at:
http://www.hunterpublishing.com

Every effort has been made to ensure that the information in this book is correct, but the publisher and author do not assume, and hereby disclaim, any liability to any party for loss or damage caused by errors, omissions, misleading information or potential problems caused by information in this guide, even if these are a result of negligence, accident or any other cause.

Prices, hours of operation, amenities and conditions change over the course of time, and readers are advised to contact the locations prior to planning a visit. The attractions, museums, restaurants, shops and businesses listed in this book have been reviewed over a period of time, and reflect the personal experiences of the author and other contributors to this guide. The author and publishers cannot be held responsible for the experiences of the reader with regard to the establishments listed herein. We welcome comments and suggestions from our readers for future editions.

Maps by Lissa K. Dailey, © Hunter Publishing, Inc.

Cover photo: *Beale Street, Memphis / B.B. King's Blues Club & Restaurant*
Courtesy Memphis Convention & Visitors Bureau

Photo of author on page iii by Rita A. Robinson

Special thanks to the many establishments, historical organizations,
tourist boards, and chambers of commerce who graciously
provided photographs for use in this guide.

3   4   5

About the Author

Wayne C. Robinson has traveled extensively throughout the United States and Canada during the last 20 years. After spending most of his childhood in Boston, Massachusetts, Wayne moved with his family to Germany as a military dependent, where he graduated from Munich American High School. He attended North Texas State University and is a graduate of the International Tour Management Institute (ITMI) in San Francisco, California. He was a Navy journalist and has worked with the *Villager* newspaper in Austin, Texas.

Wayne currently works as a seasonal tour director for tour operators around the US, and is also an international and domestic flight attendant for a major air carrier. He was previously employed by Royal Caribbean Cruise Line, Ltd. in the Caribbean Islands and Southern California.

Readers may send comments to *The African-American Travel Guide,* c/o Hunter Publishing, 239 South Beach Road, Hobe Sound, FL 33455, or by e-mail to afrotravel@msn.com.

Acknowledgments

I would like to thank the following individuals and organizations who have contributed so much to this book:

Atlanta Convention & Visitors Bureau; Georgia Peach State Black Tourism Association; Baltimore Area Convention and Visitors Association; Francis Smiley and the Alabama Bureau of Tourism and Travel, for their dedicated research and their permission to use excerpts from their travel guide, *Alabama's Black Heritage;* Birmingham Convention & Visitors Center; Greater Boston Convention & Visitors Bureau, Inc.; African Meeting House in Boston; Performance Media; Chicago Sun-Times Features, Inc. for their permission to use excerpts of their publication, *Illinois Generations; A Traveler's Guide to African American Heritage* and Dr. Gwendolyn Robinson, Muriel Wilson, Ramon Price, Willie Dixon, Dr. Charles Branham, Constance White, Ann Ridge, Dr. James Grossman, Dr. Yvonne King-Smith, Maynard Crossland, Kathryn Harris, Mildred Parette, Glenette Tilly-Turner, Dr. Donn F. Bailey, Dr. Juliette E.K. Walker, Rev. Gessel Berry, Vernon Jarrett, Amina Dickerson, Charles Sherrell, Dr. Delores Cross, Abena Joan Brown, Hermene Hartman, Dr. Harold Pates, Lisa Ely, Billy Montgomery, Susan Mogerman, Cheryl Kennedy, Joseph Banks, Rose Jennings, Gerald Cooper and Michael DeVaul for their dedicated research and contributions; Dallas Convention & Visitors Bureau; Metropolitan Detroit Convention & Visitors Bureau; African-American Tourism Council of Indiana; Indianapolis Convention & Visitors Association; Los Angeles Convention & Visitors Bureau; Greater Los Angeles African-American Chamber of Commerce; Memphis Convention & Visitors Bureau; Donna Monroe of Memphis, TN, for her editing assistance; Mobile Convention & Visitors Bureau; Montgomery Convention & Visitors Center; Greater New Orleans Black Tourism Network; Louisiana Office of Tourism; New Orleans Metropolitan Convention & Visitors Bureau; New York Convention & Visitors Bureau; Harlem Visitors and Convention Association; Philadelphia Tribune; Philadelphia Convention & Visitors Center; San Francisco African American Historical and Cultural Society; San Francisco Convention and Visitors Bureau; Oakland Convention & Visitors Authority; African American Chamber of Commerce/East Bay; Washington, DC Convention and Visitors Association for their dedicated research and contributions from their *African American Historical Attractions Guide;* Metropolitan Toronto Convention & Visitors Association; Soul in Canada/Black Tourism in Canada; William N.T. Wylie of Parks Canada; Henry Bishop and Robert French of the Black Cultural Centre for Nova Scotia; Multicultural Council of Windsor & Essex County; Windsor Essex County & Pelee Island Convention & Visitors Bureau; and Rita A. Robinson.

Contents

Maps

Dedication

I would like to thank the following people for their continued support during the writing of this book: My mother, Sylvia E. Robinson; my sisters, Robyn and Jylle; my brother, Daryl; Rita A. Robinson; and my daughter, Ashley. I would also like to thank Hunter Publishing for the opportunity that helped change the direction of my life. Most importantly, I would like to thank Jesus Christ for my salvation, His mercy and His unconditional and undeserving love toward me.

Introduction

The African-American Travel Guide provides information about the history, progress and contributions of African-Americans and African-Canadians, and provides hundreds of listings so that travelers may support the many African-American owned or operated historical sites, attractions, restaurants, businesses and restaurants.

History

The Slave Era

Probably the most tumultuous period in the history of the African and African-American people is the slave era. Spanish and Portuguese explorers and settlers profited from the sale and use of African slaves. During the early 1600s a large labor force was required to produce tobacco, cotton and other crops grown on plantations in the Caribbean Islands and in Central and South America. In 1619, African slaves arrived in the southeastern corner of what was later to become the United States.

The slaves were treated harshly during their trip to the New World and upon their arrival. They were emotionally and physically abused, bought and sold like cattle, and separated from family members and loved ones. Even small children were taken from their mothers and fathers. Paradoxically, these harsh conditions built the foundation for historical, religious and cultural legacies that would be honored centuries later.

Most southern states maintained and supported slave ownership. By 1810 there were more than six million slaves in the southeastern US, with the highest concentrations in Alabama, Florida, Georgia, Louisiana, Mississippi, South Carolina, Virginia, and Texas. However, particularly in the northern states, abolitionists spoke out in opposition to slavery. This division later became one of the primary causes of the Civil War.

In 1820, the Missouri Compromise was the first of several moves by the US government to deal with the controversial issue of slavery. Although this measure merely prohibited slavery north of the state of Missouri, it set a precedent for other states.

Opposition to slavery became widespread, especially among the slaves. Abolitionists led revolts and published newspapers in their quest to end slavery throughout the US and Canada. By 1860, the North and the South had developed distinctly different social, economic and political views. Tempers flared as each faction tried to impose their own viewpoints on the entire country. Although the two sections had compromised for many years, the situation finally became explosive in 1861, and the Civil War broke out. It ended, many bloody battles later, in 1865. In 1862, while the war still raged, President Abraham Lincoln signed the Emancipation Proclamation, which prohibited slavery in all states except those still rebelling against the Union. Finally, in 1885, the Thirteenth Amendment to the US Constitution prohibited slavery throughout the US.

The Great Migration

The abolition of slavery provided many slaves with the option of either remaining on the plantations to become sharecroppers, or migrating to northern US cities to find jobs and opportunities where they could enjoy their newfound freedom.

The "Great Migration" to northern sections of the US and Canada during the late 1800s was a major turning point for African-Americans. They were welcomed by slaves who had escaped earlier using the "Underground Railroad." Surprisingly, they were also welcomed by northern businesses who needed laborers for their growing industries.

Detroit, New York City, and Philadelphia were some of the major US cities that became melting pots for job seekers from diverse ethnic groups. Still, Blacks had to struggle to obtain and maintain employment in a society that looked upon them as inferior. In 1870, 80% of the Black population over the age of 10 was illiterate, thus making manual labor their only alternative. Those Blacks who were more educated were able to own land and hold public offices.

This turning point demonstrated the determination and persistence of African-Americans to survive in the US and become part of the ethnic diversity of a growing nation.

The Civil Rights Movement

The Emancipation Proclamation, the Missouri Compromise and the Thirteenth, Fourteenth and Fifteenth Amendments to the Constitution did abolish slavery. However, Blacks desired a basic human right: to be treated like other ethnic groups. A series of civil rights laws was passed to help achieve that objective.

In 1954, the case of Brown versus the Board of Education of Topeka, Kansas was presented to the US Supreme Court and set a precedent for equal treatment toward Blacks. A 1955 bus boycott in Montgomery, Alabama, became the pivotal point in the Civil Rights Movement when Rosa Parks refused to give up her seat to a white person. Dr. Martin Luther King, Jr. and other civil rights activists and organizations devoted their lives to fostering equal treatment for all Americans in education, housing, and voting rights, and to gaining recognition of Blacks as legitimate citizens of the United States. In 1964, the Civil

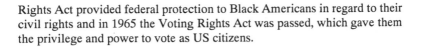

Rights Act provided federal protection to Black Americans in regard to their civil rights and in 1965 the Voting Rights Act was passed, which gave them the privilege and power to vote as US citizens.

African-Canadians

Many Black slaves escaped into Canada with hopes of finding freedom and the opportunity to start a new life. Some escaped through the Underground Railroad, settling in Ontario. Others, particularly those who favored the British Government (Black Loyalists) during the American Revolution, fled to the province of Nova Scotia and settled in Birchtown and other areas around Shelbourne County. However, many were surprised to find that Canada also had laws that were pro-slavery and pro-segregation. In 1834, slavery and segregation were banned in Canada and throughout the British Empire. After the abolition of slavery in the US, many Blacks left Canada and gladly returned to the US to take advantage of job opportunities in northern cities. However, many remained in Canada and settled there. The provinces of Nova Scotia and Ontario have consistently held the largest African-Canadian populations in Canada, and have attracted people of African descent from other parts of the world, such as Africa and the Caribbean Islands. African-Canadians also had to deal with discriminatory acts by whites who did not want a multicultural society. Black Americans, who had become loyal to the British Government and migrated to Birchtown, Nova Scotia during the American Revolution, were disappointed by the treatment they received. They were confronted by angry and violent whites who did not want Blacks competing for jobs. At one time, a riot broke out. Blacks were subsequently forced to survive on their own in a land foreign to them.

In 1967, Black Canadians who had settled in the development of Africville since the early 1800s were forcibly relocated as a result of urban renewal plans by the Halifax government. Their homes, churches and schools were destroyed to build a city park, now called Seaview Memorial Park. Residents of Africville were relocated to public housing in Halifax. Each July, former residents of Africville, along with their descendants, hold a reunion in memory of their former neighborhood.

Because Nova Scotia and Ontario have the largest Black populations in Canada, they are the focus of two chapters in this guide. Nova Scotia has a large concentration of African-Americans who escaped into Canada and has a number of historic sites, landmarks, and churches. On the other hand, Ontario has the largest concentration of Caribbean Blacks and Africans who migrated into Canada from other countries. Ontario has several African-Canadian museums, historical sites and landmarks, and an abundance of African-inspired restaurants, arts, entertainment and festivals. In Canada, visitors will find numerous historic sites and landmarks involving the Underground Railroad System. Travelers may visit historic churches that are more than 100 years old, and may also have the opportunity to speak with direct descendants of original African-Canadian settlers. There are museums that depict Canada's rich African-Canadian history, including the famed "Uncle Tom's Cabin." In addition, there are foods, music and art from Africa, the Caribbean, and the United States. Tours are offered that show and tell about places of historic significance. Both provinces have their own flavor of African-Canadian history and culture. African-Canadians also celebrate Black History (Heritage) Month during February of each year, and they especially welcome the company of their African-American cousins.

Approaching The 21st Century

As the turn of the century draws near, African-Americans can look back and recognize the experiences, progress and contributions of their predecessors. The influence of the first Africans to arrive in America has been sustained in the culture of African-Americans. Their contributions in the fields of music, art, business, entertainment, religion, politics, science and sports have finally been recognized for their quality and importance. In spite of the harsh conditions experienced by many African-Americans, their culture, history, talents and spirits will endure.

The African-American Travel Guide will become a part of that legacy, assisting travelers of all ethnic groups, ages and religions in learning about the background and future of the African-American people.

How To Use This Book

The African-American Travel Guide contains information for 17 cities across the United States plus two provinces of Eastern Canada. It includes Atlanta, Baltimore, Birmingham, Boston, Chicago, Dallas, Detroit, Indianapolis, Los Angeles, Memphis, Mobile, Montgomery, New Orleans, New York City, Philadelphia, San Francisco, Washington, DC and, in Canada, Nova Scotia and Ontario. Each area is covered in an individual chapter. Each chapter has listings for the city profiled and, in many cases, for areas nearby. Author's recommendations are marked with a ☆. The businesses profiled in the guide may be owned or operated by African-Americans, cater to an African-American clientele, provide services or cuisine enjoyed by African-Americans, or promote the historical significance and achievements of African-Americans.

The guide can be used by both leisure and business travelers. The leisure traveler, who generally has more time and flexibility to explore, can consult the guide prior to visiting a particular city to plan activities. Easy-to-read maps are provided for each city, showing the main arteries of that area and the locations of various points of interest. The guide is also an exciting way to educate family members on the history and contributions of African-Americans.

The business traveler can use the guide to find dining and entertainment options. Most business is conducted in downtown areas, and the guide can help travelers to determine time and distance from a particular establishment or activity. For those using public transportation, phone numbers for checking schedules are provided, along with contact information for local taxi services.

Before You Go

Always contact locations prior to departure to confirm hours of operation, rates or admission fees, parking information, and specific directions. If you are planning to use major credit cards, it's a good idea to call first. Many small establishments are on a cash-only basis. Although every effort has been made to ensure that the information in this guide is correct, many businesses change their hours of operation according to season or other factors. Some may move or even go out of business before this book is released. When you visit places listed in this book, be sure to mention that you read about them in *The African-American Travel Guide.*

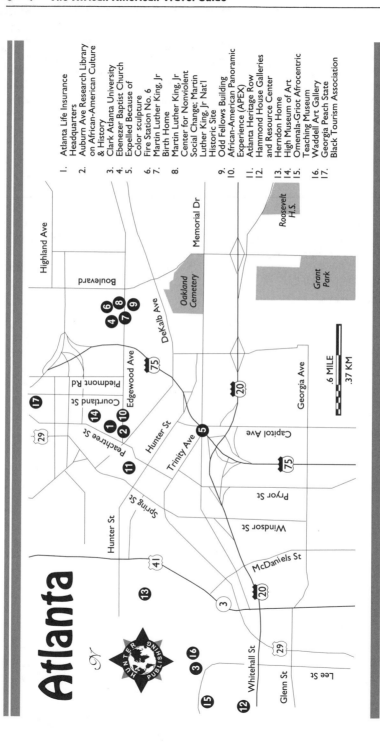

1. Atlanta Life Insurance Headquarters
2. Auburn Ave Research Library on African-American Culture & History
3. Clark Atlanta University
4. Ebenezer Baptist Church
5. Expelled Because of Color sculpture
6. Fire Station No. 6
7. Martin Luther King, Jr Birth Home
8. Martin Luther King, Jr Center for Nonviolent Social Change; Martin Luther King, Jr Nat'l Historic Site
9. Odd Fellows Building
10. African-American Panoramic Experience (APEX)
11. Atlanta Heritage Row
12. Hammond House Galleries and Resource Center
13. Herndon Home
14. High Museum of Art
15. Omenala-Griot Afrocentric Teaching Museum
16. Waddell Art Gallery
17. Georgia Peach State Black Tourism Association

Atlanta

Historic Sites & Landmarks

Atlanta Life Insurance Headquarters, 148 Auburn Ave, ☎ 404-659-2100. This historic building is now part of the Martin Luther King, Jr. Historic District, and for 60 years was home to the Atlanta Life Insurance Company, once the second largest African-American-owned insurance company in the US. There are exhibits about founder Alonzo Herndon and Atlanta's history. Mon-Thurs, 8 am-4:30 pm. Free admission.

Atlanta Preservation Center, The Desoto, 156 7th Street NE, Suite 3, ☎ 404-876-2040. Visitors can choose from any of the Atlanta Preservation Center's 10 guided walking tours through historically significant districts. Tours are led by knowledgeable guides who will escort visitors to historic districts such as the Sweet Auburn/Martin Luther King, Jr. District, one of the Southeast's most prosperous African-American business centers. Ongoing weekly. Please call for tour information. Admission charge.

Auburn Avenue Research Library on African-American Culture and History, 101 Auburn Ave NE, ☎ 404-730-4001. Open since 1994, the library contains more than 21,000 books covering African literature, art, bibliographies, biographies, essays, drama, fiction, genealogy and history. Mon-Thurs, noon-8 pm; Fri, 1 pm-5 pm; Sat-Sun, 2 pm-6 pm. Free admission.

Ebenezer Baptist Church, 407 Auburn Ave NE at the Martin Luther King, Jr. National Historic Site, ☎ 404-331-6922. This is the church where Martin Luther King, Jr. worshipped as a child and returned as co-pastor with his father "Daddy King" from 1960 to 1968. Ebenezer Baptist Church is the site where numerous civil rights activities took place. Mon-Fri, 9 am-5 pm. Saturday, 9 am-2 pm. Free admission.

Expelled Because of Color **sculpture,** at the northeast corner of the capitol, overlooking Martin Luther King, Jr. Drive at Capitol Ave. In the late 1970s, the Georgia Legislature Black Caucus commissioned Atlanta artist John Riddle to create a work depicting the history of the struggle and contributions of African-American Georgians to the state's heritage. The sculpture was dedicated in honor of the 33 African-Americans who sat in the Georgia General Assembly shortly after the Civil War. In 1868 the white legislators expelled and ousted these African-Americans from their posts, hence the sculpture's title, "Expelled Because of Color." It is a four-tier metal sculpture featuring small figures representing African-Americans as slaves, then as laborers, and finally contributing to the building of the state. In the words of the sculptor, "cinder block forms at the base of the sculpture symbolize the building of Black political awareness and self-representation in Georgia. Our enslavement, our role in the Revolutionary War, the Black Church, our labor and the right to vote are components of these Black Georgians' struggle from the slave ship to the State House."

Fire Station No. 6, 39 Boulevard, at the Martin Luther King, Jr. National Historic Site, ☎ 404-331-3922. This station was built in 1894 and served the "Sweet Auburn" community until 1991. Hear about the role the fire station played in protecting Atlanta's growing neighborhoods. Also, view a completely restored 1927 American LaFrance fire engine. Mon-Sun, 9 am-5 pm. Free admission.

Martin Luther King, Jr. Birth Home, 501 Auburn Ave NE, ☎ 404-331-6922. The late Dr. Martin Luther King, Jr. was born in this home on January 15, 1929. King lived here until the age of 12, and the house has been restored and furnished to look as it did when Dr. King was a young boy. The house is a registered National Historic Landmark. Guided tours of the birth home are every half-hour. Meet the Ranger at Fire Station No. 6 at 39 Boulevard. Mon-Sun, 10 am-5 pm. Free admission.

Martin Luther King Historic District
Courtesy of Georgia Dept. of Industry, Trade & Tourism

Martin Luther King, Jr. Center for Nonviolent Social Change, Inc., 450 Auburn Ave NE, ☎ 404-331-6922. Mrs. Coretta Scott King, the widow of the late Dr. Martin Luther King, Jr., established the Center for Nonviolent Social Change in 1968 as a means to preserve King's legacy and to continue his work. King's burial site is at this location. The Center's Freedom Hall displays exhibits of Dr. King, Mrs. Coretta Scott King, and of India's great leader,

Mahatma Gandhi (1869-1948), who also led a nonviolent movement in his native India. Mon-Sun, 9 am-5 pm. Free admission.

Martin Luther King, Jr. National Historic Site, 450 Auburn Ave NE, ☎ 404-331-5190. This national park site near downtown Atlanta memorializes America's most revered Civil Rights leader, Dr. Martin Luther King, Jr. Authorized by Congress in 1980, the site preserves the Auburn Avenue neighborhood where Dr. King was born, lived, worked, worshipped, and where he is buried. The Martin Luther King, Jr. National Historic Site is one of Atlanta's top visitor attractions, drawing an average of 1.5 million visitors a year. The site is managed by the National Park Service as one of 369 units of the National Park system. The historic site's primary attractions include a new visitor center, birth home of Dr. Martin Luther King, Jr., historic residences, Ebenezer Church, the Martin Luther King Center for Nonviolent Social Change, Inc., King burial site, Fire Station Museum and Sweet Auburn Business District. The parking fee is $3.00. Center is open daily, 9 am-5 pm. Free admission.

Odd Fellows Building, 236 and 250 Auburn Ave NE, ☎ 404-525-5027. This six-story building located in Atlanta's Sweet Auburn Historic District was built in 1912 by a team of African-American architects. Once home to the famous Yates and Milton Drugstore and Cervy Hall Haberdashery, the Odd Fellows building attracted such music legends as Count Basie, Lionel Hampton, Cab Calloway and Sam Cooke, who performed in the building's roof garden. Mon-Fri, 8 am-5 pm.

Stone Mountain Park, East of Interstate 285 and US 78. Web site: www.stonemountainpark.org. This 3,200-acre recreational park includes a number of authentically furnished slave cabins and antebellum homes. The park also includes a golf course, ice-skating rink, riverboat cruise, Swiss skylift, hiking trails and a scenic railroad. Park is open daily, 6 am-midnight, Plantation hours are 10:30 am-5:30 pm and 10 am-9 pm during the summer. Admission charge.

Trevor Arnett Library, Clark Atlanta University Campus, 111 James P. Brawley Drive SW, ☎ 404-880-8000. This library houses rare historical items and includes articles from historic African-American writers such as Phyllis Wheatley, Arna Bontemps, Countee Cullen and others. Open daily, 9 am-11 pm. Free admission.

Wren's Nest, 1050 Ralph David Abernathy Blvd, ☎ 404-753-7735. Considered Atlanta's oldest house museum, the Wren's Nest was, from 1881-1908, home to author, journalist, and folklorist Joel Chandler Harris and his family. Not only was Harris famous for the African-American stories of Br'er Rabbit and Br'er Fox, he was once editor of the *Atlanta Constitution* and authored 30 books. The Wren's Nest is a National Historic Site and city of Atlanta landmark, with tours and a series of storytelling programs for children. Br'er

Atlanta

Rabbit books and tapes are featured at the Wren's Nest Museum Store. Tues-Sat, 10 am-4 pm; Sun, 1 pm-4 pm. Admission charge.

Sites Beyond Atlanta

Morton Theater, 195 West Washington Street, Athens, GA, ☎ 706-613-3770. This theater was built by Monroe Bowers "Pink" Morton in 1910 and was the core of the downtown African-American business district. Morton was a prominent businessman, and in 1896 was made a member of the Republican National Committee. The Morton Theater became a gathering place for 19th-century African-American residents of Athens. This was the country's first theater built and owned by African-Americans. It operates today as a community performing arts center. Business hours are Mon-Fri, 9 am-2 pm and 1 pm-6 pm. Call to arrange free tours.

Atlanta History Center

Museums/Exhibits

African-American Panoramic Experience (APEX), 135 Auburn Ave NE, ☎ 404-521-2739. Atlanta's African-American History Museum features exhibitions of artistic as well as historic subjects. The museum features local history including a model of Georgia's first African-American-owned drugstore, West African artifacts, and a permanent African-American collection by nationally known artists. Tues, 10 am-5 pm; Wed, 10 am-6 pm; Thurs-Sat, 10 am-5 pm; Sun, 1 pm-5 pm. Admission charge.

Atlanta History Center, 130 W Paces Ferry Rd, ☎ 404-814-4000. This history museum offers visitors an overview of the city's history through videos, photographs and exhibits. Visitors can listen to a speech by Dr. Martin Luther King, Jr., explore a turn-of-the-century trolley, pilot a plane into Hartsfield International Airport or witness the drama of the Civil War. Tues-Sat, 10 am-5 pm; Sun, 1 pm-5 pm. Admission charge.

Hammond House Galleries and Resource Center for African-American Art, 503 Peeples Street SW, ☎ 404-752-8730. The gallery displays a variety of works throughout the year by African-American artists. Works include African masks, Haitian paintings, originals, prints, and watercolors. Tues-Fri, 10 am-6 pm; Sat-Sun, 1 pm-5 pm. Admission charge.

Herndon Home, 587 University Place NW, ☎ 404-581-9813. Once the Home of Alonzo F. Herndon, founder of the Atlanta Life Insurance Company, this 15-room Beaux Arts mansion was built in 1910 by African-American craftsmen and is on the National Register of Historic Places. Herndon rose from a slave-born barber to found one of the most successful African-American businesses of all time. His son, Norris Herndon, is the only heir to the Herndon fortune and has maintained and improved the home with Roman and Venetian glass, silver, original furnishings and antique furniture. Tues-Sat, 10 am-4 pm. Tours given on the hour. Donation requested.

High Museum of Art Folk Art & Photography Galleries, 30 John Wesley Dobbs Ave NE, main location, ☎ 404-733-HIGH. The High's permanent collection houses more than 10,000 objects and includes collections by African-American artists. Rotating exhibits also include works by African-American artists. Call for specifics on upcoming African-American exhibits. General hours are Mon-Sat, 10 am-5 pm. Some exhibits are free; others require an admission charge.

Michael C. Carlos Museum, 571 South Kilgo Street, Emory University, ☎ 404-727-4282. This museum maintains a permanent collection of over 12,000 African objects from around the world. They also put on special programs and presentations of African-American relevance. Mon-Sat, 10 am-5 pm. Suggested donation on permanent exhibits; admission charge on some special displays. Call for current schedule of exhibits and events.

Omenala-Griot Afrocentric Teaching Museum, 337 Dargan Place SW, West End, ☎ 404-755-8403. Visitors will be intrigued by the interactive educational displays here. The Omenala takes a unique approach to help visitors learn more about the African-American experience. The Omenala-Griot Afrocentric Teaching Museum has permanent and rotating exhibits and is located in the historic West End. Tours are scheduled by appointment from Mon-Fri, 9 am-3 pm. On Sat they are scheduled between 1 pm-4:30 pm with no appointment needed. Call for specific tour hours. Admission charge.

Herndon Home
Photo courtesy of the Georgia Dept. of Industry, Trade & Tourism

Waddell Art Gallery, Clark Atlanta University, lower level, 111 James P. Brawley Drive SW, ☎ 404-880-8000. This unique collection of artwork represents some of the most talented contemporary African-American artists, i.e., Henry Ossawa Turner, Ernest Crichlow, John Biggers, Elizabeth Catlett and Charles White. Tues-Fri, 10 am-4 pm. Free admission.

Museums Beyond Atlanta

Harriet Tubman African-American Museum, 340 Walnut Street, Macon, GA, ☎ 912-743-8544. African-American art, history and culture come alive at the "Tubman," Georgia's largest African-American museum. Nine galleries of exciting exhibitions, a resource center and a museum store create an enlightening and entertaining experience. The centerpiece of the Tubman is a world-class mural entitled *From Africa to America,* painted by local artist Wilfred Stroud. It chronicles the historic journey of African-Americans from slavery to modern times. Other permanent exhibits include galleries of inventors and military leaders, and there is a hands-on African musical instrument area for children. Visitors will also enjoy the permanent collection of artifacts and art from Africa and Macon, Georgia, plus rotating temporary exhibits from around the country. Mon-Sat, 9 am-5 pm; Sun, 2 pm-5 pm. Suggested donation.

Historic Colleges & Universities

Clark Atlanta University, 240 James P. Brawley Drive SW, ☎ 404-880-8000. Private university. Established in 1869.

Interdenominational Theological Center, 671 Beckwith Street SW, ☎ 404-527-7709. Private graduate theological center. Founded 1958.

Morehouse College, 830 Westview Drive, ☎ 404-681-2800. Private liberal arts college. Established in 1867.

Morris Brown College, 643 Martin Luther King, Jr. Drive NW, ☎ 404-220-0270. Private, church-affiliated historic African-American college. Established in 1881.

Spelman College, 350 Spelman Lane SW, ☎ 404-681-3643. Private historic African-American liberal arts college for women. Established in 1881.

Shopping

Galleries & Specialty Shops

African Connections and **Afrikan Interiors.** Two locations: 1107 Euclid Ave, ☎ 404-589-1834, and 250 Auburn Ave, ☎ 404-523-9458. Wide selection of African clothing, textiles, music and musical instruments. Tues-Sat, 11 am-6 pm; Sun, 2 pm-6 pm.

Bukom Textile Stores, 2680 Godby Road, ☎ 404-766-0417. African fabrics and prints. Mon-Sat, 10 am-7:30 pm.

Camille Love Gallery, 309 East Paces Ferry Road, #120, ☎ 404-841-0446. Offers a variety of contemporary African-American paintings and sculptures. Selection of artists' works on display vary throughout the year. Tues-Sat, 11 am-5 pm.

Diaspora Arts, 232 Auburn Ave NE, ☎ 404-525-7900. Varied selection of African-American art, artifacts and accessories. Located on historic "Sweet Auburn" Ave. Tues-Sat, 11 am-7 pm.

Future Image International Art Gallery, 60 Upper Alabama Street SW, ☎ 404-523-5129. Original African art, limited editions featuring prominent African-American athletes and leaders. Mon-Sat, 10 am-9:30 pm; Sun, noon-6 pm.

Gallery Abayoni, 186-B Auburn Ave NE, ☎ 404-581-1003. A gallery of fine art by African-American, African, Haitian and Caribbean artists. Features Shona sculpture from Zimbabwe, fine jewelry, textiles and books. Enjoy the coffees from their espresso bar while browsing. Mon-Sat, 11 am-8 pm.

LaNik Gallery and Fine Arts, 2298 Cascade SW, ☎ 404-758-5040. One of the largest African-American art galleries in Atlanta. Represents a large selection of paintings, prints and 1996 Olympic items. Specialty is art consultation, interior decorating and framing for the discriminating art collector. Hours are usually 11 am-7 pm daily, but special arrangements by appointment are preferred.

Level 2 Art Gallery and Special Events Venues, 385 Marietta Street, ☎ 404-522-8477. Level 2 houses an extensive collection of original fine art by international African-American artists. Collection includes lithographs, limited collection prints and unique gift and novelty items, museum quality framing and repair. Mon, 11 am-3 pm; Tues-Fri, 11 am-6 pm; Sat, noon-5 pm; Sun, by appointment only. After-work jazz sets. See listing under *Entertainment.*

Visual Images Design Studio and Art Gallery, 251 Walker Street, ☎ 404-581-1006. Offers original African-American art, designs, prints, and interior decorating. Hours vary by appointment, but flexible.

William Tolliver's Art Gallery, Inc., 2300 Peachtree Road, Suite #C-203. ☎ 404-350-0811. Originals, prints and sculpture by Atlanta's African-American artist William Tolliver. Wed-Sat, 11 am-7 pm.

Yanzum Village African Art, 285 Peachtree Street NE, ☎ 404-874-8063. Features authentic works by African, African-American, and Caribbean artists. Selections include paintings, metal art, and West African masks. Mon, by appointment; Tues-Fri, 10 am-5:30 pm; Sat, 11 am-5 pm.

Bookstores

Heritage Bookstore, 2389 Wesley Chapel Road, #201, Decatur, ☎ 770-322-7347. Specializes in a wide variety of African-American and multicultural books (religion, history, fiction, nonfiction, children's and inspirational), as well as gift items. Mon-Sat, 10:30 am-8 pm; Sun, 1 pm-6 pm.

Medu Bookstore, 2841 Greenbriar Parkway SW, ☎ 404-346-3263. Specializes in a variety of subject matter interesting to African-Americans. Mon-Sat, 10 am-9 pm; Sun, 12:30 pm-6 pm.

Shrine of the Black Madonna Bookstore, 946 Ralph David Abernathy Blvd, ☎ 404-752-6125. Has a variety of African-American items, such as children's books, psychology, religion, holistic health, and educational guides. The Shrine also has a wide selection of African paintings, authentic masks and sculptures. Mon, 3 pm-7 pm; Tues-Sat, 11 am-7 pm; Sun, 1:30 pm-3 pm. ☆ *Specially recommended.*

Truth Bookstore, 56 Marietta Street, NW, ☎ 404-523-3240 or 800-987-8841. A large selection of African-American, Caribbean, and African books, videos, audios, games and Kwanzaa items. Mon-Fri, 9 am-6 pm; Sat, noon-5 pm.

2 Friends Bookstore, 598 Cascade Rd, ☎ 404-758-7711. "Capturing the essence of Africa" in greeting cards, figurines, books, art, statues, masks and Afrocentric wedding and graduation invitations. Mon-Sat, 10 am-8 pm.

Fashions

African Connection, 1107 Euclid Ave, ☎ 404-589-1834. Wide selection of African clothing and authentic, ceremonial, exquisite and affordable art. Tues-Sat, 11 am-6 pm; Sun, 2 pm-6 pm; closed Mon.

Damar's La Boutique, 242 Auburn Ave, ☎ 404-221-0384. Features gift items, accessories, and elegant designer hats for ladies. Tues-Fri, 11 am-7 pm; Sat, noon-5 pm.

Zita Fashions, 228-230 Auburn Ave, ☎ 404-215-9912. African and custom-made formal and informal fashions; African wedding accessories. Mon-Sat, 10 am-6 pm.

Popular Shopping Centers

Underground Atlanta, Peachtree Street and Central Ave at Alabama Street, ☎ 404-523-2311. Day and night, Underground Atlanta showcases the diverse culture of a growing city. It's the city's town square, and a favorite place for festival and events. It is also an important retail center with more than 120 shops, nightclubs, services and restaurants covering parts of six city blocks. Mon-Sat, 10 am-9:30 pm; Sun, noon-6 pm. In summer, Sun, 11 am-7 pm. Restaurant and nightclub hours vary. Call first.

Restaurants

◆ Barbecue

Aleck's Barbecue Heaven, 783 Martin Luther King, Jr. Drive NW, ☎ 404-525-2062. Specialty is pork, beef and chicken barbecue, chitterling dinners and sandwiches. Mon-Thurs, 11 am-10 pm; Fri-Sat, 11 am-1 am; Sun, 1 pm-8 pm.

◆ Caribbean

The Caribbean Restaurant, 180 Auburn Ave, ☎ 404/658-9829. Mon-Thurs, 11:30 am-8 pm; Fri-Sat, 11:30 am-9 pm.

Coconut Dish, 180 Elm Street SW, ☎ 404-222-9291. Traditional Jamaican cuisine. Jerk and curried dishes, such as chicken, oxtail, beef and meat patties. Mon-Fri, 11 am-7 pm.

Heritage Cafe Caribbean Grill and Bar, 1995 Windy Hill, ☎ 770-438-9222. Full-scale tropical menu includes coconut fried chicken, conch fritters, jerk chicken, shrimp San Juan, Trinidadian vegetarian roti and tantalizing tropical drinks. Tues-Sun, 4 pm-2 am. See listing under *Entertainment.*

Lauren's Caribbean Restaurant, 32 Decatur Street, ☎ 404-688-7005. Features jerk chicken and other Caribbean dishes. Mon-Sun, 10:30 am-9 pm.

Patti Hut Cafe, 596 Piedmont Ave, A-204, Rio Mall, ☎ 404-892-5133. Authentic West Indian-style food served with a Southern accent. Cozy Jamaican atmosphere, live reggae, jazz and poetry readings. Breakfast, lunch and dinner. Televised soccer games. Mon-Thurs, 10 am-10 pm; Fri-Sat, 10 am-midnight; Sun, noon-6 pm. See Atlanta listing for "Jazz" entertainment.

Royal Caribbean Bakery and Restaurant, 4859 Memorial Drive, Rockmore Plaza, ☎ 404-299-7714. In addition to spiced buns, coco bread and other baked goods, Royal Caribbean features curried goat, oxtail, jerk chicken, roti, Chinese roast chicken, brown stew, fish and tropical drinks. Mon-Thurs, 9 am-8 pm; Fri-Sat, 9 am-9 pm.

◆ Soul Food

Beautiful Restaurant, 2260 Cascade Road SW, ☎ 404-752-5931. Soul food cuisine. Features smothered pork chops with gravy, meatloaf, baked chicken and fish, barbeque and a variety of vegetables. Sun-Wed, 7 am-midnight; Thurs-Sat, 24 hours.

Catfish Station, 618 Ponce De Leon Ave, ☎ 404-875-2454. National African-American restaurant and bar establishment. Features fried catfish and Louisiana cuisine, including red beans and rice. Mon-Sat, noon-2 am; Sun, until 1 am. See listing under *Entertainment.*

Gladys Knight & Ron Wynan's Chicken and Waffle, 618 Ponce De Leon, Ponce Square, ☎ 404-874-9393. One of Atlanta's newest soul food restaurants. Gladys Knight can be seen here on some nights. Casual dress is okay. Mon, 11 am-3 pm; Tues-Thurs, 11 am-11 pm; Fri-Sat, 11 am-3 pm; Sun, 11 am-5 pm.

J.R. Crickets, 2348 Cascade Road SW, ☎ 404-753-5191. Specialty is hot wings. Mon-Thurs, 11 am-2 am; Fri-Sat, 11 am-4 am.

Mo Better Chicken, 1829-A DeLowe Dr, ☎ 404-758-6122. Specialty is fried chicken. Mon-Fri, 11 am-9 pm; Sat-Sun, 11 am-10 pm.

Pascal Brothers, 830 Martin Luther King, Jr. Drive SW and at Hartsfield International Airport Concourses, ☎ 404-577-3150. Specialty is Southern fried chicken; menu also includes other entrées and an endless list of fresh vegetables. Features homemade peach cobbler. Considered an Atlanta tradition for nearly 50 years. Open daily, 8:30 am-10 pm.

Sylvia's, 241 Central Ave, ☎ 404-529-9692. This popular restaurant (which also has a location in Harlem, NY) features traditional soul food and American cuisine in an elegant atmosphere. Specialties include smothered pork chops and chicken, world-famous BBQ pork ribs, salmon croquettes, fried catfish and vegetable side dishes, including fried sweet potatoes. Mon-Thurs, 11 am-10 pm; Fri, 11 am-11 pm; Sat, noon-11 pm; Sun buffet, noon-8 pm. During the week they have after-work piano sets from 5:30-7:30. ☆ *Specially recommended.*

◆ Vegetarian

Domiabra Vegetarian Palace, 2329 Cascade, ☎ 404-753-2008. Specialty is Caribbean vegetarian food. Serves exotic drinks and desserts. Mon-Sun, 11:30 am-10 pm. See listing under *Entertainment.*

Entertainment

◆ Jazz Nightclubs & Lounges

Cafe 290, 290 Hilderbrand Drive, ☎ 404-256-3942. Live jazz daily. 8:30 pm-12:30 am; weekends until 2 am. No cover charge. Continental cuisine.

Heritage Cafe Caribbean Grill and Bar, 1995 Windy Hill Rd, ☎ 770-438-9222. Live entertainment weekends starting at 9 pm. See restaurant listing under *Caribbean.*

Catfish Station, 618 Ponce De Leon Ave, ☎ 404-875-2454. National African-American restaurant and bar establishment. Features live jazz and rhythm and blues nightly. Fri-Sun, 9 pm-1 am. Cover charge. See restaurant listing under *Soul Food.*

Dante's Down the Hatch, 3380 Peachtree Road, Underground Atlanta, ☎ 404-266-1600. Jazz, 7:30 pm-11:30 pm; Sat-Sun, 7:30 pm-12:30 am. Cover charge. Call for upcoming events.

Domiabra Vegetarian Palace, 2329 Cascade Road, ☎ 404-753-2008. Live jazz Fri-Sat evenings on the first and third weekends of each month. Mon-Sun, 11:30 am-10 pm. No cover charge. See restaurant listing under *Vegetarian.*

Heritage Cafe Caribbean Grill and Bar, 1995 Windy Hill Rd, ☎ 770-438-9222. Live entertainment weekends, 9 pm-2 am. See restaurant listing under *Caribbean.*

Level 2 Art Gallery and Special Events Venue, 385 Marietta Street, ☎ 404-522-8477. Fri "after work" live jazz, art, food and more. Mix and mingle New York-style in the cozy two-story loft. Level 2 features a variety of special events. Fri, 5 pm-9 pm. Call for upcoming events. See listing under *Galleries & Specialty Shops.*

Patti Hut Cafe, 595 Piedmont Ave, A-204, Rio Mall, ☎ 404-892-5133. Deejay, 8 pm-midnight; live music on Fridays, midnight-2 am; live reggae on Sat, 8 pm-midnight. No cover charge for music. See restaurant listing under *Caribbean.*

Atlanta

Yin Yang Café, 64 Third Street, ☎ 404-607-0682. Live jazz weekday evenings. Fri-Sun, "Jazz Jam." Call for specific hours and upcoming events.

◆ Dance Nightclubs

Club Anytime, 1055 Peachtree Street NE, ☎ 404-607-8050. Contemporary dance music. Multi-ethnic establishment. Open 24 hours.

Club Oxygen, 3065 Peachtree Street, ☎ 404-816-6522. Hip-hop dance club, sports bar and restaurant. Call for specific hours.

Frozen Paradise, 5580 Memorial Drive, Stone Mountain, ☎ 404-297-9977. Popular dance nightclub and restaurant. Nightclub open Mon-Sat, 10 pm-2 am.

Illusions, 3131 Campbellton, ☎ 404-349-9462. Popular contemporary dance club, especially on Sunday nights. Call for specific hours.

Tongue and Groove, 3055 Peachtree Street, ☎ 404-261-2325. Weekends feature contemporary dance music. Sat, 70s disco.

V's on Peachtree, 320 Peachtree Street, ☎ 404-522-3021.

◆ Comedy

Uptown Comedy Center, 2140 Peachtree Street, #320, Atlanta. ☎ 404-350-6990. Local and national comedians. Call for upcoming events.

Lodging

Bed & Breakfasts

The Koweeta Pines, 500 Koweeta Trail, College Park, GA 30349, ☎ 770-964-1488. This owner-occupied bed & breakfast is nestled in a wooded area of College Park, just 10 minutes from Atlanta's Hartsfield Airport and about 20 minutes from downtown Atlanta. Shared and private baths are available. Amenities include cable TV, in-room music, terrace access, complimentary fresh-baked muffins. and a selection of beverages. Call for current rates and reservations.

Roseland Manor, 6580 Church St, Riverdale, GA 30274, ☎ 770-996-1221.

Wise House, in the quiet Niskey Lake section of southwest Atlanta. ☎ 404-691-WISE (691-9473), fax 404-699-2171. E-mail: wisehouse@juno.com. Call for directions and complete address. Wise House is an owner-occupied bed and breakfast "homestay," a private residence providing overnight accommodations and hot breakfasts. The spacious ranch-style contemporary home is close to many area attractions. Their breakfast specialty is homemade biscuits, along with other favorites. Amenities include an exercise room, sun room, recreation area with a basketball hoop, Internet access, fax and airport shuttle service. Call for current rates and reservations.

Outside of Atlanta

Weekender, Sapelow Island, GA 31327. ☎ 912-485-2277, fax 912-485-2212. Off the Georgia coast on a barrier island, this African-American-owned establishment offers guests a choice of renting a room or an apartment with all the amenities. The 12 x 3½-mile island has quiet public beaches and nature trails. African-American history abounds in the area. The island can be conveniently accessed by a passenger ferry operated by the State of Georgia. All meals are extra and can be arranged with innkeepers. Call for current rates and reservations.

Travel Agents

Kimelle Kruises, 400 Colchester Drive, Stone Mountain, ☎ 770-879-2535 or 800-880-8982, after hours. Full-service travel agency. By appointment only.

Ross Charters and Associates, Inc., 5310 Rocky Pine Drive NE, Lithonia, ☎ 770-322-9189. Complete travel and tourism services. Custom and packaged tours, motorcoach charters, multicultural and city tours.

Heritage Tours

Georgia Peach State Black Tourism Association, 285 Peachtree Center Ave, #1000, ☎ 404-656-7829. Call for specific tour information and schedules. Mon-Fri, 8 am-5 pm.

Guidelines Atlanta, 5500 Pharr Rd, #305, ☎ 404-237-5154. Ask for information on their African-American Heritage Tour.

Legacy Tours, 3960 LaSalle Way, SW, ☎ 404-947-2179. African-American heritage tours. Call for specific tour information and schedules.

S.C.L.C. Women, 328 Auburn Ave, ☎ 404-584-0303. Tour options range from three hours to two days. They offer African-American heritage and civil rights tours of Atlanta, Selma, Birmingham and Montgomery. Required donation.

Atlanta

Media

Radio Stations

◆ Jazz

WCLK 91.9 FM, 111 James P. Brawley Drive, SW, ☎ 404-880-8273. Jazz, public radio. Broadcast from Clark Atlanta University. "Jazz of the city."

WJZF 104.1 FM, 190 Marietta Street NW, ☎ 404-577-2872. Smooth jazz.

◆ Urban Contemporary

WIGI 1340 AM, 1532 Howell Mill, ☎ 404-352-3943. Urban contemporary and oldies.

WVEE 103.3 FM, 120 Ralph McGill Blvd, #1000. ☎ 404-898-8900.

WHTA 97.5 FM, Atlanta's only hip-hop station.

◆ Gospel

WAEC 840 AM, ☎ 404-355-8600. "Love 86, the gospel countdown." Features James Dobson, Tony Evans, Fred Price, Bob Larson, J. Vernon McGee, Kenneth Hagin and more.

WAOK 1380 AM, 120 Ralph McGill Blvd, #1000. ☎ 404-898-8900. "The people's station." For the latest in news, entertainment and community events. Inspirational format.

WTJH 1260 AM, 2146 Dodson Drive. ☎ 404-344-2235. "Word power." Inspirational format.

WXLL 1310 AM, request line, ☎ 404-288-3206. "Reaching out to you in gospel music."

WYZE 1480 AM, 1111 Boulevard, SE, ☎ 404-622-7802. "The hot new gospel voice in Atlanta."

Newspapers

Atlanta Daily World, 145 Auburn Ave NE, ☎ 404-659-1110. Atlanta's oldest African-American newspaper. Distributed four times weekly.

Atlanta Inquirer, 947 Martin Luther King, Jr. Drive, ☎ 404-523-6086. African-American community newspaper. Distributed weekly on Thursdays.

Atlanta Bulletin, 1655 Peachtree Street, #1102, ☎ 404-874-1968. African-American-owned multicultural newspaper. Distributed weekly on Thursdays.

Atlanta Voice, 633 Pryor Street, ☎ 404-524-6426. African-American community newspaper. Distributed weekly on Thursdays.

Magazines

Atlanta Tribune, 875 Old Roswell Rd, C-100, Roswell, ☎ 770-587-0501, fax 770-642-6501. E-mail: tribune@mindspring.com; Web site: www.atlantatribune.com. Bi-monthly African-American magazine.

Black Pages of Atlanta, 3711 College Street, College Park, ☎ 404-766-1692. Directory of numerous African-American-owned businesses in the Atlanta area. Annual publication.

Publications

Atlanta Heritage, Atlanta Convention & Visitors Bureau, 233 Peachtree Street NE, Atlanta, GA 30303, ☎ 404-249-1750.

Atlanta Now, Official Visitors Guide of the Atlanta Convention and Visitors Bureau, 233 Peachtree Street, Atlanta, GA 30303, ☎ 404-249-1750.

Atlanta Black Pages Directory and Resource Guide, Euphrates, Inc., 3711 College Street, College Park, GA 30337, ☎ 404-766-1692.

Georgia's African-American Heritage Guide, Portraits and Pathways, American Visions Magazine, PO Box 37049, Washington, DC 20078-4741, ☎ 202-462-1779.

African-American Churches

AME

Alexander Memorial AME, 287 Augusta Ave SE, ☎ 404-627-4429.

Allen Temple AME, 1625 Simpson Rd NW, ☎ 404-794-3316.

Big Bethel AME Church, 220 Auburn Ave NE, ☎ 404-659-0248.

Cobb Bethel AME, 2090 County Line Rd SW, ☎ 404-344-5067.

Fidelity AME, 1913 Main Street NW, ☎ 404-794-3329.

Flipper Temple AME, 580 Fair Street, SW, ☎ 404-522-5020.

Greater Bethel AME, 2455 Lakewood Ave SW, ☎ 404-627-2802.

Greater Mount Carmel AME, 4078 Carver Drive, ☎ 770-451-1091 or 770-458-2063.

Hope New AME, 3012 Arden Road NW, ☎ 404-261-4393.

Hunter Hills AME, 1423 Akridge Street, NW, ☎ 404-758-8090.

Macedonia AME, 3267 Jonesboro Road SE, ☎ 404-363-3647.

Mount Carmel AME, 1140 Henry Thomas, ☎ 404-627-6550.

New Life AME Zion, 3399 Roosevelt Hwy, ☎ 404-669-8643.

Pleasant Hill AME, 4584 Stonewall Tell Rd, ☎ 770-969-1593.

St. John AME, 1158 Coleman Street, SW, ☎ 404-755-2738.

St. Mark AME, 3605 Campbellton Rd SW, ☎ 404-349-6800.

St. Philip AME, 240 Candler Road SE, ☎ 404-371-0749.

Shaw Temple AME Zion, 38 Hightower Road NW, ☎ 404-696-5542.

Smith Chapel AME, 183 Mayson Ave NE, ☎ 404-577-3397.

St. Peter AME, 637 Highland Ave NE, ☎ 404-688-1588.

Trinity AME, 604 Lynhurst Drive, SW, ☎ 404-696-5826.

Turner Chapel AME, 4650 Cascade Road SW, ☎ 404-699-0023.

Turner Monumental AME, 66 Howard Street NE, ☎ 404-378-5970.

Victory AME, 249 Fielding Lane SW, ☎ 404-505-0444.

Wilkes Chapel AME, 2293 Perry Blvd NW, ☎ 404-799-7511.

Baptist

Ebenezer Baptist Church, 407 Auburn Ave NE, ☎ 404-688-7263.

Antioch Baptist Church North, 540 Kennedy Street SW, ☎ 404-688-5679.

West Hunter Street Baptist Church, 1040 Ralph David Abernathy Blvd SW, ☎ 404-758-5563.

Catholic

St. Anthony's Catholic Church, 928 Ralph David Abernathy Blvd SW, ☎ 404-758-8861.

CME

Butler Street CME Church, 23 Butler Street SE, ☎ 404-659-8745.

Greater Hopewell CME, 604 Cooper Street SW, ☎ 404-523-2394.

Holsey Temple CME, 704 Charlotte Place NW, ☎ 404-794-8458.

Shy Temple CME, 2012 Memorial Dr SE, ☎ 404-377-3174.

COGIC

Holy Hill COGIC, 959 Constitution Rd SE, ☎ 404-627-7280.

One Step of Faith COGIC, 1962 Perkerson Rd SW, ☎ 404-758-0440.

Non-Denominational

Hillside International Truth Center, Inc., 2450 Cascade Rd SW, ☎ 404-758-6811.

Calendar of Annual Events

◆ **January**

Martin Luther King Birthday Celebration. Citywide activities. Georgia Peach State Black Tourism Association, 285 Peachtree Center Ave, #1000, ☎ 404-656-7829.

◆ **February**

Celebration of Black History Month Events. Citywide activities. Georgia Peach State Black Tourism Association, 285 Peachtree Center Ave, #1000, ☎ 404-656-7829.

◆ **March**

National Black Arts Festival. Multiple venues. Georgia Peach State Black Tourism Association, 285 Peachtree Center Ave, #1000, ☎ 404-656-7829.

Underground Atlanta Anniversary Celebration, ☎ 404-523-2311 or Georgia Peach State Black Tourism Association, 285 Peachtree Center Ave, #1000, ☎ 404-656-7829.

Springfest, Auburn Ave, ☎ 404-688-7011 or Georgia Peach State Black Tourism Association, 285 Peachtree Center Ave, #1000, ☎ 404-656-7829.

◆ **May**

African Diaspora Celebration, Auburn Ave, ☎ 404-688-7011, or contact Georgia Peach State Black Tourism Association, 285 Peachtree Center Ave, #1000, ☎ 404-656-7829.

Malcolm X Festival & Parade, ☎ 404-288-9880 or Georgia Peach State Black Tourism Association, 285 Peachtree Center Ave, #1000, ☎ 404-656-7829.

◆ **June**

Classic Chastain (continues through August), the Atlanta Symphony Orchestra's outdoor summer concert series. Included in the schedule are African-American R&B, jazz and popular artists. For information, contact the Woodruff Arts Center box office, ☎ 404-733-5000.

◆ **July**

Black Family Reunion Celebration, Grant Park, National Council of Negro Women, ☎ 404-524-6269.

Classic Chastain, Atlanta Symphony Orchestra. See June listing for details.

Kujichagulia Festival, Mosley Park, New Africans People's Party Organization, ☎ 404-288-9880.

Underground International Bazaar, Underground Atlanta, ☎ 404-523-2311.

◆ August

Classic Chastain, Atlanta Symphony Orchestra. See June listing for details.

Marcus Garvey Day, Mosley Park, Georgia Peach State Black Tourism Association, 285 Peachtree Center Ave, #1000, ☎ 404-656-7829.

African Pride Cultural Festival, Underground Atlanta, ☎ 404-523-2311.

◆ September

Muhammad Ali Labor Day Road Race, City Streets, ☎ 404-378-1600 or Georgia Peach State Black Tourism Association, 285 Peachtree Center Ave, #1000, ☎ 404-656-7829.

Arts Festival, Piedmont Park, Arts Festival of Atlanta, Inc., ☎ 404-885-1125.

Sweet Auburn Heritage Festival, Auburn Ave, ☎ 404-523-2311.

Underground Atlanta Labor Day Weekend Jazz Festival, Underground Atlanta, ☎ 404-523-2311.

◆ October

Peace Festival, Candler Park, ☎ 404-266-1969.

Hunter Street, Reunion, Martin Luther King Drive, ☎ 404-522-3249.

◆ November

Lighting of the Great Tree, Underground Atlanta, Rich's, ☎ 770-913-5551.

◆ December

Egleston Children's Christmas Parade, Downtown, Festival of Trees, ☎ 404-264-9348

Underground Atlanta Peach Drop New Year's Eve on Sweet Auburn, Auburn Ave, ☎ 404-523-2311.

Public Transportation

William B. Hartsfield International Airport, ☎ 404-530-6600.

Metro Area Rapid Transit Authority (MARTA), local bus and subway transportation schedule and information, ☎ 404-848-4711.

◆ **Taxicabs**

Atlanta Taxicab Association, ☎ 404-753-7759.

Checker Cab Company, ☎ 404-351-1111.

Atlanta Area Resources

Alliance Theater, 1280 Peachtree Street NE, Atlanta, GA 30309, ☎ 404-733-5000.

Atlanta African Film Society, PO Box 50319, Atlanta, GA 30302.

Atlanta Convention & Visitors Bureau, 223 Peachtree Street NE, Atlanta, GA 30303, ☎ 404-521-6600. Web site: www.acvb.com. Mon-Fri, 8:30 am-5:30 pm.

Fox Theater, 660 Peachtree Street NE, Atlanta, GA 30308, ☎ 404-249-6400.

Georgia Department of Industry, Trade and Tourism, PO Box 1776, Atlanta, GA 30301-1776, ☎ 800-847-4842 or 404-656-3590.

Georgia Peach State Black Tourism Association, 285 Peachtree Center Ave, #1000, Atlanta, GA 30303-1230, ☎ 404-656-7829.

Jomandi Theater, 1444 Mayson Street NE, Atlanta, GA 30324, ☎ 404-876-6346.

Just Us Theater Company, PO Box 42271, Atlanta, GA 30311, ☎ 404-753-2399.

National Park Service, Martin Luther King, Jr., National Historic Site, Auburn Ave NE, Atlanta, GA 30312, ☎ 404-331-5190. Daily, 9 am-5 pm.

Peach State Tourism Association, PO Box 38191, Atlanta, GA 30334, ☎ 404-656-7829 or 912-236-8326.

Variety Playhouse, 1099 Euclid Ave NE, Atlanta, GA 30307, ☎ 404-524-7354.

Atlanta

Baltimore

1. Cab Calloway Collection
2. Enoch Pratt Free Library
3. Frederick Douglass Marker
4. Joshua John Marker
5. Black Soldier Statue
6. Orchard Street Church & Museum
7. Billie Holiday Statue
8. Sharp St. United Methodist Church
9. Thurgood Marshall Bust
10. Thurgood Marshall House Marker
11. Thurgood Marshall Statue
12. Baltimore City Life Museum;
    Museum Row
13. Eubie Blake Gallery at the Brokerage
14. Great Blacks in Wax Museum
15. Baltimore Museum of Art
16. Maryland Historical Society
17. Baltimore Area Visitors
    Information Center

.5 MILE
.3 KM

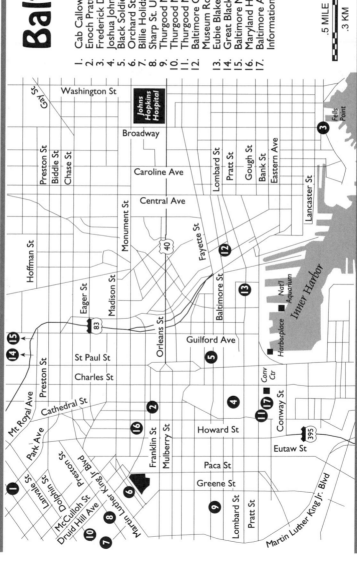

Baltimore

Historic Sites & Landmarks

Billie Holiday Statue, Pennsylvania Ave, between Lanvalve and Lafayette Streets. Born Eleanora Fagan on April 7, 1915, Billie Holiday was one of the greatest jazz singers of the 20th century. She was the subject of the major motion picture, *Lady Sings the Blues,* starring Diana Ross. Holiday died in 1959. An 8½-foot-tall bronze statue by sculptor James Earl Reid features the Baltimore native in a gown, with a gardenia in her hair.

Black Soldier Statue, Battle Monument Plaza, Calvert and Lexington Streets. In memory of American African-American soldiers from all branches of the service, the 19-foot-tall bronze figure wears a uniform with patches and medals of service and valor. His hands hold a wreath and banner listing American wars.

Cab Calloway Collection, Coppin State College Library, 2500 West North Avenue, ☎ 410-383-5926. The library contains a collection of Cab Calloway's personal memorabilia. Calloway was a renowned orchestra leader, composer and singer. He died in 1994. Free admission.

Enoch Pratt Free Library, 400 North Cathedral Street, Baltimore, ☎ 410-396-5500. Visit the Maryland Room's Afro-American Collection; explore an extensive array of books, archives, documents, photographs, publications, maps, records and more. Mon-Wed, 10 am-8 pm; Thurs, 10 am-5 pm; Sat, 10 am-5 pm. Free admission.

Frederick Douglass Marker, 500 South Dallas Street, Fell's Point. This marker honors one of the foremost African-American abolitionists and civil rights leaders, Frederick Douglass, who died in 1895.

Frederick Douglass Statue, Morgan State University, Hillen Road and Coldspring. Another monument to honor this African-American leader (see previous entry for more information). The 8½-foot-tall statue of Douglass was designed and sculpted by James Lewis.

Joshua John Marker, Hopkins Plaza at Charles and Baltimore streets. This marker honors one of this country's most renowned African-American painters, Joshua John, who created works during the 18th and 19th centuries.

NAACP Headquarters, 4805 Mount Hope Drive, ☎ 410-358-8900. Protecting and enhancing the civil rights of African-Americans, the NAACP Headquarters moved to Baltimore in 1986. The building includes a library and

Statue of Justice Thurgood Marshall
Courtesy of the Baltimore Area
Convention & Visitors Association

conference room, and a memorial garden named for writer Dorothy Parker is on the grounds. Tours by appointment only.

Orchard Street Church and Museum, 512 Orchard Street, ☎ 410-523-8150. One of Baltimore's first AME churches, this building was built by African-American slaves between 1837 to 1840. Tours by appointment only.

Sharp Street United Methodist Church, 1206 Etting Street, ☎ 410-523-7200. Organized in 1802, this church was the first African-American congregation in Baltimore.

St. Francis Xavier Catholic Church, Carolina and Oliver streets, Baltimore, ☎ 410-727-3103. Established in 1864, it is the oldest African-American Church building in the US.

Thurgood Marshall Bust, University of Maryland at Baltimore, 500 West Baltimore Street. Marshall was the first African-American elected to the US Supreme Court.

Thurgood Marshall Statue, Pratt and Sharp streets.

Thurgood Marshall House Marker, 1632 Division Street, Baltimore. Thurgood Marshall once lived in this home. Not open to the public.

Sites Beyond Baltimore

Benjamin Banneker Memorial, Mount Gilboa AME Church, Oella, MD. Banner was a mathematician, astronomer and inventor. Appointed to the District of Columbia Commission by President George Washington, Banneker worked with others to draw up plans for the design of the nation's capitol. Banneker died in 1806.

Kunta Kinte Plaque, City Dock, Annapolis, MD. African slave Kunta Kinte arrived at the colonial port of Annapolis in 1767. Kinte's descendent, author Alex Haley, wrote about his life in the popular novel and major motion picture *Roots*. The Kunta Kinte Heritage Festival is held annually in Annapolis, MD.

Matthew Henson Marker, Maryland State House, State Circle, Annapolis, MD. Henson was an explorer who co-discovered the North Pole with Rear Admiral Peary. Henson died in 1955.

Museums/Exhibits

Baltimore City Life Museums and Museum Row, 800 East Lombard Street, Baltimore, ☎ 410-396-6320. The 1840 House, the Carroll Mansion and the Courtyard Exhibition Center are only a few of the institutions to tour while visitors travel back through history at the Baltimore City Life Museum and Museum Row. The museum also features two historical dramas that highlight Baltimore's African-American community: *A Woman's Place* and *Heroes Just Like You.* Mon-Sat, 11 am-6 pm. Admission charge.

Baltimore Museum of Art, Art Museum Drive at Charles and 31st Streets, Baltimore, ☎ 410-396-6320. African art, masks and sculptures from Guinea and Angola are among the many works displayed at the Baltimore Museum of Art's Wurtzburger Gallery. The gallery exhibits works that represent diverse cultures from around the world. Wed-Fri, 10 am-4 pm; Sat-Sun, 11 am-6 pm. Admission charge.

Baltimore

Black American Museum, 1769 Carswell Street, ☎ 410-243-9600. This small art museum contains works by local contemporary African-American artists. Mon-Fri, 9 am-5 pm. Admission charge.

Eubie Blake Gallery at the Brokerage, 34 Market Place, Baltimore, ☎ 410-396-8128. Memorabilia in honor of the late jazz composer, Eubie Blake, and exhibitions of local artists. Mon-Fri, noon-5 pm. Free admission.

Great Blacks in Wax Museum, 1601 East North Avenue, Baltimore, ☎ 410-563-6415. The Great Blacks in Wax Museum chronologically presents wax figures of famous African-Americans "from slave ships to spaceships." Visitors will view figures of Martin Luther King, Jr., Rosa Parks, Frederick Douglass, Colin Powell, Harriet

Great Blacks in Wax Museum
Courtesy of the Baltimore Area
Convention & Visitors Association

Tubman and many more. The entrance to the museum has a startling exhibit of a slave ship, and depicts the harsh treatment and life of African slaves during their journey to the Americas. (Free parking is allowed along the street or in the Stop N Shop parking lot across the street.) Mon-Sat, 9 am-6 pm; Sun, noon-6 pm. Admission charge.

Maryland Historical Society, 201 West Monument Street, Baltimore, ☎ 410-685-3750. Paintings by Black Colonial portraitist Joshua Johnson are included in the collection at the library of the Maryland Historical Society. Original sheet music and memorabilia of Eubie Blake are also located at the institution. Tues-Fri, 10 am-5 pm; Sat, 9 am-5 pm. Admission charge.

Morgan State University Art Gallery, James E. Lewis Museum of Art, Coldspring Lane and Hillen Road, ☎ 410-319-3020. This art gallery features an eclectic gathering of African, American and European art. The collection also contains a number of notable pieces from West Africa, such as masks, furniture, artifacts and drums. Mon-Fri, 9 am-5 pm; weekends by appointment. Free admission.

Morgan State University Sopher Library, Coldspring Land and Hillen Road, Baltimore, ☎ 410-319-3458. Bill "Bojangles" Robinson's dancing shoes, memorabilia of Matthew Henson (one of the first men to reach the North Pole), books, pamphlets, periodicals, art works and clippings are among the considerable African-American holdings at the library's Davis Room. Visit the Benjamin A. Quarles Afro-American Studies Room and the Parren J. Mitchell room. Mon-Fri, 9 am-5 pm. Weekends vary; call ahead. Free admission.

Museums Beyond Baltimore

Banneker-Douglass Museum of Afro-American Life and History, Mount Moriah Church, 84 Franklin Street, Annapolis, MD, ☎ 410-974-2893. Constructed in 1874, the Gothic-style Mount Moriah Church was saved from demolition in the 1970s; the structure now houses an excellent museum of Afro-American life and history and includes African-American art, commissioned art, historical artifacts, historical archives, rare books, African art and artifacts, the Herbert M. Frisby Collection and the Thomas Baden Collection. Tues-Fri, 10 am-3 pm; Sat, noon-4 pm. Free admission.

Maryland Museum of African Art, 5430 Vantage Point Road, Historic Oakland at Town Center, ☎ 410-730-7105. Founded in 1980, the institution promotes a better understanding of traditional African art and culture, through programs, lectures, workshops and courses, sculptured figures, musical instruments, household items, jewelry and textiles. Tues-Fri, 10 am-4 pm; Sun, noon-4 pm. Call in advance. Free.

Historic Colleges & Universities

Coppin State College, 2500 West North Avenue. Baltimore, ☎ 410-383-5990. Founded 1900. State-supported college.

Morgan State University, Coldspring Lane and Hillen, Baltimore, ☎ 410-319-3000. Founded 1867. State-supported university.

Sojourner-Douglass College, 500 North Carolina Street, Baltimore, ☎ 410-276-0306. Web site: http://host.sdc.edu. Originally started in the early 1970s as the Homestead-Montebello Center of Antioch University, Sojourner-Douglass College became an independent four-year institution in 1980.

Shopping

Galleries & Specialty Shops

Framing Place, 8115 Liberty Road, ☎ 410-655-6468. African-American art. Limited editions and much more. Mon-Sat, 10 am-6 pm.

African-American Art Gallery, 7262 Cradle Rock Way, Columbia, MD, ☎ 410-381-1199. Fine African-American art. Mon-Sat, 11 am-7 pm; Sun, noon-5 pm.

Gallery Africa, (two locations) Beltway Plaza Mall at 6094 Greenbelt Road, Greenbelt, ☎ 301-345-2322 or Forest Village Park Mall at Donnell Drive and Pennsylvania Avenue, ☎ 301-736-8107. African wood carvings, African fabrics, hand-crafted jewelry and clothing from East and West Africa. Mon-Sat, 10 am-9:30 pm; Sun, noon-6 pm.

La Grande Vision, 408 East Eager Street, ☎ 410-837-1265. Portraits and figurative sculptures. La Grande also features the works of African-American sculptor James Earl Reid. Call for hours.

Mahogany Exchange, 111 West Saratoga Street, ☎ 410-752-5808. Afrocentric boutique featuring ladies' and men's clothing and fabric, unique gift items, collectibles, prints, ethnic greeting cards, artifacts and jewelry. Tues-Sat, 11 am-6 pm.

Of African Descent, 34 Market Place, ☎ 410-752-6838. Specializes in African artifacts, gifts, jewelry and assorted handcrafts by African-Americans. Mon-Fri, 11:30-6 pm.

Bookstores

Arawak Books, 1401 University Blvd, Langley Park, ☎ 301-434-2373. Afrocentric books: art, biography, drama, fiction, poetry, history, geography, politics, contemporary issues and much more. Sun-Fri, noon-6 pm; Sat, noon-9 pm. Closed Mon.

Gospel Notes, Rivertowne Commons Shopping Center at 6147 Oxon Hill Road, Oxon Hill, ☎ 301-839-2636. African-American Christian bookstore. Mon-Sat, 10 am-8 pm.

Karibu Books, 3500 East/West Highway, Hyattsville, ☎ 301-559-1140, fax 202-667-5278. Books by and about African-Americans. Mon-Sat, 10 am-9:30 pm; Sun, noon-6 pm.

North Star Bookstore, 7025 Liberty Rd, Windmoor Shopping Center, ☎ 410-265-8787, fax 410-265-8788. African-American fiction and nonfiction books. Mon-Sat, 10 am-8 pm; Tues, 10 am-7 pm.

Fashions

African Accents, 1724 Woodlawn Dr, ☎ 410-655-3620. Call for information on store items and hours.

African-American Fashions, Woodmoor Shopping Center at 7031 Liberty Rd, Woodlawn, ☎ 410-281-1310. African fabrics, custom-designed clothing and accessories. Mon-Sat, 9 am-8 pm; Sun, noon-5 pm.

African Fashions Culture Store, 3816 Liberty Heights Ave, Baltimore, ☎ 410-664-5141. African-American fashions for men, women and small children. Mon-Sat, 10 am-9 pm; Sun, 1 pm-6 pm.

Afrique Fashion, 1200 Mondawmin Mall, ☎ 410-669-5571. Men's, women's and children's African fashions and accessories. Mon-Sat, 10 am-9 pm.

Cally's Fashion-African Clothing, 1119 West Lombard Street, ☎ 410-752-0876. Custom-made African clothing.

Expressions Cultural Center, 222 North Paca Street, ☎ 410-783-0195. Original African and African-American art representing local and international artists including oil paintings, watercolors, sculptures, masks, and much more. Mon-Sat, 9:30-6 pm.

Maggie's Place, 213 West Read Street, ☎ 410-728-5678. High fashion women's clothing boutique. Tues-Fri, 10 am-5 pm; Sat, 10 am-3 pm.

Mahogany Exchange and **Out of Africa Boutique,** 111 West Saratoga Street, ☎ 410-752-5808. Afrocentric boutique featuring ladies' and men's clothing and African fabrics, unique gift items, collectibles, prints, ethnic greeting cards, artifacts and jewelry. Tues-Sat, 11 am-6 pm.

Pretty Please, 3032 Mondawmin Mall, upper level, ☎ 410-523-9001. Women's upscale designer fashions. Mon-Sat, 10 am-9 pm.

Rhonda's Boutique, 514-516 West Franklin Street, ☎ 410-669-8160. Women's clothing. Tues-Sat, 11 am-7 pm.

The Shirtery, 2901 Druid Park Drive, #200E, Baltimore, ☎ 410-669-2726.

Spas

Arlinda's Place Skin and Body Care Salon, 2076 Lord Baltimore Dr, ☎ 410-298-8778. Call for information.

Restaurants

◆ **Caribbean**

Caribbean Cabin and Muffin Works, 222 North Charles Street, ☎ 410-576-9257. Caribbean cuisine and bakery items. Features specialties such as jerk chicken, curry goat, rice and peas, and other Caribbean favorites. Also features 24 varieties of muffins and other baked delicacies. Mon-Fri, 8 am-3 pm.

Caribbean Kitchen, 218 North Liberty Street, Downtown, ☎ 410-837-2274. Features traditional West Indian meals and serves generous portions of oxtail, curried and jerk chicken, curried goat dinners served with rice and peas, and other soul food, Caribbean delicacies and tropical drinks. Mon-Thurs, 7 am-5 pm; Fri 7 am-9 pm; Sat, 11 am-4:30 pm. ☆ *Specially recommended.*

Negril on Thayer, 965 Thayer Ave, Silver Spring, MD, ☎ 301-585-3000. No pork served. Mon-Sat 11 am-10 pm, closed Sun.

◆ **Seafood**

Bertha's, 734 S Broadway, Fells Point, ☎ 410-327-5795. Seafood, chicken, mussels, crab cakes and variety of fresh fish. Open daily, 11:30 am-10:30 pm.

Haven, 1552 Havenwood Rd, Northwood Shopping Center, ☎ 410-366-7416. Seafood, chicken, beef pasta and much more. Features blues at night. Open daily, noon-midnight.

Shuckers Seafood Restaurant, Harborplace-Pratt Pavilion, Downtown, ☎ 410-547-9090. Their specialty is oysters on the halfshell and they feature clams, crab cakes, shrimp and much more. Informal setting in Pavilion marketplace. Daily, 10 am-10 pm.

◆ **Soul Food**

Five Mile House, 5302 Reistertown Rd, ☎ 410-542-4895. Features chicken, burgers, seafood and much more. Mon-Sat, 6 am-2 am.

Southern Diner, 6577 Coventry Way, Clinton, ☎ 301-868-0815. Specialty is fried chicken, meatloaf, fish, pork chops, chopped steak, beef ribs, pork and all the traditional soul food vegetables. Mon-Sat, 8 am-9 pm; Sun, 8 am-8 pm.

Benny's Restaurant, 2701 North Charles Street, ☎ 410-366-7779. Serves lunch and dinner and features a Sunday jazz brunch. Open Thurs-Sun.

Baltimore

Black Entertainment Network BET Sound Stage, 9640 Lottsford Ct, Largo, MD, ☎ 301-883-9500. Located about 25 miles south of downtown Baltimore next to the Washington Bullets' US Air Arena. From Baltimore, take I-95 south. This unique music video theme restaurant serves up classic American entrées with a southern flair, such as steaks, seafood, Caribbean jerk chicken, New Orleans Creole gumbo and homemade desserts. Dress code is smart informal. Sunday brunch, 11 am-3 pm, features the gospel sound of BET Network's Bobby Jones. Mon-Thurs, 11:30 am-1 am; Fri-Sat, 11:30 am-2 am; Sun, 11 am-midnight.

Entertainment

Clubs/Lounges

◆ Jazz

Silver Shadow, Lakefront North, Columbia, ☎ 410-730-0111. Contemporary dance club. Live music: jazz, disco, reggae.

◆ Dance

Arch Social Club, 2426 Pennsylvania Ave, ☎ 410-728-3837.

Poet Club, 918 East North Ave, ☎ 410-243-7609. Local establishment with jukebox music. Open daily, 6 pm-2 am. Closed Tues.

Silver Shadow, Lakefront North, Columbia, ☎ 410-730-0111. Contemporary dance club. Live music: jazz, disco, reggae.

Wall Street Bar and Lounge, 1817 Maryland Avenue, ☎ 410-625-3873. Open Wed-Sat for special events. Call first.

Club 21, 2105 Pennsylvania Ave, ☎ 410-669-8000. Contemporary dance nightclub. Open evenings, 9 pm-2 am. Jazz happy hour, Mon-Fri at 5 pm.

Dinner Theater

Encore Dinner Theater, 3801 Liberty Heights Ave, ☎ 410-466-2433. Call for upcoming events and schedules.

Comedy

Monique's Comedy House at Cochini's, 225 North Liberty Street, ☎ 410-494-7500. Call for upcoming shows and comedians.

Travel Agents

Galaxsea Cruises, 6400 Baltimore National Pike, #270-B, Catonsville, MD 21228, ☎ 800-890-6660 or 410-747-5204.

Henderson Travel Services, 7961 Eastern Ave, Silver Spring, MD 21224, ☎ 800-327-2309 or 301-650-5700, fax 301-650-5717. A premiere African-American travel agency specializing in worldwide tours and packages, and featuring such exotic places as Africa, Caribbean and Europe. A full-service travel agency.

Total Travel Services, Inc., 7554 Main Street, Pikesville, MD 21227, ☎ 410-795-8850.

Heritage Tours

About Town Tours, 10 Fox Hill Ct, Baltimore, MD 21128-9799, ☎ 410-592-7770, fax 410-592-3333. About Town Tours features a three-hour historic tour of African-American history and culture. Tour highlights include the Great Blacks in Wax Museum, Orchard Street Methodist Church, Fells Point, former home of Frederick Douglass, and Seton Hill, part of the Underground Railroad. Visitors will gain insight into the significant contributions made by famous African-American Baltimoreans such as Eubie Blake, Thurgood Marshall, Benjamin Banneker, Clarence Mitchell and Lillie Carroll Jackson.

African-American Renaissance Tour, PO Box 2402, Baltimore, MD 21203, ☎ 410-728-3837 or 410-727-0755, fax 410-396-9586. This Baltimore-based tour company highlights historic African-American churches, educational institutions, businesses and a variety of other sites depicting the history of Baltimore's African-American community. Tours feature visits to the Great Blacks in Wax Museum, Orchard Street Church, Morgan State University and a number of other cultural sites, landmarks and businesses. Ask about their "Nightlife" tours. Call for tour schedules and more information.

Rent A Tour, 3414 Philips Dr, Baltimore, MD 21208, ☎ 410-653-2998. This Baltimore tour company specializes in convention, meeting and reception services, and customized touring programs. It features an African-American Heritage tour that includes visits to Baltimore's Black historical sites, landmarks and cultural centers. Highlights of the tour include the Great Blacks in Wax Museum, the Eubie Blake Museum and Cultural Center, Orchard Street Church, Fells Point and much more. Call for schedule and additional information.

Baltimore

Media

Radio Stations

◆ Jazz

WEAA 88.9 FM, Morgan State University at Hillen and Coldspring Lane, ☎ 410-319-3564, fax 410-319-3798. Ethnic (Caribbean), jazz, gospel, public radio format.

◆ Urban

WEBB 1360 AM, 3000 Druid Park Dr, ☎ 301-367-9322. Adult contemporary format.

WWIN 95.9 FM, 200 South President Street, ☎ 410-332-8200. Urban contemporary format featuring jazz and oldies R&B.

◆ Gospel

WBJR 860 AM, 3000 Druid Park Dr, ☎ 410-367-7773, fax 410-367-4702. Gospel format.

WCAO 600 AM, 1829 Reistertown Rd, ☎ 410-653-2200, fax 410-486-8057. Gospel format.

WJRO 1590 AM, 159 Eighth Ave, ☎ 410-761-1590. Gospel format.

WWIN 1400 AM, 200 South President Street, ☎ 410-332-8200. Gospel/inspirational format.

Newspapers

Afro-American Newspaper, 2519 North Charles Street, ☎ 410-554-8200, fax 410-554-8213.

Baltimore Afro-American, 628 North Eutaw Street, ☎ 301-728-8200. Web site: www.afroam.org. Black community newspaper. Distributed weekly on Thursdays.

Baltimore Times, 12 East 25th Street, ☎ 410-366-3900. African-American community newspaper. Distributed on Fridays.

Magazines

Black Pages of America; Washington Metropolitan Edition, 101 North Sixth Street, Richmond, VA, ☎ 804-782-1000. Directory of numerous African-American-owned businesses in the metropolitan Maryland area.

Publications

Baltimore's African-American Heritage Guide, Visitors Guide, Baltimore Office of Promotion and the Baltimore Area Convention and Visitors Association, 200 West Lombard Street, Baltimore, MD 21202, ☎ 410-752-8632.

Destination Maryland, Mid Atlantic Magazine, 250 South President Street, Level One South, Baltimore, MD 21202.

Minority Business Guide, Downtown Partnership of Baltimore, 217 North Charles Street, Baltimore, MD 21201, ☎ 410-244-1030. Listing of some African-American business in the downtown Baltimore area.

Washington Metropolitan Black Pages, Black Pages of America, 101 North Sixth Street, Richmond, VA 23219, ☎ 301-567-7500.

African-American Churches

AME

Adams Chapel, 3809 Egerton Rd, ☎ 410-542-6200.

Agape Fellowship, 4804 Reistertown Rd, ☎ 410-466-4545.

Allen, 1130 West Lexington Street, ☎ 410-298-1514.

Bethel, 300 Druid Hill Ave, Baltimore, ☎ 410-523-4273. Dates back to the late 18th century✓

Davis Memorial AME, 2409 Roslyn Ave, ☎ 410-664-0106. ◇

Ebenezer AME, 20 West Montgomery Street, ☎ 410-783-0190.

Evergreen, 3342 Old Frederick Rd, ☎ 410-945-0130.

Fallsroad AME, 2145 Pine Ave, ☎ 410-922-3190.

Gaines AME, 7134 Montgomery Rd, ☎ 410-796-8530.

Hemingway Temple AME, 2701 Woodview Rd, ☎ 410-354-2518.

Imani AME, 5803 Moravia Road, ☎ 410-485-2025.

John Wesley AME Zion, 1923 Ashland Ave, ☎ 410-732-7020.

Oak Street AME, 123 West 24th Street, ☎ 410-235-6908.

Pennsylvania Avenue AME Zion, 1128 Pennsylvania Ave, ☎ 410-728-7416.

Patterson Asbury AME, 2211 Division Street, ☎ 410-523-3678.

Payne Memorial AME, 1714-1716 Madison Ave, ☎ 410-669-8739.

St. John AME, 810 North Carrollton Ave, ☎ 410-523-5468.

St. Stephen's AME, 7741 Mayfield Avenue, ☎ 410-796-9762.

Shiloh AME, 2601 Lyndhurst Ave, ☎ 410-367-8961.

Star of Bethlehem AME, 2525 Rigley Street, ☎ 410-727-1433.

Trinity AME Church, 2140 East Hoffman Street, ☎ 410-342-2320.

Wayman's AME, 1305-1307 Washington Blvd, ☎ 410-727-8626.

Baptist

First Baptist Church, 25 North Carolina Street, ☎ 410-675-2333.

Leadenhall Baptist Church, 1021 Leadenhall Street, ☎ 410-539-9334.

Union Baptist Church, 1219 Druid Hill Ave, ☎ 410-523-6880.

Catholic

St. Francis Xavier Catholic Church, Carolina and Oliver streets, ☎ 410-727-3103.

St. Peter Claver Roman Catholic Church, North Fremont Ave, ☎ 410-728-2033.

COGIC

Emmanuel Temple COGIC, 509 North Franklintown Rd, ☎ 410-233-6965.

Faith Temple COGIC, 2301 Edmonson Ave, ☎ 410-233-6705.

Prayer Mission COGIC, 1209 West Fayette Street, ☎ 410-528-0022.

Methodist

Sharp Street United Methodist Church, 1206 Etting Street, ☎ 410-523-7200.

Four Square

Lafayette Square Church, 1121 West Lanvale Street, Baltimore, ☎ 410-523-1366. Est. 1825.

Calendar of Annual Events

◆ **January**

Dr. Martin King, Jr. Celebration, Citywide activities, ☎ 410-752-8632.

Let Freedom Ring, ☎ 410-783-8000. The Baltimore Symphony Orchestra performs a musical celebration in honor of Dr. Martin Luther King, Jr. each January.

◆ **February**

Black History Month in Baltimore. From a series presented by the Baltimore Film Forum to lectures, concerts and fundraisers, there's something to do every day during the Month of February. For a listing, call ☎ 410-837-4636 or 800-282-6632.

◆ **July**

Artscape, ☎ 410-396-4575. Festival of the literary, performing and visual arts of Baltimore.

Thursday Night Jazz Concert Series. Every summer, Thursday evenings sizzle in downtown Baltimore! Free outdoor concerts offer a line-up of jazz, reggae, salsa and R&B. Music lovers groove to performances by the area's best musicians and national acts. For more information, call ☎ 410-837-4636 or 800-282-6632 for a schedule.

◆ **August**

Kunta Kinte Commemoration and Heritage Festival. This annual event in historic Annapolis features arts, crafts, exhibits and ethnic foods. For information, ☎ 410-349-0338.

Trinidad and Tobago Festival. The annual ethnic celebration transports visitors to the islands. Sample food and beverages, and swing to the sounds of steel drum bands. Contact the Trinidad and Tobago Association of Baltimore at ☎ 410-467-TTAB.

◆ **September**

AFRAM Festival, ☎ 800-282-6632 or 410-225-7896. Annual African-American exposition. Foods, arts, crafts, exhibits, entertainment.

◆ **December**

Kwanzaa Activities. Citywide. Baltimore Area Convention and Visitors Association, 100 Light Street, Baltimore, MD 21202, ☎ 800-282-6632 or 410-659-7300.

Baltimore

Public Transportation

Baltimore-Washington International Airport (BWI), ☎ 410-859-7111. Outside Baltimore, ☎ 800-I-FLY-BWI. TDD, 410-859-7227.

Baltimore Metro and Light Rail, ☎ 410-539-5000.

MARC Trains, ☎ 800-325-RAIL.

Metropolitan Area Transit Authority, ☎ 202-637-7000.

Metrobus, ☎ 202-637-7000.

MTA Buses, Metro & Light Rail Services, ☎ 410-539-5000.

Washington Dulles International Airport, ☎ 703-661-2700.

Washington Metro, ☎ 202-637-7000.

Washington National Airport, ☎ 703-419-8000.

Water Taxi, ☎ 800-658-8947 or 401-563-3901.

Baltimore Area Resources

African Culture Education and Research Foundation, 5430 Vantage Point Rd, Baltimore, MD 21044, ☎ 301-596-0051.

Baltimore Area Convention and Visitors Association, 100 Light Street, Baltimore, MD 21202, ☎ 800-282-6632 or 410-659-7300, fax 410-727-2308; Web site: www.baltconvstr.com.

Baltimore Area Visitors Information Center, 300 West Pratt Street, Baltimore, MD 21202, ☎ 410-837-4636. Mon-Fri, 9-5.

Maryland Office of Tourism and Development, 217 East Redwood, Baltimore, MD 21202, ☎ 800-543-1036 or 410-767-3400. Mon-Fri, 8:30-5.

National Coalition of Black Meeting Planners, 8630 Fenton Street, #126, Silver Spring, MD 20910, ☎ 301-587-9100.

Partnership of Baltimore, *Minority Business Guide*, 217 North Charles Street, Baltimore, MD 21201, ☎ 410-244-1030.

Birmingham

Historic Sites & Landmarks

A.G. Gaston Gardens, 1501 Fifth Ave N, A.G. Gaston Motel. Civil Rights marchers once formed ranks here in 1963. For many years, the A.G. Gaston Motel was Birmingham's only first-class hotel for African-Americans. It now serves as a residence for elderly and handicapped tenants. Not open to the public.

Alabama College of Barber Instruction, Inc., 1715 Fourth Ave, ☎ 205-328-2076. N. Clinton Simpson, Sr. founded the college as the New Breed Barber Shop. Its mission is to encourage minorities to own commercial property in the Historic Fourth Avenue Business District.

Alabama Penny Savings Bank, 310 18th Street N. The first African-American-owned bank in Alabama (1890), the Alabama Penny Savings Bank helped thousands of Birmingham's African-American citizens by financing the construction of their homes and churches. For viewing only.

Arthur H. Parker Home, 522 First Street N. This is the former residence of Arthur H. Parker, once principal of Parker High School. For many years it was the largest secondary school in the US for African-Americans. The home was built in the 1920s of handmade pressed concrete blocks. Not open to the public.

Bethel Baptist Church, 3233 29th Ave N, ☎ 205-322-5360. From 1953 to 1961, Bethel Baptist Church served as the headquarters for the Birmingham Civil Rights Movement and the Alabama Christian Movement. The Gothic-styled brick building was built in 1926 and was the first in the area to have offices for clergy and Sunday School rooms. It survived three bombings during the 1960s under the pastorate of Reverend Fred Shuttelsworth.

Black Masonic Temple, 1630 Fourth Ave. In the heart of the Fourth Avenue Historic District, the Black Masonic Temple served as the center of community activity for African-Americans for many years. The seven-story brick and steel structure was built in an early 20th-century neo-classical revival design. Not open to the public.

City Federation of Women's Club House, 551 Jasper Rd. This house was built in 1900 and has been used to house elderly and orphaned African-Americans. It is now used as a day nursery. Not open to the public.

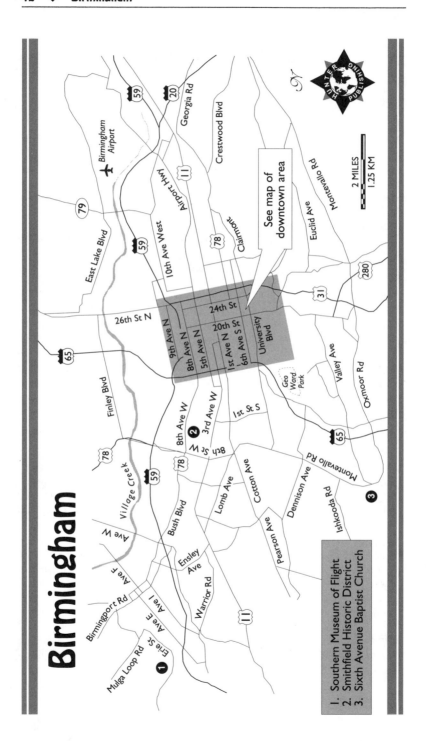

Birmingham

59
20
Georgia Rd
Crestwood Blvd
Birmingham Airport
11
Airport Hwy
79
10th Ave West
78
Clairmont
East Lake Blvd
59
See map of downtown area
Euclid Ave
Montevallo Rd
280
31
2 MILES
1.25 KM
65
26th St N
24th St
9th Ave N
8th Ave N
5th Ave N
20th St
1st Ave N
6th Ave S
University Blvd
Finley Blvd
Valley Ave
Oxmoor Rd
Geo Ward Park
8th Ave W
3rd Ave W
2
1st St S
65
8th St W
78
78
Montevallo Rd
Village Creek
59
Bush Blvd
Lomb Ave
Cotton Ave
Dennison Ave
Ishkooda Rd
3
Ave W
Ensley Ave
Pearson Ave
Warrior Rd
11
Ave F
Ave E
Ave I
Birmingport Rd
Erie St
Mulga Loop Rd
1

1. Southern Museum of Flight
2. Smithfield Historic District
3. Sixth Avenue Baptist Church

Dr. A.M. Brown Home, 319 North Fourth Terrace. Dr. A.M. Brown was the African-American physician who founded World Health Week. He was the original owner of this 1½-story home. The house is now occupied by the Birmingham Arts Club.

Fourth Avenue Historic Business District, located in the 1600-1800 blocks north and parts of the 300 block of 17th and 18th streets north. This area was once the heart of social, cultural and commercial activity for African-Americans during the early 1900s. Today, some of the area still remains active, including many small African-American-owned shops, restaurants, bars, Alabama Jazz Hall of Fame, and Kelly Ingram Park.

Greyhound Bus Station, North 19th Street. This is the site where the "Freedom Riders" were violently attacked by angry segregationists in May of 1961. The 21 Black and white Freedom Riders traveled by bus to test segregation laws and practices.

Kelly Ingram Park, 6th Ave N, at Sixteenth Street. This historic park was the site of violent attacks on peaceful civil rights demonstrators during the 1960s. Scenes of police dogs chasing African-American men, women and children and fire hoses spraying them were images that shocked the world. Sculptures depicting these scenes are on the park grounds. Violent scenes such as the ones that occurred here were instrumental in overturning segregation in the nation.

Birmingham

Kelly Ingram Park
Photo courtesy of the Greater Birmingham Convention & Visitors Bureau

Parker High School, Eighth Street, between Fifth and Third streets. Named after Arthur H. Parker, this high school (originally called Industrial High School in 1889) was, for several years, the nation's largest secondary school for African-Americans.

Rickwood Field, 1137 2nd Ave W, ☎ 205-780-0023. Built in 1910, Rickwood is America's oldest baseball park. It showcased the talents of baseball legends from Piper Davis to Willie Mays, Babe Ruth and Hank Aaron. Few African-American teams could afford their own playing facilities; the Birmingham Black Barons rented the stadium from its white owners on dates when the Birmingham Barons, a white minor league team, were not in town.

Sixteenth Street Baptist Church, 1530 Sixth Ave N, ☎ 205-251-9402. On September 15, 1963, Addie Mae Collins, Cynthia Wesley, Carol Robertson, and Denise McNair were the four young girls who were killed by a bomb that exploded near the church sanctuary. The tragedy was a major turning point in the civil rights protest in Birmingham and became a rallying cry for unity throughout the country. A memorial for the four girls is located in the church basement and includes photos and memorabilia. The church was founded in 1873. Open during the week for visitors and for Sunday services.

Sixteenth Street Baptist Church
Photo courtesy of the Greater Birmingham Convention & Visitors Bureau

Sixth Avenue Baptist Church, 1101 Martin Luther King, Jr. Drive SW, ☎ 205-251-5173. Now home to one of the largest congregations in the state, the Sixth Avenue Baptist Church dates back to 1881 when it first opened its doors for worship services. It was later rebuilt and moved to its present site in the early 1970s. Open for Sunday services.

Smithfield Historic District, Eighth Ave to Third Street W. In 1886, plantation owner Joseph Riley Smith and nine other investors subdivided 600 acres and turned them into suburban lots. They named the streets after relatives and friends, and the area later became known as Smithfield. By 1989 it had become Birmingham's fourth largest suburb. Smithfield was further developed in the early 1900s as a neighborhood for prominent African-American professionals. Many homes in the district were designed by noted African-American architect Wallace A. Rayfield. Parker High School, Birmingham's first high school for African-American students, is located here.

T.J. Johnston House, 500 Eighth Street. This house was built in 1925 by noted architect, Wallace Rayfield. It was once the site of the first YMCA branch to be located in an African-American neighborhood. Not open to the public.

Woodlawn Cemetery, Airport Boulevard. Buried here are Addie Mae Collins, Cynthia Wesley and Carol Robertson, three of the young victims of the Sixteenth Street Baptist Church bombing on September 16, 1963. The fourth victim, Denise McNair, is buried elsewhere.

Woolworth Department Store site, 1006 20th Street. This historic site was the scene of a violent lunch counter protest in the 1960s.

Sites Beyond Birmingham

Jesse Owens Monument, Jesse Owens Park, County Road 187, Oakville, near Danville and Molton. The memorial to this Olympic athlete is located near his birthplace. The park includes a playground, baseball field, basketball courts, running track, pavilions, welcome center and tenant house, as well as a replica of the home of the four-time Olympic gold medalist. The park opened during the 1996 Olympics.

Tuxedo Junction, 1728 20th Street, Ensley, AL. Named for the streetcar at Tuxedo Park, the junction gained national attention from the 1939 hit song *Tuxedo Junction,* written by Birmingham composer Erskine Hawkins. The dance hall on the second floor of the Nixon building was the social hub for Birmingham's African-American community in the 1920s and 30s.

Museums/Exhibits

Alabama Jazz Hall of Fame, 1631 Fourth Ave N, ☎ 205-254-2731. Great jazz artists from Alabama are honored here at the Alabama Jazz Hall of Fame. The contributions of Nat "King" Cole, W.C. Handy, Lionel Hampton, Erskine

Hawkins, Sun Ra and others are also displayed here. The museum is located in the historic Carver Theatre for the Performing Arts. Tues-Sat, 10 am-6 pm; Sun, 1 pm-5 pm. Free admission.

Alabama Sports Hall of Fame Museum, 2150 Civic Center Blvd, ☎ 205-323-6665. The museum features exhibits on some of Alabama's great African-American athletes, highlighting the careers of prominent basketball, football and baseball figures. Mon-Sat, 9 am-5 pm; Sun, 1 pm-5 pm. Closed Christmas and New Year's Day. Admission charge.

Birmingham Civil Rights Institute, 520 16th Street N, ☎ 205-328-9696. This "living" institution chronicles the dramatic activities in Birmingham during the 1960s. The institute has developed a series of programs, services and exhibits that depict the history of African-Americans in the struggle for civil rights. Exhibits are displayed in a variety of galleries, and there is a theater and gift shop. Tues-Sat, 10 am-5 pm; Sun, 1 pm-5 pm. Suggested donation.

Birmingham Civil Rights Institute
Photo courtesy of the Greater Birmingham Convention & Visitors Bureau

Birmingham Museum of Art, 2000 Eighth Ave N, ☎ 205-254-2565. The museum has over 1,500 works of art from diverse cultures, dating from ancient to modern times, including growing collections of African, pre-Columbian and Native American art. It is the oldest art museum in the country. Free admission. Tues-Sat, 10 am-5 pm; Sun, noon-5 pm. Closed Monday, New Year's Day, Thanksgiving and Christmas.

Downtown Birmingham

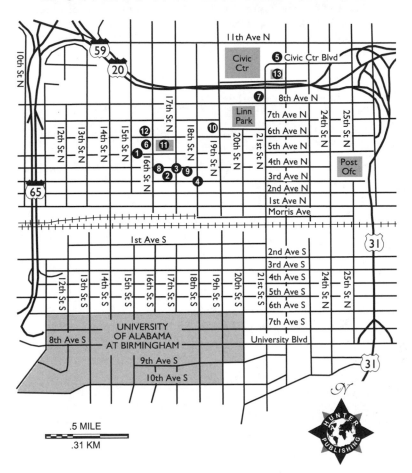

.5 MILE

.31 KM

Birmingham

1. A.G. Gaston Gardens
2. Alabama Jazz Hall of Fame
3. Alabama College of
   Barber Instruction
4. Alabama Penny Savings Bank
5. Alabama Sports Hall of Fame
6. Birmingham Civil Rights Institute
7. Birmingham Museum of Art

8. Black Masonic Temple
9. Fourth Avenue Historic Business Dist.
10. Greyhound Bus Station
11. Kelly Ingram Park
12. Sixteenth Street
    Baptist Church
13. Greater Birmingham
    Convention & Visitors Bureau

Southern Museum of Flight, 4343 73ʳᵈ Street N, ☎ 205-833-8226. Among its wide variety of exhibits and aviation memorabilia is an excellent display about the Tuskegee Airmen. Tues-Sat, 9:30 am-4:30 pm; Sun, 1 pm-4:30 pm. Closed on Mondays and major holidays. Admission charge.

W.C. Handy Birthplace and Museum, 620 West College Street, off US 72, ☎ 205-766-7642. Considered the "Father of the Blues," music legend W.C. Handy was born in this two-room log cabin in 1873. Tues-Sat, 9 am-noon and 1 pm-4 pm. Admission charge.

Historic Colleges & Universities

J.F. Drake State Technical College, 3421 Meridian Street, Huntsville, AL 35811, ☎ 205-539-8161. Founded 1961.

Lawson State Community College, 3060 Wilson Road SW, Birmingham, AL 35221, ☎ 205-925-2515.

Miles College, 5500 Ave G, Ensley, AL 35208, ☎ 205-923-2771. Established in 1908. Independent four-year Christian Methodist Episcopal college.

Oakwood College, Oakwood Road NW, Huntsville, AL 35896, ☎ 205-726-7000. Private four-year college. Founded 1896.

Stillman College, PO Box 1430, Tuscaloosa, AL 35403, ☎ 205-349-4240. Private four-year college. Founded 1876.

Talladega College, 627 West Battle Street, Talladega, AL 35160, ☎ 205-362-0206. Private four-year college. Founded in 1867.

Shopping

Galleries & Specialty Shops

Balloons Etc., 220 20ᵗʰ Street N, Downtown, ☎ 205-254-9003. All-occasion balloons, candy, chocolate, gift baskets.

From Me To You, Inc., 105 20ᵗʰ Street N, Downtown, ☎ 205-323-8492. Card and gift gallery. African-American cards, figurines, balloons, prints and gift baskets. Call for store hours.

Ophelia's Gallery, 1905 Old Bessemer Highway, ☎ 205-925-9166. A gallery of exclusive African-American art, Ophelia's sells quality paintings, sculpture, and collectibles from local and nationally recognized African-American artists. The gallery displays a scenic mural painted by a number of African-Americans and is a popular stop for tour groups. Mon-Sat, 10 am-6 pm; Sun, 1 pm-4 pm.

Positive Images-Afro-American Art Gallery, 1604 Third Ave W, ☎ 205-785-7000. Represents local and international African-American artists, featuring wood carvings, statues and T-shirts. Call for store hours.

Sweet Treats and More, 214 20ᵗʰ Street N, downtown, ☎ 205-798-7214. Call for hours.

Bookstores

Mahogony Books, 208 20ᵗʰ Street N, downtown, ☎ 205-252-1624. Afrocentric books and figurines, ethnic greeting cards and postcards, jewelry, ethnic dolls, small selection of African furniture, Kwanzaa items and African fashions. Call for store hours.

Yamini's Accessories and Books, 1727 Third Ave N, downtown, ☎ 205-322-0037. Afrocentric books, greeting cards, men's and women's clothing, jewelry, incense and oils, African masks and prints. Mon-Fri, 10 am-5:30 pm; Sat, 11 am-5 pm.

Fashions

African Fashions Unlimited, 1525 Fourth Ave N, ☎ 205-322-7010. African clothing, men's and women's accessories; handbags, hats, jewelry, art, African soaps and incense and ethnic cards. Mon-Sat, 10 am-6 pm.

Fashion Avenue, 217 North 20ᵗʰ Street, ☎ 205-324-5490. Men's and boys' clothing, sweats, sportswear, leathers, shirts, jackets, shoes, hats, vests.

Judy's Downtown, 1916 Second Ave N, ☎ 205-254-3383. Women's boutique with a selection of African women's fashions and accessories. Mon-Thurs, 9 am-5:15 pm; Fri-Sat, 9 am-5:30 pm.

Restaurants

Bro Chette's, Que & Bayou, 1709 Fourth Ave N, Fourth Avenue Historic District, ☎ 205-326-3663. Specialties are barbeque pork, chicken and rib plates and sandwiches. Menu items also include Cajun red beans and rice, gumbo, blackened fish and shrimp. Mon-Tues, 11 am-6 pm; Wed-Fri, 11 am-9 pm; Sat, 11 am-6 pm.

Exotic Wings and Things, 121 20ᵗʰ Street N, Downtown, ☎ 205-324-2424. Specialty is Buffalo hot wings, short orders, side orders, sandwiches. Call for hours.

Green Acres, 1705 Fourth Ave N, Fourth Avenue Historic District, ☎ 205-251-3875. Specialty is fried chicken wings, livers and gizzards. Menu items include a variety of sandwiches, fish and pork chop meals. Call for hours.

Birmingham

Hosie's Bar-B-Q and Fish, 321 17th Street N, downtown, ☎ 205-326-3495. Specialty is barbeque and hot wings. Menu items include fried fish, pig's ears and feet, shrimp and soul food side orders. Mon, 11 am-8 pm; Tues-Thurs, 11 am-10 pm.

Nelson's Bakery-Deli, 1623 Fourth Ave, Fourth Avenue Historic District, ☎ 205-250-0052. Short order items. Menu also includes homemade baked goods. Mon-Fri, 8 am-5 pm.

Nelson Brothers Café, 312 17th Street N, downtown, ☎ 205-254-9098. Short order fast food restaurant. Homemade pies and cakes. Open daily, 6 am-5 pm.

Rib It Up, 830 First Ave N, ☎ 205-328-7427. Popular neighborhood barbeque restaurant. Call for hours.

Entertainment

◆ Reggae

Cafe 312, 312 20th Street S, ☎ 205-324-7768. Thursdays, live Caribbean and Reggae music. Open weekends. Call for current events.

◆ Dance Nightclubs

French Quarter, 1630 Second Ave N, downtown, ☎ 205-254-2799. Popular dance club with live entertainment. Two levels of entertainment. Call for schedule of events.

Tee's, 821 Second Ave N, ☎ 205-324-0791. Popular dance nightclub. Contemporary music. Call for hours.

Heritage Tours

Landmark Tours, 4363 First Ave N, Birmingham, AL 35209, ☎ 800-338-4714 or ☎ 205-592-2001. African-American heritage tours.

S.C.L.C. Women, 328 Auburn Ave, Atlanta, ☎ 404-584-0303. Offers several tour options from three-hour tours to two-day excursions; African-American heritage and civil rights tours of Atlanta, Selma, Birmingham and Montgomery. Required donation.

Travel Agents

United Management Enterprises, 648 Center Way SW, Birmingham, AL 35211, ☎ 205-322-3219.

Media

Radio

◆ Urban

WATV 900 AM, 3025 Ensley Ave, ☎ 205-780-2014. Full service format.

WENN 107.7 FM, 424 16th Street N, ☎ 205-254-1820. Urban contemporary.

WJLD 1449 AM, Spaulding Ishkooda Road, ☎ 205-942-1776. Adult urban contemporary format.

◆ Gospel/Religious

WAGG 1250 AM, 424 16th Street N, ☎ 205-254-1820. Religious format.

WAYE 1220 AM, 1403 Third Ave W, ☎ 205-786-9293. Gospel format.

Newspapers

Birmingham Times, 115 Third Ave W, ☎ 205-251-5158. African American community newspaper. Distributed weekly.

Birmingham World, 407 15th Street N, ☎ 205-251-6523. African-American community newspaper. Distributed weekly.

Publications

Alabama's Black Heritage, Alabama Bureau of Tourism and Travel, 401 Adams Ave, #126, Montgomery, AL 36104, ☎ 800-ALABAMA.

African-American Churches

AME

Allen Chapel AME, 6213 Second Ave S, ☎ 205-595-8040.

Allen New Temple AME, 4353 Huntsville Road, ☎ 205-841-1577.

Bryant Chapel AME, 1300 First Ave W, ☎ 205-925-7151.

Gaines Chapel AME, 1104 37th Pl N, ☎ 205-595-2081.

Metropolitan AME Church, 1530 Fourth Ave N, ☎ 205-252-8503.

Mt. Hermon AME Zion, 1310 Depot Street ☎ 205-808-0434.

Oak Ridge AME Zion, 1209 Indiana Street, ☎ 205-785-6087.

Payne Chapel AME, 1833 Center Way S, ☎ 205-251-3412.

Birmingham

St. James AME, 4200 5th Ct N, ☎ 205-591-1238.

St. John AME Church, 15th and Seventh Ave, ☎ 205-251-3764.

Sixteenth Street Baptist Church, 1530 Sixth Ave N, ☎ 205-251-9402.

COGIC

Unity COGIC, 3904 Jefferson Ave NW, ☎ 205-925-7890.

Calendar of Annual Events

◆ January

Ebony Fashion Fair, ☎ 205-458-8400. Spotlight on African-American beauty and fashion.

Unity Breakfast in honor of Dr. Martin Luther King's birthday, ☎ 205-458-8400. The community comes together to honor the birthday of a civil rights legend.

◆ February

Black History Month Activities, ☎ 205-458-8400, or Greater Birmingham Black Chamber of Commerce, ☎ 800-962-6453 or 205-458-8000.

◆ July

Function at Tuxedo Jazz Festival, Ensley, AL, ☎ 205-254-2720. Famous Birmingham jazz musicians and local talents headed for the big-time entertain the crowds.

Birmingham Heritage Festival, ☎ 205-324-3333. Dedicated to preserving the legacy of African-Americans by educating through arts and entertainment.

◆ September

Black Expo, ☎ 205-458-8400.

Jazz Hall of Fame Banquet and Concert, ☎ 205-254-2720. Honoring nationally-known jazz musicians from the Birmingham area.

◆ October

Birmingham Jam Jazz, Blues and Gospel Festival, Greater Birmingham Convention and Visitors Bureau, 2200 9th Ave N, ☎ 800-962-6453 or 205-458-8000.

◆ December

Kwanzaa Celebration, ☎ 205-458-8400 or Greater Birmingham Black Chamber of Commerce, ☎ 800-962-6453 or ☎ 205-458-8000.

Public Transportation

Birmingham International Airport, ☎ 205-595-0533.

Metro Area Express (MAX). For schedule information, ☎ 205-521-0101. Operates daily, but closed Saturdays.

Birmingham Area Resources

Alabama Bureau of Tourism and Travel, 401 Adams Ave, #126, Montgomery, AL 36104, ☎ 800-ALABAMA.

Greater Birmingham Black Chamber of Commerce, ☎ 800-962-6453 or 205-458-8000.

Greater Birmingham Convention and Visitors Bureau, 2200 Ninth Ave N, Birmingham, AL 35203, ☎ 800-962-6453 or 205-458-8000; Web site: www.bcvb.org. Mon-Fri, 8:30 am-5 pm.

Travelers Aid Society, Airport location, ☎ 205-322-5426.

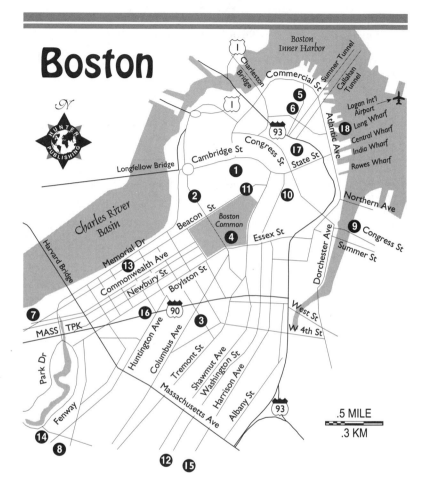

1. African Meeting House & Black Heritage Trail
2. Charles Street AME Church
3. Harriet Tubman House
4. Boston Massacre Monument
5. Copps Hill Burying Ground
6. Crispus Attucks Burial Site
7. "Free At Last" sculpture
8. Northeastern University
9. KIDS Bridge / Children's Museum
10. Old South Meeting House
11. Robert Gould Shaw & 54th Regiment Memorial
12. Prince Hall Masonic Temple
13. William Lloyd Garrison statue
14. Boston Museum of Fine Arts
15. Museum of the National Center for Afro-American Artists
16. Greater Boston Convention & Visitors Center
17. Faneuil Hall / Quincy Market
18. New England Aquarium

Boston

Historic Sites & Landmarks

African Meeting House, 46 Joy Street, Beacon Hill/Boston, ☎ 617-742-1854. Nicknamed the "Black Faneuil Hall," the African Meeting House has served as the center for political, social, educational and religious activity for Boston's Black community during the 1900s. It was constructed in 1806 by free Black craftsmen and laborers and is considered to be the oldest Black church still standing in the nation. Over the years, the Meeting House also served as the recruitment center for the celebrated 54th Regiment and the home of the New England Anti-Slavery Society. Its basement housed the first public school for Black children in the Boston area. Mon-Fri, 10 am-4 pm.

The Cambridge African-American Heritage Trail, ☎ 617-349-4683 or 617-441-2884. This self-guided walking tour highlights historic African-American sites throughout the city of Cambridge, near Boston. Major points of interest include the former home of educator W.E.B. DuBois while he was earning his doctorate at Harvard University; the home of William Wells Brown, the nation's first African-American novelist; and the home of Maria Baldwin, the first African-American headmistress at the Agassiz School. The tour also includes other African-American sites and interesting historical facts about the Cambridge area. Call for tour information.

African-American Literature Collection, Sawyer Library at Suffolk University, 8 Ashburton Place, Beacon Hill/Boston, ☎ 617-573-8535. This 5,000-volume collection by African-American writers was founded in 1971 and focuses on 18th- and 19th-century works by African-American writers associated with New England. Free admission.

Black Heritage Trail. African Meeting House, 46 Joy Street, ☎ 617-742-1854. Led by knowledgeable National Park rangers, the 1.6-mile Black Heritage Trail is a walking tour through Beacon Hill, which was a settlement for Boston's African-American community between 1800 and 1900. The Trail guides visitors to 14 historical sites such as the African Meeting House; the celebrated Robert Gould Shaw and 54th Regiment memorials; former schools, residences and Underground Railroad stations. The Trail takes visitors through one of the largest groupings of African-American historic sites in the nation. Call for tour schedules. Free brochure; free admission.

Boston Massacre Monument, Boston Commons, Tremont Street. Escaped slave Crispus Attucks was the first to die in the historic Boston Massacre on March 5, 1770, when he and several other colonists were killed by British troops. This incident marked the beginning of the American Revolution. In

1851, Black leaders William C. Nell, Charles Redmond, Lewis Hayden, and Joshua B. Smith petitioned the Massachusetts state legislature to erect a monument in memory of Attucks. The granite and bronze monument was erected in 1907 on the Boston Commons. A representation of Attucks appears in the foreground of the frieze at the base of the monument.

Copp's Hill Burying Ground, between Hull and Snowsen streets, down from the Old North Church. This burial ground holds the gravesites of many 18th century African-American heroes such as Prince Hall, who founded the first African-American Masonic organization in 1787 after being rejected from white Masonic organizations. Open until dusk.

Dillaway-Thomas House, Roxbury Heritage State Park, 183 Roxbury Street, Roxbury/Boston, ☎ 617-445-3399. This mid-18th-century Georgian gambrel-roof structure was built for Reverend Oliver Peabody. However, it is named after General John Thomas, who used it as his Revolutionary War headquarters. It is also named after Charles Dillaway, an educator who resided there for much of the 19th century. The Dillaway-Thomas house now serves as a heritage center, providing historical and cultural events, special exhibits, lectures, concerts, films and the "Griots of Roxbury," a youth group that, through developing and understanding the past, hopes to make positive changes for the future. Tour hours: Tues-Fri, 10 am-4 pm, Sat-Sun, noon-5 pm. Appointments available. Free admission.

Smith Court, Black Heritage Trail
Photo courtesy of the Greater Boston Convention & Visitors Bureau

Emancipation Group, Park Square and Stuart streets, Boston. The slave in this sculpture is a model of Archer Alexander, the last person captured under the historic Fugitive Slave Act, which provided for slaves to be returned from one state or territory to another. The cost of the $17,000 statue was raised entirely by freed slaves, and was presented to the city of Boston by Moses Kimball in 1877. It is actually a duplicate of the original bronze, which stands in Lincoln Park in Washington, DC.

"Free At Last," Marsh Plaza, Boston University, Kenmore/Boston. This 20-foot-high work of art by Sergio Castillo is made of Cor-ten steel and stands at the University's Marsh Plaza. The sculpture depicts 50 doves, symbolic of each of the 50 states, and its base is engraved with quotations by Dr. Martin Luther King, Jr.

Harriet Tubman House/United South End Settlements, 566 Columbus Ave, ☎ 617-536-8610. Harriet Tubman, nicknamed the "Black Moses" of the Underground Railroad, opened the Harriet Tubman House for the Aged and Indigent in upstate New York after the Civil War. Another was opened in Boston in 1904 at 25 Holyoke Street by six Black women who donated their time, money and property to assist Black working girls from the South. This current site was opened in 1988, and continues to provide a range of social services and activities. It has a collection of books, periodicals, documents, photographs, and a videotaped interview with one of Tubman's great nieces. It provides research and information on Harriet Tubman. An art gallery representing local artists is open Mon-Fri, 9 am-8 pm; Sat, 10 am-2 pm.

John D. O'Bryant African-American Institute, Northeastern University, 40 Leon Street, Roxbury, ☎ 617-373-3141. The institute serves as an academic, cultural and personal support service for Northeastern University's African-American students. The library houses a collection of print and nonprint materials concerning African-Americans and African Diaspora. Mon-Fri, 9 am-4:30 pm.

KIDS Bridge - The Children's Museum, 300 Congress Street, Downtown Boston, ☎ 617-426-6500. Developed by Boston's Children's Museum in 1990, this interactive anti-discrimination exhibit was designed to help kids explore their ethnic identity and to deal with racial prejudice. The exhibit's goals are to teach children to value themselves and others, and to work against racism. It presents this in a fun and thought-provoking way. Tues-Sun, 10 am-5 pm; Fri, 9 am-5 pm. Summer hours: Mon-Thurs, 10 am-5 pm; Fri, 9 am-5 pm; Sat, 10 am-5 pm. Admission charge.

King Reading and Exhibition Room, Mugar Library, Boston University, Commonwealth Ave, Kenmore/Boston, ☎ 617-353-3696. This memorial library honoring the late Dr. Martin Luther King, Jr. features rotating exhibits of his papers, including sermon manuscripts, essays, speeches, correspondence, his telephone book, drafts of the manuscript for his book, *Stride Toward*

Boston

Freedom, photographs, tape recordings of speeches and interviews, citations, and awards. Mon-Fri, 9-5.

Muhammad's Mosque #11, 10 Washington Street, Dorchester, ☎ 617-442-6082. The late Malcom X founded this Mosque in 1954 after returning to Boston from his Islamic studies with Nation of Islam leader Elijah Muhammad. It is the Boston headquarters for the Nation of Islam. Malcolm X served briefly as the Mosque's minister before being transferred to Philadelphia and New York City. Louis Farrakhan, who became the national leader of the Nation of Islam in 1977, was born and raised in Roxbury.

Martin Luther King, Jr. Graduate Student Home, 397 Massachusetts Ave, South End/Boston. The late Dr. Martin Luther King, Jr. resided here from 1952-53 while enrolled at Boston University's School of Theology. On January 15, 1989 (which would have been Dr. King's 60th birthday) a plaque was placed on the building commemorating his life there. Not open to the public.

Old South Meeting House, 310 Washington Street, Downtown Boston, ☎ 617-482-6439. Prominent African-Americans such as Booker T. Washington and W.E.B. Dubois have lectured in this building, which has served as a forum for free speech. Author Phyllis Wheatley, the first African-American to publish a book, was a member of the Meeting House. Her worship here provided inspiration for her book, *Poems on Various Subjects Religious and Moral,* published in 1773. An original copy of it is on permanent display here as part of an exhibit on her life and work. Call for current hours.

A. Philip Randolph Memorial Statue & Tribute to Pullman Porters, Back Bay Station, Dartmouth Street. The history of the African-American railroad worker is depicted in this sculpture by African-American sculptress Tina Allen. The memorial commemorates A. Philip Randolph, the founding president of the Brotherhood of Sleeping Car Porters, the first successful Black trade union. Randolph (1889-1979) was an active civil rights leader and is credited with influencing Franklin Roosevelt to bar racial discrimination in the defense industries during World War II.

Prince Hall Masonic Temple, 18 Washington Street, Dorchester/Boston, ☎ 617-445-1145. Prince Hall founded the first African Masonic Lodge in the US in 1787. Boston's Lodge No. 459 is one of the few lodges that holds its original Royal Charter. The Prince Hall Freemasons is one of the most prominent Black masonic organizations in the US and Caribbean, and many noted African-American leaders have been members. Prince Hall was also an active civil rights leader, Methodist minister, and Revolutionary War soldier. Hall, along with 1,000 other freed colonial Blacks, is interred at Copp's Hill Burying Ground in Boston's North End.

Robert Gould Shaw and the 54th Regiment Memorial, Corner of Park and Beacon, directly across from the Old State House at Boston Commons. In July of 1863, Robert Gould Shaw and 900 Black volunteer soldiers led an assault at Fort Wagner, SC prior to the capture of the city of Charleston. They were outnumbered and the attack failed, and nearly half the soldiers of the heroic 54th Regiment were killed, wounded, or missing in action. Their bodies were buried in a mass grave at the fort. The high-relief bronze sculpture by August St. Gaudens commemorating these heroic men took 14 years to complete, and it is considered one of the finest war memorials anywhere. The actions of the 54th Regiment were portrayed in a major motion picture, *Glory,* starring African-American actors Morgan Freeman and Denzel Washington.

Robert Gould Shaw/54th Regiment Memorial,
a testimony to the service of Afro-Americans in the Civil War.
Photo courtesy of the Greater Boston Convention & Visitors Bureau

William Lloyd Garrison House, 125 Highland Street, Roxbury/Boston, ☎ 617-445-8961. Garrison was an active anti-slavery crusader. He helped found the New England Antislavery Society and was publisher of *The Liberator,* an anti-slavery newspaper. He traveled throughout the northern parts of the US and to England to bitterly attack the issue of slavery. Garrison lived in this home from 1864 and died in New York City on May 24, 1879.

The house is now used as a convent by The Society of St. Margaret. Open by appointment only. A statue of Garrison is located at the Commonwealth Avenue Mall at Dartmouth & Exeter streets in the Boston/Back Bay area.

William Trotter House, 97 Sawyer Ave, Dorchester/Boston. Now a National Historic Landmark, this house was the residence of William Monroe Trotter (1872-1934), founder and publisher of the *Boston Guardian*, a newspaper that assisted in the fight for civil rights. Trotter was also founder of the Boston Civil Rights League (1901), a precursor to the NAACP. The house was built in 1893. Not open to the public.

League of Women, 558 Massachusetts Ave, South End/Boston. Martha and William Carnes owned this house during the Civil War and used the property to shelter fugitive slaves. It was purchased in 1920 by the League of Women for Community Service, under the leadership of Maria Baldwin. Today, the league continues to provide a variety of community and social service programs for those in need. On the National Register since 1975, 558 Massachusetts Ave also stands as a monument to the continuing service of African-American women.

Sites Beyond Boston

Old Burial Ground, Garden Street and Massachusetts Ave, Cambridge. African-American Revolutionary War soldiers Neptune Frost and Cato Steadman are buried here. Open until dusk.

Peter Salem's Gravesite, Old Burial Ground, Main Street, Framingham. Salem was an African-American slave who fought in many Boston area battles against the British at Lexington and Bunker Hill. For more information regarding Salem's gravesite, contact the Framingham town clerk at ☎ 508-620-4862.

Phyllis Wheatley Collection, Houghton Library, Harvard University, 1350 Massachusetts Ave, Cambridge, ☎ 617-495-2441. This Harvard University library holds a rare collection of manuscripts by African-American 18th-century poet Phyllis Wheatley. Collection includes portions of Wheatley's correspondence. Mon-Fri, 9 am-4 pm; Sat, 9 am-1 pm. Free admission.

Ink Well Beach, Martha's Vineyard. This popular beach area resort has attracted African-Americans for years. Once home to a thriving African-American and American Indian population, Ink Well Beach is now a summer vacation spot for many African-Americans. Two African-American-owned bed & breakfasts are located on the island: Shearer Cottage and Twin Oaks. See the *Lodging* section for information.

Nantucket Whaling Museum, Broad Street, Nantucket, ☎ 508-228-1736. Hundreds of African-American seamen lived and worked in the Nantucket area as part of New England's thriving 19th-century whaling industry. Some of their history is exhibited at the Nantucket Whaling Museum. From June-August, open daily from 10 am-5 pm; from September-May, open Sat-Sun, 11 am-3 pm.

Museums/Exhibits

African-American Master Artists in Residency Program (AAMARP), Northeastern University, 76 Atherton Street/Jamaica Plain-Boston, ☎ 617-373-3139. This Northeastern University gallery exhibits paintings, collages, illustrations, fabrics, photographs and written materials by well-known African-American artists. The AAMARP was founded by artist-activist professor Dana Chandler and exhibits works of 18 renowned artists. Open to the public. Call for an appointment.

Boston Museum of Fine Art, 465 Huntington Ave, ☎ 617-267-9300. The array of authentic African and African-American art pieces and paintings is among the world's finest. Tues, 10 am-4:45 pm; Wed, 10 am-9:45 pm; Thurs-Sun, 10 am-4:45 pm. Admission charge.

Museum of the National Center of Afro-American Artists, 300 Walnut Ave, ☎ 617-442-8614. This center houses more than 4,000 works by contemporary African-American artists. Works reflect the heritage, culture and diaspora of the African and Caribbean people. Tues-Sun, 1 pm-5 pm. Admission charge.

Historic Colleges & Universities

Roxbury Community College, 1234 Columbus Ave, Roxbury, MA 02120, ☎ 617-541-5310. State-supported two-year college. Founded 1973.

Shopping

Art Galleries & Specialty Shops

A Nubian Notion, Inc., 146 Dudley Street, Roxbury, ☎ 617-442-2622. Afrocentric gifts, imported artifacts, oils, Kwanzaa kits, candles, books, jewelry, West Indian bangles, calendars, T-shirts, sweatshirts, cards and more. Mon-Sat, 10 am-7 pm.

Boston

Oasis Boutique, 3 Main Street, Brockton, ☎ 508-588-8842. Afrocentric gifts from West Africa, West Indies and Cabo Verde Islands. Creative T-shirt designs, carvings, masks, canes, plates, wall ornaments, imported from Kenya, Ghana and Nigeria. Books, greeting cards, hats and oils. Mon-Sat, 10 am-6 pm. Summer hours: Mon-Fri, 10 am-6 pm; Sat, 10 am-7 pm; Sun, noon-6 pm.

Rose of Sharon Gifts, 1601 Blue Hill Ave, Suite 202, Mattapan, ☎ 617-298-0609. Afrocentric art, books and gift items. Tues-Fri, 2:30 pm-6:30 pm; Sat, 9:30 am-6 pm.

Treasured Legacy, Copley Place (around the corner from Neiman Marcus), Boston, ☎ 617-424-8717. Exquisite African art, books and gifts. Mon-Sat, 10 am-7 pm.

Ujamaa Mart (Roxbury's Mini Mall), 62 Warren Street, Roxbury, ☎ 617-445-9446. African-American stores specializing in Afrocentric products. Eleven stores under one roof; religious scriptural plaques, T-shirts, sweatshirts, hats, books, cards, jewelry, collectible dolls, men's fashions, women's fashions, children's fashions, accessories, skin care, hair braiding, bridal items and fabrics. Mon-Thurs, 10 am-6 pm; Fri-Sat, 10 am-7 pm.

Visham Arts and Crafts, Assemble Square Mall, Somerville (Route 3, Exit 29), ☎ 617-628-9868. African clothing, handcrafted wood, jewelry and accessories, custom clothing, musical instruments, canes, chairs and baskets. Mon-Sat, 10 am-9:30 pm; Sun, 11 am-6 pm.

Book Stores

Afrobooks, 927 Main Street, #A, Worcester, ☎ 508-799-9799.

Cultural Collections, 754 Crescent Street, Brockton, ☎ 508-580-1055, fax 508-580-5197.

Fashions

Nouveau Fashions, Copley Place, Boston, ☎ 617-266-1114. Women's fashion boutique. Mon-Sat, 10 am-7 pm.

Restaurants

◆ Barbecue

Red Bones Barbecue, 55 Chester Street, Somerville, ☎ 617-628-2200. Mon-Sat, 11 am-10 pm; Sun, noon-10 pm.

◆ Caribbean

Rhythm and Spice Caribbean Grill and Bar, 315 Massachusetts Ave, Cambridge, ☎ 617-497-0977. Specialties include Amerindian, West African, West Indian, East Indian, Chinese, British and Spanish cuisine. Menu items include jerk barbecue, rice, beans, peas, roti, curries and chutneys, pickled mixed vegetables, chicken, goat, beef and vegetarian items. Sun-Thurs, 5:30 pm-9:30 pm; Fri-Sat, 5:30 pm-10 pm.

◆ Soul Food

Bob the Chef's, 604 Columbus Ave, South End/Boston, ☎ 617-536-6204. Call for restaurant hours. Cajun/Southern cuisine. Tues-Wed, 5-10. Thurs-Sat, 5-12. Sunday brunch, 11-3:30, dinner 5-9.

Chef Lee's, 1140 Blue Hill Ave, Dorchester, ☎ 617-436-6634. Specializes in soul food; chicken, ribs, fish, pork chops, rice, black-eyed peas, collard greens, pig's feet and more. Mon-Sat, 7 am-8 pm.

Magnolia's Southern Cuisine, 1193 Cambridge Street, Cambridge, ☎ 617-576-1971. Specializes in New Orleans Cajun cuisine. Fish, beef, seafood entrees. Tues-Sat, 6 pm-10 pm.

Entertainment

Jazz/Blues Nightclubs/Lounges

Rhythm and Spice Caribbean Grill and Bar, 315 Massachusetts Ave, Cambridge, ☎ 617-497-0977. Weekly reggae, calypso and Caribbean dance music. Call first for upcoming events. Cover charge. Fri-Sat, 10:30 am-1 am.

Sculleries Jazz Club, Doubletree Guest Suites, 400 Soldiers Field Road, Boston, ☎ 617-562-4111. Call for specific events.

Dance Clubs

Rolls Club, 477 River Street, Mattapan/Boston, ☎ 617-296-5136.

Lodging

Bed & Breakfasts

Shearer Cottage, Rose Ave, Oak Bluffs, MA 62557, ☎ 508-693-2364.

Boston

Twin Oaks Inn Bed & Breakfast

Twin Oaks Inn, 8 Edgartown Road, PO Box 1767 Vineyard Haven, MA 02568, ☎ 508-693-8633, fax 508-522-1122. This Dutch Colonial-style inn was built in 1906 and is located on the popular resort island of Martha's Vineyard, within walking distance of the ferry terminal and the downtown area. There are two buildings on the premises. The main house has two spacious antique-filled bedrooms with private baths, and two smaller rooms with a shared bath; two of the rooms are suites. Also, there is a separate one-bedroom apartment with its own entrance, sun room, fireplace and kitchen. A continental-plus breakfast is served each morning and includes the innkeeper's homemade "Morning Crunch Granola." Twin Oaks Inn has been awarded the 1996 Crême de la Crême Award from *Boston Best Guide* for "Best Atmosphere." Call for current rates and reservations.

Travel Agents

Centurion World Travel, 160 Speen Street, #305, Framingham, MA 01701, ☎ 800-631-5943.

Media

Radio Stations

◆ Urban Contemporary

WILD 1090 AM, 90 Warren Ave, ☎ 617-427-2222.

WLVG 740 AM, 670 Cummins Way, ☎ 617-576-2895. Religious, urban contemporary format.

◆ Eclectic

WMLN 91.5 FM, 1071 Blue Hill Ave, ☎ 617-333-0311.

Newspapers

Bay State Banner, 68 Fargo Street, Dorchester, ☎ 617-357-4900. African-American community newspaper. Distributed weekly on Thursdays.

Magazines

Caribbean Voice Magazine, PO Box 285, Mattapan, ☎ 508-584-6833.

Publications

Black Pages of New England, PO Box 1848, Brockton, MA 02403, ☎ 508-584-5656 or ☎ 617-298-3000. Directory of numerous African-American businesses in New England, primarily in the greater Boston area.

Boston: African-American Discovery Guide, Greater Boston Convention & Visitors Bureau, Inc., Prudential Tower, Boston, MA 02199-0468, ☎ 800-888-5515 or ☎ 617-536-4100.

African-American Churches

AME

Charles Street AME, 551 Warren Street, Roxbury, ☎ 617-427-1298.

Columbus Avenue AME Zion, 60 Columbus Ave, ☎ 617-266-2758.

St. Paul AME Church, 37 Bishop Allen Drive, Cambridge, ☎ 617-661-1110.

Baptist

Concord Baptist, 190 Warren Ave, Boston/South End, ☎ 617-266-8062.

Morning Star Baptist, 1257 Blue Hill Ave, Boston/Mattapan, ☎ 617-298-0278.

New Hope Baptist, 740 Tremont Street, Boston/South End, ☎ 617-437-1439.

People Baptist, 132 Camden Street, Boston/South End, ☎ 617-427-0424.

Twelfth Street Baptist, 150 Warren Street, Roxbury, ☎ 617-442-7855.

Episcopal

St. Augustine and St. Martin Episcopal, 29-31 Lenox Street, Boston/South End, ☎ 617-442-6395.

St. Cyprian, 1073 Tremont Street, Boston/South End, ☎ 617-427-6175.

Methodist

Union United Methodist, 485 Columbus Ave, Boston/South End, ☎ 617-536-0872.

Wesley United, 1076 Washington Street, Boston/Dorchester, ☎ 617-298-1886.

Boston

Non-Denominational

New Covenant Christian Center, 1500 Blue Hill Ave, Boston/Dorchester, ☎ 617-445-0636.

Pentecostal

Holy Tabernacle, 70 Washington Street, Boston/Dorchester, ☎ 617-427-8510.

Mount Calvary Holy Church of America, 9 Otisfield Street, Boston/Roxbury, ☎ 617-427-7596.

Seventh Day Adventist

Seventh Day Adventists, 108 Seaver Street, Boston/Dorchester, ☎ 617-427-2201.

Calendar of Annual Events

◆ January

Martin Luther King, Jr. Day, ☎ 617-536-4100. The third Monday of every January is set aside to honor, commemorate and celebrate the life and words of Dr. King. The day is filled with special meetings, gospel concerts, memorial services, exhibits and performances.

Charles Hotel Jazz Festival, Cambridge (January-May), ☎ 617-876-7777.

◆ February

Black History Month. February is dedicated to discovering and celebrating Black History. There are numerous lectures, readings and special events throughout the city.

◆ June

Boston Globe **Jazz Festival** (seven days in mid-June), ☎ 617-929-2649.

◆ July

Abolitionists March and Rally, African Meeting House, Beacon Hill, ☎ 617-742-1854. Held annually on the weekend closest to July 18.

◆ December

Black Nativity, National Center for Afro-American Artists, ☎ 617-442-8614. Musical version of Langston Hughes' storytelling of the birth of Christ.

Kwanzaa, Children's Museum and Art of Black Dance and Music, ☎ 617-666-1859. City-wide activities.

Public Transportation

Logan International Airport, ☎ 800-23-LOGAN.

Massachusetts Bay Transportation Authority (MBTA). For local bus and subway schedules and information for the Greater Boston area, ☎ 617-722-3200.

Taxi Services

Checker Taxi Co, ☎ 617-536-7500.

Brighton Cab, ☎ 617-536-5010.

Town Taxi, ☎ 617-536-5000.

Boston Area Resources

African Meeting House, 8 Smith Court, Boston, MA 02114, ☎ 617-742-1854. Open daily, 9 am-5 pm.

Boston National Historical Visitor Center, 15 State Street, Boston, MA 02109, ☎ 617-242-5642. Open daily, 9 am-5 pm.

Greater Boston Convention & Visitors Bureau, Inc., Prudential Tower, Boston, MA 02199-0468, ☎ 800-888-5515 or 617-536-4100; Web site: www.bostonusa.com. Mon-Fri, 8:30 am-5 pm.

Massachusetts Office of Travel and Tourism, 100 Cambridge Street, 13th Floor, Boston, MA 02202, ☎ 800-447-6277 or 617-727-3202. Mon-Fri, 8:45 am-5 pm.

Travelers Aid Society of Boston, ☎ 617-542-7286.

Boston

Metropolitan Chicago

1. Harpo Studios / Oprah Winfrey
2. Carter G. Woodson Regional Library
3. Chess Records
4. Chicago Daily Defender
5. Chicago Urban League
6. Eternal Flame AME Church
7. Johnson Products
8. Johnson Publishing
9. Muhammad Ali Residence
10. Soft Sheen Products
11. Operation PUSH / Rainbow Coalition
12. Art Institute of Chicago
13. Chicago Historical Society Museum
14. DuSable Museum of
    African-American History
15. Field Museum of Natural History
16. Graue Mill & Museum
17. Chicago Convention & Tourism Bureau

2 MILES
1.25 KM

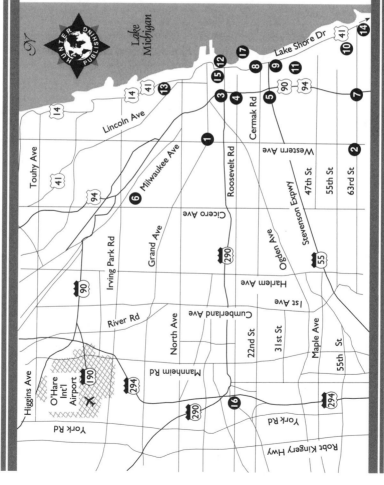

Chicago

Historic Sites & Landmarks

Alpha Kappa Alpha Sorority International Headquarters, 5656 S Stony Island Ave, ☎ 312-684-1282. The four-story building is the headquarters of this African-American women's sorority. The organization was founded in 1908.

Bessie Coleman Burial Site, Lincoln Cemetery, 123rd Street and Kedzie Ave, ☎ 773-445-5400. Aviator, barnstormer and activist Bessie Coleman earned international recognition during the 1920s by performing dangerous aerial stunts. Coleman was born in 1896 and developed an interest in flying after hearing her brother's stories about his experiences during World War I. Determined to enter flight school, she applied for a pilot's license, but to no avail. She was rejected repeatedly until Chicago African-American business leaders Robert Abbott and Jessie Binga lent their financial support and encouraged her to pursue a career in aviation. Coleman finally earned her pilot's license in France in 1915 and encouraged other African-Americans to pursue a similar career. Bessie Coleman tragically died in 1926 during one of her performances. Open Mon-Sun, 8 am-4:30 pm. Maps available at entrance.

Captain Ernest A. Griffin Place, Douglas Plaza, 3232 S Martin Luther King, Jr. Drive, ☎ 312-642-2420. The funeral home constructed by Capt. Griffin is located on the former site of Camp Douglass, where he was born. The base was initially used as a Union Army induction center and then as a prison for Confederate soldiers. Private Charles H. Griffin, Capt. Griffin's grandfather, served in the US Colored Infantry Unit, the "Fighting 29th." Army insignias, weapons and battle logs are on display in the parking lot of the funeral home. Photographs and other memorabilia are exhibited in the building. Open daily 10 am-5 pm.

Carter G. Woodson Regional Library, 9525 S Halsted Street, ☎ 312-747-6900. The Woodson Library, part of the Vivian Harsh Collection of Afro-American History and Literature, has one of the largest collections in the US of African-American history and culture. Vivian Harsh was the first African-American woman to head a branch of the Chicago Public Library, who compiled the works. The Carter G. Woodson Regional Library is named in honor of the Black scholar and founder of the Association for the Study of Negro Life and History and the *Journal of Negro History.* Also known as the "Father of Negro History," Woodson was responsible for the recognition of "Black History Month," designated by President Gerald Ford in 1976. Mon-Thurs, 9 am-9 pm; Fri-Sat, 9 am-5 pm.

Chess Records, 2120 S Michigan Ave, ☎ 312-808-1286. Ramsey Lewis, Wynton Kelly, Ahmad Jamal, James Moody, Sonny Stitt, Yusef Lateef and Muddy Waters are just a few of the jazz and blues artists who recorded here at Chess Records. Leonard Chess, the successful nightclub owner who owned the popular Macomba at 39th and Cottage Grove and other South Side clubs during the 1940s, bought a share of what was Aristocrat Records. The label was changed to Chess Records after Leonard and his brother bought out their Aristocrat partner. The Blues Heaven Organization purchased the site to help blues artists promote blues education in local schools and to help them collect their royalties. Tours during Black History Month only.

Chicago Daily Defender, 2400 S Michigan Ave, ☎ 312-225-2400. Founded by Robert Sengstacke Abbott in 1905 and subsequently taken over by his nephew, John Sengstacke, in 1940, the *Daily Defender* became the nation's most widely circulated Black newspaper. It attacked segregation, discrimination and lynching and encouraged southern Blacks to migrate north. The publication has an estimated 1.2 million weekly readers. The *Defender* is the first of many newspapers owned by the Sengstacke family; others include the *Pittsburgh Courier,* the *Tri-State Defender* and the *Michigan Chronicle.* Mon-Fri, 9 am-4:30 pm. Call for tours.

Chicago Urban League, 4510 S Michigan Ave, ☎ 773-285-5800. Established in 1916, the Chicago Urban League has helped guide the African-American community in their social and economic progress. They were initially founded to assist during the "Great Migration," when southern Blacks moved to the north for better opportunities. The league has traditionally helped Blacks toward obtaining fair practices in employment, housing, government and health care. Today, it has 130 employees and an operating budget of $6 million. The organization moved to this modern, multi-level office facility in 1984. Mon-Fri, 8 am-6 pm.

Daniel Hale Williams Home, 445 E 42nd Street. Dr. Daniel Hale Williams (1856-1931) was a heart surgeon and one of the founders of Chicago's Providence Hospital. He was the first physician to perform surgery on the human heart, served on the Illinois State Board of Health, surgeon-in-chief at Freedman's Hospital in Washington, D.C., taught at Chicago Medical College and advocated for Meharry Medical College in Nashville, Tennessee and at Howard University. Dr, Daniel Hale Williams lived in this home from 1905 to 1929. The site was designated a National Historic Landmark in 1975. Not open to the public.

Eighth Regiment Army Armory, 3533 Giles Ave, ☎ 773-493-9840. This armory is the home of the "Fighting Eight" Infantry of the Illinois National Guard and was built to house a regiment of African-American officers. It was established in 1898 during the Spanish-American War as an all-Black volunteer regiment. They served along the Mexican/US border in 1916 under the command of Col. Franklin A. Dennison during World War I. The Armory and the nearby sculpture are listed on the National Register of Historic places.

Elijah Muhammad Former Residence, 4847 S Woodlawn. Elijah Muhammad was the former leader of the Nation of Islam, one of the largest African-American religious organizations in the nation. The Nation of Islam is now under the leadership of Louis Farrakhan, who currently resides here. The home was also the former residence of World Heavyweight Boxing Champion Muhammad Ali. Not open to the public.

Eternal Flame AME Church, 1412 Greenfield, North Chicago ☎ 773-473-3722. Rev. E.J. Cole, father of famed singer Nat "King" Cole, was at one time pastor of this church. Rev. Cole was active in the 1960s Civil Rights Movement and led his congregation to the historical March on Washington in 1963. Call for tours.

The Harold Washington Library Center
© Willy Schmidt, City of Chicago, Courtesy of the Chicago Office of Tourism

Harold Washington Library Center, 400 S State St, ☎ 312-747-4300. The 10-story building opened in 1991, and was named in honor of former Chicago Mayor Harold Washington. The Center is a state-of-the-art complex complete with a 385-seat auditorium and a computer reference center. Special features of the library are the Harold Washington Archives and Collections (on the 9th floor), and the Chicago Blues Archive, representing several African-American artists. A mural-sized mosaic by African-American artist Jacob Lawrence is on the north wall of the central lobby. The work is entitled *Events in the*

Chicago

Life of Harold Washington. Tue & Thurs, 11 am-7 pm; Wed, Fri and Sat, 9 am-5 pm; Sun 1 pm-5 pm.

Harpo Studios, 1058 W Washington Blvd, ☎ 312-591-9222. This is the home of the Oprah Winfrey Show. Winfrey purchased this complex in 1988; it is the first and only studio complex owned by an African-American woman. The building was erected in the early 1900s and has been used as an armory for the US Army, a car barn for streetcars serving Chicago's West Side, and as a roller skating rink. The studio now has state-of-the-art film production and post-production capabilities. For tickets to the Oprah Winfrey Show, call at least one month in advance. No tapings during summer months.

Historic North Pullman Organization, 10432 S Maryland Ave, ☎ 773-928-6300. This organization educates and enlightens the public on the role of the Pullman porters. The name Pullman comes from George Mortimer Pullman (1831-1897), who invented the modern railroad sleeping car.

Jean Baptiste Pointe DuSable High School, 4934 S Wabash Ave. This predominantly African-American high school was named in honor of the founder of Chicago. Because of overcrowding at predominantly Black Wendell Phillips High School, DuSable was opened in 1935 and was the first high school built for Chicago's Blacks. During the 1930s and 1940s, the school produced more jazz musicians than any other school of its kind in the country. Pianist Dorothy Donegan, comedian Redd Foxx, Mayor Harold Washington and author Dempsey Travis are among the school's most prominent alumni.

Jean Baptiste Pointe DuSable Home and Trading Post Site, 401 N Michigan Ave, north of Wacker Drive. This historic site played an important part in Chicago's history. A Haitian-born immigrant, Jean Baptiste Pointe DuSable (1745-1818), arrived in Chicago in 1779 and was the first non-Indian to settle in the area. The industrious DuSable built and opened a trading post. His home originally measured only 20 feet by 40 feet; however, he later added two barns, a workshop, a bake house, a smoke house and a poultry house. He also earned a living as a miller and fur trader. The home and trading post site (now indicated by a marker) are listed on the National Register of Historic Places and were designated National Historical Landmarks in 1976.

Joe Louis Residence, 4326 S Michigan Ave. Former Heavyweight Boxing Champion Joe "The Brown Bomber" Louis once lived in this Chicago home. Louis earned the title in 1937 by defeating James J. Braddock and held it for almost nine years until his retirement in 1949. Not open to the public.

Johnson Products, 8522 S Lafayette Ave, ☎ 312-483-4100. Known for its successful line of Black hair products, Johnson Products was launched in 1953 when chemist George Johnson and hairstylist Orville Nelson developed a new hair straightener. A year later, the partnership dissolved and Johnson produced the Ultra Wave Hair Culture. Johnson Products moved to its present location in 1960 and in 1965 hit the $1 million sales mark. It became the first Black-owned business to trade on the New York Stock Exchange and was a sponsor of the television hit show, *Soul Train*. Johnson Products was sold in 1933 to IVAX of Dallas, Texas. Call to arrange tours.

Johnson Publishing, 820 S Michigan Ave, ☎ 312-322-9320. In 1942, John H. Johnson took a $500 loan and developed what later became the second largest African-American-owned business in the nation. Johnson published the *Negro Digest,* which later became *Black World.* In 1945, Johnson founded the popular *Ebony* magazine which brought the Johnson Publishing company national recognition. Johnson also publishes the popular *Jet* and *EM (Ebony Many)* magazines and owns Fashion Fair Cosmetics, Ebony Fashion Fair Show, WJPC AM and FM radio stations and the Ebony/Jet Showcase television show. The corporate office has one of the largest collections of African-American art in the nation. Mon-Fri, 9 am-5 pm.

Lloyd Hall Home, 420 E 65th Street. Lloyd Hall was a successful chemist who was known for patenting more than 100 methods for sterilizing foods and spices. He was born in 1894 in Elgin, Illinois and graduated from Northwestern University. In 1916, Hall was appointed as a chemist at the Chicago Board of Health and continued to develop new products while employed at Griffin Laboratories (1437 W 37th Street). The colonial-style home was built in the 1940s and is not open to the public.

Margaret Burroughs Home, 3806 S Michigan Ave. Burroughs was an artist, educator, writer, social activist and the founder of the DuSable Museum of African-American History. This beautiful mansion was built in 1903 by contractor John Griffin and in the late 1930s was converted into the Quincy Club, a private establishment. In 1961, it became the site of the Ebony Museum of Negro History. Located in South Chicago across the street from the South Side Community Arts Center, the Quincy Club became a social center and a rooming house for Black railroad workers who could not lodge in most Chicago hotels. Not open to the public.

Milton L. Olive Park, 640 Ontario Street on the lake side of Lake Shore Drive. This park was named in honor of a Vietnam War hero, Private First Class Milton L. Olive, who threw himself upon a grenade to save the lives of his platoon. He was the first African-American to be awarded the Congressional Medal of Honor for valiant service in the Vietnam War.

Mosque Maryum (formerly Nation of Islam Temple No. 2), 7351 Stony Island Ave, ☎ 773-324-6000. The Nation of Islam was founded by Wallace Fard Muhammad. After his death, the organization split into two factions. One remained in Detroit, while the other, led by Elijah Muhammad, moved to Chicago in 1934 and became the Nation of Islam Temple #2. When Elijah Muhammad died in 1975, the organization again split into two factions; one group supported Muhammad's son, W. Deen Muhammad; the other group

Chicago

supported the current Nation of Islam leader, Louis Farrakhan, who eventually purchased this temple. Call for tour information.

Muhammad Ali Residence, 4800 block of South Woodlawn. This is the home of the former Heavyweight Boxing Champion. Not open to the public.

New Regal Theater, 1649 E 79th Street, ☎ 773-721-9301. Duke Ellington, Nat "King" Cole, Jackie Wilson, Smokey Robinson and Louis Armstrong were just a few of the notable performers at the infamous Regal Theater. The original Regal opened in 1928 and was demolished in 1973. The 3,000-seat auditorium was part of the South Center Department Store and the Savoy Ballroom. The New Regal Theater, which has 2,300 seats, is the largest African-American owned multi-purpose theater in Chicago. Call for upcoming events.

Noble Drew Ali Burial Site, Lincoln Cemetery Mausoleum, 123rd Street and Kedzie Ave, ☎ 773-445-5400. Ali was founder and leader of the Moorish Science Temple during the 1920s, which claimed a membership of 2,100 by 1929, the year of his death. The Islamic group's banner consisted of a Moorish star and crescent with a red background, similar to that used today by the Nation of Islam. Apparently Noble Drew Ali's religious traditions influenced the founding of the Nation of Islam. Open Mon-Sun, 8 am-4:30 pm. Maps available at the entrance.

Oak Woods Cemetery, Greenwood Ave at 67th Street, ☎ 773-288-3800. This cemetery has been in existence since the late 1860s, and many prominent African-Americans have been buried here. They include Mayor Harold Washington; Jesse Owens, Olympic Gold Medalist; Edna Rose Abbott, wife of Robert S. Abbott, founder of the *Chicago Defender* and widow of Tuskegee Airman George S. Denison, who is also buried at the site; civil rights and women's suffrage advocate Ida Wells; Ferdinand Barnett, newspaperman, politician and lawyer; and Thomas A. Dorsey, the "father of gospel music." Mon-Fri, 8:30 am-4:15 pm; Sat, 9 am-3 pm. Closed Sunday. Tower of Memories Mausoleum open 10 am-4 pm daily. Maps available at main office.

Operation PUSH (People United to Serve Humanity), 930 E 50th Street, ☎ 773-373-3366. Rev. Jesse Jackson founded Operation PUSH on Christmas Day in 1971 after he resigned from his position as director of Operation Breadbasket. Because of Jackson's charismatic leadership, Operation PUSH became one of the nation's most recognized civil rights organizations. Known for its economic and educational programs, it quickly emerged as a negotiating body for African-Americans and local and national corporations in the areas of employment, promotion, subcontracting and franchising. Mon-Fri, 9 am-5 pm.

Oscar Stanton DePriest Home, 4536-4538 S Martin Luther King, Jr. Drive. Oscar DePriest (1871-1951) was born in Florence, Alabama. He moved to

Chicago and became the first African-American to serve on the Chicago City Council and in the United States Congress (1929-1934), representing a district north of the Mason-Dixon Line. Most of DePriest's constituents were also from the South. While in the House of Representatives, DePriest fought for civil rights legislation and for adequate funding for African-American educational institutions. In 1965, this home was designated a National Historic Landmark. Not open to the public.

Percy Julian and Anna Johnson Julian Home, 515 N E Ave, Oak Park. Dr. Percy Julian (1899-1975), was one of the nation's leading scientists. A graduate of DePauw, Harvard and the University of Vienna, and a recipient of 18 honorary degrees, Dr. Julian was responsible for developing a treatment for arthritis and a fire-fighting substance during World War II. He received the Proctor Prize and was elected to the elite Academy of Sciences. However, when this top 20th-century African-American scholar moved to Oak Park, he received hostile treatment because of his race. Racists set fire to his house, threw dynamite on his lawn and sent threatening letters to him and his family. In response, Julian hired guards to watch his house until the threats ended. He remained in the house until his death. In 1991, the United States Postal Service commemorated Dr. Julian by placing his portrait on a postage stamp. Not open to the public.

Provident Hospital, 500 E 51st Street, ☎ 312-572-2977. For many years, the Provident Hospital was the only hospital in the city that would provide health care services for African-Americans. Founded in 1891 by pioneer heart surgeon Daniel Hale Williams with the combined assistance and citywide fundraising efforts, Provident Hospital opened on South Dearborn Street with 12 beds, and has since established the first training school dedicated to African-Americans who want to pursue a career in medicine or nursing. The hospital continues to serve Chicago's South Side and the southern suburbs of Cook County. Tours available.

Quinn Chapel AME Church, 2401 S Wabash Ave, ☎ 312-791-1846. This is the oldest African-American church in Chicago, and is listed on the National Register of Historic Places. Named in honor of Bishop William Paul Quinn, the church was once a station for the Underground Railroad.

Robert S. Abbott House, 4742 S Martin Luther King, Jr. Drive. Robert Sengstacke Abbott (1870-1940) founded the *Chicago Defender* newspaper in 1905. Abbot was born and raised in Georgia and published a weekly newspaper that attracted Southern Blacks. During World War I, Abbott encouraged Southern Blacks to move to the North for better opportunities; This became an integral part of what has since been called "The Great Migration." The *Chicago Defender* provided the news and information that many Blacks needed to migrate to Chicago. In 1917, the newspaper became the largest-selling Black newspaper in the nation. Abbott's home was designated a National Historic Landmark and listed on the National Register of Historic Places.

Chicago

Soft Sheen Products, 1000 E 87ᵗʰ Street, ☎ 773-978-0700. Edward and Betti Ann Gardner created Soft Sheen products out of their home in 1964. Their desire to develop high quality health and beauty aids for Blacks resulted in what is now one of the largest African-American-owned businesses in the nation. Still a family-run business, Soft Sheen today has over 600 employees who produce more than 50 products distributed worldwide. Soft Sheen owns *Shop Talk* magazine and Brainstorm Communications. Contact the Human Resources Department at Ext. 2038 to schedule tours.

Southside Community Arts Center, 3831 S Michigan Ave, ☎ 773-373-1026. This popular community arts center was dedicated by First Lady Eleanor Roosevelt in May 1941. Housed in Old Comisky Mansion, the center has been noted for its diverse cultural activities in this African-American community for more than 50 years. Wed-Fri, noon to 5 pm; Sat, 9 am-5 pm; Sun, 1 pm-5 pm. Free admission.

Supreme Life Insurance Company Building, 3501 S Martin Luther King, Jr. Drive. Founded as Liberty Life in 1919 by a group headed by Frank Gillespie, Supreme Life Insurance Company became one of the largest Black-owned insurance companies during the Great Depression. Earl B. Dickerson, a Chicago civil rights leader, served as the company's chief counsel. The company is now owned by Johnson Publications.

Victory Sculpture, 35ᵗʰ Street and Martin Luther King, Jr. Drive. This very visible sculpture commemorates the achievements of the 8ᵗʰ Illinois Regiment and comprises three panels: the first portraying a Black soldier, the second a woman symbolizing African-American motherhood, and the third the familiar patriotic symbol of "Columbia" holding a tablet recording the locations of the regiment's noted battles. At the top of the monument is a uniformed African-American doughboy (World War I soldier).

Vivian Harsh Collection of Afro-American History and Literature, 9525 S Halsted Street, ☎ 312-747-6910. Vivian Harsh was a collector of works by some of the most prominent African-American artists since the early 1900s. She has nurtured a collection of over 70,000 volumes by Langston Hughes, Richard Wright, Gwendolyn Brooks, Arna Bontemps and others as part of the Special Negro Collection at the Chicago Southside Community Public Library (also see Carter G. Woodson Regional Library). Mon-Thurs, 10 am-8 pm; Fri-Sat, 9 am-5 pm. Free admission.

Sites Beyond Chicago

Baldwin Ice Cream, 935 W 175ᵗʰ Street, Homewood. Originally called Seven Links Ice Cream Company, the business was created in 1921 by seven African-American postal workers. The company gained popularity when they allowed the public to view the production of the ice cream at their Chicago location. The company changed its name to Baldwin in 1946, and in 1992 it was acquired by Eric Johnson, formerly of Johnson Products. The ice cream is available in major food stores throughout the Midwest, East Coast and the South.

Burr Oak Cemetery, 4400 W 127th Street, Alsip, ☎ 773-233-5676. The gravesites of such notables as singer Dinah Washington and *Chicago Defender* founder Robert S. Abbott are located at this cemetery. The 120-acre burial ground originally created much controversy among area residents, who did not want Blacks buried here. Open daily during daylight hours.

Mt. Glenwood Cemetery South, 18301 Glenwood-Thornton Rd, Glenwood, ☎ 708/758-5663. Nation of Islam leader Elijah Muhammad, Dr. Charles Gavin, the first African-American admitted into the National College of Orthopedic Surgeons, and Fred "Duke" Slater, the first African-American elected to the National Football Hall of Fame, are buried at this historic African-American cemetery. Open daily 8 am until dusk. Office hours are Mon-Fri, 8 am-4 pm.

Rev. Amanda Berry Smith Burial Site, Washington Memorial Gardens Cemetery, 701 Ridge Rd, Homewood, IL, ☎ 708/798-0645. This world famous evangelist/writer is buried at this site. Her 1893 book, *An Autobiography, The Story of the Lord's Dealing with Amanda Smith, the Colored Evangelist,* was a bestseller. Smith opened up an orphanage in Harvey, Illinois for Black children. Cemetery is open daily until dusk.

Sarah Springs Store, 13910 Claire Blvd, Robbins. In the late 1920s, store owner Sarah Springs rented the second story of this building to Marcus Garvey. The site became the local headquarters of Garvey's Universal Negro Improvement Association (UNIA).

S.B. Fuller Mansion, 13500 Kedzie Ave, Robbins. S.B. Fuller has become an icon within the African-American business community. With only a third-grade education, Fuller became one of the nation's first African-American multi-millionaires by selling cosmetics and soap door-to-door. He helped *Ebony* magazine publisher, John S. Johnson, George Johnson of Johnson Products and others to achieve success. Fuller's wife, Lestine, designed this prairie-style home, built in 1954 for nearly $300,000. Not open to the public.

Museums/Exhibits

Art Institute of Chicago, 111 S Michigan Ave, ☎ 312-443-3600. This institute owns and displays important pieces of art by African-American artists. Exhibits include sculptures and artifacts from many African cultures. Mon, Wed, Fri, 10:30 am-4:40 pm; Tues, 10:30 am-8 pm; Sat, 10 am-5 pm; Sun noon-5 pm. Admission charge.

Bronze lions outside of Art Institute of Chicago
© Peter J. Schulz, City of Chicago, Courtesy of the Chicago Office of Tourism

Chicago Historical Society Museum, Clark Street at North Ave, ☎ 312-642-4600. The Chicago Historical Society houses an extensive collection of materials relating to the history of African-Americans. Among its permanent exhibits are portraits of John Jones and his wife, Mary, and *A House Divided,* an exhibit which focuses on the Civil War and the Reconstruction. The museum's manuscript collections include the scrapbooks of former alderman and civil rights leader Earl B. Dickerson, papers of various Chicago area notables such as former Congressman Arthur Mitchell, the Rev. Archibald Carey, Sr. and businessman and journalist Claude Barnett. Mon-Sat, 9:30 am-4:30 pm; Sun, noon-5 pm. Mondays free; admission charge other days.

DuSable Museum of African-American History, 740 E 56th Pl, ☎ 773-947-0600. One of the premier African-American Museums in the nation, the DuSable Museum is named in honor of Jean Baptiste Pointe DuSable (see entry for DuSable in the *Historic Sites & Landmarks* section). The museum has been open since 1961 as the Ebony Museum in the home of Dr. Margaret Goss Burroughs (additional information on the Burroughs home is in the *Historic Sites & Landmarks* section). The museum moved to its present location at Washington Park in 1973 and is now one of the nation's largest African-American museums. Among its holdings is an extensive collection of artifacts, art objects, books, civil rights documents, original slave documents and various memorabilia. DuSable also has a diverse array of cultural and educational programs. Mon-Sat, 10-4; Sun, noon-4. Admission charge.

Field Museum of Natural History, Roosevelt Rd at Lake Shore Drive, ☎ 312-922-9410. A special feature of the Field Museum is the 15,000-square-foot *Africa* exhibit, designed to help visitors understand the diversity of African culture and its influences upon the Americas. The African Diaspora, a re-creation of a Senegal street market, the African desert ecosystem and the issue of slavery are all explored here. Open daily, 9 am-5 pm. Admission charge.

Colleges & Universities

Chicago State University, 9501 S Martin Luther King Drive, Chicago, IL 60628, ☎ 312-995-2387. State-supported university founded in 1867.

Malcolm X College, 1900 W Van Buren, Chicago, IL 60612, ☎ 312-850-7000. Junior college.

Shopping

Galleries & Specialty Shops

Affordable Art Gallery, 7745 S Halsted Street, ☎ 773-874-1295. Features paintings by Chicago's African-American artists. Mon-Fri, 10 am-6 pm; Sat, 10 am-5 pm.

African-American Images Books and Gifts, 1909 W 95th Street, ☎ 773-445-7822. Books by African-American authors – fiction, non-fiction, men's and women's studies, African-American history and religion. Mon-Thurs, 11 am-7 pm; Sat, 9 am-5 pm.

Afrika North, 4629 N Broadway, ☎ 312-907-0005. Books, incense, ethnic jewelry and accessories, silver jewelry, greeting cards and posters. Mon-Sat, noon-8 pm; Sun, 11 am-5 pm.

Annie Lee & Friends Art Gallery, 37 E Main Street, Glenwood, ☎ 708-757-7100. Features the paintings of African-American artist Annie Frances Lee, whose works have been featured in the motion picture *Coming to America,* which starred Eddie Murphy and Arsenio Hall, and the sitcom *A Different World.* Gift shop, bookstore and coffee shop. Mon-Sat, 11 am-7 pm.

Artwerk Gallery, 5300 S Blackstone Ave, ☎ 773-684-5300. Features a collection of African-American lithographs, original prints and sculptures. Mon-Fri, 11 am-8 pm; Sat-Sun, 11 am-7 pm.

Bag It Black Art Group International. Two locations: 2425 E 72nd Street, ☎ 773-768-4200, open Tues-Thurs, 10 am-8 pm; Sat, 10 am-7 pm; and 455 N Milwaukee Ave, Tues-Thurs, noon-6 pm; Sat, 11 am-6 pm. Sundays by appointment at both locations. Museum-quality antiques, African-American art, oils, paintings, sculpture and African-American memorabilia. Specializes in famous African-American autographs. For serious collectors and investors.

Chicago

Kwanzaa Shop, 1729 E 71ˢᵗ Street, ☎ 773-955-8989. Select collection of cultural items and gifts. African-Chicano items. Tues-Thurs, 11 am-6 pm; Sat, noon-5 pm.

Nicole Gallery, 734 N Wells Street, ☎ 312-787-7716. Zimbabwe, Haitian and African-American paintings and sculpture. Sun-Mon, by appointment only; Tues-Sat, 10:30 am-5 pm.

Satori Fine Art, 230 W Superior, ☎ 312-751-1883. Contemporary art by African-Americans and other artists of color; books on African-American Art. Tues-Fri, 11 am-6 pm; Sat-Sun, 11 am-5 pm.

Susan Woodson Gallery, 5121 S Drexel Blvd, ☎ 773-288-6063. African-American fine art and sculptures. By appointment only.

Unan Imports, 6971 N Sheridan, ☎ 773-274-4022. African arts and crafts, unique gift items. African artifacts, batiks, carvings, clothing, jewelry and leather products. Mon-Sat, 11 am-7 pm; Sun, noon-5:30 pm.

Window to Africa, 5210 S Harper, ☎ 773-955-7742. Traditional and contemporary African paintings, sculpture, beads, jewelry and textiles. Mon-Thurs, noon-7 pm; Sat, 10 am-7 pm; Sun, noon-5 pm.

Woodshop Art Gallery and Frame Service, 441 E 75ᵗʰ Street, ☎ 773-994-6666. African-American art by local artists. Mon-Fri, 9 am-6 pm; Sat, 10 am-3 pm.

Bookstores

African-American Book Center, 7524 S Cottage Grove Ave, ☎ 773-651-0700, fax 773-651-7286. African-American fiction and nonfiction books, contemporary themes. Mon-Thurs, 10 am-6 pm; Sat, 10 am-5 pm.

African-American Images Books & Gifts, 1909 W 95ᵗʰ Street, ☎ 773-445-7822. Books by African-American authors – fiction, non-fiction, men's and women's studies, African-American history and religion. Mon-Thurs, 11 am-7 pm; Sat, 9 am-5 pm.

Afrocentric Bookstore, 333 S State Street, Downtown, ☎ 312-939-1956. Mon-Thurs, 9:30 am-6:30 pm; Sat, 10 am-5 pm.

Black Light Fellowship Bookstore, 128 S Paulina Street, ☎ 312-563-0081. African-American Christian books, Bibles, African-American art, African fabrics, gifts, occasion cards and church materials. Mon-Thurs, 10 am-7 pm; Sat, 10 am-5 pm.

Family Health Education Service Bookstore, 8525 S State Street, ☎ 773-488-0229. African-American history books, Bible stories, medical guides, bedtime stories and magazines. Mon-Thurs, 8:30 am-5:30 pm. Closed weekends.

Freedom Found Books, 5205 S Harper Ave, ☎ 773-288-2837. African-American literature, African-American apparel, African-American art, jewelry and Afrikan fabrics. Call for hours.

Images In Reading, 2056 E 71st Street, ☎ 773-643-3391. African-American children's books, adult best sellers, history and philosophy. Mon-Thurs, 11:30 am-6 pm; Sat, 10 am-3 pm.

The Reading Room; African Centered Books and Gifts, 112 S State Street, ☎ 312-658-0824. African-American fiction, non-fiction, religion, history and current affairs. Open daily, 9 am-6 pm.

Fashions

Dornita's, 6251 S Halsted Street, ☎ 773-488-4055. Distinctive clothes for distinctive women. Mon-Sat, 9:30 am-6:30 pm.

Ebony Kid's Boutique and School Uniforms, 233 E 79th Street, ☎ 312-483-4296. Boys' and girls' clothing, school uniforms, ladies leg wear. Tues-Sat, 9 am-7 pm.

Glitz to Grandeur, 727 E 79th Street, ☎ 312-488-3400. Designer Afrocentric clothing for men and women.

Labeled Black Apparel, 857 E 79th Street, ☎ 773-994-0858. Clothing and accessories from an Afrocentric point of view, adult and children's clothing, art, oils, T-shirts, fabric, jewelry and household items. Mon-Thurs, 9 am-6 pm; Sat, 10 am-5 pm. Seasonal hours. Call first.

Remmy's Boutique, 820½ E 79th Street, ☎ 773-723-8311. Authentic African clothing, Kente strips, crowns, head wraps, jewelry, accessories, bags, shoes and artifacts. Mon-Thurs, 10 am-7 pm; Fri-Sat, 10 am-8 pm.

Sew-Fine Fabrics & Fashions, Inc., 1333 E 75th Street, ☎ 773-363-1547. Specializes in Afrocentric fabrics, clothing, cultural jewelry and African greeting cards. Mon-Sat, 10 am-6 pm.

Window to Africa, 5210 S Harper Ave, ☎ 312-995-7742. Afrocentric clothing for men and women, African art, artifacts, jewelry and other gift items. Mon-Fri, 11 am-7 pm; Sat, 10 am-7 pm; Sun, noon-5 pm.

Restaurants

◆ African

Moulibet, 3521 N Clark Street, ☎ 312-929-9383. Authentic Ethiopian vegetarian and meat dishes. Live entertainment on weekends. Mon-Thurs, 5 pm-10 pm; Fri-Sat, 4 pm-midnight; Sun, 4 pm-10 pm.

Chicago

Vee-Vee's African Restaurant and Cocktail, 6343 N Broadway, ☎ 773-465-2424. Nigerian restaurant featuring chicken, fish, goat, Sunday buffet. Mon-Sat, noon-11 pm; Sun, noon-9 pm.

◆ American

Michael Jordan's Restaurant, 500 N Lasalle Street, ☎ 312-644-3865. American cuisine, including barbeque, pasta entrées, seafood and steaks. The three-level establishment includes a sports bar, gift shop, and private dining/banquet rooms. Mon-Thurs, 11 am-10 pm; Fri-Sat, 11 am-10:30 pm.

◆ Caribbean

A Taste of Jamaica, 1372 E 53rd Street, ☎ 773-955-4373. Traditional Jamaican cuisine features grilled chicken, jerk chicken and curried goat. Mon-Fri, 11 am-10 pm; Sat 11 am-8 pm.

Island Bar & Grill, 940 W North Ave, ☎ 312-951-1700. Caribbean cuisine, featuring Trinidadian, Cuban and Hawaiian dishes. Mon-Thurs, 6 pm-10 pm; Fri-Sat, 6 pm-11 pm. Bar opens at 5 pm.

Island Delites, 1461 E Hyde Park Blvd, ☎ 773-324-3100. Caribbean cuisine featuring jerk chicken, catfish, kingfish escobeche, curried goat and red snapper. Sun-Thurs, 11 am-9:30 pm; Fri-Sat, 11 am-11 pm.

Jan's Jerk Pit, 8115 S Ashland, ☎ 773-723-2866 or ☎ 773-723-2686. Specializes in jerk chicken, curried goat and chicken, oxtails, red snapper, red beans and rice, and plantains.

Maxine's, 1232 E 87th Street, ☎ 773-933-0500. Caribbean cuisine, featuring jerk chicken. Sun, 11 am-6 pm; Mon-Thurs, 11 am-9 pm; Fri-Sat, 11 am-11 pm.

◆ Creole

C'est Si Bon, Ltd., 5225 S Harper Ave, ☎ 312-363-4124. Features soul food, creole, Cajun and American cuisine. Specializes in gourmet bakery items. Tues-Sat, 10:30 am-6:30 pm; Sunday brunch, 11 am-4 pm.

◆ Soul

Alexander's Restaurant, 3010 E 79th Street, ☎ 773-768-6555. Specializes in prime rib and roast beef. Thursdays, live jazz at 6:30 pm. Mon-Thurs, 11 am-11 pm; Fri-Sat, 11 am-1 am; Sun, noon-11 pm.

Alice's Restaurant, 5638 W Chicago Ave, ☎ 312-921-1100. Soul food. Open for breakfast, lunch and dinner daily, 6:30 am-8 pm.

Barbara's Restaurant, 422 E 75th Street, ☎ 773-624-0087. Traditional soul food dishes including fish, chicken, beef, roast and ham hocks. Mon-Sat, 5 am-6 pm; Sun, 5 am-2 pm.

Brown's Chicken & Pasta, 8015 S Halsted Street, ☎ 773-783-3145. Soul food menu; red beans and rice, chicken gumbo, mixed greens and catfish, etc. Call for hours.

Captain's Hard Time Dining, 436 E 79th Street, ☎ 312-487-2900. Specialties are soul, creole, Cajun and continental items. Open for breakfast, lunch and dinner, 8 am-11 pm.

Edna's, 3175 W Madison Ave, ☎ 312-638-7079. Soul food cuisine. Open since 1966, Edna's was once a popular spot for civil rights workers. Tues-Sun, 6 am-9 pm.

Fish Hut, 724 S Wabash Ave, ☎ 312-922-2819. Seafood, pastas, chicken, home-cooked vegetables and peach cobbler are their specialties. Mon-Thurs, 10 am-midnight; Fri-Sat, 10 am-3 am; Sun, 2 pm-10 pm.

Gina's Cafeteria, 4735 W Chicago Ave, ☎ 773-379-8010. Traditional soul food dishes. Daily specials under $3.00. Tues-Sun, 8 am-8 pm.

Glady's, 4527 S Indiana Ave, ☎ 773-548-4566. Home-cooked meals featuring ham hocks, neck bones, turkey wings, chicken, corned beef, oxtail, beef stew, roast pork, catfish and perch served with traditional soul food vegetable items. Top your meal off with peach or apple cobbler. Call for daily specials. Open for breakfast, lunch and dinner. Tues-Sun, 7 am-10 pm; closed Mon.

Harold's Chicken Shack, 7310 S Halsted Street, ☎ 773-723-9006 and 100 W 87th Street, ☎ 312-224-3314. Specialty is fried chicken dinners. Sun-Thurs, 11 am-midnight; Fri-Sat, 11 am-2 am.

Jackie's Place, 226 E 71st Street, ☎ 312-483-4095. Features a variety of soul food items, like ham hocks, neck bones, short beef ribs, chicken wings, steaks, fried catfish and a host of other favorites. Open 24 hours for breakfast, lunch and dinner.

Nina's Restaurant, 5810 W Madison Street, ☎ 773-921-5062. Soul food menu. Daily lunch specials. Tues-Sat, 6 am-7 pm; Sun, 6 am-4 pm.

Mr. Rick's The Note Restaurant and Lounge, 118 E Cermack, ☎ 312-842-0400. Elegant soul food restaurant, cozy, family settings. Specialty is soul food items, including barbeque. Daily specials. Sun-Thurs, 10 am-11 pm; Fri-Sat, 10 am-2 am.

Ruby's Soul Food, 10043 S Halsted, ☎ 773-779-6857. Short ribs of beef, greens, candy sweets and a wide variety of beans. Chicken and ham hocks. Mon-Thurs, 6 am-6 pm; Sat, 6 am-3 pm.

Soul Queen, 9031 Stony Island Ave, ☎ 312-731-3366. Soul food buffet. Mon-Thurs and Sun, 11 am-11:30 pm; Fri-Sat, 11 am-1 am.

Chicago

◆ Vegetarian

Soul Vegetarian Restaurant, 205 E 75th Street, ☎ 312-224-0104 or 312-224-5851. Vegetarian cuisine that features low-fat and healthy vegetarian soul cuisine. Mon-Thurs, 9 am-9 pm; Fri-Sat, 9 am-11 pm; Sun, 9 am-8 pm.

Entertainment

Music

◆ Blues

Arti's, 1249 E 87th Street, ☎ 773-734-0491. Live blues Sunday and Monday nights. Open daily, noon-2 am.

Buddy Guy's Legends, 754 S Wabash Ave, ☎ 312-427-0333. Live blues nightly. Serves Louisiana-style soul food. Mon-Thurs, 5 pm-2 am; Fri, 4 pm-2 am.

Checker Board Lounge, 423 E 43rd Street, ☎ 773-624-3240. Live blues nightly; 11 am-2 am.

Lee's Unleaded Blues, 7401 S Chicago Ave, ☎ 773-493-3477. Live blues; Sun-Fri, noon-2 am; Sat, 9 pm-3 am.

◆ Jazz Nightclubs/Lounges

Andy's, 11 E Hubbard Street, ☎ 312-642-6805. Very popular jazz nightclub that features Chicago jazz, blues and rock. Three bands daily. Multiethnic crowd. Serves lunch weekdays at 11:30. Call for band lineup and specific hours.

Back Room, 1007 N Rush Street, ☎ 312-751-2433. Contemporary jazz. Multiethnic crowd. Sun-Thurs, 9 pm-2 am; Sat, 9 pm-3 am.

Bop Shop Jazz Club, 1807 W Division Street, ☎ 773-235-3232. Contemporary Chicago-style jazz. Multiethnic crowd. Different shows daily at 10 pm.

Bull Jazz Night Club, 1916 N Lincoln Park W, ☎ 312-337-3000. Local contemporary jazz nightclub. Sun-Thurs, 9:30 pm-2:30 am; Fri, 9:30 pm-3 am; Sat, 9:30 pm-4:30 am.

Club Alexander's, 3010 E 79th Street, ☎ 773-768-6555. Live jazz on Thursdays; live blues on Saturdays. Also known as Alexander's Steak House. Mon-Thurs, 11:30 am-11 pm; Fri-Sat, 11:30 am-1 am; Sun, 1 pm-10:30 pm.

Cotton Club, 1710 S Michigan, ☎ 312-341-9787. Jazz and Latin rhythms, Dixieland and blues. Open daily 8 pm-3 am. Dinner on weekends. Variety of food items.

Europia, 2828 N Lincoln Ave, ☎ 312-528-5339. Jazz, rock and blues music. Live jazz Thurs-Sat. Cover charge.

Green Dolphin Street, 2200 N Ashland Ave, ☎ 773-395-0066. This upscale restaurant has a 1940s look and features live jazz Tues-Sat, 8 pm-3 am.

Jazz Showcase, 59 W Grand at Clark Street, ☎ 312-670-2473. Hot jazz shows, non-smoking. Tues-Thurs, 8 pm-10 pm; Fri-Sat, 9 pm-11 pm; Sun, 4 pm matinees, 8 pm and 10 pm. Cover charge. Call for upcoming shows.

New Checkerboard Lounge, 423 E 43rd Street, ☎ 773-624-3240. Live blues music. Sun-Fri, 9:30 pm-1 am; Sat, 9:30 pm-3 am.

OZ, 2917 N Sheffield, ☎ 773-975-8100. Contemporary jazz fusion. Storefront surrounding, upscale crowd. Staged shows: Thurs-Fri, 9:30 pm-1:30 am; Sat, 10 pm-2:30 pm.

Pop's for Champagne, 2934 N Sheffield, ☎ 312-427-1000. Ritzy jazz club featuring over 100 varieties of champagne. Romantic (and pricey), jazz brunch on Sundays, 10:30 am-2 pm. Sun, Mon, Wed, Thurs, 8 pm-midnight; Fri-Sat, 9 pm-1 am.

Dance Nightclubs

Brother's Palace, 939 N Pulaski Rd, ☎ 773-384-2875. Disc jockey plays contemporary rhythm and blues on Saturdays. Open nightly.

Clique, 2347 S Michigan Ave, ☎ 312-326-0274. Multi-activity entertainment establishment that attracts a mostly 25-and-up crowd. Dance nightclub at the top of the Clique with a deejay, live bands and comedy; open daily, Mon-Thurs, 4 pm-2 am; Fri and Sun, 4 pm-4 am; Sat, 4 pm-5 am. Comedy shows, 9:30 pm and 12:30 pm. VIP and Executive Room for VIPs and celebrities. Food items on weekends, which include variety of appetizers, sandwiches, hot wings, buffalo wings, chicken breasts, filet of fish, corned beef and more. All inclusive with cover charge.

Club Inta's, 308 W Erie, ☎ 312-664-6880. Elegant nightclub featuring contemporary dance music. Friday after-work sets. Tues-Thurs, 5 pm-2 am; Fri, 5 pm-4 am; Sat, 8 pm-5 am.

Culpeppers Night Spot Dance Club, 11441 S Michigan Ave, ☎ 773-568-6752. Wednesdays, female dancers for the men; Tuesdays, male dancers for the ladies. Fri-Sat, college night.

Equator Nightclub, 4715 N Broadway, ☎ 312-728-2411. Dance nightclub featuring Afro-pop, Caribbean, disco and calypso. DJ. Wed-Fri and Sun, 9:30 pm-2 am; Sat, 9:30 pm-3 am.

Fifty Yard Line, 69 E 75th Street, ☎ 773-846-0005. Dance club for mature patrons. Sun-Fri, 10 pm-2 am; Sat, 10 pm-3 am. Kitchen serves short orders. Free on Thursdays.

Red Dog Club, 1958 W North Ave, ☎ 773-278-5138. One of the city's hottest dance clubs. Mon-Wed, 10 pm-4 am; Fri, 10 pm-5 am.

◆ Reggae

Wild Hare & Singing Armadillo Frog Sanctuary, 3530 N Clark Street, Northside, ☎ 773-327-4273. Live reggae daily. Sun-Fri, 9 pm-2 am; Sat, 9 pm-3 am.

Theater

New Regal Theater, 1645 E 79th Street, ☎ 312-721-9230. Variety of jazz, blues and gospel performances. Dinner theater, scheduled events. Call for update information.

Comedy Clubs

All Jokes Aside, 100 S Wabash Ave, ☎ 312-922-0577. Upscale comedy club featuring local and national artists. Call for show times.

Clique, 2347 S Michigan Ave, ☎ 312-326-0274. Comedy shows featuring local and national performers. Thurs-Sat, 9:30 pm and 12:30 pm.

Heritage Tours

Black CouTours, PO Box 201896, Chicago, IL 60620-1896, ☎ 773-233-8907 or ☎ 773-538-5454, fax 773-233-5237. E-mail: coutours@aol.com; Web site: www.travelfile.com/get/coutours.html. Black CouTours specializes in African-American heritage sightseeing tours of Chicago and other US and Canadian cities. Chicago tours feature visits to Oprah's Studio, DuSable Museum, famous residences, Michael Jordan's playground, Underground Railroad stations and much more. Call for rates and schedule information.

Tour Black Chicago, 35 E Wacker Drive, #222, Chicago, IL 60601, ☎ 312-332-2323; fax 773-684-9434. Established in 1990, this is a top cultural and historic African-American tour company. Knowledgeable guides will take visitors to some of the historic sites and fun spots in the city's African-American community.

Travel Agents

LCW Travel, ☎ 773-947-5199. 24-hour travel service. Airline, bus, rail, tours, incentive programs and bus charters.

Uniglobe Top Flight Travel, 750 S Halsted #2000, Chicago 60607, ☎ 312-996-4488. African-American travel specialists. Africa, Caribbean, Mexico, family reunions, cruises and tour groups.

Media

Radio

◆ Jazz

WSSD 88.1 FM, 11026 S Wentworth Ave, ☎ 312-928-8800. Blues, jazz, gospel and talk show format.

◆ Gospel

WSBC 1240 AM, 4949 W Belmont Ave, ☎ 312-282-9722. Black gospel, ethnic format.

WYCA 92.3 FM, 6336 Calumet Ave, Hammond, IN, ☎ 312-734-4455. Gospel format.

◆ Urban Contemporary

WGCI 107.5 FM, 332 S Michigan Ave #600, ☎ 312-984-1400.

WJPC 950 AM, 820 S Michigan Ave, ☎ 312-322-9400.

WLNR 106.3 FM, 820 S Michigan Ave, ☎ 312-322-9400.

WVAZ 102.7 FM, 800 S Wells, #250, ☎ 312-360-9000.

◆ Full Service

WKKC 89.3 FM, 6800 S Wentworth Ave, ☎ 312-846-8531.

Newspapers

Chicago Citizen, 412 E 87th Street, ☎ 312-487-7700. African-American community newspaper. Distributed Thursdays.

Chicago Crusader, 6429 S Martin Luther King, Jr. Drive, ☎ 312-752-2500. African-American community newspaper. Distributed Saturdays.

Chicago Daily Defender, 2400 S Michigan Ave, ☎ 312-225-2400. African-American community newspaper.

Chicago Independent Bulletin, 2037 W 95th Street, ☎ 312-783-1040. African-American community newspaper. Distributed Thursdays.

Chicago Metro News, 3437 S Indiana Ave, ☎ 773-488-1100. African-American community newspaper. Distributed Saturdays.

Chicago Shoreland News, 11740 S Elizabeth, ☎ 312-568-7091. African-American community newspaper. Distributed Thursdays.

Chicago South Shore Scene, 7426 S Constance, ☎ 312-363-0441. African-American community newspaper. Distributed Thursdays.

Chicago Standard News, 615 S Halsted, ☎ 708/755-5021. African-American community newspaper. Distributed weekly.

Chicago Weekend, 412 E 87th Street, ☎ 312-487-7700. Weekend newspaper serving Chicago's African-American community. Distributed Thursdays.

Magazines

Afrique News Magazine, 4554 N Broadway, Suite 320, ☎ 312-989-8138. News magazine targeted towards Africans, African-Americans, Caribbean and Afro-Latinos. Regularly features articles on African profiles, Caribbean affairs, editorials, travel, entertainment, education and Africans. Distributed monthly.

Black Pages of Chicago, 407 E 25th Street, ☎ 312-808-1800. Listing of some African-American-owned businesses in Greater Chicago area.

Ebony, Johnson Publishing, 820 S Michigan Ave, Chicago, IL 60605, ☎ 312-322-9200. Monthly African-American magazine.

Ebony Man, Johnson Publishing, 820 S Michigan Ave, Chicago, IL 60605, ☎ 312-322-9200. Monthly African-American male magazine.

Jet, Johnson Publishing, 820 S Michigan Ave, Chicago, IL 60605, ☎ 312-322-9200. Monthly African-American magazine.

Publications

Illinois Generations: A Traveler's Guide to African-American Heritage, Performance Media; Chicago Sun-Times Features, Inc., 401 N Wabash Ave, Chicago, IL 60611.

The Guide to Black Chicago, The Guide Group, 843 W Van Buren, Suite 378, Chicago, IL 60607, ☎ 312-509-6815.

African-American Churches

AME

Allen Temple AME, 18 W 30th Street, ☎ 312-842-6733.

Arnett Chapel AME, 1444 W 112th Street, ☎ 773-881-9238.

Blackwell Memorial AME, 3956 S Langley Ave, ☎ 773-624-4573.

Carey Temple AME, 7157 S Greenwood, ☎ 773-324-7766.

Coppin Memorial AME, 5627 S Michigan, ☎ 773-667-5881.

Grant Memorial AME, 4017 Drexel Boulevard, ☎ 773-285-5819.

Greater Institutional AME, 7800 S Indiana, ☎ 773-873-0880.

Greater Walters AME Zion, 8422 S Damen, ☎ 773-779-8400.

Gregg Memorial AME, 740 W 59th Street, ☎ 773-487-8683.

Greater Street John AME, 6207 S Throop, ☎ 773-925-2262.

Hyde Park AME, 12058 S Eggleston, ☎ 773-785-5890.

Martin Temple AME Zion, 6930 S Cottage Grove Ave, ☎ 773-493-8624.

Mary Butler AME, 320 S California Ave, ☎ 773-533-3217.

Mount Oliver AME, 4600 S Evans Ave, ☎ 773-536-9610 or ☎ 773-624-7946.

Quinn Chapel AME, 2401 S Wabash Ave, ☎ 312-791-1846.

Robinson Chapel AME, 7950 S Burnham Ave, ☎ 773-221-9177.

Ruby's Memorial AME, 1005 N Pulaski Rd, ☎ 773-384-2103.

St. James AME, 9256 S Lafayette Ave, ☎ 773-785-9733.

St. Mark AME Zion, 7358 S Cottage Grove Ave, ☎ 773-994-4222.

St. Mary AME, 5251 S Dearborn Street, ☎ 773-548-2100.

St. Matthew-Gordon AME Zion, 9448 S Eggleston Ave, ☎ 773-224-4350.

St. Paul AME, 8911 S Mackinaw Ave, ☎ 773-734-4522.

St. Paul AME, 4236 W Cermak Rd, ☎ 773-522-4812.

St. Stephen AME, 2000 W Washington Blvd, ☎ 312-666-4164.

Samuel Israel AME, 1350 W Erie Street, ☎ 312-421-2954.

Turner Memorial AME, 3610 S Giles Ave, ☎ 773-548-4111.

Baptist

Olivet Baptist, 401 E 31st Street, ☎ 312-842-1081.

Episcopal

St. Thomas Episcopal Church, 3801 S Wabash Ave, ☎ 312-268-1900.

Catholic

St. Elizabeth Roman Catholic Church, 4058 S Michigan Ave, ☎ 312-373-6035.

Chicago

COGIC

A Gift from God COGIC, 8607 S Ashland Ave, ☎ 773-445-5645.

All Souls COGIC, 3637 W 16th Street, ☎ 773-762-1142.

Apostolic Church of God, 6320 S Dorchester Ave, ☎ 773-667-1500.

Bethel Deliverance COGIC, 5350 W Division Street, ☎ 773-626-7451.

BPGP Pickens Memorial Temple COGIC, 5659 S Union Ave, ☎ 773-488-0300.

Carol Divine Temple COGIC, 1508 S Millard Ave, ☎ 773-522-8328.

Center of Hope COGIC, 336 N Laramie Ave, ☎ 773-378-8859.

Faith and Deliverance COGIC, 4666 W Fulton Street, ☎ 773-261-2400.

First Rock of Ages COGIC, 11153 S Vincennes Ave, ☎ 773-239-4453.

House of Prayer Temple COGIC, 622 W 120th Street, ☎ 773-928-0958.

New Deliverance COGIC, 5431 W Madison Street, ☎ 773-921-1115.

Old Ship of Zion COGIC, 5040 W Chicago Ave, ☎ 773-261-7158.

One Way COGIC, 5857 W Division Street, ☎ 773-379-1140.

Peoples Outreach Missionary COGIC, 6852 S Racine Ave, ☎ 773-488-8809.

Prince of Peace Tabernacle COGIC, 7822 S Halsted Street, ☎ 773-846-6344.

Straightway Evangelistic COGIC, 11801 S Sangamon Street, ☎ 773-995-7721.

True Temple COGIC, 6536 S Ashland Ave, ☎ 773-737-4160.

Unity Sanctuary Mission COGIC, 26 E 69th Street, ☎ 773-874-3549.

Calendar of Annual Events

Unless otherwise noted, contact the **Chicago Mayor's Office of Special Events** at ☎ 312-744-3315 for information on the following:

◆ January
Dr. Martin Luther King, Jr. Day – various activities around Chicago.

◆ February
Black History Month – city-wide activities.

◆ **April**

Annual Proud Lady Beauty Show, American Health and Beauty Aids Institute, ☎ 312-321-6824.

◆ **June**

Annual Chicago Gospel Festival

DuSable Museum Walk-A-Thon

◆ **July**

Black Expo Chicago

Chicago Bacchanal Caribbean Parade

DuSable Museum Art & Crafts Festival

National Council of Negro Women Black Family Reunion

Roots Festival

West Garfield Street Festival

◆ **August**

Annual Chicago Jazz Festival

Ghana Festival

Jazz Unites JazzFest

Jazz in the Alley

Taste of Midway Festival

West Garfield Park Summer Fest

World's Largest Stepper's Contest

◆ **September**

African Festival of the Arts - Labor Day Weekend.

African-Caribbean International Festival of Life

◆ **December**

Kwanzaa

Public Transportation

Chicago O'Hare International Airport, ☎ 800-832-6352.

Chicago Transit Authority (CTA), ☎ 312-836-7000.

METRA Train, ☎ 312-836-7000.

Chicago

Chicago Area Resources

Black Ensemble Theater, 4520 N Beacon Street, Chicago, IL 60640, ☎ 312-769-5516.

Chicago Convention and Tourism Bureau, 2301 S Lake Shore Drive, ☎ 312-567-8500, fax 312-567-8533. Web site: www.chicago.il.org. Mon-Thurs, 8:30 am-4:30 pm.

Chicago Office of Tourism, Chicago Cultural Center, Michigan Ave and Washington Street, Chicago, IL 60602, ☎ 312-744-2400.

Mayor's Office of Special Events, City Hall, 121 N LaSalle Street, Room 703, Chicago, IL 60602, ☎ 312-744-3315.

New Regal Theater, 1645 E 79th Street, Chicago, IL 60649, ☎ 312-721-9230.

Travelers Aid, Chicago O'Hare Airport, ☎ 773-894-2427.

Dallas

Museums/Exhibits

African-American Museum, 3536 Grand Ave, Fair Park, ☎ 214-565-9026. The museum houses displays and exhibits that explore the African-American experience. Historical artifacts and art housed in four vaulted galleries display the rich heritage of the African-American people. Tues-Fri, noon-5 pm; Sat, 10 am-5 pm; Sun, 1 pm-5 pm. Free admission.

The African-American Museum

Dallas Museum of Art, 1717 North Harwood, ☎ 214-922-1200. The Museum of Africa and Asia are a part of the permanent collections of the Dallas Museum of Art. The museum displays a number of African artifacts and authentic African art works. Tues, Wed and Fri, 11 am-4 pm; Thurs, 11 am-9 pm; Sat-Sun, 11 am-5 pm. Admission charge.

Museums/Exhibits Beyond Dallas

Cattleman's Museum, 1301 West Seventh Street, Fort Worth, ☎ 817-332-7064. The Cattleman's Museum houses a small display of memorabilia from Texas' 19th-century African-American cowboys. Mon-Fri, 8:30 am-4:30 pm. Free admission.

Dallas Area

1. Museum of African-American Life and Culture
2. Dallas Museum of Art
3. Black Images Book Store
4. Red Bird Shopping Mall
5. Wynnewood Village Shopping Mall
6. Dallas Convention & Visitors Bureau

1.5 MILES

.93 KM

Historic Colleges & Universities

Paul Quinn College, 3837 Simpson Stuart, Dallas, TX. 75241, ☎ 214-376-1000. Church-affiliated college.

Shopping

Galleries & Specialty Shops

Art Gallery at New Orleans, 1001 North Beckley, Pleasant Run Shopping Center, Desota, ☎ 214-357-7053. African-American art by local and international artists. Mon-Fri, 9 am-5 pm.

Arthello's Gallery, 1922 South Beckley Ave, ☎ 214-941-2276. African-American artworks by local and national artists, paintings, pencil drawings, watercolors and portraits.

Art Masters, 207 South Tyler, #105, ☎ 214-948-6557. Original African-American art representing local and national artists. Mon-Fri, 10 am-6 pm; Sat, 10 am-4 pm.

Ebony Fine Art & Custom Framing, 631 South Hwy 67, south of Hwy 20, ☎ 214-298-4092. African-American art. Tues-Sat, 10 am-7 pm; Sun, 1 pm-6 pm.

Pan-Africa Connection, 623 South Jefferson Street, ☎ 214-943-8262. Authentic African art, statues, masks, books and much more. Mon-Sat, 9 am-7 pm.

Stephanie's Collection of African-American Art, 6955 Greenville, ☎ 214-369-4438. Mon-Sat, 10 am-7 pm.

Vera's Card Boutique, 2435 West Kiest, ☎ 214-330-9918. Ethnic greeting cards. Mon-Sat, 9 am-7 pm.

Bookstores

Afro Awakenings Books, 2415 South Collins, Arlington, ☎ 817-265-0001. Specializes in African-American books, newspapers, art, audios, greeting cards, and incense. Mon-Fri, 10 am-7 pm; Sat, 10 am-6 pm.

Black Book Worm, 605 South Berry, #114, Fort Worth, ☎ 817-923-9661. Specializes in African-American books, greeting cards, magazines and educational games.

Black Images Book Store, 230 Wynnewood Village Shopping Center, ☎ 214-943-0142. Black Images has an enormous assortment of African-American books, gift items, tapes, cards, games, posters, incense oils, T-shirts, prints, Kwanzaa supplies and more. Black Images features monthly autograph sessions by nationally known African-American writers and artists. Mon-Sat, 10 am-7 pm; Sun, 1 pm-6 pm.

Ebony Expressions Books, Gifts, Etc., 3701 South Cooper, #153, Arlington, ☎ 817-467-7107. African-American books, collectibles, gift bags, children's books, African-American dolls, greeting cards, art, Negro League apparel and features storytelling for children. Mon-Fri, 10 am-7 pm; Sat, 10 am-6 pm.

Jokae's African-American Books, 3917 West Camp Wisdom, #107, ☎ 214-283-0558 or 800-749-7725. African-American books, greeting cards, papyrus and African-American art. Jokae's also features a reading and tutorial center for children. Call for current hours.

Fashions

Adam's Boutique, 4226 South Lancaster, ☎ 214-372-9756. Fashions for African-American women, including designer suits, evening wear, jewelry, make-up, accessories and women's hats. Mon-Sat, 9 am-5:30 pm.

Ellene's Kids, Red Bird Mall, #2040, ☎ 214-780-1703. Specializes in children's clothing: dresses, tuxedos, suits and ties, sportwear, summerwear, and accessories. Mon-Sat, 10 am-9 pm; Sun, noon-6 pm.

Howards' Boutique, 4210 West Camp Wisdom, #170, Independent Square Shopping Center, ☎ 214-780-0176. Specializes in fashions for African-American women, featuring designer suits, evening wear, jewelry and hats. Tues-Sat, 10 am-6 pm.

Ngozi's, 137 Wynnewood Village, ☎ 214-942-1775. Specializes in authentic African fashions, fabrics, leather, costume jewelry, women's suits, dresses, head wraps and African wedding attire.

Red's Selective Men's Wear, 4210 West Camp Wisdom, #210, ☎ 214-709-0994. Specializes in fashions and styles for the African-American males. Features suits, ties, leathers and a complete line of men's clothing and accessories. Mon-Sat, 10 am-6 pm.

Uniquely African, 3917 West Camp Wisdom, #102, ☎ 214-709-9611. Specializes in African men's, women, and children's clothing. Feature flamboyant fashions, accessories, artifacts, handwoven Kente strips, dolls, Greek strips, jewelry, African ties and hats. Mon-Sat, 10 am-8 pm.

Popular Shopping Centers

Red Bird Mall, 3662 West Camp Wisdom Rd, ☎ 214-296-1491. Mall hours are Mon-Sat, 10 am-9 pm; Sun, noon-6 pm.

Wynnewood Village Mall, Illinois Ave & Zang Blvd, ☎ 214-943-4351. The mall has several stores featuring African-American wares. Hours vary with each store.

Restaurants

◆ Barbecue

Brown & Hayes Bar-B-Que & Grill, 4845 Lancaster Rd, ☎ 214-371-8687. Features ribs and sausage link baskets, smoked turkey breasts, catfish fillets, homemade hamburgers and potato and chess pies. Catering available. Mon-Thurs, 10 am-10 pm; Fri-Sat, 10 am-midnight.

Daniel's Bar-B-Que & Game Room, 2319 South Beckley, ☎ 214-946-3157 or ☎ 214-946-3158. Specializes in hickory-smoked barbecue ribs, beef, sausage links and ham. Also features homemade burgers, chopped beef, salads, cakes and banana pudding. Restaurant has on-site video games and pool tables. Mon-Thurs, 11:30 am-10 pm; Fri-Sat, 11 am-midnight; Sun, noon-8 pm.

Phil's Bar-B-Que, Catering and Sub Shop, 3801 French Settlement, ☎ 214-637-5565. Full service restaurant that features ribs, catfish, hickory-smoked barbecue, roast beef, burgers, beef, fried okra, subs, homemade pound cake and banana pudding. Serves breakfast and lunch. Mon-Fri, 7 am-3 pm.

◆ Caribbean

Cafe Gecko, 5290 Beltline Rd, #118, Addison, ☎ 972-458-9884. Caribbean cuisine tinged with south-of-the-border Mexican flavors. Their specialty is conch chowder. Open daily, 11 am-3 am.

Elaine's Kitchen, 1912 Martin Luther King Blvd, ☎ 214-565-1008. Their specialties are curried goat and jerk chicken. Mon, noon-9 pm; Tues-Sat, noon-10 pm; closed Sun.

◆ Soul

Mama Joe's Market Grill, 3622 Camp Wisdom, Oak Cliff, ☎ 214-298-0454. Variety of soul food entrées and vegetables, such as fried chicken, pork chops, meat loaf, beef, a salad bar and cobbler desserts. Located in the Red Bird Shopping Mall in South Dallas. Family atmosphere. Mon-Sat, 11 am-8 pm; Sun, 11 am-5 pm. ☆ *Specially recommended.*

Soul Embassy Cafe, 3840 West Northwest Hwy, #480, Plaza on Bachman Creek, ☎ 214-357-SOUL. Soul cuisine includes ribeye steaks, fried green tomatoes, black-eyed pea soup. Live jazz many nights. Sunday Gospel brunch. Lunch Mon-Fri, 11 am-2 pm. Dinner Wed-Sun, 6 pm-11 pm.

Sweet Georgia Brown, 2840 South Ledbetter, ☎ 214-375-2020. Specializes in "down-home" cooking, like candied yams, sausage links, ribs, corn, collard and turnip greens, potato salad and homemade peach, blueberry and apple cobblers. Catering available. Mon-Thurs, 11:30 am-11 pm; Fri-Sat, 11:30 am-1 am; Sun, 11:30 am-9 pm.

Williams Fried Chicken, 238 West Illinois, off Interstate 35, ☎ 214-943-4001.

◆ Vegetarian

Strictly Vegetarian, 243 Wynnewood Shopping Center, ☎ 214-912-9796. Features vegetarian soups and sandwiches, deli items. Mon-Sat, 11:30 am-8 pm.

Entertainment

◆ Jazz

Gigi's Jazz, 5915 South Northwest Hwy, ☎ 214-692-7088. Popular Dallas adult jazz club.

Soul Embassy Café, 3840 West Northwest Hwy, #480, Plaza on Bachman Creek, ☎ 214-357-SOUL. Live jazz many nights. Call first. Sunday Gospel brunch. Lunch Mon-Fri, 11 am-2 pm; dinner Wed-Sun, 6 pm-11 pm.

Travel Agents

A-Plus Travel, Inc., 16901 North Dallas Pkwy, #109, Dallas, TX 75248, ☎ 214-250-1992.

A & J Cruises, 4620 Country Creek, #1188, Dallas, TX 75236, ☎ 214-337-1358.

Cruise Holiday of Desoto, 900 North Polk, #106, Dallas, TX 75208, ☎ 214-228-4600.

Favorite Places Travel, 2735 Villa Creek, #160, Dallas, TX 75234, ☎ 214-406-8898.

Four Seasons Travel, 400 South Zang Blvd, #912, Dallas, TX 75208, ☎ 800-228-3501 or 214-943-2583.

Mid-Town Travel Agency, 100 North Central #202, Dallas, TX 75201, ☎ 214-741-3075.

Robinson's Tour & Travel, 2331 Gus Thompson, #129A, Casa View Shopping Center, Dallas, TX 75228, ☎ 800-590-5445 or 214-324-9876.

Uptown Travel Service, 2808 McKinney, #101, Dallas, TX 75204, ☎ 214-999-5800.

Wyndham Travel Partners, 1909 Hi Line, #J, Dallas, TX 75207, ☎ 214-573-4236.

Heritage Tours

Citisites, PO Box 225233, Dallas, TX 75222, ☎ 214-371-8995.

Media

Radio

◆ Jazz

KNTU 88.1 FM, University of Texas, Denton, ☎ 817-565-3688.

◆ Urban

KJMZ 100.3 FM, 545 South John Carpenter Hwy, #1700, ☎ 214-988-7525.

◆ Gospel

KHVN 970 AM, 545 South John Carpenter Hwy, #1700, ☎ 214-988-7525.

KSGB 1540 AM, 3105 Arkansas Ave, Arlington, ☎ 817-469-1540.

KSKY 660 AM, 4144 North Central Expressway #266, ☎ 214-352-3975.

Newspapers

Dallas Examiner, 111 Dragon, ☎ 214-651-7066. African-American community newspaper. Distributed weekly on Thursdays.

Dallas Post Tribune, 2726 South Beckley, ☎ 214-946-7678. African-American community newspaper. Distributed weekly on Thursdays.

Dallas Weekly, 3101 Martin Luther King, Jr. Blvd, ☎ 214-428-8958. African-American community newspaper. Distributed weekly on Wednesdays.

Minority Business News, 11333 North Central Expressway, #201, ☎ 214-369-3200.

Publications

Black Pages of Dallas/Fort Worth, 3806 Marvin D. Love, #130, Dallas, TX 75224, ☎ 214-375-5200; fax 214-375-5223. Directory of numerous African-American-owned businesses in the Dallas/Fort Worth area. Annual publication.

Dallas: A Guide to African-American Life and Culture, The Dallas Convention & Visitors Bureau, 1201 Elm Street, Dallas, TX 75270, ☎ 214-746-6677.

Membership Directory and Referral Guide, Dallas Black Chamber of Commerce, 2838 Martin Luther King, Jr. Blvd, Dallas, TX 75215, ☎ 214-421-5200; fax 214-421-5510.

African-American Churches

AME

Bethel AME, 1638 South Ann Arbor Ave, ☎ 214-375-0144.

Ezra Chapel AME, 855 North Masters Drive, ☎ 972-557-4950.

Gaines Chapel AME, 1502 South Haskell Ave, ☎ 214-826-5031.

Rice Chapel AME, 4122 South Marsalis Ave, ☎ 214-376-6527.

St. James AME, 200 North Jim Miller Rd, ☎ 214-391-5541.

St. Mark's AME Zion, 2311 South Illinois Ave, ☎ 214-376-7750.

St. Paul AME, 2420 Metropolitan Ave, ☎ 214-421-1344.

St. Paul AME, 12230 Coit Rd, ☎ 972-233-7335.

Smith Chapel AME, 2406 Childs Street, ☎ 214-948-9482.

Tenth Episcopal District AME, 4347 South Hampton Rd, ☎ 214-333-2632.

Baptist

Concord Missionary Baptist, 3410 South Polk, ☎ 214-372-4543.

Friendship West Baptist, 616 West Kiest Blvd, ☎ 214-371-2029.

Golden Gate Baptist, 1101 Sabine, ☎ 214-942-7414.

Greater Cornerstone Baptist, 8219 Bunch Drive, ☎ 972-437-3325.

Mt. Pisgah Missionary Baptist, 11611 Webb Chapel, ☎ 214-241-6151.

New Birth Baptist, 444 West Ledbetter Dr, ☎ 214-374-0828 or 214-374-0829.

New Mount Zion Baptist, 9550 Sheppard Rd, ☎ 214-341-6459.

People's Baptist, 3119 Pine Street, ☎ 214-421-1098.

Peace Full Rest Baptist, 402 Cliff, ☎ 214-625-0893.

St. John Missionary Baptist, 2600 South Marsalis Ave, ☎ 214-375-4876.

Trinity Missionary Baptist, 5400 Elgin Street, ☎ 817-535-8567.

Church of Christ

Bridge of Life Christian Fellowship, 4129 Ball Street, ☎ 214-375-3661.

Dallas West Church of Christ, 3510 Hampton Rd, ☎ 214-631-5448.

Cedar Crest Church of Christ, 2134 Cedar Crest Blvd, ☎ 214-943-1340.

COGIC

Christ Holy Temple Cathedral COGIC, 2423 South Buckner Blvd, ☎ 214-388-9000.

Cornerstone COGIC, 2027 Lamont Ave, ☎ 214-948-1752.

Greater New Birth United COGIC of America, 3200 Ramona Ave, ☎ 214-372-5670.

Lively Stone COGIC, 8240 Carbondale Street, ☎ 214-371-9040.

United Pentecostal Temple COGIC, 4002 Kostner Ave, ☎ 214-371-1441.

Methodist

St. Paul United Methodist, 5710 East R.L. Thornton Hwy, ☎ 214-821-2970.

Non-Denominational

Oak Cliff Bible Fellowship, 1908 West Camp Wisdom, ☎ 214-228-1281. Radio personality Tony Evans is Pastor here.

Calendar of Annual Events

◆ January

Dr. Martin Luther King, Jr. Celebration, ☎ 214-421-5200.

Martin Luther King B'Ball Tournament, ☎ 214-821-9000.

Martin Luther King, Jr. Annual Art-Fest, ☎ 972-461-7174.

◆ February

Black History Month activities, ☎ 214-421-5200.

◆ March

Annual Spring Revival, St. Luke Community United Methodist Church, ☎ 214-821-2970.

Annual "Here's Hope Spring Revival," Cathedral of Faith Baptist Church, ☎ 214-398-7553.

Annual Career Expo, Oak Cliff Bible Fellowship Church, ☎ 214-228-1281.

Annual Scholarship Banquet, Black Data Processors Associates – Dallas Chapter, ☎ 972-407-6895. The organization selects a high school senior to receive scholarship funds.

◆ **May**
African-American Museum Annual Ball & Auction, ☎ 214-565-9026.

◆ **June**
Juneteenth Celebration Activities, ☎ 214-421-5200.

Public Transportation

Dallas Area Rapid Transit (DART). For bus schedules and information, ☎ 214-979-1111 or ☎ 214-749-3278.

Dallas/Fort Worth International Airport (DFW), ☎ 972-574-8888.

Dallas Love Field, ☎ 214-670-6073.

Taxi Services

Checker Cab, ☎ 214-565-9132.

Lone Star Cab, ☎ 214-352-5822.

Taxi Dallas, ☎ 214-823-3950.

Yellow Cab, ☎ 214-426-6262.

Dallas Area Resources

Dallas Black Chamber of Commerce, 2838 Martin Luther King, Dallas, TX 75270, ☎ 214-421-5200. Mon-Fri, 9 am-5 pm.

Dallas Black Dance Theater, 2627 Flora Street, Dallas, TX 75201, ☎ 214-871-2387.

Dallas Convention & Visitors Bureau, 1201 Elm Street, Dallas, TX 75270, ☎ 800-232-5527. Web site: www.gdc.org.

East Dallas Black Chamber of Commerce, 718 North Buckner Blvd, #332, Dallas, TX 75218-2720, ☎ 214-321-6446.

Fort Worth Black Chamber of Commerce, 3607 South Rosedale, Fort Worth, TX 76105, ☎ 817-531-8510.

Junior Black Academy of Arts and Letters, 650 Griffin, Dallas, TX 75208, ☎ 214-658-7144.

On the Internet: **http://cityview.com/dallas** has information about the Dallas area.

Detroit

Historic Sites & Landmarks

Black Bottom and Paradise Valley, Gratiot and St. Antoine. Between 1910 and 1930 Detroit's African-American population grew from around 6,000 to a staggering 120,000. The "Great Migration" of Blacks from the South to Detroit was a result of jobs available at the Ford Motor plant. Most African-Americans lived in the area known as "Black Bottom," which was located between Brush and Elmwood streets from Gratiot South to Larned. Although the job outlook was promising for some, many were unemployed and lived in sub-standard, overcrowded housing conditions. The area called "Paradise Valley" served as the business center for Detroit's African-American community during the 1930s and 1940s. At that time, nearly all businesses in Paradise Valley were African-American-owned and included nightclubs, restaurants, hotels and bowling alleys. The area had previously been inhabited by other immigrant groups until the turn of the century.

Burton Historical Collection/E. Azalia Hackley Memorial Collection, Detroit Public Library Main Branch, 5201 Woodward Ave, ☎ 313-833-1480. The Burton Historical Collection houses extensive information and resources for African-American genealogical research. The Hackley Collection is considered the oldest collection of historical memorabilia in North America. Open Sat, 9:30 am-5:30 pm; Wed, 1 pm-9 pm; Tues-Sat, 9:30 am-5:30 pm.

Elmwood Cemetery, 1200 Elmwood. This cemetery contains the graves of 14 of the 102nd US Colored Troops. Other prominent African-Americans from Detroit who are buried here include African-American abolitionist George DeBaptiste and William Lambert, manager and treasurer of the Underground Railroad's Detroit Terminal.

Fox Theatre, 2211 Woodward Ave, ☎ 313-396-7600. This historic landmark was built in 1928 and continues to provide topnotch variety, drama, comedy and musical events.

Grand Lobby, historic Fox Theatre
Photo by Mike Ditz, © MDCVB

Detroit

1. Black Bottom and Paradise Valley District
2. Detroit Public Library
3. Elmwood Cemetery
4. Frederick Douglass and John Brown Meeting Marker
5. George DeBaptist Homesite
6. Joe Louis Memorial/Cobo Center
7. Omega Psi Phi Fraternity House
8. Orchestra Hall
9. Orsel McGhee House
10. Phyllis Wheatley Homesite
11. Second Baptist Church
12. Underground Railroad Crossing Site
13. African-American Heritage Cultural Ctr
14. Concept East II/The Black Cinema Gallery
15. Detroit Historical Museum
16. Detroit Institute of the Arts
17. Graystone International Jazz Museum
18. Institute of African-American History
19. Motown Historical Museum
20. Museum of African-American History
21. Nat'l Museum of the Tuskegee Airmen at Historic Fort Wayne
22. Your Heritage House, Inc.
23. Henry Ford Museum & Greenfield Village
24. Metropolitan Detroit Convention & Visitors Bureau

Exterior of the historic Fox Theatre
Photo by Marji Silk, © MDCVB

Frederick Douglass and John Brown Meeting Marker, Congress and St. Antoine. This site marks the historic meeting on March 12, 1859, between antislavery orator, leader and writer Frederick Douglass and John Brown, an antislavery leader. Along with several other African-American leaders, Douglass and Brown met to discuss their tactics for abolishing slavery in the US. Douglass advocated political means while Brown advocated insurrection. The site is also recognized as the location where John Brown planned his West Virginia Raid at Harper's Ferry.

George DeBaptiste Homesite, East Larned and Beaubien. DeBaptiste was born and raised in Fred-ericksburg, Virginia and settled in Madison, Indiana in 1838. There he became involved with the Underground Railroad and worked as a valet for William Henry Harrison, who later became President. Following Harrison's death, DeBaptiste moved to Detroit and started a clothing business. After that, he purchased the *T. Whitney*, an excursion steamboat, which he sold a few years later to start a catering business. He was active in assisting runaway slaves cross over into Canada, and helped organize the First Michigan Colored Regiment during the Civil War. His obituary reads, "His gifts and benefactions during his life would amount to a small fortune. No one in need appealed to him in vain."

Joe Louis Arena, 600 Civic Center, next to the Cobo Center. This sports and concert arena was named in honor of the boxing champ.

Joe Louis Memorial, Cobo Conference/Exhibition Center, One Washington Blvd, ☎ 313-224-0226. A 12-foot-high statue of boxing champ Joe Louis, designed and sculpted by Edward N. Hamilton, is located in the atrium near the Exhibition Center's main entrance. The center also has an exhibit area with memorabilia relating to the champ's life.

Joe Louis Memorial at Woodward Ave and Jefferson. The 24-foot-tall sculpture, titled "The Fist," was designed by sculptor Robert Graham.

Omega Psi Phi Fraternity House, 235 East Ferry. Omega Psi Phi (The Qs) was founded at Howard University in 1911. This fraternity was the first of its kind of a higher learning institution for African-Americans. Nu Omega was founded by Dr. DeWitt T. Burton, O.T. Davis and Francis Dent in 1923 at Omega Psi Phi's Detroit graduate chapter at Wayne State University in 1938. The Nu Omega Detroit chapter purchased this three-story Victorian building in 1942 and continues to sponsor projects which include tutoring and scholarship programs.

Orchestra Hall (formerly Paradise Theater), Woodward at Parsons. From jazz to big band swing and gospel, Orchestra Hall was the most famous stage for African-Americans in the US during the early to mid-1900s. The building was originally built for the Detroit Symphony Orchestra, but they later relocated to the Masonic Temple. After closing for some time, Orchestra Hall was temporarily re-opened as Reverend James L. Lofton's Church of Our Prayer. The building eventually was abandoned, becoming dilapidated by the late 1950s. In 1964 it was headed for destruction until local citizens rallied to restore the facility and use it again as a concert hall.

Orsel McGhee House, 4626 Seebaldt. The McGhees were an African-American family who fought and won a legal suit against nonwhite residents. The suit was filed in 1944 by their next-door neighbors, citing a "restrictive covenant." The McGhees received a court order to vacate the premises. With the assistance of the NAACP and African-American attorney Thurgood Marshall, the case was appealed to the US Supreme Court, who in 1948 abolished restrictive covenants. Marshall was later named a Supreme Court justice.

Phyllis Wheatley Homesite, East Elizabeth near St. Antoine. This facility was named after 18th-century African-American poet Phyllis Wheatley, the first African-American woman, first slave and second woman to publish books of poetry in the US. Wheatley was brought to the US as a slave at the age of seven and wrote her first poetic work at the age of 14. The Phyllis Wheatley home was organized in 1898 by Fannie Richards and a group of other dedicated women who used the facility to provide care for elderly and needy African-American women.

Second Baptist Church, Monroe at Beaubien. This historic church was established in 1836 by 13 former slaves. It is the oldest African-American church in the Midwest and has been an integral part of Detroit's African-American community since the late 1930s. In addition to serving as a station to Detroit's Underground Railroad, the Second Baptist Church established the Amherstburg Baptist Association, a central location in which Detroit and Canadian Baptist churches aided the increasing population of freed slaves. Reverend William C. Monroe used the church basement to teach and direct a school for African-American children between 1842 and 1846.

Soldiers and Sailors Monument, Woodward Ave, and Campus Martius. This monument honors Detroit's local African-American Civil War veterans and is rumored to portray the 19th-century abolitionist and feminist Sojourner Truth. The "Emancipation" figure represents freedom.

Underground Railroad Station Marker at Griswold and State. This was the location of the Finney House Barn, built by Seymour Finney in 1846. Finney was a "Superintendent of the Underground Railroad" who used his barn as a major station for hiding and assisting fleeing slaves.

Underground Railroad Crossing Site, West Jefferson Ave and Sixth Street This site was one of the most popular crossings for escaped slaves fleeing to Canada for freedom during the last quarter of the 18th century. Several other crossing points have been identified by historians between Lake Erie and Lake St. Clair along the Detroit River. Detroit became a major Underground Railroad terminal for runaway slaves, and many of southwestern Ontario's African-American Canadians have traced their ancestry to the area.

Walter P. Reuther Library Archives of Labor and Urban History, Wayne State University Campus, 5401 Cass Ave, ☎ 313-577-4024. This facility holds an extensive collection on African-American history. Mon and Wed-Fri, 9 am-4:45 pm; Tues, 9 am-9 pm.

Sites Beyond Detroit

Sojourner Truth Memorial and Gravesite, Oakhill Drive at Oakhill Cemetery, Battle Creek. Take Exit 3 off Interstate 94 north from Detroit, head eastbound on Dickman St., right at South St., left at Oakhill Drive. Born Isabelle Baumfree of New York, Sojourner Truth was a former slave set free by her earthly master and by her Heavenly Master, our Lord, Jesus Christ. She dedicated the remainder of her life to serving God by traveling throughout the Eastern US "showing people their sins and being a sign unto them." This African-American abolitionist also helped slaves escape into Canada. She died in 1883 in Battle Creek, Michigan. A memorial at her gravesite was later erected in her honor.

Museums/Exhibits

African-American Heritage Cultural Center, 2511 West McNichols, ☎ 313-494-7452. Developed and operated by the Detroit Public School System, this museum features exhibitions of ancient African culture. Mon-Sat, 10 am-4 pm.

Concept East II/The Black Cinema Gallery, 1194 Pingree, ☎ 313-972-1030. African-American cinema collector James Wheeler has assembled one of America's most extensive collections of films, videos and memorabilia related to the history of African-Americans in the performing arts. Call for schedule and/or appointment. Admission charge.

Detroit Historical Museum, 5401 Woodward Ave, ☎ 313-833-1805. The museum displays memorabilia of former African-American sports figures, such as Joe Louis, Willis Ward and Thomas Tolan. It also includes material representing the growth of Detroit's African-American community dating from the late 1800s. Wed-Sun, 9:30-5. Admission charge.

Detroit Institute of Arts, 5200 Woodward Ave, ☎ 313-833-7900. Works by famous African-American artists such as Romare Bearden and Detroit artist Charles McGhee are on permanent display. One of America's largest museums, the DIA also displays portions of its extensive African art collection, including bronzes from Benin (Nigeria). Wed-Fri, 11 am-4 pm; Sat-Sun, 11 am-5 pm. Suggested donation.

Hitsville USA, the Motown Record Corporation
Photo by Susan Stewart, © MDCVB

Graystone International Jazz Museum, Book Tower Building, 1249 Washington Blvd, #201, ☎ 313-963-3813. A jazz history museum inspired by the late Duke Ellington, Graystone exhibits instruments, photographs and video presentations which focus on America's jazz history. Call for hours. Admission charge.

Institute of African-American Arts, 2641 West Grand Blvd, ☎ 313-872-0332. This museum showcases the works of some of Detroit's contemporary African-American artists such as LeRoy Foster and Oscar Graves. Each weekend, the institute also hosts music, drama, and dance performances. Admission charge.

Motown Historical Museum, 2648 West Grand Blvd, ☎ 313-875-2264. Music producer Berry Gordy, Jr. began his remarkable career as a songwriter after he quit his job at the Ford Motor Company in 1957. Gordy borrowed $800 from his family and became a producer and founder of Motown. He originally purchased the property at 2648 West Grand Blvd for $10,000; it currently houses the collection of Motown memorabilia. During the 1960s, the house served as a home for Gordy and his family, and as the headquarters and studio of the Motown Record Corporation (Hitsville USA). Visitors can view the infamous "Studio A" and the actual equipment used to produce such hits as *My Girl, Baby Love, Please Mr. Postman* and *My Guy* by the Temptations, Supremes and other Motown stars. Sun-Mon, noon-5 pm; Tues-Sat, 10 am-5 pm. Admission charge.

Museum of African-American History, 315 East Warren, ☎ 313-494-5800. Web site: www.detnews.com/maah/. The largest African-American museum in the country, the Museum of African-American History is dedicated to education and documentation of the life, history and culture of Africans and African-Americans and their struggle for dignity and freedom. Field to Factory is the museum's permanent exhibition, documenting the Great *Migration* of African-Americans who moved from the rural South to the industrialized North during the 20th century. The museum features a 350-seat theater and galleries dedicated to technology, the arts and historical archives. Tues-Sun, 9:30 am-5 pm. Admission charge.

National Museum of the Tuskegee Airmen at Historic Fort Wayne, 6325 West Jefferson Ave, ☎ 303-843-8849. This museum, located at Historic Fort Wayne, is dedicated to the achievements of the Tuskegee airmen. Their role as combat aviators within the segregated ranks of the US Armed Forces in 1941 was to fight in World War II, and their training at the Army Air Corps base in Tuskegee, Alabama, prepared them for the 1,500 missions flown over Europe. The squadron shot down enemy aircraft, bombed barges and enemy power stations, and successfully escorted other fighter pilots to their missions. Their success led to President Truman's decision to integrate the military. Detroit's Mayor Coleman Young is among the Tuskegee heroes. Donation requested.

Tight Pack, *a sculpture portraying enslaved Africans, featured at the Museum of African-American History. Detroit students posed for the sculpture.*
Photo courtesy of the Museum of African-American History

Your Heritage House, Inc., 110 East Ferry, ☎ 313-871-1667. The 100-year-old Victorian house and museum offers a multicultural experience for children. The large collection of rare books, artifacts, works of art and information documents African-American achievements in the arts. Mon-Fri, 10 am-5 pm. Admission charge.

Museums Beyond Detroit

Henry Ford Museum & Greenfield Village, 20900 Oakwood Blvd, Dearborn, ☎ 313-271-1620. Some of the most interesting inventions that you'll find in the Henry Ford Museum are works of African-Americans. Pick up a tour brochure on African-American inventors near the central hands-on area, and discover for yourself the significant contributions made by Granville Woods, Andrew Beard, Garrett Morgan, Lewis Latimer and Elijah McCoy. Test your ear at mixing a Motown hit, become a DJ for a few minutes and dance the "Frog." Fabulous cars from the 1960s line the entrance to the Motown exhibition. The new multimedia exhibition, The Motown Sound: The Music & The Story, is presented in partnership with the Motown Historical Museum. Museum hours: Mon-Sun, 9 am-5 pm. Village hours: Mon-Sun, 10 am-5 pm. Admission charge.

National Afro-American Museum and Cultural Center, 1350 Brush Row, Wilberforce, Ohio, 10 minutes from downtown Dayton, ☎ 513-376-4944. The National Afro-American Museum and Cultural Center is a national treasure established to present African-American history and culture from the African origins to the present. The Center boasts a remarkable permanent exhibit: From Victory to Freedom: Afro-American Life in the Fifties, which focuses on Black America between the years 1945 and 1965. The Museum has over 10,000 artifacts acquired from the world over in its permanent collection. It also features award-winning exhibitions like Songs of My People and Uncommon Beauty in Common Objects; The Legacy of African-American Craft. Mon-Sat, 9 am-5 pm; Sun, 1 pm-5 pm. Admission charge.

Historic Colleges & Universities

Lewis College of Business, 17370 Meyers Rd, Detroit, MI 48235, ☎ 313-862-6300. Independent two-year college. Founded 1929.

Shopping

Galleries & Specialty Shops

African Imports (Karamu Art Gallery), Shrine of the Black Madonna Cultural Center and Bookstore, 13535 Livernois, ☎ 313-491-0777. Call for hours.

Art Gallery, 19534 Grand River, Rosedale Park, ☎ 313-534-4400. Tues-Fri, 1 pm-7 pm; Sat, 11 am-7 pm.

Dabl's Perette's Gallery, 1257 Woodward Blvd, ☎ 313-964-4247. African beads, carvings, fabrics and clothing. Mon-Sat, noon-7 pm.

Donald Morris Gallery, 105 Townsend, Birmingham, ☎ 248-642-8812. Specializes in museum-quality tribal African art. Tues-Sat, 10:30 am-5:30 pm.

Galerie Haitien, 4363 Kensington, ☎ 313-885-2704. Features Haitian art exclusively. Shown by appointment only.

G.R. N'Namdi Gallery, 161 Townsend, Birmingham, ☎ 248-642-2700. Represents a number of major African-American artists, including Richard Hunt, Al Loving, Jr., Howardena Pindell and Jacob Lawrence. Tues-Sat, 11 am-5:30 pm; Sun, 1 pm-4 pm.

Moore African Art, 1301 Broadway, ☎ 313-965-4540. Features Zimbabwean stone sculpture and paintings from Soweto, Zambia, Zimbabwe and Zaire. Works by Ronnie Dongo, Brighton Sango, Richard Mteki, Lazarus Takawira and Israel Chikumbirike. Mon-Sat, 10 am-5:30 pm.

Nkomii Youth Center & International Art Gallery, Inc., 630 Woodward, ☎ 313-961-4210. The gallery features west and southeast African art while the center sponsors programming designed to introduce youth to authentic African language, music, dance and history. Nkomii's international gallery is complemented by a unique after-school and weekend educational and cultural center for children and adults. Mon-Fri, 9 am-5 pm; Sat, 10 am-2 pm; Sun, by appointment only.

Pyramids, 18100 Meyers, ☎ 313-921-0200. Sportswear and accessories and Afrocentric merchandise. Mon-Sat, 10 am-8 pm.

Reflections of Color Gallery, 18951 Livernois, ☎ 313-342-7595. Specializes in hand-painted Egyptian papyrus and African art. Mon-Fri, 11 am-8 pm; Sat, 11 am-5 pm.

Sherry Washington Gallery, 1274 Library, Downtown, ☎ 313-961-4500. Repertoire of artists includes Gilda Snowden, Charles Burwell, David Fludd, William T. Williams and Nadine DeLawrence as well as younger, largely undiscovered talents. Tues-Fri, 10 am-5 pm; Sat, noon-5 pm.

Spirit in the Park, 297 East Grand River, ☎ 313-965-4919. African-American art, i.e., original oil paintings, textiles, dolls, quilts, Moroccan pottery, and jewelry. Tues-Sat, 11 am-6 pm.

Umoja Fine Arts, 16250 Northland Drive, #104, Crossroads Building, Southfield, ☎ 248-552-1070, fax 248-553-6392. Said to be the largest distributor of African-American art in the Midwest. Mon, Wed, Fri, noon-5 pm; Sat, 1 pm-5 pm.

Zawadi Gift Shop, 8411 East Forest, Inner City Sub-Center, ☎ 313-921-0200. Small gift shop featuring Afrocentric merchandise, including sportswear, books and artifacts. Mon-Fri, noon-8 pm; Sat, 10 am-6 pm.

Bookstores

Apple Book Center, 790 West Outer Drive, ☎ 313-255-5221, fax 313-255-5230. E-mail: apple001@aol.com. African-American fiction and non-fiction books and general interest books. Mon-Sat, 10 am-9 pm; Sun, 10 am-7 pm.

Baker Bible & Books Store, 10200 Grand River, ☎ 313-933-5507. General interest and some African-American books. Mon-Sat, 9 am-6 pm.

Book Corner, 19555 James East Wadsworth, Jr. Ave (West McNichols Rd), ☎ 313-532-1520. Offers an array of religious books and bibles, as well as cultural, children's and general educational books. Also features African artifacts, authentic Kente pieces, jewelry, designer Afrocentric fashions and greeting cards. Mon-Thurs, 11 am-8 pm; Fri-Sat, 11 am-5 pm; Sun, after each church service.

Gospel House Bible Bookstore, 15920 Grand River, ☎ 313-272-2772.

Kuumba Korners, 9980 Gratiot Ave, ☎ 313-921-0723. African and African-American books. Mon-Fri, noon-5 pm; Sat, 11 am-6 pm.

Shrine of the Black Madonna Cultural Center and Bookstore, 13535 Livernois, ☎ 313-491-0777. For 22 years, this bookstore (the largest African-

American bookstore in the country) and gallery has offered an array of Afrocentric items from the world over, including fabrics, leather goods and rare cultural items. Tues-Thurs, 11 am-6 pm; Fri-Sat, 11 am-7 pm.

Vaughn's Bookstore, 16525 Livernois, ☎ 313-863-1940. Proprietor Ed Vaughn is a legend in Detroit's African-American community because of his involvement in the African-American consciousness movement in the 1960s and 1970s, as well as his expertise in the history of people of African heritage. Detroit's first African-American bookstore carries such a range of books on history and culture of African peoples that it draws scholars from the world over. Mon-Sat, noon-7 pm.

Fashions

Africa House, 19445 Livernois Ave, ☎ 313-341-7423. African clothing for men, women and children, and gift items. Tues-Sat, 10 am-6 pm.

Bernie's Closet on the River, 18256 Grand River, ☎ 313-836-7307. Vintage Clothing featuring vintage hats, purses, exotic hard-to-find items, furs, jewelry and collectibles. Wed-Fri, 10 am-7 pm; Sat, 10 am-6 pm.

Lajo's Private Collection, 208 East Grand River, Harmonie Park, ☎ 313-962-5256. Exclusive fashions for women. Mon-Sat, 10 am-6 pm.

Hot Sam's Quality Clothier, 1317 Brush Street, ☎ 313-961-6779, fax 313-961-6919. Designer name men's clothing and shoes. Big and tall sizes available. Mon-Sat, 9 am-6:30 pm.

Nathan's Fashions, Inc., 9101 Grand River Ave, ☎ 313-935-1111. Men's and boy's clothing. Big and tall fashions, men's dress shoes and women's clothing. Mon-Sat, 9 am-7 pm; Sun, 10 am-4 pm.

Nene's International Fashions and More, 19323 Livernois, ☎ 313-341-7954. Upscale fashion boutique for men, women and children featuring designs from Africa, Europe and the US. Also carries ethnic greeting cards, jewelry, lingerie, arts and crafts and variety of gift items. Mon-Sat, 10 am-7 pm.

The Urbanite Men's Clothing, 18960 Greenfield, ☎ 313-272-1163. Custom tailored suits, sport coats, trousers and dress shirts. Also features name-brand designs and Flic ties and clothing. Mon-Sat, 10 am-10 pm; Sun, noon-8 pm.

Women Size Suits & Dresses, 57 West Milwaukee, ☎ 313-871-5552. Fashions for full figured women, size 14 and up. Mon-Sat, 10 am-6 pm.

Spas

Mel's Salon & Associates, 6080 Woodward Blvd, ☎ 313-872-6630; voice mail 810-788-5905. Massage therapy. Wed-Thurs, 7 pm-10 pm; Sat, 11 am-3 pm.

Detroit

Stressage Health Spa, 16587 Wyoming, ☎ 313-864-8355. Features a variety of stress relief and relaxation services, such as aromatherapy, ancient Thai massage, holistic health support, facials, manicures, pedicures, day spa treatment, bath and beauty items, natural foods, lectures and workshops. Mon-Fri, 11 am-6 pm; Sat, 11 am-5 pm.

Restaurants

◆ Caribbean

Captain Tony's Key West Bar & Grill, 3335 N. Woodward, Royal Oaks, ☎ 248-288-6388. Features tropical dishes that include plenty of fruits and vegetables from the Dominican Republic and Honduras. Mon-Thurs, 11 am-10 pm; Fri-Sat, 11 am-11 pm; Sun, 1 pm-8 pm.

◆ Seafood

Mr. FoFo's, 8902 Second at Hazelwood, ☎ 313-873-4450. Deli, seafood, barbecue, specialty desserts. Lunch and dinner items, carry-out only. Open every day, 24 hours.

Shrimp Hut, 15725 Livernois, ☎ 313-864-6742. Several locations throughout Detroit metro area. French-fried shrimp, fish, chicken, catfish and homemade pies. Sun-Thurs, until 3 am; Fri-Sat, until 4 am.

◆ Soul Food

East Franklin, 1440 Franklin, Rivertown, ☎ 313-393-0018. Lunch and dinner. Tues-Thurs, 11 am-9 pm; Fri, 11 am-10 pm; Sat, noon-10 pm; Sun, noon-9 pm.

Bea's Comedy Kitchen, 541 East Larned, Downtown, ☎ 313-961-2581. Dinner. See their listing under *Comedy Clubs.* Open daily 7 pm-2 am.

Edmund Place Restaurant, 69 Edmund, just north of downtown, ☎ 313-831-5757. Soul food in restored Victorian ambiance. Lunch and dinner. Mon, noon-3 pm; Tues-Sun, noon-9 pm.

Steve's Soul Food, 8443 Grand River Ave, ☎ 313-894-3464. Lunch and dinner. Cafeteria-style sit-down restaurant or carry-out. Mon-Sun, 11 am-9 pm.

◆ **Vegetarian/Muslim**

Aknartoon's Eatery, 10310 Woodward Ave, at Calvert ☎ 313-867-3102. Vegetarian Muslim cuisine. Lunch and dinner. Monday-Sun, 11 am-4 am.

Restaurants Beyond Detroit

◆ **Cajun**

Jambalaya Johnnie's, 26555 Evergreen, Southfield, ☎ 810-948-8964. Hot 'n sassy Cajun/Creole cuisine. Lunch and dinner. Mon-Fri, 11 am-11 pm; Sat, 4 pm-11 pm. Closed Sun. See listing under *Entertainment Beyond Detroit.*

◆ **International**

Dempsey's Place, 3000 East Jefferson Ave, Rivertown, ☎ 313-259-9806. International cuisine, contemporary surroundings. Lunch, dinner and Sunday brunch. Mon-Thurs, 11 am-10 pm; Fri-Sat, 11 am-11 pm; Sun, 10 am-9 pm. Entertainment. See listing under *Jazz Clubs/Lounges.*

Entertainment

◆ **Jazz Nightclubs/Lounges**

Baker's Keyboard Lounge, 20510 Livernois, ☎ 313-345-6300. Live jazz. Call for specifics. "The oldest jazz club in the world."

Bert's Marketplace, 2727 Russell, Eastern market, ☎ 313-567-2030. Live jazz, comedy-jazz nights, weekends. Great jazz "until the wee hours."

Bo Mac's Lounge, 281 Gratiot, ☎ 313-961-5152. Live jazz. Call for specific hours and entertainment.

Club Penta, 3011 West Grand Blvd, ☎ 313-972-3760. Live jazz, blues and R&B. "Upbeat sophistication."

Flood's Bar & Grille, 731 St. Antoine, Downtown, ☎ 313-963-1090. Jazz, R&B, live music. Light dinner and lunch.

Rhinoceros, 265 Riopelle, ☎ 313-259-2208. Live jazz, lunch and dinner. "Intimate urbane sophistication."

◆ **Dance Nightclubs**

Detroit West Club, 14400 Wyoming, ☎ 313-834-3233. Oldies upstairs, contemporary music downstairs, dancing. "Brush up on your hustle and electric slide."

Fountain Room, 8443 Grand Ave, ☎ 313-894-5560. Blues, oldies, Top 40 for the over-35 set. Snack baskets available.

Legends Nightclub, 415 East Congress St., ☎ 313-961-5005. A popular premiere dance club and entertainment complex. The four-level club includes dance floor, sports bar and game room. Multiethnic, young crowd.

◆ **Comedy Clubs**

All Jokes Aside, 2036 Woodward Ave, Downtown, ☎ 313-962-2100. Detroit's own comedy jam. Full drink menu, live comedy. Call for current schedule.

Bea's Comedy Kitchen, 541 East Larned, Downtown, ☎ 313-961-2581. Hot local comedy. See listing under *Soul Food* restaurants.

Entertainment Beyond Detroit

◆ **Jazz/Blues Nightclubs/Lounges**

Dempsey's Place, 3000 East Jefferson Ave, Rivertown, ☎ 313-259-9806. Live jazz pianist and gospel entertainment. Sunday brunch. Sun, 10 am-9 pm. See listing under *Restaurants Beyond Detroit.*

Jambalaya Johnnie's, 26551 Evergreen, Southfield, ☎ 810-948-8964. Live jazz on Fri nights. Lunch and dinner Mon-Fri, 11 am-1 am. Sat, 4 pm-11 pm. Closed Sun. See listing under *Restaurants Beyond Detroit.*

Soup Kitchen Saloon, 1585 Franklin Street, Rivertown, ☎ 313-259-2643. Live big band and blues. "Laid-back dining and entertainment."

◆ **Dance Nightclubs**

Feathers Nightclub, 1538 Franklin, Rivertown, ☎ 313-567-2763. Urban contemporary, Top 40, live band Weds, DJ on Sun. Soul food snacks, appetizers.

Warehouse, 2999 Woodbridge, Rivertown, ☎ 313-567-1292. Contemporary music and dancing. After-work buffet on Fridays. "Dance till you drop."

Media

Radio Stations

◆ **Jazz**

WJZZ 105.9 FM, 2994 East Grand Blvd, ☎ 313-871-0590.

◆ **Urban Contemporary**

WGPR 107.5 FM, 3146 East Jefferson Ave, ☎ 313-259-8862.

WJLB 97.9 FM, 645 Griswold Street, # 633, ☎ 313-965-2000.

WQBH 1400 AM, Penobscot Building, ☎ 313-965-4500.

◆ Gospel

WCHB 1440 AM, 32790 Henry Ruff Rd, ☎ 313-278-1440. Gospel and blues format.

Newspapers

Detroit Sunday Journal, 11000 West McNichols, #19, ☎ 313-964-5655. African-American community newspaper. Distributed weekly.

Michigan Chronicle, 479 Ledyard, ☎ 313-963-5522. Detroit's oldest African-American-owned newspaper. Distributed weekly on Wednesdays.

Magazines

Detroit Black Yellow Pages, ☎ 313-342-1717. Directory of Detroit's African-American-owned businesses.

Northwest Courant, 10600 West McNichols, ☎ 313-255-3536. African-American community news magazine.

Publications

Detroit; A Visitor's Guide to Detroit's African-American Community and *Metropolitan Detroit Metro Visitors Guide;* Detroit Convention & Visitors Bureau, 100 Renaissance Center, Detroit, MI 48243-1056. ☎ 313-567-1170.

Travel Agents

Dynasty Travel & Tours, 11000 West McNichols, #302, Detroit, MI 48221, ☎ 313-863-1750. Individual, group and corporate travel professionals.

Jomar International Travel, Inc., 21500 Greenfield Rd, #207, Oak Park, ☎ 810-967-1514. ITAS. Can arrange African-American tours of Detroit.

Group Travel & Tours, Inc., 19454 James Couzens, Detroit, MI 48235, ☎ 888-354-7687 or 313-342-4744. Specializes in travel plans for individuals, groups, churches and schools.

People's Travel/American Express, 2065 Rawsonville Rd, Belleville, MI 48111, ☎ 313-487-2359. Special packages targeted towards African-Americans.

The Tour and Travel Co., 18505 West 8 Mile #114, Detroit, MI 48219, ☎ 313-538-3400, fax 313-538-3634. Professional travel consultants.

Heritage Tours

Action Tours, 5663 Haverhill Rd, West Bloomfield, MI 48322, ☎ 810-851-7893. Tour includes stops on Detroit's Underground Railroad and the Museum of African-American History. Call for more information.

Detroit Upbeat, 18430 Fairway Drive, Detroit, MI 48221, ☎ 313-341-6808. Various tours, including Detroit overview, Underground Railroad and the Black music and art of Motown.

Ellis Tours and Charters, Inc, ☎ 800-435-1885 or 313-425-1885, fax 313-425-2852. This six-hour tour features various historic and cultural sites in Detroit's African-American community and may include visits to the Motown Historical Museum, Tuskegee Airmen Museum, Underground Railroad stops and the new Museum of Afro-American History.

Grayline Tours – Detroit Department of Transportation, ☎ 313-833-1805 or 313-935-3808. The Detroit Historical Museum's Black Historic Sites Committee offers customized group tours based on the *Black Historic Sites in Detroit* booklet. Tours include major Underground Railroad sites in Detroit and Ontario, and 20th-century sites related to the Great Migration and the legendary Paradise Valley community.

Tours Beyond Detroit

African-American Heritage Tour, 611 Broadway, Lorain, Ohio 44052, ☎ 800-334-1673. African-American Heritage Tour of Lorain County, Ohio. Knowledgeable guides will take visitors to Lorain County's rich historical sites where many slaves escaped to freedom. Call or write for their 12-page African-American Heritage Tour brochure.

African-American Churches

AME

AME Zion, 4400 Bewick Street, ☎ 313-571-3360.

Allen Temple AME, 4101 Helen Street, ☎ 313-925-8311.

Baber Memorial AME, 15045 Burt Rd, ☎ 313-255-9895.

Bethel AME Church, 5050 St. Antoine, ☎ 313-831-8810.

Blackwell Temple AME Zion, 7116 Fenkell Street, ☎ 313-862-5060.

Clinton Chapel AME Zion, 3381 23rd Street, ☎ 313-897-5866.

Ebenezer AME, 5151 West Chicago, ☎ 313-933-6943.

Grace Chapel AME, 490 Conner Street, ☎ 313-824-1533.

Greater Quinn AME, 13501 12th Street, ☎ 313-867-8380.

Gregg Memorial AME, 10120 Plymouth Rd, ☎ 313-491-1704.

Greater St. Peter AME Zion, 4400 Mount Elliott, ☎ 313-923-3161.

John Wesley AME Zion, 6419 Beechwood Street, ☎ 313-894-5600.

Lomax Temple AME Zion, 17441 Dequindre Street, ☎ 313-893-1463.

Mt. Calvary AME, 1800 East 7 Mile, ☎ 313-892-0042.

New St. James AME, 9321 Rosa Parks Blvd, ☎ 313-867-2851.

Oak Grove AME, 19801 Cherrylawn Street, ☎ 313-341-8877.

St. Andrews AME, 12517 Linwood Street, ☎ 313-868-3156.

St. Mary's AME Zion, 5330 East McNichols Rd, ☎ 313-892-1060.

St. Stephens AME, 6000 John East Hunter Drive, ☎ 313-895-4800.

Baptist

Burnett Baptist, 16801 Schoolcraft, ☎ 313-837-0032.

Chapel Hill Baptist, 5000 Joy Rd, ☎ 313-931-6805.

Elyton Missionary Baptist, 8903 St. Cyril, ☎ 313-921-4072.

First Baptist Institutional, 17101 West 7 Mile, ☎ 313-838-0166.

First Progressive Missionary Baptist, 10103 Gratiot, ☎ 313-925-9337.

Galilee Baptist, 14201 Arlington, ☎ 313-893-1472.

Hartford Memorial Baptist, 18700 James Couzens, ☎ 313-861-1200.

Messiah Baptist, 8100 West 7 Mile, ☎ 313-864-3337.

New Bethel Baptist, 8430 C.L. Franklin Blvd, ☎ 313-894-5788.

New Providence Baptist, 19901 Kentucky, ☎ 313-863-2725.

Second Baptist Church, 441 Monroe, ☎ 313-961-0920.

Second Ebenezer Baptist, 2760 East Grand Blvd, ☎ 313-872-7322.

Spring Hill Baptist, 19371 Greenfield, ☎ 313-837-7225.

Sweet Home Baptist, 2764 West Grand Blvd, ☎ 313-837-5672.

Tabernacle Missionary Baptist, 6125 Beechwood, ☎ 313-898-3325.

COGIC

Brotherly Love COGIC, 15700 Hubbell Street, ☎ 313-835-4890.

El Beth-El Temple COGIC, 15801 Schaefer Highway, ☎ 313-835-3326.

Detroit

Evangelistic Center COGIC, 8915 Puritan Street, ☎ 313-864-7380.

Fountain of Life COGIC, 16911 W. McNichols Rd, ☎ 313-493-0706.

Glad Tidings COGIC, 624 East 7 Mile Rd, ☎ 313-366-4378.

God's Oasis COGIC, 8132 Fullerton Street, ☎ 313-933-9732.

God's Temple Church of COGIC, 8257 Joy Rd, ☎ 313-934-5361.

Holy Temple of Truth COGIC, 10627 Puritan Street, ☎ 313-342-5255.

New Christ Temple COGIC, 10001 Hayes, ☎ 313-521-4586.

New Life COGIC, 13427 East McNichols Rd, ☎ 313-527-4930.

Revival Center COGIC, 10511 West Chicago Street, ☎ 313-834-0055.

St. Joseph Tabernacle COGIC, 13041 West Chicago Street, ☎ 313-834-6161.

United Temple COGIC, 16219 Meyers, ☎ 313-341-6346.

Victory Worship Center COGIC, 18347 West McNichols Rd, ☎ 313-531-5290.

Calendar of Annual Events

◆ January

Dr. Martin Luther King, Jr. Holiday Luncheon Program, Wayne State University, ☎ 313-577-2246.

◆ February

African-American Heritage Month, citywide activities. Metropolitan Detroit Convention and Visitors Center, ☎ 313-567-1170.

2648 Grand Celebration, Motown Historical Museum pays tribute to legendary Motown artists, ☎ 313-875-2264.

◆ March

Salute to Distinguished Warriors Dinner. Detroit Urban League honors those who have made outstanding contributions for the cause of human and Civil rights, ☎ 313-832-4600.

◆ April

NAACP Freedom Fund Dinner, ☎ 313-871-2087. Fundraising dinner, featuring nationally known speakers and entertainment.

◆ May

Bal Africain, Detroit Institute of Arts. Black-tie gala and fundraiser for Museum's Friends of African and African-American Art, ☎ 313-833-0247.

◆ **June**

A Celebration of Emancipation, Juneteenth celebration at Henry Ford Museum and Greenfield Village. Music, storytelling, dramatic readings, ☎ 313-271-1620. .

Gospelfest, Gospel music celebration, ☎ 810-851-3993.

◆ **July**

Afro-American Music Festival, Metropolitan Arts Complex, Inc. Three days of entertainment: jazz, blues, gospel, hip-hop. Third weekend of July, ☎ 313-863-5554.

◆ **August**

African World Festival, Museum of African-American History. Three-day festival at Hart Plaza celebrates African heritage with music, clothing, art, food and cultural items. Third weekend in August, ☎ 313-833-9800.

◆ **September**

Montreaux-Detroit Jazz Festival, Music Hall Center for the Performing Arts. Largest jazz festival in North America. Labor Day weekend, ☎ 313-963-7622.

Urban League Annual Golf Outing. Detroit Urban League. Public golf outing, dinner and charity auction to benefit youth development, ☎ 313-832-4600.

◆ **October**

Ancestors Day. Museum of African-American history celebrates this African tradition in lieu of Halloween. Costuming, storytelling, dancing, feasting and the pouring of libations, ☎ 313-833-9800.

◆ **December**

Kwanzaa. City-wide events. Consult local newspapers for current listings of celebration times and locations.

Public Transportation

Detroit Department of Transportation (local bus service), ☎ 313-933-1300.

Detroit Metro Airport, ☎ 313-942-3550.

Detroit People Mover, downtown rail system, ☎ 800-541-7245 or 313-962-7245.

Detroit Trolley, ☎ 313-933-1300 or 313-933-8020.

Taxi Services

Checker Cab Co, ☎ 313-963-5005.

Southfield Cab Co, ☎ 810-356-1090.

Detroit Area Resources

Detroit Association of Black Organizations, 4450 Oakman Blvd, Detroit, MI 48204, ☎ 313-491-0003.

Metropolitan Detroit Convention & Visitors Bureau, 100 Renaissance Center, Detroit, MI 48243-1056, ☎ 313-259-4333, fax 313-259-7583. Web site: www.visitdetroit.com. The Bureau is open Mon-Fri, 9 am-5 pm; Sat-Sun, 10 am-5 pm.

Travel Michigan, PO Box 30226, Lansing, MI 48909, ☎ 517-373-0670. Mon-Fri, 8 am-5 pm.

Visitor Hotline, ☎ 800-DETROIT. Up-to-date information on Detroit area events.

Indianapolis

Historic Sites & Landmarks

Crispus Attucks High School Building and Center, 1140 North Martin Luther King, Jr. Street, ☎ 317-226-4611. Named in honor of the first to die at the Boston Massacre, Crispus Attucks, this high school was the first in the city specifically built for African-Americans in 1927. Mon-Fri, 8 am-4:45 pm. See listing under *Museums/Exhibits* for additional information.

Historic Ransom Place, 830 Dr. Martin Luther King, Jr. Street, ☎ 317-632-8482. Called the "Negro Meridian Street" of Indianapolis, this neighborhood dates back to the late 1800s and early 1900s as an exclusive section for African-American lawyers, doctors and businessmen. Named after Freeman B. Ransom, manager and attorney for the famed Madame C.J. Walker, the neighborhood developed as a result of the northern migration of African-Americans from the South.

Madame Walker Center, 617 Indiana Ave, ☎ 317-236-2099, fax 317-236-2099. E-mail: mmewalker@aol.com. Listed on the National Register of Historic Places and a National Historic Landmark, the Madame Walker Building and Theatre was named after America's first female self-made millionaire, Madame C. J. Walker. Walker, an African-American, built her fortune from a hair-straightening formula and a host of beauty schools around the US. Today, the center remains very active in performing arts and other cultural and civic activities, and maintains permanent exhibits of the late Madame Walker and history of the center. Mon-Thurs, 9 am-5 pm. Free tours of the center. Admission during events.

Major Taylor Velodrome, 3649 Cold Spring Rd, ☎ 317-327-8356. Marshall Walter Taylor was the first African-American athlete who achieved championship status. Taylor "Major" dedicated 16 years to a career of cycling and won three US championships and two world titles. Taylor was nicknamed major because of the military style uniform he wore during his career.

Sites Beyond Indianapolis

Levi Coffin House, North Main Street, Fountain City, ☎ 317-847-2432. Called the "President of the Underground Railroad," Quakers Levi Coffin and his wife, Catherine, as well as other concerned citizens successfully assisted 2,000 escaped slaves to safety during their journey north to freedom. The attic in their Fountain City home, an Underground Railroad Station, was used to hide slaves. Seasonal hours. Call first. Tues-Sun, 1 pm-4 pm. Admission charge.

Downtown Indianapolis

1.5 MILES

.9 KM

1. Crispus Attucks Museum
2. Historic Ransom Place
3. Madame Walker Center
4. Major Taylor Velodrome
5. Children's Museum
6. Freetown Village Museum
7. Indianapolis Museum of Art

8. Indiana World War
   Memorial Museum
9. Indianapolis Convention
   & Visitors Bureau
10. Indiana Black Expo
11. Indianapolis Black Chamber
    of Commerce

Lick Creek "Little Africa" Settlement, USDA Forest Service, Hoosier National Forest, 811 Constitution Ave, Bedford, IN 47421, ☎ 812-275-5987, TTY 812-279-3423. Remnants of "Little Africa" can be seen at the Hoosier National Forest along Lick Creek. Many of the graves within the site are the remains of African-Americans who had settled with a group of sympathetic Quakers. Having escaped the persecution of slavery from their homes in North Carolina, they settled along Lick Creek between 1815 and 1820. According to an 1860 census, more than 260 African-Americans had acquired land and lived in the area, and in 1837 an African Methodist Episcopal Church was built. All that remains of the area are a few of the church's foundation stones and the bare white crosses and weathered tombstones of the graves. It is estimated that between 70-100 African-Americans were buried at the site.

Museums/Exhibits

Children's Museum, 3000 North Meridian Street, ☎ 317-924-5431. "African-American Scientists from A-Z" is featured at the Children's Museum. The exhibit is located on the fifth floor of the museum and highlights contributions by African-Americans in the field of science. Exhibits include several inventions made by famous and not-so-famous African-Americans. Mon-Sat, 10 am-5 pm; Sun, noon-5 pm. Admission charge.

Crispus Attucks Museum, 1140 Dr. Martin Luther King, Jr. Street, ☎ 317-226-4613. This history museum recognizes and honors the contributions made by African-Americans, particularly those graduates of Crispus Attucks High School. Attucks was not only the first man to die in the Boston Massacre, but also the first African-American. Mon-Fri, 10 am-2 pm, or by appointment.

Freetown Village Museum, Madame Walker Urban Life Center, 617 Indiana Ave, ☎ 317-631-1870, fax 317-631-0224. E-mail: freetown.org@iquest.com. Web site: www.freetown.org. This unique museum concept is African-American history at its finest. Depicting the life of African-Americans in the 1870s, Freetown Village produces touring plays, craft and heritage workshops, and evening dinners with African-American cuisine and authentic period entertainment. There is also a museum store and a permanent exhibit at the Indiana State Museum at 202 North Alabama, ☎ 317-232-1631. The museum store, along with the Madame Walker Urban Life Center, should be on every visitor's itinerary while in Indianapolis. Free admission to museum store. Call ahead for evening dinner dates, schedules and events.

Indiana World War Memorial Museum, "Military Heritage of African-American Americans in National Defense." Located in the lower concourse on the plaza between New York, St. Clair, Pennsylvania and Meridian streets, it is part of the "Hoosiers in the Armed Forces" exhibit. Open daily, 8:30 am-4:30 pm. Free admission.

Indianapolis

Indianapolis Museum of Art, 1200 West 38th Street, ☎ 317-923-1331. One of the oldest art museums in the country, the museum has African art pieces among its extensive collections. Tues, Wed, Fri and Sat, 10 am-5 pm; Thurs, 10 am-8:30 pm. Free admission.

Shopping

Galleries & Specialty Shops

Agape Enterprises Gift Shop, 3140 North Illinois Street, ☎ 317-283-1454. Distinctive quality gift items from 35 various countries.

Awesome Gifts and Decorations by Linda, 4025 Rommel Drive, ☎ 317-291-9343. Gift baskets, floral designs and wedding coordinator.

Be Real Fine Art Gallery, 1060 North Capitol, ☎ 317-630-5000. Afrocentric sculptures, paintings, (abstract, oil, and watercolor) by African-American artist William C. J. By appointment only.

Bijoux, by Beverly, 49 West Washington Street, Circle Centre Mall, ☎ 317-226-9647. Afrocentric scarves, handbags and other accessories and jeweled items. Mon-Sat, 10 am-9 pm; Sun, noon-6 pm.

Bonnie Marche Framing and Gift, 2021 East 52nd Street, ☎ 317-257-6746. African-American and contemporary art and fine gifts.

Magnifiscents, 5207 East 38th Street, Sam's Mini Mall Shopping Center, ☎ 317-549-3880. Afrocentric incense, oils and gift items. Mon-Thurs, 11 am-7 pm; Sun, noon-5 pm.

Niang African Art, C49 West Maryland Street, Circle Centre Mall, ☎ 317-638-5629, fax 317-638-5635 and 3919 Lafayette Rd, Lafayette Square Mall, ☎ 317-216-9634. Authentic African art, papyrus, wood carvings, beads, African music and instruments, brass items, custom-made African clothes and prints. Mon-Sat, 10 am-9 pm; Sun, noon-6 pm.

Universal Gift Shop, 155 West Washington Street, Merchant's Plaza, Hyatt Hotel, ☎ 317-681-9012. Specializes in authentic African art and features clothing, jewelry, purses, briefcases and various African art pieces.

X-Pressions Art Gallery, 5912 North College Ave, ☎ 317-257-5448. African-American art pieces. Mon-Sat, 10 am-7 pm; Sun, noon-5 pm.

Bookstores

Respect for Life Bookstore, 4040 North Millersville Rd, ☎ 317-541-1720.

X-Pressions Book Store, 5912 North College, ☎ 317-257-5448. Afrocentric book store.

Fashions

Adam's Apple Menswear, 4640 North Keystone Ave, ☎ 317-726-1804. Contemporary African-American men's clothing and accessories. African-American print ties. Mon-Sat, 10 am-7 pm.

Beth's Boutique, 1005 West 30th Street, ☎ 317-926-2254.

Classic Fashions, 3825 North Illinois, ☎ 317-924-9451.

Flora's Unique Boutique, 16 West 22nd Street, ☎ 317-926-5449. Contemporary women's fashions and accessories. Tues-Sat, 10 am-5 pm.

Interstate Jobbers, 2020 East 46th Street, ☎ 317-253-7081. Contemporary men's store. High-fashion designs and accessories. Tues-Sat, 10 am-6 pm.

Gold Coast, 5454 East Fall Creek Pkwy, North Drive, ☎ 317-545-2355. African clothing for men, women and children and African art. Mon-Sat, 10 am-7 pm.

Marie's Boutique, 820 East Westfield, ☎ 317-251-2606. Contemporary women's clothing. Mon-Thurs, 11 am-6 pm; Sat, noon-5 pm.

Mac's Fine Jewelry and Fashion, 3790 North Arlington Ave, ☎ 317-543-2586. Contemporary men's clothing and accessories. Mon-Sat, 11 am-7 pm.

Niang African Art, C49 West Maryland Street, Circle Centre Mall, ☎ 317-638-5629, fax 317-638-5635 and 3919 Lafayette Rd, Lafayette Square Mall, ☎ 317-216-9634. See listing under *Galleries & Specialty Shops.* Mon-Sat, 10 am-9 pm; Sun, noon-6 pm.

Players Modern Clothing, 5915 East 38th Street, ☎ 317-545-3221. Contemporary men's clothing and accessories. "Definitely the type of clothes that the brothers wear." Mon, noon-6 pm; Tues-Thurs, 11 am-6 pm; Thurs-Sat, 10 am-7 pm.

Serendipity House, 7505 North Michigan Rd, ☎ 317-291-3451. Full figure custom-designed women's clothing and accessories. Most clothes are designed and manufactured by Serendipity. Mon-Sat, 10 am-5 pm; Sun, by appointment.

Health Clubs

Redfit Fitness Consultants, Inc. 3905 Vincennes Rd, Indianapolis, IN 46268, ☎ 317-471-8090. Aerobics classes Mon-Wed, 6:30 pm-7:30 pm; Sat, 11 am-noon. Personal training sessions by appointment.

Praisercise, Inc., 7399 North Shadeland Ave, #141, Indianapolis, IN 46250, ☎ 317-465-8979.

Restaurants

African

Queen of Sheba, 936 Indiana Ave, ☎ 317-638-8426. Ethiopian cuisine. Call for restaurant hours.

Barbeque

Bar-B-Que Heaven, 2515 Dr. Martin Luther King, Jr. Street, ☎ 317-926-1667. Mon-Wed, 11 am-2 am. Thurs-Sat, 11 am-3 am.

King Ribs, 4130 North Keystone, ☎ 317-543-0841; also five other locations. Popular barbeque rib restaurant featuring pork rib dinners and sandwiches with all the trimmings. Mon-Thurs, 11 am-midnight; Fri-Sat, 11 am-2 am; Sun, noon-midnight.

Purnell's Barbecue and Fish, 2535 North Lafayette Rd, ☎ 317-923-6191. Pork rib dinners, beef barbeque sandwiches, perch, catfish and other fish dinners and sandwiches. Mon-Thurs, 10 am-11:30 pm; Fri-Sat, 10 am-1:30 am; Sun, 10 am-10 pm.

International

Daddy-O's Express Grill, 3744 North Keystone Ave, ☎ 317-921-1922. International cuisine and Chicago-style sausage, stromboli, blackened chicken salad, turkey and chicken sandwiches, hot wings and much more. Mon-Thurs, 10:30 am-11 pm; Fri-Sat, 10:30 am-1 am.

Seafood

Shrimp Hut Seafood, 5401 East 38th Street, ☎ 317-545-3989. Popular neighborhood restaurant that features a variety of seafood dinners and sandwiches. Mon-Thurs, 11 am-midnight; Fri-Sat, 11 am-4 am.

Soul Food

Big Mama's Soul Food, 1002 East 38th Street, ☎ 317-931-9680. Traditional soul food cuisine. Tues-Sun, noon-7 pm.

Marble's Southern Cookery, 2310 Lafayette Rd, ☎ 317-687-0631. Traditional soul food cuisine. Open daily, 11 am-7 pm.

Entertainment

Jazz

Jazz Kitchen, 5377 North College Ave, ☎ 317-253-4900. Premiere jazz club. Call for club hours and events. Cover charge.

Chatterbox Tavern, 435 Massachusetts Ave, Downtown, ☎ 317-636-0584. Live jazz six nights a week. Call for club hours and events.

Jazz Cooker, 925 Westfield Boulevard, ☎ 317-253-2883. Southern-style cuisine. Open daily 5 pm-10 pm; Sun, until 9 pm. Jazz during dinner hours and on weekends from 7pm-10 pm.

Keystone Grill, 8650 Keystone at the Crossing, ☎ 317-848-5202. Call for club hours and events.

Melody Inn, 3826 North Illinois Street, ☎ 317-923-4707. Call for club hours and events.

Rick's Café Americain, Union Station, ☎ 317-634-6666. Call for club hours and events.

Dance

Barritz Nite Club, 71st Michigan Rd, New Augusta Shopping Centre, ☎ 317-329-4083. Popular dance night club.

Cosmo Knights Club, 3338 North Illinois Street, ☎ 317-923-0230. Call for club hours and events.

Culture Club, 235 South Meridian, ☎ 317-756-9606. Call for club hours and events.

Faces Midtown Club, 2145 North Talbott, ☎ 317-923-9886. Premiere dance night club. Call for club hours and events.

The Crib, 4458 North Allisonville, ☎ 317-253-4500. Call for club hours and events.

The Sunset Pub, 719 Indiana Ave, ☎ 317-636-0603. Call for club hours and events.

Comedy

Act IV, 5299 East 38th Street, ☎ 317-541-9343. Call for upcoming schedule of events and hours.

Indianapolis

Lodging

Bed & Breakfasts

Le Chateau Delaware Bed & Breakfast Inn, 1456 North Delaware Street, Indianapolis, IN 46202, ☎ 317-636-9156. Guests enter the doors of the beautiful Le Chateau Delaware and feel as if they are in a French castle. Le Chateau Delaware was built in 1906, and is adorned with antique furnishings, hardwood floors, brass and poster beds, and has four beautiful bedrooms with private or shared baths. In the mornings, guests are greeted with the aroma of freshly brewed coffee or tea, homemade rolls, muffins, fruits of the season and juices. Close to area attractions. Call for current rates and reservations. ☆ *Specially recommended.*

Travel Agents

Advance Travel & Cruise Planner, Inc., ☎ 800-492-3033 or 317-568-1304.

International Travel Service, 2920 North Keystone Ave, #2, PO Box 18649, Indianapolis, IN 46218, ☎ 317-924-3877, fax 317-924-5285.

Just Friends Travel Agency, 2021 East 52nd Street, #210, Indianapolis, IN 46205, ☎ 317-255-8520.

Rainbow Travel International, 1508 East 86th Street, Indianapolis, IN 46240, ☎ 800-797-6915 or 317-283-6388, fax 317-283-7622.

Heritage Tours

Historic Ransom Place, 830 Dr. Martin Luther King, Jr. Street, Indianapolis, IN 46202, is the starting point for a 31-stop walking tour offered by the Heritage Learning Center, ☎ 317-632-2340, fax 317-685-2760. The tour covers the "Heritage Tourism Corridor." Some of its highlights include the Madame C.J. Walker Building and Urban Life Center, Walker's home, Historic Ransom Place (Indianapolis' African-American historic district), the Crispus Attucks Museum and the Heritage Learning Center Museum. Contact the Heritage Learning Center for further information.

Media

Radio

◆ Jazz

WVPE 88.1 FM, 2424 California Rd, ☎ 219-262-5660. Jazz, National Public Radio.

◆ Urban Contemporary

WGGR 106.7 FM, 6264 La Pas Trail, ☎ 317-293-9600. Urban hits and oldies format.

WTLC 105.7 FM, 2126 North Meridian Street, ☎ 317-923-1456.

◆ Gospel

WPZZ 95.9 FM, 2021 East 52nd Street, ☎ 317-255-4569.

◆ Newspapers

Indiana Herald, 2170 North Illinois Street, ☎ 317-923-8291. Indiana's largest minority-owned newspaper. Distributed weekly on Thursdays.

Indianapolis Recorder, 2901 North Tacoma Ave, ☎ 317-924-5143. African-American community newspaper. Distributed weekly on Thursdays.

◆ Magazines

African-American Network, PO Box 681556, Indianapolis, IN 46218, ☎ 317-466-0440.

Black Focus, PO Box 53-1151, Indianapolis, IN 46218, ☎ 317-293-4708. African-American magazine.

EN Magazine, 2901 North Tacoma Ave, Indianapolis, IN 46218, ☎ 317-924-5143. Bi-annual African-American entertainment news magazine.

◆ Publications

Griot; A Traveler's Guide to Indiana's African-American Heritage, African-American Tourism Council of Indiana, ☎ 317-876-0853.

Indianapolis Cultural Guide, Entertainment News Magazine, 2901 North Tacoma Ave, Indianapolis, IN 46218, ☎ 317-924-5143.

This is Indianapolis, Indianapolis Convention & Visitors Association, One RCA Dome, #100, Indianapolis, IN 46225-1060, ☎ 317-639-4282, fax 317-639-5273.

Indianapolis

African-American Churches

AME

Allen Chapel AME, 637 East 11th Street, ☎ 317-638-9963.

Bethel AME, 414 West Vermont Street, ☎ 317-634-7002.

Jones Tabernacle AME Zion, 2510 East 34th, ☎ 317-547-7828.

Liberation AME, 4906 Crittenden Ave, ☎ 317-259-9250.

Providence AME, 980 Burdsal Parkway, ☎ 317-925-0053.

Robinson Community AME, 4602 North College Ave, ☎ 317-924-4044.

St. John AME, 1669 Columbia Ave, ☎ 317-924-7780.

Apostolic

Apostolic House of Prayer, 3201 Dr. Andrew J. Brown Ave, ☎ 317-925-6424.

Christ Church Apostolic, 6601 Grandview Drive, ☎ 317-255-8761.

Christ Temple, 430 West Fall Creek Boulevard N, ☎ 317-923-7278.

Emmanuel Temple, 6138 Michigan Rd, ☎ 317-257-2895.

Grace Apostolic, 649 East 22nd Street, ☎ 317-925-8103.

Baptist

Christ Missionary Baptist, 1202 Eugene Street, ☎ 317-925-4132.

Eastern Star Missionary Baptist, 5730 East 30th Street, ☎ 317-591-5050.

Eastside Baptist, 2845 Baltimore, ☎ 317-926-5436.

Messiah Missionary Baptist, 2701 North California, ☎ 317-925-7435.

Mount Olive Baptist, 1003 West 16th Street, ☎ 317-634-9178.

Mount Vernon Baptist, 709 North Belmont, ☎ 317-636-4964.

New Bethel Baptist, 1519 Dr. Andrew J. Brown, ☎ 317-636-6622.

St. John's Missionary Baptist, 1701 Andrew J. Brown, ☎ 317-636-5775.

Catholic

St. Rita's Catholic, 1733 Dr. Andrew J. Brown, ☎ 317-635-9349.

Christian

Light of the World Christian, 5640 East 38th Street, ☎ 317-547-2273.

CME

Phillip's Temple CME, 101 East 34th Street, ☎ 317-925-2000.

Trinity CME, 2273 Dr. A.J. Brown Ave, ☎ 317-925-8275.

Pentecostal

Pentecostal Liberty Tabernacle, 4825 West Beecher, ☎ 317-241-2710.

Calendar of Annual Events

◆ January

Dr. Martin Luther King, Jr. Celebration, Indianapolis Convention & Visitors Bureau, ☎ 317-639-4282.

◆ February

Black History Month Celebration, Indianapolis Convention & Visitors Bureau, ☎ 317-639-4282.

◆ May

Yellow Brick Road Celebration, African-American Tourism Council, ☎ 317-876-0853.

◆ June

Indianapolis Black Expo Soulfest, ☎ 317-925-2702. Largest and longest-running African-American exposition in the US.

◆ August

Major Taylor Day and Antique Bicycle Festival, ☎ 317-327-8356.

Annual Indiana Ave Jazz Festival Indianapolis Convention & Visitors, ☎ 317-639-4282 or 317-236-2099.

◆ October

Indiana Black Expo Golf Tournament Classic Gala, Indiana Black Expo, Inc, ☎ 317-925-2702.

Indianapolis Black Alumni Council's Annual College Fair, Indiana Black Expo, Inc, ☎ 317-925-2702.

Indianapolis

Public Transportation

Indianapolis International Airport, ☎ 317-487-7243.

Indianapolis Metro Customer Service, ☎ 317-632-1900. Local bus transportation schedule and information.

Taxi Services

Yellow Cab Company, ☎ 317-487-7777.

Indianapolis Area Resources

African-American Tourism Council of Indiana, ☎ 317-876-0853.

Indianapolis Convention & Visitors Bureau, One Hoosier Dome, #100, Indianapolis, IN 46225, ☎ 317-639-4282. Web site: www.indy.org/. Mon-Thurs, 8:30 am-5 pm.

Indiana Black Expo, Inc., 3145 North Meridian Street, Indianapolis, IN 46208, ☎ 317-925-2702, fax 317-925-6624.

Indianapolis Chamber of Commerce, 320 North Meridian Street, Indianapolis, IN 46204-1719, ☎ 317-464-2200, fax 317-464-2217. E-mail: chamber@indylink.com. Web site: www.indychamber.com.

Indiana Department of Tourism, One North Capitol, #700, Indianapolis, IN 46204-2288, ☎ 317-232-8860; hotline, ☎ 800-289-6646. Web site: www.state.in.us/tourism.

Indianapolis Black Chamber of Commerce, 3145 North Meridian Street, #240, Indianapolis, IN 46208, ☎ 317-925-0533, fax 317-925-0568. Web site: www.blackchamber.org.

Madame Walker Theatre and Urban Life Center, 617 Indiana Ave, Indianapolis, IN 46202.

Los Angeles

Historic Sites & Landmarks

Clark Hotel, 1917 Central Ave. This historic hotel was built to accommodate Black train porters. Not open to the public.

Golden State Mutual Insurance Company, 4261-4263 South Central Ave, ☎ 213-296-6565. Founded in 1925, this was the original site of the first African-American-owned insurance company. Golden State also has a collection of African-American art depicting the African-American pioneers of California and the West. Call for more information. Open by appointment only, Mon-Thurs, 9 am-4 pm; Fri, 9 am-1 pm.

Nat "King" Cole burial site, Forest Lawn Memorial Park, 1712 South Glendale Ave, Glendale, ☎ 818-241-4151. Cole's burial site is located in the Freedom Hall Mausoleum at the Sanctuary of Heritage. Cole died of lung cancer in 1965 at the age of 45.

Sammy Davis, Jr. burial site, Forest Lawn Memorial Park, 1712 South Glendale Ave, ☎ 818-241-4151. The talented singer and performer died in 1990.

Hollywood Walk of Fame, Hollywood Blvd. Numerous prominent African-American radio, film, music and television personalities are among those names engraved on the more than 2,000 terrazzo and brass stars here.

Watts Walk of Fame, 1333 East 103rd Street, southeast border of Will Rogers Memorial Park, Watts, ☎ 213-974-2222. This ceramic artwork is a historic tribute to active African-American community leaders.

Museums/Exhibits

California Afro-American Museum, 600 State Drive, Exposition Park, ☎ 213-744-7432. This museum has a number of hanging exhibits that focus on the achievements of Africans and African-Americans in history and art. Opened during the 1984 Olympic Arts Festival. Free admission. Tues-Sat, 10 am-5 pm.

Dunbar Hotel Black Historical Cultural Museum, 4225 Central Ave, ☎ 213-234-7882. The Dunbar was the first US hotel built for African-Americans. The hotel operated from the 1930s to the 1950s. Photos and other memorabilia are featured. Mon-Fri, 9 am-6 pm. Call for tours.

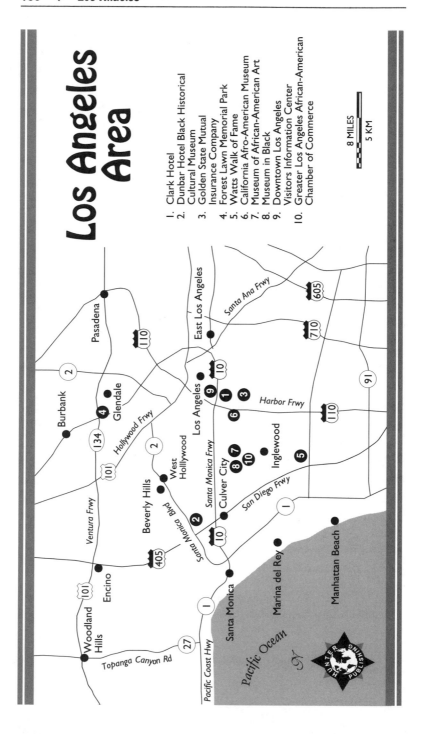

Los Angeles Area

1. Clark Hotel
2. Dunbar Hotel Black Historical Cultural Museum
3. Golden State Mutual Insurance Company
4. Forest Lawn Memorial Park
5. Watts Walk of Fame
6. California Afro-American Museum
7. Museum of African-American Art
8. Museum in Black
9. Downtown Los Angeles Visitors Information Center
10. Greater Los Angeles African-American Chamber of Commerce

8 MILES
5 KM

El Pueblo De Los Angeles Historic Park, 622 North Main Street. This historical 44-acre park was originally the Spanish section of Los Angeles when it was founded in 1781 by 44 people, many of whom were of African-American descent. The self-guided walking tour will show visitors several restored historic buildings, including the home of Pio Pico, a mulatto who served as Governor of California when it was controlled by Mexico. The popular Pico Blvd in Los Angeles is named after Pio Pico. The Founders Plaque sets on the south side of the plaza and lists the names of the first settlers from 1781. The Sepulveda House Visitor Center at 622 North Main Street is open Tues-Sat, 10 am-4 pm, and will provide additional information about the site. Free admission.

Fowler Museum of Cultural History, UCLA, 405 Hilgard Ave, ☎ 310-825-9672. Collections of African, Oceanic and Native American art. Wed-Sun, noon-5 pm; Thurs, noon-8 pm. Free admission.

Los Angeles County Museum of Art, 5905 Wilshire Blvd, ☎ 213-857-6000. Extensive collection of Egyptian and sub-Saharan art dating from pre-Dynastic to some of the Roman eras. Tues-Thurs, 10 am-5 pm; Fri, 10 am-9 pm; Sat, 11 am-6 pm. Admission charge.

Museum of African-American Art, 4005 South Crenshaw Blvd. May Company Store, Third Floor, ☎ 213-294-7071. The works of African-American Harlem Renaissance artist Palmer Hayden are the highlight of this museum. Much of Hayden's works portray life in Harlem during the early 1900s. The museum also houses paintings, masks, carvings, sculptures and ceremonial pieces of the African diaspora throughout the Americas and the Caribbean. Wed-Sat, 11 am-6 pm; Sun, noon-5 pm. Free admission.

Museum in Black, 4331 Degnan Blvd, ☎ 213-292-9528. This museum exhibits both African and African-American art, including masks, dolls, beads and statues of African culture and numerous pieces of African-American materials. Tues-Sat, noon-6 pm; Sun-Mon, by appointment only. Free admission.

Historic Colleges & Universities

Charles R. Drew University of Medicine and Science, 1621 East 120th Street, ☎ 213-563-4960. Federally-funded private university. Founded in 1978.

Shopping

Galleries & Specialty Shops

The Abyssinia, 6727 Hollywood Blvd, ☎ 213-467-5453. Imported African arts from 20 different African countries. Features African masks, sculptures, clothing, jewelry and much more. Mon-Thurs, 10:30 am-7:30 pm; Fri-Sat, 10:30-8 pm.

African Princess, 6666 Hollywood Blvd, ☎ 213-463-1713. African and Jamaican jewelry and masks. Daily, 11 am-6 pm.

Aswad International Gallery, 1539 Centinela Ave, Inglewood, ☎ 310-677-8283. African-American fine art, prints and posters. Wed-Fri, noon-7 pm; Sat, 10 am-7 pm; Sun, Mon and Tues, by appointment only.

Bak-tu-Jua, 4330 Degnan Blvd, ☎ 213-295-8406. African imports, arts, jewelry and leather goods. By appointment only.

Black Gallery & Black Photographers of California, 107 Santa Barbara Plaza, ☎ 213-294-9024. Photos by African-American photographers. Wed, Fri and Sat, 1 pm-6 pm.

Boston Hallmark, 5317 West Centinela Ave, Ladera Shopping Center, ☎ 310-216-9688. African-American gifts, cards, jazz pieces, statues, collectibles and much more. Mon-Fri, 10 am-7:50 pm; Sat, 10 am-7 pm; Sun, 11 am-4 pm.

The Collectors Safari, 1401 North La Brea, Inglewood, ☎ 213-969-1740. African-American books, cards, art, music and collectibles.

Designs by Denise, 4444 West Slauson Ave, ☎ 213-291-4456. African-American prints, furnishings and collectibles, lamps, crystals, metal, pewter and much more. Thomas Blackshear, Duncan Royale collections. Open daily, 11 am-6 pm.

Galerie Lakaye, 1550 North Curson Ave, ☎ 213-850-6188, fax 213-850-1259. Exclusively Caribbean art featuring mostly Haitian works. Mediums include watercolors, oils, acrylics and much more. Galerie LaKaye produces the Caribbean Art Series. Intimate setting located in a craftsman-style house built in the late 1920s. Mon-Fri, noon-5 pm; Sat-Sun, by appointment only.

Gallery Tanner, 5271 West Pico Blvd, ☎ 213-933-0202. African-American artworks. Themes and variations in drawings, paintings and sculpture. Thurs-Sun, 2 pm-6 pm; Mon-Wed, by appointment only.

Kongo Square, 4334 Degnan Blvd, ☎ 213-291-6878. African-American collectibles, posters, ethnic jewelry and Afrocentric greeting cards. Mon, Tues and Thurs, 11 am-6 pm; closed Wed. Open some Sundays.

M. Hanks Gallery, 3008 Main Street, Santa Monica, ☎ 310-392-8820. Original African-American paintings, drawings, prints, sculpture, and posters by such artists as Palmer Hayen, Elizabeth Catlett, William Pajaud and Phoebe Beasely. Art appreciation classes are also offered. Hours by appointment.

Vibrant Fine Art, 3444 Hillcrest Drive, ☎ 213-766-0818. African-American imagery. Hours by appointment.

Bookstores

Dawah Bookshop, 4801 Crenshaw, ☎ 213-299-0335. Books on African heritage and African-American experiences. Open daily, 10 am-7 pm.

Eso Won Books, 3655 South La Brea Blvd, ☎ 213 -294-0324. African-American books. Mon-Fri, 10 am-7 pm; noon-5 pm.

Malik's Book Palace, 4058 Crenshaw Blvd, ☎ 213-294-1311. African-American books. Mon-Sat, 11 am-7 pm.

Moondance Bookshop, 11633 Santa Monica Blvd, ☎ 310-996-2665. African-American books. Mon-Sat, noon-7 pm.

Windsor Hills Christian Book Center, 4438 West Slauson Ave, ☎ 213-290-3079. African-American and religious books, gift items and fine collectibles. Mon-Sat, 10 am-6 pm.

Word of Life Christian Bookstore, 7223 South Main Street, ☎ 213-758-2733. African-American and religious books. Mon-Sat, 9:30 am-5:30 pm.

Fashions

Africa 2 U, 673 East University, Carson City, ☎ 310-217-1449. Imported West African clothing for men, women and children. Africa 2 U also manufactures clothing with fabrics from Nigeria, Niger, Benin and other African countries. Mon-Sat, 11 am-7 pm; Sun, noon-6 pm.

African Color Scheme, 3971 South Western Ave, ☎ 213-298-9837. Custom-made and ready-made African clothing for men, women and children. African fabrics and art works. Mon-Sat, 9:30 am-7 pm; Sun, 1 pm-6 pm.

Africana Imports, 3430 West Slauson Ave, ☎ 213-294-8151. African fashions for men, women and children. Some African art works. Mon-Sat, 10 am-7 pm.

African Princess International, 6666 Hollywood Blvd, ☎ 213-463-1713. Imported African fashions for men, women and children; hats and jewelry. Mon-Sat, 10 am-6:30 pm; Sun, noon-6 pm.

Designers Network International, 3419B West 43rd Pl, Fashion Heritage Showroom, ☎ 213-291-2535. Fashionable African clothing and accessories. 11 am-7 pm. By appointment only.

Kilimanjaro International Boutique, 2601 Martin Luther King, Jr. Blvd, ☎ 213-290-0685. Imported African garments by Aisha Majid, custom designs, ready-to-wear, wedding gowns and formal wear. African carvings and statues. Mon-Sat, 10:30 am-7 pm.

West Love Cultural Crafts, 6050 South Sepulveda Blvd, Fox Hills Mall, second level, Culver City, ☎ 310-313-6736. Afrocentric clothing, books and African artifacts.

Health Clubs

Jack's Health & Fitness, 1069 S La Brea, ☎ 213-938-3851. Free weights, Lifecycles. Clientele is primarily African-American. Non-membership fees available on a daily basis for a nominal fee. Mon-Fri, 6 am-10 pm; Sat, 8 am-7 pm; Sun, 10 am-7 pm.

Restaurants

◆ African

Nyala's, 1076 South Fairfax Blvd, ☎ 213-936-5918. Ethiopian and Italian cuisine. Mon-Fri, 11 am-11 pm; Sat-Sun, noon-midnight.

Rosalind's West African Cuisine, 1044 South Fairfax Ave, ☎ 213-936-2486. West African and Ethiopian cuisine. Open daily, 11 am-midnight.

◆ Barbecue

Bar-B-Q Unlimited, 3101 West Rosecrans Blvd, Hawthorne, ☎ 310-644-3415. Variety of barbeque dinners choices, such as pork, beef, and chicken with all the trimmings. Mon-Thurs; 10 am-9 pm; Fri-Sat, 10 am-10 pm; Sun, 11 am-7 pm.

Leo's Barbeque, 2619 Crenshaw Blvd, ☎ 213-733-1189. Carry-out barbeque; beef, chicken, pork and sausage dinners and sandwiches. Tues-Thurs, 11:30 am-10:30 pm; Fri-Sat, 11:30 am-midnight.

◆ Caribbean

Babalu, 1002 Montana Street, Santa Monica, ☎ 310-395-2500. Caribbean, Cuban, Mexican, Italian and Thai cuisine. Serves breakfast, lunch and dinner. Tues-Sun, 8 am-10 pm; Sunday brunch 11:30 am-3 pm.

Coley's Place, 5035 West Slauson Ave, Los Angeles, ☎ 213-291-7474. Traditional Jamaican cuisine. Jerk chicken, roti, meat patties, etc. Mon-Sat, 11 am-10 pm; Sun, 11 am-8 pm.

Jamaican Café, 424 Wilshire Blvd, Santa Monica, ☎ 310-587-2626. Traditional Jamaican cuisine. Open daily, 11:30 am-11 pm.

◆ Creole / Cajun

Aunt Gussye's Place, 2057 North Los Robles Ave, Pasadena, ☎ 818-794-6024. Mon-Sat, 7 am-9 pm. Creole.

B.B. King's Blues Club and Restaurant, Universal City Walk, 1000 Universal Center Drive, Universal City, ☎ 818-622-5480. Southern and Cajun cuisine; barbeque. Live blues entertainment nightly. Mon-Thurs, 7 pm until last band set; Fri-Sat, 5 pm until last band set. Sunday Gospel Brunch, call for hours.

Edouard's, 3300 West Manchester Ave, Inglewood, ☎ 310-673-5031. Creole and Southern cuisine. Wings, catfish, other favorites. Tues-Thurs, 8 am-9 pm; Fri-Sat, 8 am-10 pm; Sun, 7 am-8 pm.

Gagnier's, 3650 Martin Luther King, Jr. Blvd, ☎ 213-292-8187. Mon-Wed, noon-9 pm; Thurs-Sat, noon-10:30 pm.

Harold & Belle's, 2920 W Jefferson Blvd, ☎ 213-735-9023. Louisiana-style cuisine, featuring a variety of seafood, ribs, gumbo, and much more. Mon-Thurs, 11:30 am-10 pm; Fri-Sat, 11:30 am-11 pm; Sun, 11:30 am-10 pm.

House of Blues Restaurant, 8439 West Sunset Blvd, second level, West Hollywood, ☎ 213-650-0247. Cajun-American cuisine. Live blues nightly. Open for lunch Mon-Fri, 11:30 am-4:30 pm; dinner Mon-Fri, 5:30 pm-11 pm. Sunday Gospel Brunch at noon and 2:30 pm.

La Louisanne Creole Cuisine, 5812 Overhill, Los Angeles, ☎ 213-293-5073.

The Townhouse, 6835 La Tijera Blvd, ☎ 310-649-0091. Dance nightclub featuring rhythm and blues. Live jazz and DJ. Serves Creole soul cuisine. Open daily, 3 pm-2 am.

◆ Soul Food

Aunt Kizzy's Back Porch, 4325 Glencoe Ave, Marina Del Rey, ☎ 310-578-1005. Mon-Sat, 11 am-11 pm; Sun, 11 am-10 pm. Gospel brunch, Sat and Sun, 11 am-3 pm.

Bertha's, 1714 West Century Blvd, ☎ 213-777-3373. Mon-Fri, 11 am-9 pm; Sat, noon-9 pm.

Dulan's, 4859 Crenshaw Blvd, ☎ 213-296-3034. Traditional Southern-style breakfast, lunch and dinner. Features fried and baked chicken, short ribs, oxtail, pork chops and much more. Open weekends only; Sat, 8 am-7 pm; Sun, 10 am-7 pm.

Georgia, 7250 Melrose Ave, ☎ 213-933-8420. Owned by Denzel Washington and Eddie Murphy, who occasionally drop by. Fried chicken and other Southern dishes. 6:30 pm-11 pm; Sun, 5:30 pm-11 pm. Reservations only.

Mamie's Southern-Style Kitchen, 11102 West Olympic Blvd, West Los Angeles, ☎ 310-478-8857.

Los Angeles

Maurice's Snack and Chat, 5549 West Pico Blvd, ☎ 213-931-3877. Popular soul food restaurant frequented by many of Hollywood's African-American performers.

Roscoe's House of Chick and Waffles, 1514 North Gower Street, Hollywood and several other Los Angeles area locations. Popular soul food restaurant frequented by many of Hollywood's African-American performers. ☎ 213-466-7453. Sun-Thurs, 9 am-midnight; Fri-Sat, 9 am-4 am.

Stevie's on the Strip, 3403 Crenshaw Blvd, ☎ 213-734-6975. Soul food and seafood. Chicken, catfish, red snapper, shrimp, oysters, short ribs and pork ribs. Sun-Thurs, 11 am-10 pm; Fri-Sat, 11 am-11 pm.

Serving Spoon, 1403 Centinela Ave, Inglewood, ☎ 310-412-3927. Mon-Fri, 7 am-3 pm; Sat-Sun, 7 am-5 pm.

Entertainment

Jazz/Blues Nightclubs/Lounges

B.B. King's Blues Club and Restaurant, Universal City Walk, 1000 Universal Center Drive, Universal City, ☎ 818-622-5471. Live blues entertainment nightly. Sunday Gospel Brunch. Call for schedule.

Jerry's Flying Fox Restaurant & Nightclub, 3724 Martin Luther King, Jr. Blvd, ☎ 213-293-5544. Serves a variety of soul food favorites. Features jazz, rhythm & blues. DJ. Open daily, 11 am-2 am.

Dance Nightclubs

Current Affair Night Club, 234 West Manchester Ave, Inglewood, ☎ 310-674-3764. Features live band and DJ nightly. Seafood dinners available.

Kingston 12, 814 Broadway, Santa Monica, ☎ 310-451-4423. LA's premier reggae dance club. Features local and international reggae artists. Open daily, 9 pm -2 am.

Savannah West, 12100 Wilshire Blvd, ☎ 310-207-3333.

The Townhouse, 6835 La Tijera Blvd, ☎ 310-649-0091. Dance nightclub featuring rhythm and blues, live jazz and DJ. Serves appetizers and bar menu items. Open daily, 3 pm-2 am; entertainment starts at 9 pm.

Comedy Clubs

Maverick Flat, 4225 Crenshaw Blvd, ☎ 213-295-4179. Features primarily African-American comedians. Made popular during the '60s by Richard Pryor, Earth, Wind & Fire, and other famous African-American artists. Comedy shows begin at 10 pm; cover charge.

Television Studios, Production Studios & Show Tapings

Call or write for ticket information as far in advance as possible for any of the following shows; some shows fill up very quickly. Minimum age restrictions for admission may apply, so ask when making reservations.

Black Entertainment Network (BET), 2801 West Olive Ave, Burbank, CA 91505, ☎ 213-849-2728.

Between Brothers, Audiences Unlimited, Inc., 100 Universal City Plaza, Building 153, Universal City, CA 91608, ☎ 818-753-3470, ext 212. New FOX comedy starring Kadeem Hardison, Dondre T. Whitfield, Kelly Perrine, Tommy Davidson and Rachel Crawford. Films Fridays at 7 pm at Sony Pictures Studios in Culver City.

Built to Last, Audiences Unlimited, Inc., 100 Universal City Plaza, Building 153, Universal City, CA 91608, ☎ 818-753-3470, ext 212. New NBC comedy starring Royale Watkins, Denise Dowse and Jeffrey Owens. Films Wednesdays at 6 pm at Warner Bros. Studios in Burbank.

Family Matters, Audiences Unlimited, Inc., 100 Universal City Plaza, Building 153, Universal City, CA 91608, ☎ 818-753-3470, ext 212. Hit CBS comedy starring Reginald VelJohnson, Jo Marie Payton Noble and Jaleel White. Films Fridays at 6 pm at Warners Bros. Studios in Burbank.

Good News, Audience Coordinator, ☎ 213-960-4752. Stars David Ramsey, Roz Ryan, Guy Torry, Alexia Robinson and Tracey Cherette Jones. Filmed in Hollywood. Call for tickets.

In The House, Paramount Audiences, ☎ 213-956-1777. Stars rapper LL Cool J, Alfonso Ribeiro, Kim Wayans and Maia Campbell. Filmed in Hollywood. Call for ticket information.

Living Single, Audiences Unlimited, Inc., 100 Universal City Plaza, Building 153, Universal City, CA 91608, ☎ 818-753-3470, ext 212. FOX hit starring Kim Coles, Queen Latifah and Kim Fields Freeman. Films Tuesdays at 3:30 pm and 7 pm at Warner Bros. Ranch in Burbank.

Malcolm and Eddie, Audiences Unlimited, Inc., 100 Universal City Plaza, Bldg 153, Universal City, CA 91608, ☎ 818-753-3470, ext 212. UPN comedy starring Malcolm-Jamal Warner and Eddie Griffin. Films Fridays at 7 pm, Sunset Gower Studios in Hollywood.

Moesha, Paramount Audiences, ☎ 213-956-1777. Stars pop sensation Brandy. Filmed in Hollywood. Call for tickets and information.

Smart Guy, Audiences Unlimited, Inc., 100 Universal City Plaza, Building 153, Universal City, CA 91608, ☎ 818-753-3470, ext 212. New WB comedy starring Tahj Mowry. Films Fridays at 6:30 pm, Walt Disney Studios in Burbank.

Los Angeles

Sparks, Audience Coordinator, ☎ 213-960-4752. Stars James Avery, Robin Givens, Miguel A. Nuñez, Jr., Terrence Howard, Kym Whitley and Arif S. Kinchen. Filmed in Hollywood. Call for ticket information.

The Gregory Hines Show, Audiences Unlimited, Inc., 100 Universal City Plaza, Building 153, Universal City, CA 91608, ☎ 818-753-3470, ext 212. New CBS showstarring Gregory Hines and Brandon Hammond. Films at the Culver Studios in Culver City on Fridays at 7 pm.

The Jamie Foxx Show, Audiences Unlimited, Inc., 100 Universal City Plaza, Building 153, Universal City, CA 91608, ☎ 818-753-3470, ext 212. Hit WB comedy starring Jamie Foxx, Garrett Morris and Ella English. Films on Tuesdays at 6:30 pm at Warner Bros. Studios in Burbank.

The Parent 'Hood, Audiences Unlimited, Inc., 100 Universal City Plaza, Building 153, Universal City, CA 91608, ☎ 818-753-3470, ext 212. UPN comedy starring Robert Townsend and Suzzane Douglas. Films Fridays at 6 pm at Warner Hollywood Studios in Hollywood.

Vibe, Audiences Unlimited, Inc., 100 Universal City Plaza, Building 153, Universal City, CA 91608, ☎ 818-753-3470, ext 212. New syndicated entertainment program. Taped at CBS Television City in Hollywood, Mon-Fri at 4:30 pm.

Travel Agents

BRM Travel, 317 East Hillcrest Blvd, Inglewood, CA 90301, ☎ 310-677-0707.

Compton Travel, 1804 West Rosecrans Ave, Compton, CA 90220, ☎ 213-774-8510.

Fox Hills Travel, 6050 South Sepulveda Blvd, Culver City, CA 90230, ☎ 310-398-6248.

Great Escapes Cruise & Travel, 8530 Wilshire Blvd, Los Angeles, CA 90211, ☎ 310-841-2580, fax 310-841-2542. E-Mail: greateskap@aol.com. Plans "Jamaica Jam," an annual African-American cruise package featuring African-American entertainment; travels to various Caribbean ports of call.

Kola Nut Travel and Tours, 500 East Manchester Blvd, Inglewood, CA 90301, ☎ 310-674-0291.

Land, Air, & Sea Travel, 5820 Rodeo Rd, Los Angeles, CA, ☎ 310-839-2475.

Orbit Travel and Tour Services, Inc., 971 North La Brea Ave, Inglewood, CA 90302, ☎ 310-677-9400.

Romantic Travel, 1518 Piru Street, Compton, CA 90222, ☎ 310-715-4698.

Travel Fever, 720 East Manchester Blvd, Inglewood, CA 90301, ☎ 310-673-9999.

Trio Travel, 3000 West Manchester Blvd, Inglewood, CA 90305, ☎ 213-778-4370.

Heritage Tours

Black L.A. Tours, 3450 West 43rd Street, #108, Los Angeles, CA 90008, ☎ 213-750-9267, fax 213-299-0117. This tour company features a variety of packages that include visits to tapings of popular African-American television shows, historical sites and landmarks, museums, art galleries and amusement parks.

Gloria Vinson Tours, 5286 Village-Green, ☎ 213-295-0888. Specializes in tours of Los Angeles area television studios. Tour groups participate in live tapings of African-American shows, such as *The Arsenio Hall Show, Jamie Foxx, In The House, Family Matters, Sister Sister,* and many more. Also features tours of some of LA's finest restaurants, shops and movie studios.

Homes & Former Homes of Famous Personalities

Diana Ross (Motown singer) former home, 701 North Maple Drive, Beverly Hills.

Ethel Waters (actress) former home, 1910 Harvard Street, Los Angeles.

Hattie McDaniel (actress in *Gone With the Wind*) former home, 1909 Harvard Street, Los Angeles.

Little Richard (singer) former home, 1710 Virginia Rd, Los Angeles.

Louise Beavers (actress) former home, 1919 Harvard Street, Los Angeles.

Michael Jackson (singer/record producer) former home, 4641 Hayvenhurst Ave, Encino.

Nat "King" Cole (singer) former home, 401 Muirfield Rd, Hancock Park.

Ralph J. Bunche (former US diplomat, first African-American to receive Nobel Peace Prize) former home, 1221-1223 40th Place, Los Angeles.

Richard Pryor (comedian, actor) former home, 17267 Parthenia Street, Northridge.

Sammy Davis, Jr. (singer, actor) former home, 1151 Summit Drive, Beverly Hills.

Sidney Poitier (actor) home, 1007 Cove Way, Beverly Hills.

Los Angeles

Media

Radio

◆ Jazz

KTWV 94.7 FM, 5746 West Sunset Blvd, ☎ 213-466-9283. 24 hours of smooth jazz.

◆ Urban Contemporary/R&B

KACE 103.9 FM, 161 North La Brea Ave, ☎ 310-330-3100.

KGFL 1230 AM, 1100 South La Brea Ave, ☎ 213-930-9090. R&B, oldies.

KJLH 102.3 FM, 3847 Crenshaw Blvd, ☎ 213-299-5960.

KKBT 92.3 FM, 6535 Yucca Street, ☎ 213-466-9566. 24 hours of soul and rap music.

KPWR 105.9 FM, 2600 West Olive Ave, ☎ 818-953-4200. 24 hours of rhythm & blues and hip-hop.

◆ Gospel

KACE 103.9 FM, 610 South Ardmore Ave, ☎ 213-427-1039.

KKBT 92.3 FM, 6535 Yucca Street, ☎ 213-466-9566.

KMAX 107.1 FM, 3350 Electronic Drive, Pasadena, ☎ 213-681-2486.

KPFK 90.7 FM, 3729 Cahuenga Blvd, ☎ 818-985-2711. The Gospel caravan.

Newspapers

Los Angeles Scoop Newspaper, 3742 South King Blvd, ☎ 213-291-9491. Available at local newsstands. Weekly.

Los Angeles Sentinel, 3800 Crenshaw Blvd, ☎ 213-299-3800. Los Angeles' largest African-American newspaper. Distributed on Thursdays to selected newsstands and retail stores.

The Pasadena/San Gabriel Valley Journal, 1541 North Lake Ave, ☎ 818-798-3972. African-American newspaper covering the San Gabriel Valley. Available at Pasadena City Hall and various Pasadena businesses. Free.

Watts Times, 3731 Stocker Street, ☎ 213-290-6000. Weekly on Thursdays. Available at selected newsstands. Free.

Wave Community Newspaper, 2621 West 54th Street, ☎ 213-290-3000. Weekly on Thursdays. Available at Wave Community Newspaper office. Free.

Magazines

Black Meetings & Tourism Magazine, Sun Glo Enterprises, 20840 Chase Street, Winnetka, CA 91306-1207, ☎ 818-709-0646. Monthly publication. Subscription only.

Greater Los Angeles Black Directory, 12333½ A Washington Blvd, Los Angeles, CA 90066, ☎ 718-638-9675. Directory of African-American-owned businesses in greater Los Angeles area.

◆ Publications

Destination Los Angeles; Festivals of Los Angeles; Los Angeles Cultural Kaleidoscope, African-American Edition. Los Angeles Convention & Visitors Bureau, 633 West Fifth Street, Los Angeles, CA 90071, ☎ 213-624-9746.

Greater Los Angeles Black Directory, 12333 ½ A Washington Blvd, Los Angeles, CA 90066, ☎ 718-638-9675. Directory of African-American-owned businesses in greater Los Angeles area.

African-American Churches

AME

Bethel AME, 7916 South Western, ☎ 213-750-3240.

Brookins AME, 4831 South Gramercy, ☎ 213-296-5610.

Bryant Temple AME, 2525 Vernon, ☎ 213-293-6201.

Emmanuel AME, 5200 South Compton, ☎ 213-232-6300.

First AME, 2270 South Harvard, ☎ 213-730-.9180.

St. James AME, 655 West 70th Street, ☎ 213-758-6786.

St. Stephen AME, 1265 East 64th Street, ☎ 213-583-8268.

Walker Temple AME, 2525 Trinity, ☎ 213-747-7454.

Price AME, 4000 West Slauson, ☎ 213-296-2406.

Baptist

Antioch Baptist, 8725 South Central, ☎ 213-589-2551.

Baldwin Hills Baptist, 4700 West Martin Luther King, Jr. Blvd, ☎ 213-294-3200.

Bright Throne Baptist, 9801 South Figueroa, ☎ 213-757-3994.

Calvary Baptist, 6000 South Compton, ☎ 213-583-2013.

Los Angeles

Faithful Central Missionary Baptist Church, 333 West Florence Ave, Inglewood, ☎ 313-330-8000.

Greater Cornerstone Baptist, 5946 South Figueroa, ☎ 213-971-8893.

Mount Gilead, 9201 South Normandie, ☎ 213-755-4319.

New Temple Baptist, 8734 South Broadway, ☎ 213-758-3137.

COGIC

Assembly Church of God in Christ, 2156 West Slauson, ☎ 213-295-4095.

Faith COGIC, 7320 South Hoover Street, ☎ 213-759-8208.

Faith Prayer Assembly COGIC, 2825 West Jefferson Blvd, ☎ 213-732-1502.

Holy Way COGIC, 1722 Firestone Blvd, ☎ 213-589-5531.

Greater Good News Church of God in Christ, 5840 South Broadway, ☎ 213-234-6733.

Vision of God COGIC, 4321 Long Beach Ave, ☎ 213-235-5059.

West Angeles Church of God in Christ, 3045 Crenshaw, ☎ 213-733-8300.

Calendar of Annual Events

◆ January

Image Awards, NAACP, ☎ 213-931-6331. Awards to recognized African-American entertainers.

◆ February

Annual Artists Salute to Black History Month, ☎ 310-559-8868 or 213-933-2614. Festival of works by West Coast artists. Admission charge.

Afrikans are Coming Extravaganza, Veterans Memorial Auditorium, ☎ 310-412-1136. African drums and dancing.

Black History Month Tour, Our Authors Study Club, ☎ 213-482-8671. Los Angeles history tour and featuring tours of celebrity homes.

Pan-African Film Festival, ☎ 213-896-8221. Motion pictures, shorts and documentaries portraying people of African descent. Admission charge.

Reggae Muffin Festival, Long Beach Convention Center, ☎ 310-515-5355. Celebration of life and music of the late reggae king, Bob Marley.

◆ April

Los Angeles Black Business Expo, Los Angeles Convention Center, ☎ 310-572-7555. Features African-American business owners.

◆ May

African International Village Festival, ☎ 213-427-3713. African, Korean and Chinese-American food and art.

Annual Black Talkies on Parade Film Festival, Black American Film Society, ☎ 213-737-3292. Features works by top African-American filmmakers.

UCLA Jazz & Reggae Festival, ☎ 310-825-9912. Memorial weekend festival on the UCLA Campus. Free.

Belize Caye Festival, Cultural Belize Association, ☎ 213-731-2927. Music festival celebrating culture and customs of Belizean people. Admission charge.

◆ June

Africa Fete, ☎ 213-687-2159. Festival celebrating African music. International acts. Free.

Playboy Jazz Festival, ☎ 310-449-4070 or 310-450-9040. Two-day jazz celebration. Big band, fusion, Latin and more. Admission charge.

Cajun & Zydeco Festival, ☎ 310-427-3713. Two days of Cajun and Zydeco music, cuisine, dance and more.

Juneteenth Festival, William Grant Still Arts Center, ☎ 213-734-1164.

◆ July

Central Ave Jazz Festival, Jazz Mentorship Program, ☎ 213-485-0709. Festival of aspiring young jazz musicians. Free.

Inner City Cultural Center's Talent Fest, ☎ 213-962-2102. Competition for youth in the fields of drama, music and songwriting, film and videomaking, poetry and screenwriting.

Whittier Uptown Street Festival, ☎ 310-696-2662. Two days of continuous jazz on three stages. Crafts, foods. Free.

◆ August

Black Family Reunion, National Council of Negro Women, ☎ 213-292-6269.

Long Beach Jazz Festival, ☎ 310-436-7794. Jazz festival with food and variety of vendors. Admission charge.

Los Angeles African Marketplace & Cultural Faire, ☎ 213-734-1164 or ☎ 213-237-1540. Celebration of African Diaspora. Includes food, entertainment, art, business expo and more. Admission charge.

Marcus Garvey Day Parade and Festival, ☎ 213-735-9642. Celebration of birth, life and philosophies of Marcus Garvey. Food, entertainment, dance and more. Free admission.

Los Angeles

◆ **September**

Day in the Park, Concerned Belizean Association, ☎ 213-732-9742. Celebration featuring Afro-Caribbean culture, music and arts.

Leimart Park Jazz Festival, ☎ 213-960-1625. Local jazz artists. Arts and crafts, foods, ethnic wear and more. Free.

Simon Radio Watts Towers Jazz Festival, ☎ 213-847-4646. Gospel, rhythm and blues and jazz.

Watts Towers Day of the Drum, Watts Towers Art Center, ☎ 213-485-1795 or 213-847-4646. Features drummers and percussionists from Afro-Cuban, folkloricos, Afro-Brazilian, Jamaican, American and other international drummers. Free.

◆ **October**

Catalina Island Jazz Trax Festival, Casino Ballroom, ☎ 619-458-9586. Three-day jazz festival on beautiful Catalina Island. Admission charge.

International Festival of Masks, ☎ 213-937-5544. Two-day celebration of masks, culture and arts from around the world, including Africa.

Jazz at Drew, Charles R. Drew University of Science and Medicine, ☎ 213-563-5850. Celebration of jazz in music, foods and arts.

Taste of Africa, ☎ 310-915-5200. Smorgasbord of African cuisine.

Watts Third World Arts Festival, Watts Health Center, ☎ 310-412-3572. Multicultural festival of artists; theater, dance, music, storytelling, international foods. Free.

◆ **December**

Kwanzaa Candlelighting Ceremony Festival, ☎ 213-299-0964. Seven-day Kwanzaa festival.

Kwanzaa Gwaride Festival, ☎ 213-789-5654. Celebration of Kwanzaa in music, customs, rituals and ethnic marketplace. Free.

Public Transportation

LAX Airport, ☎ 310-646-5252.

Los Angeles County Metropolitan Transit Authority (MTA), local Los Angeles area bus service, ☎ 800-COMMUTE or 213-922-6235.

Taxi Services

City Cab/Yellow Cab, ☎ 818-848-1000.

L.A. Checker Cab Company, ☎ 310-330-3720.

Yellow Cab Company, ☎ 213-808-1000.

Los Angeles Area Resources

African-American Business Association, 8721 South Broadway, Los Angeles, CA 90003, ☎ 213-752-4300.

African-American Cultural Center, 2560 West 54th Street, Los Angeles, CA 90043, ☎ 213-299-6124.

Black Resource Center, A.C. Bilbrew Library, 150 East El Segundo Blvd, Los Angeles, CA 90061, ☎ 310-538-3350.

California African-American Genealogical Society, 5130 Village Green, Los Angeles, CA 90016, ☎ 213-296-6792.

Center for African-American Studies at UCLA, UCLA, 160 Hainse Hall, Los Angeles, CA 90095, ☎ 310-825-7403.

Downtown Los Angeles Visitor Information Center, 685 Figueroa Street, Los Angeles. Hours Mon-Fri, 8 am-5 pm; Sat, 8:30 am-5 pm.

Inner City Cultural Center's New Ivar Theater, 1605 North Ivar Ave, Los Angeles, CA 90028, ☎ 213-962-2102, fax 213-386-9017.

Greater Los Angeles African-American Chamber of Commerce, 3910 West Martin Luther King, Jr. Blvd, ☎ 213-292-1297, fax 213-292-1451.

Los Angeles Convention & Visitors Bureau, 633 West Fifth Street, Los Angeles, CA 90071, ☎ 213-624-9746, fax 213-624-9746.

Tourism Industry Development Council, 634 South Spring Street, #1016, Los Angeles, CA 90014, ☎ 213-486-9880, fax 213-486-9886.

Our Author's Study Club, Study of Negro Life & History, 4806 Third Ave, Los Angeles, CA 90043, ☎ 213-295-0521.

Watts Tower Arts Center, 1727 East 107th Street, Los Angeles, CA 90002, ☎ 213-847-4646.

William Grant Still Arts Center, 2520 West View Street, Los Angeles, CA 90016, ☎ 213-734-1164.

On the Internet: www.city.net/countries/united_states/california/los_angeles.

Los Angeles

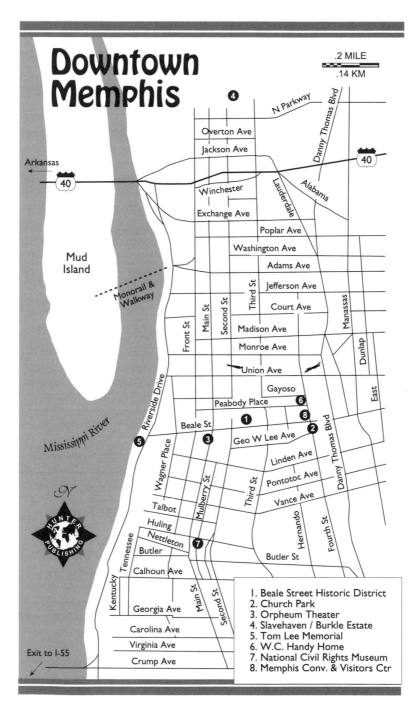

Downtown Memphis

.2 MILE
.14 KM

N Parkway

Danny Thomas Blvd

40

Overton Ave

Jackson Ave

Arkansas

40

Winchester

Alabama

Lauderdale

Exchange Ave

Poplar Ave

Washington Ave

Mud Island

Adams Ave

Monorail & Walkway

Third St

Jefferson Ave

Court Ave

Manassas

Main St

Second St

Madison Ave

Front St

Monroe Ave

Dunlap

Union Ave

Riverside Drive

Gayoso

East

Peabody Place

6

Beale St

1

8

Mississippi River

5

Wagner Place

3

Geo W Lee Ave

2

Danny Thomas Blvd

Linden Ave

Mulberry St

Third St

Pontotoc Ave

Vance Ave

Talbot

Hernando

Huling

Fourth St

Nettleton

7

Tennessee

Butler

Butler St

Calhoun Ave

Kentucky

Main St

Second St

Georgia Ave

1. Beale Street Historic District
2. Church Park
3. Orpheum Theater
4. Slavehaven / Burkle Estate
5. Tom Lee Memorial
6. W.C. Handy Home
7. National Civil Rights Museum
8. Memphis Conv. & Visitors Ctr

Carolina Ave

Virginia Ave

Exit to I-55

Crump Ave

HUNTER PUBLISHING

Memphis

Historic Sites & Landmarks

Beale Street Historic District. Beale Street was a thriving and bustling neighborhood for African-Americans at the turn of the century. "The home of the blues" and "the Memphis sound" are just a few of the phrases used to describe this historic strip of blues clubs, shops and restaurants. Music legends W.C. Handy and Rufus Thomas were among many African-American musicians whose careers started on Beale Street. Along this historic one-mile street is the Beale Street Baptist Church, built shortly after the Civil War, and a statue of W.C. Handy. A plaque for Ida B. Wells was placed on Beale Street at the site where she published her newspaper, *Free Speech*. Wells was one of the first female African-American publishers in the country, and she used her newspaper to publicize the injustices done to African-Americans during the early 1900s. African-American-owned vendors along Beale Street include Gestine's Gallery and the Old Negro League Sport Shops. Just off Beale Street is the headquarters for the Church of God in Christ.

Church Park, Beale Street. Built by Memphis' first African-American millionaire, Robert Church, this six-acre park was once the site of an amusement center that included a 2,000-seat auditorium. Church Park was the only public building that could be used by African-Americans during the early 1900s.

Nashoba Plantation, Germantown, in East Memphis. From Interstate 240, take the Poplar Street exit and head east to Riverdale. Nashoba Plantation, now a residential development, is on the right. It was originally purchased in 1826 by Frances Wright, a wealthy young Scot, for the purpose of educating and "upr aising" African-American slaves in preparation for a life of freedom. The plan never materialized and the slaves were sent to the West Indies.

Orpheum Theater, 192 South Main Street (at the intersection of Beale Street), ☎ 901-523-6049. Originally built in 1889 as Hopkin's Opera House, the Orpheum Theater later became part of a chain of vaudeville theaters. After fire destroyed the original building in 1923, the present Orpheum Theater was built in 1928. In the late 1930s such greats as Louis Armstrong, Duke Ellington, the Mills Brothers and Cab Calloway performed here. The Orpheum is currently used for live performances and films. Call for current schedule. Admission charge.

Slavehaven/Burkle Estate, 826 North Second Street, ☎ 901-527-3427. Adventure, intrigue and mystery are all part of the experience in exploring this waystation on the Underground Railroad. Secret tunnels and trap doors reveal the escape route of the runaway slaves. Startling displays of ads, auctions, and artifacts help tell the story of the slave era. Advanced reservations required. Admission charge.

Tom Lee Memorial, Beale Street, along the bank of the Mississippi River. African-American Tom Lee was honored for his heroic actions when he saved 32 people from a capsized excursion boat in the Mississippi in 1925. The city supported him for the remainder of his life, and the monument was raised after his death in 1954.

W.C. Handy Home, Beale Street, at Fourth Street, ☎ 901-522-1556. Home of the "father of the blues," this small wood-frame house displays memorabilia depicting Handy's life and music. Mon-Sat, 10 am-5 pm; Sun, 1 pm-5 pm. Admission charge.

W.C. Handy home

Historic Sites Outside of Memphis

Fort Pillow State Park, 17 miles west of Henning (about 55 miles northeast of Memphis, via US 51) on State Hwy 87, ☎ 901-738-5581. Site where African-American soldiers were massacred by Confederate raiders on April 13, 1864. The ruins of the Civil War works are maintained at the interpretive center of the park. Open daily. Interpretive center hours vary. Free admission.

Museums & Exhibits

Art Museum, University of Memphis, ☎ 901-678-2224. Holds permanent collections of Egyptian antiquities and West African art, plus changing exhibitions. Tues-Fri, 9 am-5 pm; Sat-Sun, 1 pm-5 pm. Free admission.

Alex Haley House and Museum, Henning, TN, ☎ 901-738-2240. In nearby Henning, Tennessee (about 55 miles northeast of Memphis) is the boyhood home of Alex Haley, Pulitzer Prize-winning author of *Roots* and co-author of *The Autobiography of Malcolm X*. In a burial site nearby is the grave of Chicken George. The Henning House and Museum has some of the original furnishings used in the 1918 house. Some of the tour guides here were friends of the Haley family. Tues-Sat, 10 am-5 pm; Sun, 1 pm-5 pm. Admission charge. ☆ *Specially recommended.*

Alex Haley House and Museum
Courtesy Memphis Convention & Visitors Bureau

National Civil Rights Museum, Lorraine Motel, 450 Mulberry Street, ☎ 901-521-9699. Historic site where Dr. Martin Luther King, Jr. was assassinated on April 4, 1968. The nation's first museum dedicated to the history of the American Civil Rights Movement. Buffalo Soldiers apparel items for sale. Special events throughout the year. Call for updated information. Mon-Sat, 10 am-6 pm; Sun, 1 pm-6 pm. Closed Tuesdays, Thanksgiving, Christmas and New Year's Day. Admission charge.

Memphis

Historic Colleges & Universities

LeMoyne-Owens College, 807 Walker Ave, Memphis, TN 38126, ☎ 901-774-9090. Established in 1968, a merger between two traditional African-American colleges. Church-affiliated liberal arts college.

Shopping

Galleries & Specialty Shops

All That Jazz, 1295 Southland Mall, ☎ 901-332-5200. Affordable and quality custom framing and African-American art. "An art lovers paradise." Mon-Sat, 10 am-9 pm; Sun, 1 pm-6 pm.

Art-titudes Fine Arts Gallery, 5183 Winchester Rd, ☎ 901-797-8491. Specializes in fine African-American art and features original oils, prints, serigraphs and sculptures, including verdite stone, pottery, ethnic greetings cards and custom framing. National and local artists include LaShun Beal, Charles Bibbs, William Tolliver, Leroy Campbell, George Hunt, Margaret Warfield and Kathleen Wilson. Mon-Sat, 10 am-7 pm.

Art Village Gallery, 412 South Main Street, ☎ 901-521-0782. African-American art. Mon-Sat, 11 am-5 pm.

Carlton Cards by Diane, 1215 Southland, #218, Southland Mall, ☎ 901-345-7999. Ethnic cards and gift items. Mon-Sat, 10 am-9 pm; Sun, 1 pm-6 pm.

Gestine's Gallery, 156 Beale Street, ☎ 901-526-3162. Variety of oils, prints and sculptures. An art gallery dedicated to the enrichment and exposure of the African-American culture. Mon-Thurs, 11 am-7 pm; Fri-Sun, 11 am-10 pm. Closed Tuesdays.

Old Negro League Sports Shop, 154 Beale Street, ☎ 901-527-5577. Sportswear, memorabilia, shirts, caps, postcards of Memphis' old African-American baseball leagues. Call for current hours.

Bookstores

Afrobooks, 1206 Southland Mall, ☎ 901-396-3490. African-American books.

Kemet Bookstore, 988 Mississippi Boulevard, ☎ 901-942-5064. Asian-African-American books and African accessories. Mon-Sat, 9 am-8 pm.

Sidewalk University International Booksellers, 2287 Union Ave, ☎ 901-722-2110. Largest African-American bookseller in the mid-South. Afrocentric gifts, coffee bar, deli. Mon-Sat, 11 am-7 pm.

Tennessee Regular Baptist Bookstore, 1055 South Bellevue, ☎ 901-946-9669. Supplies and written material for all denominations. Bibles, books, robes, communion ware, deacon and usher guides. Mon-Sat, 9 am-5 pm.

Fashions

Afrikan Emporium, 3984 Elvis Presley Boulevard, ☎ 901-396-3999. African clothing for men and women, accessories and artifacts. Mon, noon-7 pm; Tues-Sat, 10 am-7 pm.

Classique Boutique & Salon, 4692 Spottswood, ☎ 901-682-5544. Women's apparel: casual wear, after five, career, cruise wear, bags, jewelry and hats. Mon-Fri, 10 am-6 pm; Sat, 10 am-5 pm.

Clothes Hangar, 139 Madison, ☎ 901-526-5527. Ladies fashions: suits, sportswear, dresses and accessories. Mon-Sat, 9 am-5:30 pm.

Lew Weinberg, 102 South Main Street, ☎ 901-526-4935. Men's fashions: suits, pants, shirts, accessories. Mon-Thurs, 9:30 am-5:30 pm; Fri-Sat, 9:30 am-6 pm.

Lucille's Boutique, 2574 Lamar, ☎ 901-745-1305. African clothing for men, women and children. Business suits, church dresses, African hats and accessories, African-American art, prints, oils, incense and silk flower arrangements.

Miss BeNea's House of Fashions, 2091 Union Ave, ☎ 901-272-2112. Features a variety of women's fashions of name brand designers, jewelry and accessories. Mon-Fri, 5 pm-8 pm; Sat, 3 pm-8 pm.

Restaurants

◆ Barbecue

Chuck's BBQ, 1621 Getwell, ☎ 901-745-5306. Call for current hours.

Jim Neely's Interstate Bar-B-Que, 2265 South Third, ☎ 901-775-2304. Pork and beef barbecue rib dinners and sandwiches with trimmings. This roadside restaurant received national recognition in *People* magazine as #2 in the US in 1989, and was featured in the May 1996 issue of American Airlines' *American Way* magazine. Rated "best little pork house in Memphis" in 1989 by Memphis' *Commercial Appeal* daily newspaper. Mon-Thurs, 11 am-11 pm; Fri-Sat, 11 am-2 am; Sun, noon-10 pm. ☆ *Specially recommended.*

Payne's Bar-B-Q, 1762 Lamar Ave, ☎ 901-272-1523. Beef and pork barbeque dinners and sandwiches. Open daily, 10:30 am-10 pm.

Tops Bar-B-Q, 15 locations throughout the Memphis area, ☎ 901-682-8113. A Memphis tradition. Barbeque dinners and sandwiches. Small dining area.

Memphis

◆ Soul Food

Fishnet Restaurant, 2731 Lamar, ☎ 901-744-3656. Specialties are catfish, carp, perch and shrimp dinners and sandwiches. Other menu items include homemade hamburgers, buffalo ribs and side orders.

Four Way Grill, 998 Mississippi, ☎ 901-775-2351. Mon-Sun, 7 am-11 pm.

Clark's Diner, 2839 Lamar Ave, ☎ 901-743-2719. Menu changes daily. Very quaint and informal restaurant.

Crumpy's Restaurant, 1584 Alcy, ☎ 901-775-1777. Home cooking and catering. Mon-Sun, 11 am-10 pm.

Crumpy's Hot Wings, 3 locations: 1381 Elvis Presley Boulevard, ☎ 901-942-3427; 1724 South White Station, ☎ 901-685-8356; 1056 East Brooks, ☎ 901-345-1503. Call for hours.

Melanie's, 1070 North Watkins, ☎ 901-278-0751. Mon-Sun, 11 am-5 pm.

◆ Short Orders

Pow-Wow, 794 West Raines, ☎ 901-789-0947. Short orders such as hamburgers and fish sandwiches. Open daily, 7 am-9:30 pm.

Entertainment

Jazz/ Rhythm & Blues Clubs/Lounges

Blues City Cultural Center, 205 North Main Street, ☎ 901-525-3031. Presents plays and musicals about the South and the African-American experience in the South. Past performances include Black Nativity, God's Trombones and Beale Street, Back Again. Call for upcoming events.

Days Inn, 164 Union Downtown, ☎ 901-527-4100. Cool jazz and hot blues. "The best in live entertainment" at Memphis Sounds Lounge. Wed-Sun nights.

B.B. King's Blues Club, 143 Beale Street, ☎ 901-524-5464. Live blues entertainment nightly showcasing top blues artists. Southern dining. Gift shop features exclusive B.B. King music and merchandise.

Willie Mitchell's Rhythm and Blues, 326 Beale Street, ☎ 901-523-7444. Variety of local and nationally acclaimed artists, including Kirk Whalum and Al Green. Call for upcoming shows.

Comedy Clubs

Comedy Zone, 2125 Madison Ave, Overton Square, ☎ 901-726-4242. African-American Comedy Jam on Wednesdays. Call for reservations and information.

Crumpy's Comedy Club, 2649 Hollywood at Hwy 240, ☎ 901-358-4000. This new Memphis comedy club has been attracting an array of national artists, such as Little Bo P of HBO's *Def Comedy Jam,* and Bro Man, star of Fox-TV's *Martin.* Shows Thurs-Sat. On Wednesdays, there is "U Do It Comedy," and jazz on Sundays. Call for reservations and upcoming events.

Lodging

Bed & Breakfasts

Fort-Daniel Hall LLC Bed & Breakfast, 184 South Memphis, Holly Springs, MS 38635, ☎ 601-252-6807. Located just 35 miles south of Memphis, this colonial-style home is one of 61 antebellum structures in the Holly Springs area; it was built in 1850 for the Hugh Craft family. There are three spacious guest rooms, each decorated in a different style: Early American, European, or Asian. Private and shared baths are available. A full Southern-style breakfast is served each morning. Call for current rates and reservations.

Travel Agents

Gavin/Robinson Travel, Jackson, Mississippi, ☎ 601-948-2253. ITAS.

Globestyle Travel & Tours/Creative Communications, 405 Buntyn, Memphis, TN 38111, ☎ 901-458-3900 or 800-484-5476, PIN 3900. Customized cross-cultural tours. Distributors of Nu-Concepts in travel. Call for tour packages.

Odyssey Travel, 859 McCallie Ave, #101, Chattanooga, TN 37403, ☎ 423-756-6566.

T & T Travel, 1444 East Shelby Drive, Memphis, TN 38116, ☎ 901-332-9467. Cruises, airlines, honeymoons, reunions, bus tours, worldwide travel services.

Heritage Tours

Heritage Tours, 280 Hernando, ☎ 901-527-3427. Specializing in African-American history tours of the Memphis area, including Henning, Tennessee, location of the Alex Haley Museum and the burial site of Haley's ancestors;

Memphis

Martin Luther King, Jr. Memorial/Lorraine Motel; National Civil Rights Museum, Slavehaven; House of Underground Railroad; Slave Market District; Beale Street/Memphis Blues Heritage; Cotton Row history; Civil War history; historical African-American churches and much more. Travel, transportation and step-on guide services. Call for schedules.

Media

Radio

◆ Jazz

WUMR 92 FM, University of Memphis. For the latest in jazz events around Memphis, call the 24-hour jazz connection hotline, ☎ 901-678-2766. Memphis' only jazz station. Broadcast from the University of Memphis.

◆ Urban

KJMS 101 FM, "Jams," 80 North Tillman, ☎ 901-323-0101. Urban rap station.

WDIA 1070 AM, 112 Union Ave, ☎ 901-529-4300. Urban contemporary/talk station. Founded in 1948, it was the first radio station (founded 1948) in the nation to have an African-American format and African-American DJ. Among those who have appeared on WDIA are B.B. King, Dwight Moore and Rufus Thomas.

WHRK 97.1 FM, 112 Union Ave, ☎ 901-529-4300. Urban contemporary. Multi-ethnic listening audience.

◆ Christian/Gospel

KSUD 720 AM, 102 North 5, West Memphis, Arkansas, ☎ 501-735-6622. Request Line, ☎ 501-735-6646. Contemporary Christian radio station. Bible study programs.

WCRV 640 AM, 4990 Poplar Ave, ☎ 901-763-4640; listener comment line, ☎ 901-681-9278. Christian information radio station.

WVIM 95.3 FM, 5557 McCracken Road, Hernando, ☎ 800-400-9533. Contemporary Christian radio station.

Newspapers

Memphis Times, 1444 East Shelby Drive, #40.1 ☎ 901-345-0650. African-American newspaper serving Memphis area. Distributed weekly.

Tri-State Defender, 124 East Calhoun Street, ☎ 901-523-1820. "Mid South's alternative newspaper." Covers news in Tennessee, Arkansas and Mississippi. Distributed weekly.

Publications

Black Business Directory, 1177 Madison, #302, ☎ 901-272-1077. Annual directory of some African-American-owned Memphis businesses.

Heritage Memphis; an African-American Heritage Guide, Memphis Convention & Visitors Bureau, 40 South Front Street, Memphis, TN 38103, ☎ 901-543-5300.

Memphis Black Business Directory, 1177 Madison Ave, #302, Memphis, TN 38104, ☎ 901-323-5777.

Memphis Quick Reference Guide & City Map, Memphis Convention & Visitors Bureau, 40 South Front Street, Memphis, TN 38103, ☎ 901-543-5300.

African-American Churches

AME

Clayborn Temple AME, 294 Hernando, ☎ 901-527-7283.

St. Andrew AME, 867 South Parkway E, ☎ 901-948-6441.

St. James AME, 600 North Fourth, ☎ 901-525-2017.

White Chapel AME, 1712 Fields, ☎ 901-785-0078.

CME

Collins Chapel CME, 678 Washington, ☎ 901-525-2872.

Mount Pisgah CME, 2480 Park Ave, ☎ 901-324-0429.

Zion Hill CME, 7180 Dexter, ☎ 901-382-9259.

Baptist

Beale Street Baptist, 379 Beale Street, ☎ 901-527-4832.

First Baptist Church, 379 Beale Street, ☎ 901-522-9073.

Hopewell Baptist, 334 Ashland, ☎ 901-527-2610.

Lake Grover Missionary Baptist, 4941 Weaver, ☎ 901-785-2750.

Metropolitan Baptist, 767 Walker, ☎ 901-946-4095.

Monument Baptist, 704 South Parkway E, ☎ 901-946-2529.

Mount Pisgah Baptist, 3636 Weaver, ☎ 901-785-1888.

New Salem Missionary Baptist, 2231 South Parkway E, ☎ 901-452-7265.

Olivet Baptist, 3084 Southern Ave, ☎ 901-454-7777.

Memphis

Rock of Ages Baptist, 192 Kirk Ave, ☎ 901-946-1357.

COGIC

Abiding Faith COGIC, 775 Tanglewood Street, ☎ 901-722-2433.

Darwin COGIC, 5078 Millbranch, ☎ 901-398-8959.

Greater Deliverance COGIC, 394 South Third Street, ☎ 901-527-5418.

Grace Temple COGIC, 1429 Hemlock, ☎ 901-942-9126.

Liberty COGIC, 544 East Raines Road, ☎ 901-396-3272.

New Life COGIC, 1241 South Main Street, ☎ 901-774-5062.

Pentecostal Temple COGIC Institutional, 229 South Danny Thomas Blvd, ☎ 901-527-9202.

South Parkway COGIC, 21 South Parkway W, ☎ 901-774-6463.

Calendar of Annual Events

◆ January

Dr. Martin Luther King, Jr. Holiday Celebration, ☎ 901-521-9699.

◆ February

Black History Month. Citywide activities, ☎ 901-543-5333.

The Tennessee Black Heritage Celebration, ☎ 901-272-0831. Honors contributions and achievements of African-Americans to state of Tenneessee.

◆ March

Black History Month Activities. Citywide, ☎ 901-543-5333.

Ebony Fashion Fair, Delta Sigma Theta Sorority, ☎ 901-543-5333.

◆ April

Africa in April Cultural Awareness Festival, ☎ 901-947-2133. Five-day celebration honoring different African countries with arts, crafts, music, theatrical performances, dance and Afrocentric exhibits and seminars.

◆ May

Memphis in May International Festival, ☎ 901-525-4611. Variety of international cultural, culinary and music activities.

◆ June

Juneteenth Freedom Festival, ☎ 901-385-4943. Celebration of Emancipation of Proclamation.

◆ July

Memphis Music and Heritage Festival, Center for Southern Folklore, ☎ 901-525-3655. Downtown event featuring music, art and food.

◆ August

National Civil Rights Museum's Culture in the Courtyard Concert Series, ☎ 901-521-9699.

◆ September

WLOK Radio Stone Soul Picnic, ☎ 901-527-9565. R&B, gospel music festival in picnic atmosphere.

Black Family Reunion, National Council on Negro Women, ☎ 901-948-5000. Cultural activities and educational forums.

Public Transportation

Main Street Trolley, ☎ 901-577-2640.

Memphis Area Transit Authority (MATA). Information line, ☎ 901-274-6282.

Memphis International Airport, ☎ 901-922-8000.

Taxi Services

Checker Cab, ☎ 901-577-7700.

City Wide Cab Company, ☎ 901-324-4202.

Yellow Cab Company, ☎ 901-577-7700.

Memphis Area Resources

Blues City Cultural Center, 205 North Main Street, ☎ 901-525-3031.

Memphis Convention & Visitors Bureau, 40 South Front Street, Memphis, TN 38103, ☎ 901-543-5300, fax 901-543-5350. Web site: www.memphis-travel.com. The Bureau is open Mon-Fri, 9 am-4:30 pm.

Memphis Visitor Information Center, 340 Beale Street, Memphis, TN 38104, ☎ 901-543-3333.

Tennessee Department of Tourism Development, 320 Sixth Ave N, Nashville, TN 37202, ☎ 615-741-1904.

Watoto De Africa Dance Group, 1000 South Cooper, ☎ 901-274-8101.

Memphis

Mobile

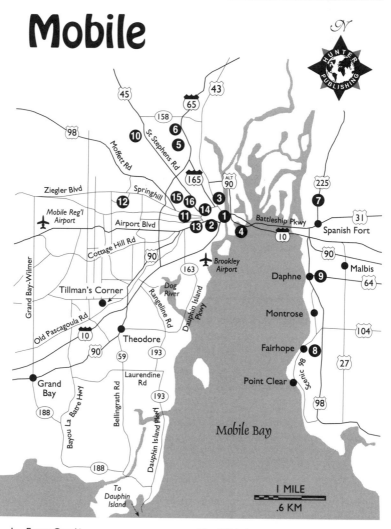

1. Forte Condé
2. Magnolia Cemetery
3. Slave Market Site
4. USS Alabama /
   Battleship Memorial Pk
5. AfricaTown
6. Cudjoe-Lewis Memorial
7. Historic Blakely Park
8. Lebanon Chapel AME Church
9. Little Bethel Baptist Church
10. Whistler
11. Bishop State Black History Museum,
    Bishop State Community College
12. Fine Arts Museum of the South
13. Heritage Museum of the
    City of Mobile
14. Mobile Black History Museum
15. National African-American
    Archives & Museum
16. Stone Street Baptist Church

Mobile

Historic Sites & Landmarks

Forte Condé, 150 South Royal Street, ☎ 334-434-7304. This replica of Forte Condé is used as the city's visitor's center; it has artifacts and a Black Heritage Display. The fort was built in 1735 and was the headquarters of the French colony in Mobile. Open daily 8 am-5 pm. Closed Christmas and during Mobile's Mardi Gras in January.

Magnolia Cemetery, Ann and Virginia Streets. Black soldiers who died during the attack on Fort Blakely on April 9, 1865 are buried in the southwest corner of this national cemetery. The attack occurred just before the capture of Mobile at the conclusion of the Civil War.

Slave Market Site, Corner of St. Louis and Royal Streets. For more than a hundred years Blacks were bought and sold as slaves at this site, despite the federal government's 1808 ban on the importation of slaves.

Stone Street Baptist Church, 311 Tunstall Street. The church's congregation dates back to the early 1800s. The building was redesigned in 1931 during the Depression.

Stone Street Baptist Church
Photo courtesy Mobile
Convention & Visitors Corp.

USS Alabama Battleship Memorial Park, 2703 Battleship Pkwy, ☎ 334-433-2703. The *Calamity Jane,* a plane used by the Tuskegee Airmen, is on display at this memorial park commemorating the battleship *USS Alabama.* Open daily, 8:30-sunset. Closed Christmas. Admission charge.

Sites Beyond Mobile

AfricaTown USA, Prichard, Mobile County, Northeast of Mobile. The towns of Happy Hill, Plateau and Magazine, Alabama make up what has been called "AfricaTown." The residents of AfricaTown are direct descendants of West African Blacks who were forced upon the ship *Clotilde* to be sold as slaves in the United States. The ship, made in Mobile, was the last one built for the purpose of smuggling Blacks into the United States. By the time the *Clotilde* landed in the US, federal legislation had been enacted to prohibit the importation of slaves to the US, and the ship's captain was forced to free his "cargo." The original residents of AfricaTown were members of the Tarkar tribe of Ghana, West Africa, and were captured and sold by the Dahomeyan warriors, also of West Africa. AfricaTown descendants hold an annual Festival (See AfricaTown Folk Festival in the *Calendar of Annual Events*), and have formed their own corporation, ADI.

Cudjoe Lewis Memorial
Photo courtesy of Mobile
Convention & Visitors Corp.

Cudjoe Lewis Memorial, Union Baptist Church, 506 Bay Ridge Road, Plateau, ☎ 334-456-6080. Cudjoe Lewis (Ka Zoola) was the last survivor of the slaveship, *Clotilde* (see AfricaTown, above). Lewis, along with 100 other members of the Tarkar tribe, settled in AfricaTown. They were buried at the Plateau Cemetery across from the Union Baptist Church.

Historic Blakely Park, 33707 Alabama Hwy 225, off I-10, Exit 30, north of Spanish Fort. Nine Black regiments of General Hawkins helped defeat Confederate defenses at Fort Blakely on April 9, 1865. The capture of the fort occurred at the end of the Civil War. Many Black soldiers who gave their lives at the battle were buried at Magnolia Cemetery (see *Magnolia Cemetery*) in Mobile. Open daily 9 am-dusk. Closed Christmas. Admission.

Lebanon Chapel AME Church, Young Street, Fairhope, south off I-10, Exit 35. Located in Fairhope's historic Black neighborhood, the Lebanon Chapel AME Church is one of the most elaborately constructed buildings in the area, and one of the finest examples of the county's concrete block construction for a church building.

Little Bethel Baptist Church, Main Street, Daphne, south off I-10, Exit 35. Church trustees Benjamin Franklin, Narcis Elwa, Stamford Starlin (now Sterling) and Nimrod Lovett were deeded two acres for this church property by Major Lewis Starke in 1867. Lucy, the mother of Daphne resident Russell Dick, was one of the last survivors of the slave ship *Clotilde*. Dick is remembered by Daphne residents as an outstanding citizen who once owned much land in Daphne, including all of the downtown area. He is buried in the church cemetery.

Whistler, Alabama, I-65 to State Hwy 45 to Prichard Corporate limits, bounded by Eight Mile Creek, just north of Mobile. Whistler is the state's largest predominantly African-American town, and has a number of landmark historic homes and Black-owned businesses.

Museums & Exhibits

Bishop State Black History Museum, Bishop State College, Central Campus, 1365 Martin Luther King, Jr. Ave, ☎ 334-405-4457. This small museum located on the Campus of Bishop State College contains artifacts, manuscripts and audio-visual productions and exhibits. Many items focus on early Mobilians and the development of the Davis Avenue Historic District. Mon-Fri, 8 am-4:30 pm.

Fine Arts Museum of the South, 4850 Museum Drive, ☎ 334-343-2667. African art works are among its international collection. Tues-Sun 10 am-5 pm; closed Mondays and major holidays. Free admission.

Heritage Museum of the City of Mobile, 355 Government Street, ☎ 334-434-7569. Among the museum's extensive collection of cultural artifacts are African-American items. Tues-Sat, 10 am-5 pm; Sun, 1 pm-5 pm; closed Mondays. Free parking next to the museum. Free admission.

Mobile Black History Museum, 269 North Broad Street, ☎ 334-433-1333. House museum highlighting Mobile County's African-American history from the early 19th century. There is a fascinating pictorial display of the people and places important to the development of the local community. Mon-Fri, 9 am-5:30 pm; Sat, 10 am-5 pm; Sun, noon-5 pm. Admission charge.

National African-American Archives and Museum, 564 Dr. Martin Luther King, Jr. Dr, ☎ 334-433-8511. The museum was built in 1930, two years after the main public library, which African-Americans were not allowed to use. Collections include portraits and biographies of famous African-Americans and a section devoted to carvings, artifacts, books and documents. Tues-Sat, 10 am-4 pm. Admission charge.

Historic Colleges/Universities

Bishop State Community College, 351 N Broad Street, Mobile, ☎ 334-690-6419. State-supported junior college.

Mobile

Shopping

Galleries & Specialty Shops

Heritage Gallery of African-American Art, 123 South Ann Street, ☎ 334-690-7222. Paintings and sculptures by local and regional artists in addition to African carvings and sculptures. Special exhibits are showcased throughout the year. Mon-Thurs, 10:30 am-3 pm; Fri 10:30 am-5pm.

M-Club Art Gallery, 58 South Royal Street, ☎ 334-432-9494. Artworks from Africa and America include paintings, prints, carvings and cards. Special exhibits at different times of the year. Mon-Fri, 11 am-4 pm; Sat by appointment.

Variety Tree, 1916-B Dauphin Island Parkway, ☎ 334-473-7171. This small service-related shop sells small gift items, such as African-American figurines, all-occasion gift baskets, jewelry, perfumes and children's clothing. Mon-Sat, 10 am-5 pm.

Victorian Teal, 357 Congress, ☎ 334-432-9022. An art gallery specializing in works by African-American artists. The main house, built in 1890, is attached to an older structure that is listed among the "Negro Shanties" on the Sanborn Map of 1855. An old African-American technique of wallpapering with collaged newspapers and magazines is used in a hallway and adjoining room. Mon-Fri, 9 am-5 pm.

Bookstores

English Book & Gift, 2811 Government Blvd, ☎ 334-478-8535. Christian book store. Religion, theology. Mon-Fri, 9:30 am-6 pm; Sat, 1 pm-5:30 pm.

Fashions

Allie's Boutique, 1070 Dr. Martin Luther King, Jr. Ave, ☎ 334-432-4082. Women's clothing store. Contemporary fashions, business suits, after-five wear, lingerie and hats. Mon-Sat, 10 am-5 pm.

Gentlemen's Den, 911 South Wilson Ave, Versailles Mini Mall, Prichard ☎ 334-452-0330. Specializes in contemporary clothes for men. Suits, slacks, shirts, ties. Mon-Sat, 10 am-6pm.

Janice's Boutique, 4055 Cottage Hill Road, ☎ 334-602-1090. Specializes in accessories for full-figured women. Mon-Fri, 10 am-7 pm; Sat 10 am-6 pm.

Myles Men's Shop, 233 South Wilson Ave, Prichard ☎ 334-457-2225. Specializes in contemporary clothes for men. Suits, slacks, ties, African caps, vests. Mon-Sat, 9 am-5 pm.

The Other Woman, 911 South Wilson Ave, Versailles Mini Mall, Prichard ☎ 334-452-8076. Specializes in contemporary full-figured women's clothing, accessories, evening wear and wedding gowns. Mon-Sat, 11 am-4:30 pm.

V & V's Specialty Shop, 1966 Springhill Ave, ☎ 334-479-3535. Upscale women's specialty clothing shop. Business attire, elegant after-five, sportswear, churchwear. Mon-Sat, 10 am-5:30 pm.

Shopping Centers

Versailles Mini Mall, 911 South Wilson Ave, Prichard, ☎ 334-456-9994. This mall features African-American-owned businesses and includes a photo shop, bridal salon, sports and clothing shop, beauty salon, Federal Express service, men's and women's clothing stores and special event rooms. Mon-Sat, 10 am-6 pm.

Restaurants

◆ Barbeque

Rodgers Bar-B-Que, 2350 Stephens Road, Prichard, ☎ 334-330-0285. Specializes in pork ribs, dinner plates, sandwiches and slabs. Mon-Thurs, 11 am-10 pm; Fri-Sun, 11 am-midnight.

Saucy-Q Bar-B-Que, 2702 Spring Hill Ave, ☎ 334-479-2727. Carry-out restaurant specializing in pork barbeque, dinner plates and sandwiches. Mon-Sat, 11 am-7 pm.

◆ Caribbean

Caribbean Island Connection, 821 Dauphin Island Pkwy, ☎ 334-476-0494. Traditional Caribbean cuisine. Jerk and curried chicken, stew, pork chops, seafood, rice and peas and other favorites. Mon-Sat, 11 am-10 pm.

◆ Soul Food

Roberson's Cafeteria #1 & 2, 920 Dr. Martin Luther King, Jr. Ave, ☎ 334-432-2923, and 504 South Wilson Ave, Prichard, ☎ 334-457-0464. Soul food cuisine. Open daily 7 am-3 pm.

Entertainment

◆ Jazz

Ferdinand's, 1803 Bear Fork Road, Prichard, ☎ 334-457-0453. Jazz & blues dance club. 25+ crowd. Appetizers. Open daily, 24 hours.

Mobile

◆ Dance Nightclubs

George's Playhouse & Lounge, 1380 Davis Ave, ☎ 334-433-9387. Urban Contemporary and R & B. Caters to a young crowd. Weekdays until 9 pm; weekends until midnight.

Silverspoon's Night Club, 1572 St. Stephens Road, ☎ 334-432-1876. Hip-hop, rap, dance nightclub catering to ages 25 and older. Open Fri-Sun, 9 pm-2 am.

Lodging

Cottonwood Mineral Hot Springs and Motel, 600 Hot Springs Rd, Cottonwood, AL 36320, in the southeast corner of the state; ☎ 800-526-7727 or 334-691-4101. Web site: www.wiregrassarea.com/classifieds/hot-springs.html. A subsidiary of *Upscale* Magazine and Bronner Bros. Cosmetics Mfg., this "Rolls Royce" of mineral hot springs is a full-service spa and motel featuring delicious meals, lodging, therapeutic massages and other rejuvenating packages, RV hook-ups, bicycle rentals and much more. Don't be surprised if you see famous African-American personalities here.

Travel Agents

American World Travel Agency & Tours, 1560 St. Stephens Road, Mobile, AL 36603 ☎ 334-433-9200, fax 334-438-4933. Full-service travel agency. Also provides personalized tours.

Heritage Tours

American World Travel Agency & Tours, see above listing.

Wrights Tours, 2328 St. Stephens Road, Mobile, AL 36617, ☎ 334-478-0064, fax 334-479-3299. Provides travel and transportation services for tours in Mobile, and transportation to other cities throughout the US and Canada.

Media

Radio

◆ Urban Contemporary

WBLX 660AM, 1204 Dauphin Street, ☎ 334-432-7609. Adult format.

WBLX 92.9FM, 1204 Dauphin Street, ☎ 334-432-7609.

WGOK 900AM, Gum Street, ☎ 334-432-8661.

WYOK 104.9FM, 800 Gum Street, ☎ 334-694-1049.

Newspapers

Mobile Beacon, 2311 Costarides Street, ☎ 334-479-0629. African-American community newspaper. Distributed weekly on Wednesdays.

Magazines

Greater Mobile Area Directory of Minority-Owned Businesses, University of South Alabama Small Business Development Center, ☎ 334-460-6004.

Publications

Alabama's Black Heritage, Alabama Bureau of Tourism and Travel, 401 Adams Ave, #126, Montgomery, ☎ 800-ALABAMA.

Mobile; the Heritage Trail Begins Here, Mobile Convention & Visitors Corporation, PO Box 204, Mobile, AL 36601, ☎ 800-5-MOBILE.

African-American Churches

AME

Big Zion Church, 112 S. Bayou Street, ☎ 334-433-8431.

Ebenezer AME Zion Church, 268 St. Charles Ave, ☎ 334-479-9873.

Emanuel AME Church, 654 St. Michael Street, ☎ 334-438-5141.

Greater Pine Grove AME Church, 800 S. Thomas Ave, ☎ 334-452-8924.

Hope Chapel AME Zion Church, 1644 Wolf Ridge Rd, ☎ 334-456-7638.

Mount Hebron AME Zion Church, 3800 Springhill Ave, ☎ 334-341-0330.

St. Paul AME Church, 1255 Montrose Street, ☎ 334-432-5207.

St. Stephens AME Church, 2707 Josephine Street, ☎ 334-479-3053.

Smith Memorial AME Church, 6501 Felhorn Rd, North ☎ 334-344-5753.

State Street AME Zion Church, 520 Sate Street, ☎ 334-432-3965.

Texas Street AME Church, 1110 Texas Street, ☎ 334-438-9294.

Baptist

Aimwell Baptist Church, 500 Earle Street, ☎ 334-433-2183.

Franklin Street Baptist Church, 2113 St. Stephens Rd, ☎ 334-479-3477.

Greater Union Baptist Church, 961 Lyons Street, ☎ 334-433-2059.

Mt. Zion Baptist Church, 461 Texas Street, ☎ 334-438-1146.

Revelation Baptist Church, 1711 Taylor Ln, ☎ 334-473-2333.

Shiloh Baptist Church, 609 Warren Street, ☎ 334-433-7661.

Stone Street Baptist, 311 Tunstall Street, ☎ 334-433-3947.

Truevine Baptist Church, 1850 Martin Luther King, Jr, ☎ 334-473-6906.

COGIC

First Church of God in Christ, 1308 St. Stephens Rd, ☎ 334-438-2115.

Calendar of Annual Events

◆ January

Mobile Mardi Gras, Mobile Convention & Visitors Corporation, PO Box 204, Mobile, AL 36601, ☎ 800-5-MOBILE.

◆ February

Black History Month, Mobile Convention & Visitors Corporation, PO Box 204, Mobile, AL 36601, ☎ 800-5-MOBILE.

The AfricaTown Folk Festival, Prichard, AfricaTown Descendents, Inc., Mobile Area Chamber of Commerce, ☎ 334-433-6951.

Taxi Services

Mike's Cab Company, ☎ 334-457-9448.

Yellow Cab, ☎ 334-476-7711.

Mobile Area Resources

AfricTown Descendents, Inc., 1710 Stile Ave, Whistler, AL 36612, ☎ 334-456-1033.

Alabama Bureau of Tourism and Travel, 401 Adams Ave, #126, Montgomery, ☎ 800-ALABAMA.

Mobile Convention & Visitors Corporation, PO Box 204, Mobile, AL 36601, ☎ 800-5-MOBILE.

Montgomery

Historic Sites & Landmarks

Abernathy Residence, 1327 Hall Street. Praetorium for First Baptist Church at the time Ralph David Abernathy was pastor. It was bombed during the Civil Rights Movement. Not open to the public.

Alabama Department of Archives and History, 624 Washington Ave, State Capitol Complex, ☎ 334-242-4443. The nation's first Department of Archives and History displays a unique collection of paintings honoring famous Alabamians and others whose achievements are connected with the state. There are portraits of Martin Luther King, Jr., George Washington Carver, Booker T. Washington, Nat "King" Cole, W.C. Handy, Harper Trenholm and others. Mon-Fri, 8 am-5 pm; Sat-Sun, 9 am-4:30 pm. Research library closed Sundays and state holidays. Free admission.

Alabama State Capitol, One Dexter Ave, ☎ 334-242-3935. The Capitol was built in 1851; in 1861 the Ordinance of Secession which withdrew Alabama from the Union was signed here. It was the capital of the Confederacy for the first three months. The circular interior staircases are the work of Horace King, a noted African-American contractor and bridge builder. In 1965, civil rights marchers gathered here on the front steps after their march from Selma. Mon-Sat, 9 am-5 pm; closed Sun and state holidays.

Alabama State Supreme Court, Dexter Ave, across from Dexter Ave King Memorial Baptist Church. It served the state's highest court for years. Many civil rights cases were tried here before being appealed to the federal courts. Alabama's first African-American Supreme Court justice, Oscar Adams, served here and was an early civil rights attorney. Justice Adams was also the first African-American to win a statewide public office since Reconstruction.

Alabama State University, 809 South Jackson Street, ☎ 334-229-4100. Founded in Marion, Alabama in 1874 as the State Normal School and University for Colored Students and Teachers. It was relocated to its present site in 1887. Historic campus buildings include the Tullibody Fine Arts Center, John W. Beverly Hall, William Hooper Council Hall, William Burns Paterson Hall, George W. Trenholm Hall, Bibb Graves Hall and Kilby Hall. Marion is the hometown of Coretta Scott King.

Ben Moore Hotel, Corner of Jackson and High streets. Built in the early 1950s, the hotel had a prominent place during the bus boycott. White city officials and African-American boycott leaders met in the Roof Garden Restaurant to discuss problems.

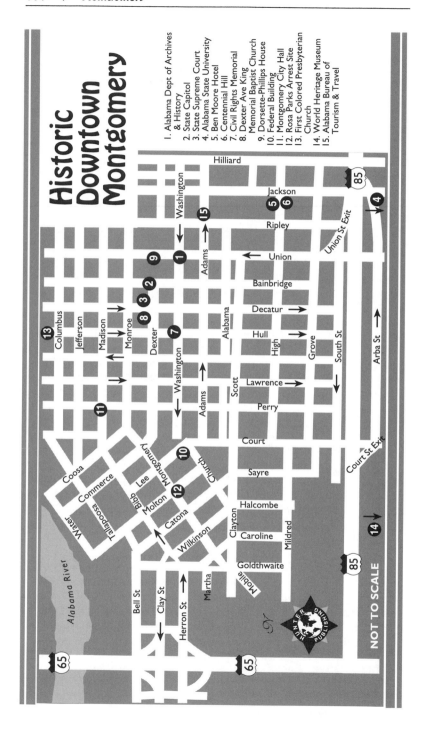

Historic Downtown Montgomery

1. Alabama Dept of Archives & History
2. State Capitol
3. State Supreme Court
4. Alabama State University
5. Ben Moore Hotel
6. Centennial Hill
7. Civil Rights Memorial
8. Dexter Ave King Memorial Baptist Church
9. Dorsette-Phillips House
10. Federal Building
11. Montgomery City Hall
12. Rosa Parks Arrest Site
13. First Colored Presbyterian Church
14. World Heritage Museum
15. Alabama Bureau of Tourism & Travel

NOT TO SCALE

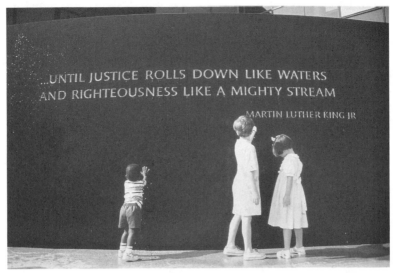

Civil Rights Memorial
Photo courtesy of the Montgomery Area Chamber of Commerce,
Convention & Visitor Development

Beulah Baptist Church, 3703 Rosa Parks Ave, ☎ 334-265-2697. Beulah Baptist Church was incorporated in 1919. Singer Nat "King" Cole and his family attended the church while he was a young boy. His father was one of the original members who assisted with the church's incorporation, and his mother played the piano for the choir. Like many other area churches, Beulah Baptist was used for meetings and services during the struggle for racial equality.

Centennial Hill, in the vicinity of Jackson and High streets. Centennial Hill was developed in the late 1870s and 1880s and was the first prominent African-American residential area to develop in the city after the Civil War. The neighborhood contains three structures listed in the National Register and 13 locally designated historic buildings.

City of St. June Historic District, 2048 Fairview Ave. Montgomery's first African-American hospital was located here. Protesters on the Selma-to-Montgomery march camped out here before walking the final few miles to the state capitol. The complex was built under the direction of Father Harold Purcell, a white priest who came to Montgomery in 1934 to establish a health clinic for African-Americans. Until his death in 1952, he worked to improve the lives of Montgomery's African-American citizens. The hospital has been converted to apartments, but the school and church are still in use.

Civil Rights Memorial, corner of Washington and Hull streets, ☎ 334-264-0286. Located on the Southern Poverty Law Center grounds, the memorial was designed by Vietnam Memorial artist Maya Lin. Engravings chronicle key events in the 1955 to 1968 struggle for racial equality and include the names of 40 people who gave their lives during that time.

Cleveland Court Apartments, 620-638 Rosa Parks Ave. Erected in 1941, Cleveland Court was one of Montgomery's first public housing facilities. Mrs. Rosa McCauley Parks, whose arrest started the bus boycott, lived in apartment number 634 from 1951 to 1957, along with her husband Raymond A. Parks and her mother, Mrs. Leona Edwards McCauley.

Cole-Samford House, 1524 St. John Street. This modest one-story frame house was the birthplace and early childhood home of well-known musician Nat "King" Cole. Not open to the public.

Dexter Avenue King Memorial Baptist Church, 454 Dexter Ave, ☎ 334-263-3970. Dr. Martin Luther King, Jr. began his leadership in the Civil Rights Movement while serving as a minister here. A mural depicts major events in his life. The church is also noted as the birthplace of the Civil Rights Movement and is an example of the role played by African-American churches in social reform. An historic marker on the grounds of the church also depicts highlights of the Civil Rights Movement. Tours, Mon-Fri, 10 am-2 pm; weekends by appointment. Free admission.

Dexter Avenue King Memorial Baptist Church
Photo courtesy of the Montgomery Area
Chamber of Commerce, Convention & Visitor Development

Dorsette-Phillips House, 422 Union Street. Purchased in 1886 by Dr. Cornelius, Montgomery's first African-American physician, who later became the chief of staff at Hale Infirmary. Not open to the public.

Dr. E.D. Nixon Collection, Alabama State University Campus, Levi Watkins Learning Arts Center, ☎ 334-229-4100. The Archives and Special Collections include Dr. Nixon's letters, papers and commendations. Other interesting African-American history items are displayed in the Library. Mon-Wed, 8 am-6 pm; Thurs-Fri, 8 am-9 pm; Sat, 8 am-6 pm; Sun, 1 pm-6 pm.

Dr. E.D. Nixon Residence, 647 Clinton Street. Nationally recognized as a pioneer of the modern Civil Rights Movement, Dr. Nixon posted bail for segregation law violator Rosa Parks. In her defense, Dr. Nixon gathered the support of Montgomery African-Americans in implementing the successful 1955-1956 Montgomery Bus Boycott. In spite of the bombing of his home and countless threats against his life, Dr. Nixon persistently fought racial segregation throughout the mid-20th century. Not open to the public.

Federal Building, 15 Lee Street, ☎ 334-223-7132. Completed in 1933 in the classical Greek style, this building originally housed the post office and other federal offices, including the US Court of Appeals and US District Court. It was here that Judge Frank M. Johnson, Jr. issued the injunction that enabled the Selma-to-Montgomery march to take place. Building open Mon-Fri, 8 am-5 pm; no tours.

Georgia Gilmore Home, 453 Dericote Street. Staunch boycott supporter Georgia Gilmore (1920-1990) welcomed participants in the Civil Rights Movement to her home and table, and was once arrested on a bus. She organized the "Club from Nowhere," whose members sold homemade pies and cakes to benefit both Blacks and whites. Not open to the public.

Greyhound Bus Station, Court Station. On May 20, 1961, 21 Freedom Riders, hoping to end discrimination in the interstate transportation system, were met by an angry mob when their bus arrived at the Montgomery terminal. The riot that ensued was one of the many events that prodded the Kennedy administration along the road to civil rights reform. The station is now an historic landmark and will house a civil rights museum.

Holt Street Baptist Church, 903 South Holt Street, ☎ 334-263-0522. On Monday, December 5, 1955, after Rosa Parks refused to relinquish her bus seat to a white man, Holt Street Baptist Church was the site of a mass meeting to determine how long the Black community would abstain from riding city buses. More than 5,000 African-Americans attended. The church was often used for meetings and rallies.

Horace King Historical Marker, Dillingham and Broad streets, Phenix City. King was known for his rise to fame from unknown slave to renowned architect. He and his master were responsible for building the Dillingham Street Bridge over the Chattahoochee River. King was subsequently freed by his master, John Godwin. He later designed and repaired bridges for the Civil War Confederates. He also served in the Alabama Legislature for 40 years. After the death of King's former master, King placed a memorial on his grave and supported his widow financially.

Jackson Community House, 409 South Union Street. The two-story clapboard house, built in 1853, is significant for its association with Jefferson Franklin Jackson, a prominent Montgomery attorney during the 1950s and for its association with the City Federation of Women and Youth Clubs. The house has served Montgomery's African-American community as an Old Folks and Orphan Home, a site for meetings and seminars and, during one period, as the only library available to the African-American community. Not open to the public.

Montgomery City Hall, 103 North Perry Street, ☎ 334-241-4400. The present building was erected in 1936, after an earlier building was destroyed by fire. In the recorder's court chamber, Rosa Parks was tried on December 5, 1955, for refusing to give up her bus seat when driver Fred Blake ordered her to do so. Mrs. Parks was convicted of the offense by Judge John B. Scott. Building open Mon-Fri, 8 am-5 pm; no tours.

Montgomery County Courthouse, 142 Washington Ave. The site of numerous sit-ins during the Civil Rights Movement. Alabama State University students were among the first to stage protests here.

North Lawrence-Monroe Street Historic District, an area including parts of Monroe and Lawrence streets. Noted as the major African-American business district developed after the passage of Jim Crow Laws in the late 19th century, the area is indicative of the African-American community's attempt to fulfill its social, cultural and economic needs within the restrictive confines of racial segregation and discrimination.

Oakwood Cemetery, Jefferson and Columbus streets. Montgomery's oldest cemetery. Veterans of all American wars are buried here, as well as local and state notables. There is a section for slaves.

Pastorium, Dexter Avenue Baptist Church, 309 South Jackson. Having served as the Pastorium of the Dexter Avenue Baptist Church since 1919, this was the home for Dr. Martin Luther King, Jr. during his ministry in Montgomery and the Montgomery Bus Boycott. Not open to the public.

Rosa Parks Arrest Site, Corner of Moulton and Montgomery streets. It was on this site on December 1, 1955 that the infamous arrest of Rosa Parks took place for her refusal to give up her bus seat.

Swayne School Site, southwest corner of Union and Grove streets. Swayne School was organized in 1885 by the American Missionary Association and the Freedmen's Bureau.

Sites Beyond Montgomery

Booker T. Washington Memorial, Tuskegee University, Tuskegee. *The Veil of Ignorance* monument portrays Booker T. Washington lifting the veil of ignorance from his fellow man.

Booker T. Washington Grave Site, Tuskegee University, Tuskegee. Washington, his family, Dr. Carver, Levi Dawson and other noted persons associated with the university are buried in the University Cemetery.

Moton Field (Tuskegee Army Air Field), Tuskegee Municipal Airport, off Chappie James Drive. Site of an annual Fly-In, Tuskegee has been called the "Home of Black Aviation." Moton is where the Tuskegee airmen, World War II Black aviators, learned to fly.

The Daniel "Chappie" James Center for Aerospace Science, Tuskegee University, Tuskegee. Daniel "Chappie" James, the first African-American four-star general, is honored with a memorial hall in his name at Tuskegee University's Department of Army and Aerospace Sciences.

The Oaks, Tuskegee University, ☎ 334-727-6390. Booker T. Washington's home (circa 1899) has been restored and is operated as a house museum by the National Park Service. Designed by Robert Taylor and built by Tuskegee students, it is one of the few surviving structures of the era designed and built by African-Americans. Open daily, 10 am-4 pm. Closed Thanksgiving, Christmas and New Year's. Tours on the hour, starting at the Tuskegee Institute National Historic Site. Free admission.

Tuskegee University, Old Montgomery Highway, Tuskegee, ☎ 334-727-8011. This well-known African-American educational institution was created in 1881 by a legislative act sponsored by Louis Adams, a former slave, and George W. Campbell, a former slave owner. Booker T. Washington was the school's first president. More than 27 buildings listed on the National Register of Historic Places are associated with the work of Booker T. Washington and Dr. George Washington Carver. Tuskegee University is the lasting legacy of these two great Americans.

Tuskegee University Administration Building (Kresge), Tuskegee University. This was originally the office of Booker T. Washington. A Centennial Visual Mural, 12 by 26 feet, is permanently displayed here.

Westwood Plantation, Uniontown, Perry County. Within its boundaries are former slave camps with house foundations, barns, well, cisterns and a cotton gin. A number of residents are direct descendants of Westwood Plantation slaves. The plantation is an excellent example of a Southern, antebellum agricultural enterprise. Not open to the public.

Museums/Exhibits

Art Objects, 2050 Woodley, ☎ 334-262-5349. More than 400 art works can be seen in the gallery, including pieces by African-American artists Lonnie Holley, Charlie Lucas, Jimmie Lee, Sudduth, Mose Tolliver, and Bill Taylor. The gallery has the largest collection of Alabama folk art in the state and one of the largest in the Southeast. Mon-Fri, by appointment only.

First Colored Presbyterian Church, Old Alabama Town Historic District, 310 North Hull Street, ☎ 334-240-4500. The small frame church dates from 1890, when the Black and white Presbyterians divided the congregation. It has been restored to its authentic state. Mon-Sat, 9:30 am-3:30 pm; Sun, 1:30 pm-3:30 pm. Admission charge.

Montgomery Museum of the Arts, One Museum Drive, in the Wynton M. Blount Cultural Art Center, ☎ 334-244-5700. The museum houses many works by Southern artists and regularly features exhibits by African-Americans. Tues-Sat, 10 am-5 pm (Thurs until 9 pm); Sun, noon-5 pm; closed Mon and major holidays. Free admission.

World Heritage Museum, 119 West Jeff Davis Ave, ☎ 334-263-7229. Features photos and displays of the Civil Rights Movement in the city of Montgomery. One of its many special events is the Annual Labor Day Heritage Run. By appointment only. Donation.

Museums Beyond Montgomery

Museum of Black History, 1006 Lancaster Street, Wetumpka, Elmore County, ☎ 334-567-6336. The building was erected in 1925. This was the original location of the first county training school for African-Americans in Elmore County. The museum contains all types of memorabilia depicting the life of Elmore County's African-American residents.

Carver Museum, Tuskegee, ☎ 334-727-6390. Established by the Tuskegee Institute in 1938, the museum's exhibits include needlework, paintings, vegetable specimens and samples of products derived from peanuts and sweet potatoes; all part of Dr. Carver's scientific contributions. Tour schedules are available at the museum, which now serves as the Visitor Orientation Center for the National Historic Site. Open daily, 9 am-5 pm. Closed Thanksgiving, Christmas and New Year's. Free admission.

Commodores Museum, 208 Martin Luther King Highway, Tuskegee, ☎ 334-727-5034. Visitors can view the former recording and rehearsal studio of popular performers. The museum features uniforms and equipment from the 1970s and 1980s along with pictures, film footage and a gift shop. Mon-Sat, 8 am-7 pm. Admission charge.

Historic Colleges & Universities

Alabama State University, 915 South Jackson Street, Montgomery, AL 36101, ☎ 205-293-4291. State-supported university. Founded 1874.

Concordia College, 1804 North Green Street, Selma, AL 36701, ☎ 205-874-5736. Two-year private college. Founded 1922.

Selma University, 1501 Lapsley, Selma, AL 36701, ☎ 205-872-2533. Independent four-year Baptist-affiliated college. Founded 1878.

Trenholm State Technical College, 1225 Air Base Blvd, Montgomery, AL 36108, ☎ 205-832-9000. Founded 1965.

Tuskegee University, Tuskegee, AL 36088, ☎ 205-727-8500. Independent university. Founded 1881.

Shopping

Galleries & Specialty Shops

Roots & Wings, A Cultural Book Place, 1345 Carter Hill Road, ☎ 334-262-1700. Conceived by attorneys Delores R. Boyd and Vanzetta Penn McPherson as a tribute to the literary cultural and artistic heritage of African-Americans, Roots & Wings opened in November 1989. The magnificent wood structure houses an art gallery, theater and a book store. It is Alabama's premier marketplace and a cultural landmark for the literary heritage of African-Americans. Roots & Wings showcases African-American paintings and graphic arts. Lectures, films and programs for children and adults are scheduled throughout the year. Mon-Sat, 10 am-6 pm. Closed Sun and major holidays. Group presentations available.

Fashions

The New Hob Nob, 1603 South Decatur Street, ☎ 334-263-2254. Women's and men's clothing and accessories, hats, scarves, gloves, ties and more. Mon-Sat, 9 am-6 pm.

Bookstores

Freedom Life Bookstore, 223 Fleming Road, ☎ 334-281-3138. Mon-Fri, 9 am-4 pm.

Restaurants

Dem Bones, Barbequed seafood, ribs (baby back, Cajun), bourbon sauce. Tues-Wed, 5 pm-10 pm; Thurs, 5 pm-11 pm; Fri-Sat, 5 pm-2 am. Live entertainment on Thurs nights at 8 pm, and on Fri-Sat, 10:30 pm until ?.

Martha's Place, 458 Sayre Street, ☎ 334-263-9135. Soul food restaurant. Buffet. Mon-Fri, 11 am-3 pm. Extended dinner hours from May-September, Fri-Sat, 5 pm-10 pm; Sun, 11 am-3 pm.

Moses & Crawford Café & Catering, 700 Columbus Street, corner of North Union and Columbus, ☎ 334-265-3520. Specializes in home cooking. Selection of homemade baked goods.

Entertainment

Dance Clubs

Top Flight Nightclub, 954 High Street, Montgomery, near Alabama State University, ☎ 334-264-2975. Wed-Thurs, 5 pm-9 pm; Fri-Sat, 9 pm-?

Travel Agents

World Over Travel, 335 Coosa Street, Montgomery, ☎ 334-265-2300.

Heritage Tours

S.C.L.C. Women, 328 Auburn Ave, Atlanta, ☎ 404-584-0303. Offers several tour options from three-hour to two-day African-American heritage and civil rights tours of Atlanta, Selma, Birmingham and Montgomery. Required donation.

Media

Radio

◆ Jazz/Blues
WXVI 1600 AM, 422 South Court, ☎ 205-263-3459. Blues format.

Newspapers

Montgomery-Tuskegee Times, 3900 University Highway, ☎ 334-262-5026. African-American community newspaper.

Magazines

Montgomery Black Pages, 314 West Wilding Drive, Montgomery, AL 36116, ☎ 334-271-1555.

Publications

Alabama's Black Heritage, Alabama Bureau of Tourism and Travel, 401 Adams Ave, #126, ☎ 800-ALABAMA.

African-American Churches

◆ Baptist
Bethel Baptist Missionary Church, 2106 Mill Street, ☎ 334-262-6825.

Beulah Baptist Church, 3703 Rosa Parks Ave, ☎ 334-265-2697.

Day Street Baptist Church, 861 Day Street, ☎ 334-269-1251.

First Baptist Church, 347 North Ripley Street, ☎ 334-264-6921.

Holt Street Baptist Church, 903 South Holt Street, ☎ 334-263-0522.

Dexter Avenue King Memorial Baptist Church, 454 Dexter Ave, ☎ 334-263-3970.

Mount Gillard Baptist Church, 3323 Day Street, ☎ 334-263-2171.

COGIC

Gospel Tabernacle Church of God in Christ, 465 South Perry Street, ☎ 334-264-5171.

New Life Church of God in Christ, 4116 Narrow Lane Road, ☎ 334-286-8207.

Calendar of Annual Events

◆ September

Annual Labor Day Heritage Run. For more information, contact the World Heritage Museum, ☎ 334-263-7229.

Site of an **Annual Fly-In,** Tuskegee has been called the "Home of Black Aviation." Moton is where the Tuskegee Airmen, World War II Black aviators, learned to fly. For more information, contact the Alabama Bureau of Tourism & Travel, ☎ 1-800-ALABAMA.

Public Transportation

Montgomery Area Transit System (MATA), ☎ 334-262-7321.

Taxi Services

Checker-Deluxe, ☎ 334-263-2512.

Original Queen's Cab, ☎ 334-263-7137.

People's Cab, ☎ 334-264-9898.

Shepherd Taxi, ☎ 334-269-9086.

Town Service Cab, ☎ 334-264-9006.

Yellow Cab, ☎ 334-262-5225.

Montgomery Area Resources

Alabama Bureau of Tourism and Travel, 401 Adams Ave, #126, Montgomery, AL 36104, ☎ 1-800-ALABAMA.

Montgomery Black Chamber of Commerce, 3480 Eastern Blvd, Montgomery, AL 36116, ☎ 334-271-1555.

Montgomery Convention & Visitors Center, 401 Madison Ave, Montgomery, AL 36104, ☎ 334-240-9437. Visitor Information, ☎ 334-262-0013.

New Orleans

Historic Sites & Landmarks

Amistad Research Center, Tilton Hall, Tulane University, 6823 St. Charles Ave, ☎ 504-865-5535. Amistad is one of the nation's largest repositories of African-American history. Papers of African-Americans and records of organizations and institutions of the African-American community make up about 90% of the center's holdings. Collections include over 6,000 linear feet of manuscripts, 250,000 photographs, 400 video and audio tapes, 20,000 books, 1,000 periodicals, 30,000 pamphlets, 1.5 million clippings, 14,000 reels of microfilm and the Aaron Douglas Collection, which has 270 paintings, drawings, and pieces of sculpture by African-American artists of the 19th and 20th centuries. Over 200 pieces of African art are in the William Bertrand, John Byers, Jessie C. Dent, and Victor DuBois collections. Some are rare and unusual examples of traditional African art; others are contemporary works. Mon-Fri, 8:30 am-5 pm; Sat, 1 pm-5 pm. Free admission.

Chalmette Battlefield, Jean LaFitte National Historic Park, six miles east of New Orleans (take Hwy LA46 to St. Bernard Hwy, Chalmette), ☎ 504-589-4430. This historic battlefield was the site of the Battle of New Orleans, a decisive victory over the British at the end of the War of 1812. General Andrew Jackson recruited free African-Americans to fight in this battle. Open daily, 8 am-5 pm. Free admission.

Historic New Orleans Collection, Williams Research Center, 410 Chartres Street, ☎ 504-598-7171. Collections reflect the history and culture of the Gulf South, Louisiana, and New Orleans. Research fields include colonial Louisiana, Louisiana Purchase, Civil War, cartography, plantations, urban development, Louisiana artists, architecture, jazz, the French Quarter and Mardi Gras. Tues-Sat, 10 am-4 pm. Free admission.

Hogan Jazz Archive, Howard Tilton Memorial Library, Tulane University, 6823 St. Charles Ave, ☎ 504-865-5688. The Hogan Jazz Archive houses materials pertaining to jazz music, and includes records and papers, oral histories, recorded music, photographs, sheet music and clippings. Mon-Fri, 8:30 am-5 pm; Sat, 9 am-1 pm. Free admission.

Jazz and Heritage Foundation Archive, 1205 North Rampart Street, ☎ 504-522-4786. Documentation of the foundation's programs and enterprises are housed in this archive and include the Jazz & Heritage Festival, Congo Square Lecture Series, Heritage School of Music and WWOZ radio station. By appointment only. Free admission.

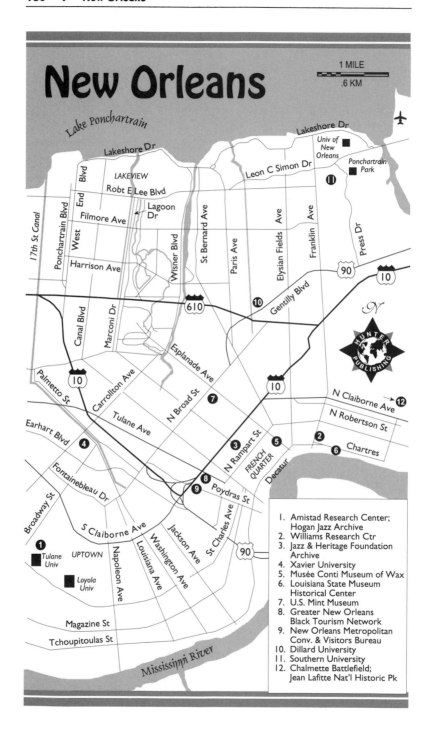

New Orleans

1 MILE
.6 KM

Lake Ponchartrain

Lakeshore Dr

Lakeshore Dr

Univ of New Orleans

Ponchartrain Park

Leon C Simon Dr

LAKEVIEW

Robt E Lee Blvd

End Blvd

Ponchartrain Blvd

West End

17th St Canal

Filmore Ave

Lagoon Dr

Harrison Ave

St Bernard Ave

Paris Ave

Elysian Fields Ave

Franklin Ave

Press Dr

Wisner Blvd

Canal Blvd

Marconi Dr

610

Gentilly Blvd

90

10

Esplanade Ave

Palmetto St

10

Carrollton Ave

N Broad St

10

N Claiborne Ave

N Robertson St

Tulane Ave

Chartres

Earhart Blvd

N Rampart St

FRENCH QUARTER

Decatur

Fontainebleau Dr

Poydras St

Broadway St

S Claiborne Ave

Jackson Ave

Washington Ave

St Charles Ave

90

Tulane Univ

UPTOWN

Loyola Univ

Napoleon Ave

Louisiana Ave

Magazine St

Tchoupitoulas St

Mississippi River

1. Amistad Research Center; Hogan Jazz Archive
2. Williams Research Ctr
3. Jazz & Heritage Foundation Archive
4. Xavier University
5. Musée Conti Museum of Wax
6. Louisiana State Museum Historical Center
7. U.S. Mint Museum
8. Greater New Orleans Black Tourism Network
9. New Orleans Metropolitan Conv. & Visitors Bureau
10. Dillard University
11. Southern University
12. Chalmette Battlefield; Jean Lafitte Nat'l Historic Pk

Martin Luther King, Jr. Statue. A statue of the famed civil rights leader is located at Martin Luther King Boulevard and South Claiborne Ave.

Southern University, Center for African & African-American Studies, 6400 Press Drive, ☎ 504-286-5296. The archives at the center focus on Africa and the African-American experience; it also has an extensive African art collection. Mon-Fri, 9 am-1 pm. Free admission.

Tulane University, Howard-Tilton Memorial Library, 6823 St. Charles Ave, ☎ 504-865-5685. Tulane pioneered the compilation of New Orleans collection archives in 1889, beginning with a letter from Thomas Jefferson to a New Orleans resident. Over the years, Tulane's collecting efforts have evolved into a suite of specialized archival resources. See listings on *Amistad Research Center* and *Hogan Jazz Archive.* Mon-Fri, 8:30 am-5 pm; Sat, 9 am-1 pm. Free admission.

Xavier University Archives and Special Collections, 7325 Palmetto Street, ☎ 504-483-7655. The Archives preserves the university's official records and houses special collections on African-American history, the American South, the Gulf-Caribbean region, and US Catholicism. Mon-Fri, 8:30 am-5 pm. Free admission.

Museums/Exhibits

Musee Conti Museum of Wax, 917 Conti Street, ☎ 504-525-2605. This unusual museum has life-size wax figures of famous New Orleans African-Americans from the 18th through the 20th centuries. From the famed Marie Laveau (the "Voodoo Queen") to Louis "Satchmo" Armstrong, the history of New Orleans is presented with wax figures depicting the African-American presence from slavery through the development of jazz. Open daily, 10 am-5:30 pm. Admission charge.

Louisiana State Museum Historical Center, 751 Chartres Street, ☎ 504-568-8214. The museum contains French Superior Council (1714-1803) and Spanish judicial records (1769-1903), as well as information about social, political, economic and medical conditions of Louisiana from the 18th century to the present. Includes extensive records of African-American history.

US Mint Museum, 400 Esplanade Ave, ☎ 504-568-6968. This old US Mint Complex houses the Jazz Museum, Carnival Museum, Louisiana Historical Center and New Orleans Jazz Club collections. The museum has an impressive collection of rare photographs, musical instruments and other items from famous jazz pioneers. An original horn of the great Louis Armstrong is also on display. Wed-Sun, 10 am-6 pm. Admission charge.

New Orleans

Sites Beyond New Orleans

River Road African-American Museum and Gallery, Tezcuco Plantation on the River Road in Burnside, LA, ☎ 504-644-7955. This museum is dedicated to collecting, preserving and interpreting artifacts that provide information about the history and culture of African-Americans. The museum pays tribute to the hundreds of slaves who were purchased and brought to Burnside, Louisiana in 1858. Many of their descendants continue to live in the rural communities along the Mississippi River, and visitors to the museum can research African-American ancestry in the extensive records here, as well as learn about the history of African-Americans who lived and worked on the sugarcane and rice plantations in the parishes along the river. Wed-Sun, 1 pm-5 pm. Winter hours may vary. Mon and Tues, by appointment only. Admission charge.

Historic Colleges & Universities

Dillard University, 2601 Gentilly Boulevard, New Orleans, LA 70122, ☎ 504-286-4666. Private liberal arts college. Founded in 1869.

Grambling State University, 100 Main Street, Grambling, LA 70121, ☎ 318-274-2330. State-supported university. Founded 1901.

Southern University of New Orleans, 6400 Press Drive, New Orleans, LA 70126, ☎ 504-286-5000. Senior state institution; established in 1959.

Xavier University, 7325 Palmetto Street, New Orleans LA 70118, ☎ 504-486-7411. Predominantly African-American Roman Catholic university. Founded in 1915.

Shopping

Galleries & Specialty Shops

African Art Gallery, 5700 Read Boulevard, ☎ 504-246-3936. Mon-Sat, 10 am-9 pm; Sun, 12:30 pm-5:30 pm.

African Art & Wears, 5700 Read Blvd, Lake Forest Plaza, ☎ 504-246-3936. African paintings, prints, statues, ladies and men's apparel. Mon-Sat, 10 am-9 pm; Sun, 12:30 pm-5:30 pm.

Bergen Galleries, 730 Royal Street, ☎ 504-523-7882. Extensive selection of African-American art, featuring the works of Tolliver, Barnes, Bibbs, Fennell and others. Sun-Thurs, 9 am-9 pm; Fri-Sat, 9 am-11 pm.

Bruce Brice Gallery, New Orleans Centre, 1400 Poydras, #244, ☎ 504-586-0668, fax 504-586-0872. Prints, paintings, folkart, sculptures, photos, and African artifacts. Mon-Sat, 10 am-8 pm; Sun, noon-6 pm.

Gallery on the Square, 514 St. Peters Street, ☎ 504-523-2821. African-American art, originals and limited editions. Mon-Sun, 10 am-5 pm.

LaBelle Gallerie, 309 Chartres Street, ☎ 504-529-3080. Large selection of African-American and multi-ethnic art. Mon-Sun, 10 am-7 pm.

Neighborhood Gallery, 217 North Broad Street, ☎ 504-822-2665. African-American art. Performing and creative art network. Call for hours.

Stella Jones Gallery, Place Street, 201 St. Charles Ave, ☎ 888-400-9100 or 504-568-9050, fax 504-568-0840. Web site: www.stellajones.com. Located in the heart of the New Orleans' Central Business District, this premier gallery specializes in original artwork by local, national and internationally known African-American artists such as Jacob Lawrence, Dr. Samella Lewis, Elizabeth Catlett, Herbert Gentry, Artis Lane and many others. Works include oils, watercolors and sculpture in bronze, wood and marble. Mon-Sat, 10 am-6 pm and by appointment.

Visual Jazz Art Gallery, 2337 St. Claude Ave, ☎ 504-949-9822. The works of New Orleans artist Richard C. Thomas are displayed here. Thomas, one of the city's prominent artists, focuses on African-American art with New Orleans jazz themes. Tues-Sat, 10 am-5 pm.

Xpressions Unlimited of New Orleans, New Orleans Centre, 1400 Poydras, #160, ☎ 504-588-1177. African-American art prints, figurines, greeting cards, and sorority and fraternity paraphernalia, such as T-shirts, hats, license plates, jackets and jerseys. Mon-Sat, 10 am-8 pm; Sun, noon-6 pm.

Bookstores

Afro-American Bookstop, New Orleans Centre, #1400 Poydras, Second Floor, ☎ 504-588-1474. Small bookstore with a great selection of books by African-American writers on various Afrocentric subjects. Mon-Sat, 10 am-8 pm; Sun, noon-6 pm.

Community Book Center, 217 North Broad Street, ☎ 504-822-2665. African-American books, cards, gifts, and games. Mon-Sat, 10 am-7 pm.

Little Professor Bookstore, 1000 South Carrolton Ave, ☎ 504-866-7646, fax 504-866-0946. Call for hours.

Fashions

B.B.H. Fashion Gallery, 117 South Rampart Street, ☎ 504-523-6700. Custom leather apparel and Negro Baseball League items. Mon-Sat, 10:30 am-6:30 pm.

New Orleans

Cultural Crossroads, 3009 Carrollton Ave, ☎ 504-866-8823. Authentic African clothing and accessories for men and women. Mon-Sat, noon-6 pm.

Enigma, New Orleans Centre, 1400 Poydras, #486, ☎ 504-588-9967. An upscale women's high-fashion boutique, featuring styles from casual to after-five and formal. Sizes range from 4 to 24. International and upcoming fashion designers are represented. Mon-Sat, 10 am-8 pm; Sun, noon-6 pm.

Imani, 813 North Broad Street, ☎ 504-482-4744. Authentic African clothing and accessories for men, women and children. Tues-Sat, 11 am-7 pm.

Restaurants

◆ African

Bennachin Restaurant, 133 North Carrollton Ave, ☎ 504-486-1313. Traditional West African cuisine. Beef, chicken, lamb and seafood entrées. Mon-Thurs, 11 am-9 pm; Fri, 11 am-10 pm; Sat, 5 pm-10 pm.

◆ Bakeries

Omar's Pies, 4637 New Orleans Street, ☎ 504-283-4700, fax 504-282-9012. A New Orleans tradition. "The Pie Man" specializes in sweet potato, lemon, custard and pecan pies. Popular home-based business. Call to arrange for pickup.

◆ Barbecue

Ms. Hyster's Barbecue, 2000 South Claiborne Ave, ☎ 504-522-3028. Specializes in hickory-smoked barbeque chicken, ribs and soul food side orders. Sun-Thurs, 11 am-midnight; Fri-Sat, 11 am-2 am.

◆ Cafés

Riverside Café, 1 Poydras Street, Riverwalk, ☎ 504-522-2061. Best place for Southern desserts. Located along the Mississippi. Mon-Thurs, 10:30 am-9 pm; Fri-Sat, 10:30 am-10 pm; Sun, 10:30 am-7 pm.

◆ Caribbean

Palmer's Jamaican Creole Restaurant, 135 North Carrollton Ave, ☎ 504-482-3658. Caribbean/Creole cuisine featuring roast pork, chicken, fish and shrimp entrées. Tues-Fri, 11:30 am-2 pm and 6 pm-10 pm; Sat, 6 pm-10 pm.

Restaurant Paris-Dakar, 1506 South Carrollton Ave, ☎ 504-866-7232. Mediterranean, African, French, and Caribbean cuisine. Mon-Wed, 11 am-10 pm; Thurs-Sat, 11 am-11 pm.

◆ Creole

Café Rue Bourbon, 241 Bourbon Street, ☎ 504-524-0114. Cajun-Creole cuisine. Elegant atmosphere in the heart of the French Quarter. Open daily, 11:30 am-3 pm; 5:30 pm-midnight.

Café Baquet, 3925 Washington Ave, ☎ 504-822-1376. Creole/soul food. Specialty is gumbo and catfish jourdiane. Mon-Thurs, 6 am-3 pm; Fri-Sat, 6 am-8 pm; Sun, 7:30 am-1:30 pm.

Dooky Chase's, 2301 Orleans Ave, ☎ 504-821-2294 or 504-821-0600. Creole cuisine and contemporary continental cuisine with a combination of African-American, French and Spanish entrées. New Orleans landmark restaurant. Sun-Thurs, 11:30 am-midnight; lunch buffet. Weekends, 11:30 am-1 am.

Dunbar's, 4927 Freret Street, ☎ 504-899-0734. Neighborhood restaurant that serves up a variety of Creole and soul food items. Mon-Sat, 7 am-9 pm.

Eddie's, 2119 Law Street, ☎ 504-945-2207. Traditional Creole-soul cuisine. A specialty at Eddie's is pork chops with oyster dressing. Mon-Wed (lunch only), 11 am-3 pm; Thurs, 11 am-10 pm; Fri-Sat, 11 am-11:30 pm.

Chez Helene's, 1536 North Robertson, ☎ 504-947-0111. Open daily 11:30 am-10 pm.

House of Blues, 225 Decatur Ave, ☎ 504-529-2583. Contemporary New Orleans cuisine, bar, dance hall. Live blues, various artists nightly. Multiethnic crowd. Dinner, Sun-Thurs, 11 am-midnight.

Montrell's Creole Café, 4116 Marigny Street, ☎ 504-288-6374. Creole, soul food, French.

Praline Connection Gospel & Blues Hall, 901-907 South Peters Street, ☎ 504-523-3973. Creole-soul cuisine. Sundays gospel brunch (11 am-2 pm). Live jazz some nights. Call first.

Olivier's Creole Cuisine, 204 Decatur Street, ☎ 504-525-7734. Authentic Creole cuisine that serves great catfish Orleans, gumbo, homemade bread pudding and peach cobbler. Elegant and intimate atmosphere. Lunch, Mon-Sun, 11 am-3 pm; dinner, Mon-Sun, 5 pm-10 pm.

Palm Court Jazz Café, 1204 Decatur Street, ☎ 504-525-0200. Classic Creole cuisine, live jazz. Wed-Sun, 7 pm-11 pm.

Rita's Olde French Quarter Restaurant, 945 Chartres Street, ☎ 504-525-7543. Cajun-Creole cuisine. Mon-Sun, 11 am-10 pm.

◆ Seafood

Felix's Restaurant & Oyster Bar, 739 Iberville Street, ☎ 504-522-4440. Specialty is oysters on the half shell. Mon-Thurs, 10:30 am-midnight; Fri-Sat, 10:30 am-1:30 am; Sun, 10:30 am-10 pm.

Jaegar Seafood, 1701 Elysian Fields Ave, ☎ 504-947-0111. Popular New Orleans seafood establishment. Jazz sets, 10 pm-2 am; food service, Tues-Fri, 11:30 am-9 pm.

◆ Soul Food

4-Seasons Cuisine, 5790 Crowder Boulevard, ☎ 504-246-3800. Traditional soul food with all the side dishes. Mon-Wed, 11 am-5 pm; Thurs, 11 am-9 pm; Fri, 11 am-11 pm; Sat, noon-11-pm.

Davis Chicken Deluxe, 4204 St. Anthony, ☎ 504-282-2557. Traditional soul food, featuring Davis' own special fried chicken recipe and a horde of soul food vegetables. Mon-Thurs, 11 am-6 pm; Fri, 11 am-9 pm; Sat, noon-6 pm.

Dunbar's, 4927 Freret Street, ☎ 504-899-0734. See listing under *Creole* restaurants.

Eddie's, 2119 Law Street, ☎ 504-945-2207. See listing under *Creole* restaurants.

Henry's Soul Food (two locations), 2501 Claiborne Ave, ☎ 504-821-7757, or 209 North Broad Street, ☎ 504-821-8635. Offers a wide variety of soul food items.

Jayde's Jazzy Soul Food, 2523 Perdido Street, ☎ 504-822-6814 and 7204 Hayne Boulevard, ☎ 504-245-1235. Traditional soul food cuisine. Mon-Fri, 11 am-3 pm (lunch); Mon-Fri, 6 pm-9 pm (dinner); Fri, 6 pm-10 pm; Sat, 3 pm-11 pm.

Praline Connection Gospel & Blues Hall, 901-907 South Peters Street, ☎ 504-523-3973. See listing under *Creole* restaurants.

Two Sisters, 223 North Derbigny Street, ☎ 504-524-0056. Popular neighborhood restaurant with a wide selection of traditional Southern soul food items. Mon-Fri, 8 am-6:30 pm; Sat, 8 am-5:30 pm.

Zachary's, 8400 Oak Street, ☎ 504-865-1559. Creole/soul food. Lunch Mon-Fri, 11 am-2:30 pm; dinner, Tues-Fri, 5 pm-9:30 pm; Sat, 5:30-10 pm.

Entertainment

◆ Jazz/Blues

Flabor's, 252 St. Bernard Ave, ☎ 504-947-6581. Jukebox music with oldies, jazz, blues and soul. Caters to mature crowds.

House of Blues, 225 Decatur Ave, ☎ 504-529-2583. Live blues. Various artists nightly. Contemporary New Orleans cuisine, bar, dance hall. Neville Brothers are regularly featured. Gift shop offers authentic House of Blues souvenirs. Sun-Thurs, 11 am-midnight.

Jaegar Seafood, 1701 Elysian Fields Ave, ☎ 504-947-0111. Jazz sets on weekends, 10 pm-2 am; Tues-Fri, 11:30 am-9 pm. Popular New Orleans seafood establishment. Cover charge.

New Showcase Lounge, 1915 North Broad Street, ☎ 504-945-5612. Live jazz, blues nightly. 6 pm-until ?

Palm Court Jazz Café, 1204 Decatur Street, ☎ 504-525-0200. Live jazz, classic Creole cuisine. Wed-Sun, 7 pm-11 pm.

Praline Connection Gospel & Blues Hall, 901-907 South Peters Street, ☎ 504-523-3973. Creole-soul cuisine. Sunday gospel brunch, 11 am-2 pm. Live jazz some nights. Call first.

Preservation Jazz Hall, 726 St. Peter Street (French Quarter), ☎ 504-523-8939. Popular jazz nightclub. Multiethnic crowd. Great New Orleans-style jazz artists. Be prepared to wait during some weekends and special events.

◆ Reggae

Oasis Nightclub, 2285 North Bayou Rd, ☎ 504-944-2000. Open weekends only.

Tipitina's, 501 Napoleon Ave, concert line ☎ 504-897-3943. Features national and international reggae artists. Call for upcoming events and times.

Whisper's Nightclub, 8700 Lake Forest Boulevard, ☎ 504-245-1059. Features local reggae artists.

Lodging

Bed & Breakfasts

Lagniappe, 1925 Peniston Street, ☎ 800-317-2120 or 504-899-2120. This 19th-century, Spanish-influenced bed and breakfast has eight bedrooms and a luxury suite, all with private baths. The innkeepers spoil their guests with fresh flowers, wine, use of a bicycle for touring the city, and a business center – not to mention the deluxe continental breakfast choices. Lagniappe has been designed so that guests have access to the entire house, making them feel at home. Located in the Uptown Historical District, close to the French Quarter and other area attractions. Call for rates and reservations.

La Maison á L'Avenue Jackson, 1740 Jackson Ave, ☎ 504-522-1785, fax 504-566-0405. E-mail: aaa@I-way.net. Web site: www.bja.com/aaa. This Greek Revival and Italianate-style bed and breakfast dates back to the 19th-century and was once the home of noted New Orleans architect Henry Howard. The suites-only bed and breakfast welcomes guests with wine and homemade cake, and serves an in-suite breakfast of fresh fruit, cereal, breads, muffins and beverages. Located in the Garden District about two blocks from the historic St. Charles Ave streetcar and only 10 minutes from the French Quarter. Call for rates and reservations.

Lagniappe Bed & Breakfast

Travel Agents

AAA Reservations Services, 1740 Jackson Ave, ☎ 504-522-1785 or 888-232-1785, fax 504-566-0405. E-Mail: aaa@I-way.net; Web site: www. bja.com/aaa. The free service offers reservations at African-American-owned accommodations in the New Orleans area. Listings include bed and breakfasts, guest homes, apartments, cottages, and penthouses.

American Worldwide Travel Agency, 11208 Hayne Boulevard, New Orleans, LA 70128, ☎ 504-244-6145.

Express Travel, 1400 Poydras Street, #980, New Orleans, LA 70112, ☎ 504-524-2424.

Four Corners Travel, 1000 North Broad Street, New Orleans, LA 70119, ☎ 504-822-6244. ITAS member.

Johnson Tour & Travel Agency, 310 South Broad Street, New Orleans, LA 70119, ☎ 504-822-2888, fax 504-822-5700.

Leisure Tyme Travelers, 5928 Spain Street, New Orleans, LA 70122, ☎ 504-283-2870.

Nu Concepts in Travel, 11000 Morrison Rd, #109, New Orleans, LA 70127, ☎ 504-242-6178, fax 504-242-1004.

SJM World Travel, 1739 North Miro Street, New Orleans, LA 70119, ☎ 800-208-3736, fax 504-242-4891.

Sunshine Travel Agency, 6027 Chef Menteur Highway, #100, New Orleans, LA 70126, ☎ 800-383-3773 or 504-245-3773.

T & S Travel Services, 4333 Woodland Drive, New Orleans, LA 70131, ☎ 504-394-5828, fax 504-394-2108.

USA Travel Agency, 1212 St. Charles Ave. New Orleans, LA 70130, ☎ 800-229-1872 or 504-523-7818, fax 504-523-0246.

Worldwide Concepts Cruise & Travel, 1972 Florida Ave, New Orleans, LA 70119, ☎ 504-944-9564, fax 504-944-1763.

Heritage Tours

Creole Tours & Travel, PO Box 4233, New Orleans, LA 70178, ☎ 504-288-7271, fax 504-944-8650.

Custom Bus Charter, 200-C Wright Ave, ☎ 504-368-9090, fax 504-368-8005.

Le'Ob's Tour & Transportation Service, 4635 Touro Street, ☎ 504-288-3478.

Louis Armstrong Foundation Jazz Tours, ☎ 504-523-0855. This New Orleans tour company uses jazz historians to escort visitors to the homes of such jazz greats as "Papa" Jack Laine, Buddy Bolden, Jelly Roll Morton, Sidney Becket, Nick La Rocca, Reverend Boatner and many more. Tours also include the Louisiana State Museum Jazz Collection at the Old US Mint Building, Storyville, and a ride up the Mississippi to view many of the great plantations. A special visit to the Howard-Tilton Library at Tulane University, home to the William Ransom Hogan Jazz Archive, is also included. Call for tour packages, schedules and rates.

Madeline Jones, Inc., 2532 General Pershing Street, ☎ 504-891-3971. Customized African-American heritage tours. Features "Taste of New Orleans" restaurant and catered meals.

Mid-City Carriages, Inc., 1615 St. Phillip Street, ☎ 504-581-4415.

Mr. Peter's Tours, 2300 St. Roch Ave, ☎ 504-943-7896.

Roots of New Orleans, A Heritage City Tour, "The Soul of New Orleans." ☎ 504-596-6889, fax 504-522-7414. E-Mail: rootsno@chamber.gnofn.org.

Tours by Richard, 6939 Neptune Court, ☎ 504-241-2375.

New Orleans

USA Convention Planners & Heritage Tours, 1212 St. Charles Ave, ☎ 504-523-7818.

Williams Tours, PO Box 8532 , New Orleans, LA 70182, ☎ 504-945-3047.

Media

Radio

◆ Jazz

WWOZ 90.7 FM, PO Box 51840, ☎ 504-568-1239. Heritage format.

◆ Urban Contemporary

WQUE 93.3 FM, 1440 Canal Street, ☎ 504-581-1280.

WYLD 940 AM, 2228 Gravier, ☎ 504-822-1945. Religious and urban contemporary.

◆ Gospel/Religious

WBOK 1230 AM, 1639 Gentilly Boulevard, ☎ 504-943-4600.

WYLD 940 AM, 2228 Gravier, ☎ 504-822-1945. Religious, urban contemporary format.

Newspapers

Data News Weekly, 3501 Napoleon Ave, ☎ 504-822-4433, fax 504-821-0320. African-American community newspaper. Distributed weekly.

Louisiana Weekly, 1001 Howard Ave, #2600, ☎ 504-524-5563. African-American community newspaper. Distributed weekly on Thursdays.

New Orleans Tribune, 2335 Esplanade Ave, ☎ 504-945-0772.

Magazines

Black Collegian, 140 Carondale Street, ☎ 504-523-0154, fax 504-523-0171.

Graffiti Magazine, 1227 North Villere Street, ☎ 504-525-9759.

Style Magazine, 650 South Pierce Street, ☎ 504-947-0007.

Publications

A Fabric of our Culture; A Directory of Louisiana's African-American Attractions, The Louisiana Office of Tourism, PO Box 94291, Department 5701, Baton Rouge, LA 70804-9291, ☎ 800-334-8626.

Soul of New Orleans, Greater New Orleans Black Tourism Network, 1520 Sugar Bowl Drive, New Orleans, LA 70130, ☎ 800-725-5652 or 504-523-5652, fax 504-522-0785.

African-American Churches

AME

Payne Memorial AME, 3306 South Liberty Street, ☎ 504-899-7421.

Petty AME Zion, 2800 Milan Street, ☎ 504-891-8971.

St. James AME, 222 North Roman Street, ☎ 504-586-9989.

St. Luke AME Methodist, 2500 Louisa Street, ☎ 504-944-6864.

St. Paul AME, 8540 Cohn Street, ☎ 504-861-3988.

St. Peter AME, 3424 Eagle Street, ☎ 504-482-5418.

St. John AME, 1017 Belleville Street, ☎ 504-366-3713.

Union Bethel AME, 2321 Thalia Street, ☎ 504-522-2658.

Wilson Chapel AME, 10121 Old Gentilly Rd, ☎ 504-246-9771.

Baptist

Beacon Light Baptist Church, 1551 Mirabeau Ave, ☎ 504-283-8757.

Christian Unity Baptist Church, 1700 Conti Street, ☎ 504-522-3493.

First African Baptist Church, 3524 LaSalle Street, ☎ 504-891-5069.

First African Baptist Church of New Orleans, Gretna, 2216 Third Street, Gretna, ☎ 504-366-9712.

First Emmanuel Baptist Church, 1829 Carondelet Street, ☎ 504-524-8891.

Franklin Avenue Baptist Church, 2515 Franklin Ave, ☎ 504-947-2408.

New Zion Baptist Church, 2319 Third Street, ☎ 504-891-4283.

Pilgrim Progress Baptist Church, 3600 Loyola Ave, ☎ 504-899-7383.

St. John Divine Baptist Church, 1763 Derbigny Street, ☎ 504-949-6624.

Catholic

Blessed Sacrament, 5018 Constance Street, ☎ 504-897-0955.

Corpus Christi Catholic Church, 2022 St. Bernard Ave, ☎ 504-945-8931.

St. Augustine Church, 1210 Governor Nicholls Street, ☎ 504-525-5934.

New Orleans

COGIC

Berea COGIC, 912 Belleville Street, ☎ 504-366-6300.

Church of God in Christ, 4304 America Street, ☎ 504-246-6149.

Fifth COGIC, 3007 Law Street, ☎ 504-945-8182.

First COGIC, 2453 Josephine Street, ☎ 504-523-6232.

Full Gospel Church of God in Christ, 2308 South Liberty Street, ☎ 504-895-6800.

Full Gospel Church of God in Christ, 5600 Read Boulevard, ☎ 504-244-6800.

Lutheran

Mount Zion Lutheran, 1401 Simon Bolivar Ave, ☎ 504-522-9951.

Zion Lutheran, 1924 St. Charles Ave, ☎ 504-524-1025.

Methodist

Peck United Methodist Church, 3631 Washington Ave, New Orleans, ☎ 504-821-1292.

St. James Methodist Church, 1925 Ursuline Ave, New Orleans, ☎ 504-822-8138.

Trinity United Methodist Church, 1028 Valence Street, New Orleans, ☎ 504-895-7155.

Wesley United Methodist Church, 2517 Jackson Ave, New Orleans, ☎ 504-524-8270.

Non-Denominational

Word of Faith, 13123-10 Service Rd, New Orleans, ☎ 504-241-1234.

Calendar of Annual Events

◆ January

Mardi Gras Festival, citywide, ☎ 504-566-5068.

Martin Luther King, Jr. Birthday Celebration, citywide, Greater New Orleans Black Tourism Network, ☎ 800-725-5652 or 504-523-5652.

◆ February

Black History Month Activities, ☎ 504-566-5068, Greater New Orleans Black Tourism Network, ☎ 800-725-5652 or 504-523-5652.

Mardi Gras, citywide celebration, ☎ 504-566-5068.

◆ March

Louisiana Black Heritage Festival, ☎ 504-288-8867, Greater New Orleans Black Tourism Network, ☎ 800-725-5652 or 504-523-5652.

◆ April

New Orleans Jazz & Heritage Festival, ☎ 504-522-4786.

◆ June

Juneteenth Celebration, ☎ 504-522-4786 or 581-2245, or Greater New Orleans Black Tourism Network, ☎ 800-725-5652 or 504-523-5652.

Reggae Fest, ☎ 504-367-3554 or 504-367-1313.

◆ August

Multicultural Tourism Summit, Greater New Orleans Black Tourism Network, ☎ 800-725-5652.

African Heritage Festival International, African Heritage Foundation, ☎ 504-949-5610.

Public Transportation

New Orleans International Airport, ☎ 504-464-3536.

Taxi Services

Coleman Cab Company, ☎ 504-891-5818

New Orleans Area Resources

Black Arts National Diaspora, 4008 Odin Street, New Orleans, LA 70126, ☎ 504-282-7975.

Greater New Orleans Black Tourism Network, 1520 Sugar Bowl Drive, New Orleans, LA 70112, ☎ 800-725-5652 or 504-523-5652, fax 504-522-0785, Web site: www.gno.com/soulgnobtn@ix.netcom.com.

New Orleans Metropolitan Convention & Visitors Bureau, 1520 Sugar Bowl Drive, New Orleans, LA 70112, ☎ 504-566-5005. Web site: www.nawlins.com.

New Orleans Visitors Information Center, 7450 Paris Rd, New Orleans, LA 70128, ☎ 504-246-5666 or 504-246-5511.

Southeast Louisiana Black Chamber of Commerce, 1600 Canal Street, #606, New Orleans, LA 70112, ☎ 504-539-9450 or 504-539-9451, fax 504-539-9452.

New York City

Historic Sites & Landmarks

African Burial Ground and Five Points Archeological Projects, Six World Trade Center, US Customs House, Room 239, ☎ 212-432-5707, fax 212-432-5920. In May of 1991, the skeletal remains of more than 400 men, women and children, primarily of African descent, were recovered from the Broadway block bordered by Duane, Elk and Reade streets in lower Manhattan. The African Burial Ground, referenced as the "Negroes Burying Ground" on 18th-century maps, was unearthed as a result of building construction initiated by the General Services Administration (GSA), a federal agency. Members of New York's African-American community protested the excavation of the site, and pressure mounted by this group and other concerned citizens eventually brought the plight of this historic cemetery to the attention of Congress, who temporarily halted excavation in July, 1992. The remains were recovered and subsequently transferred to Howard University in Washington, DC. Call for information on touring the site. See also listing under *Heritage Tours.*

Apollo Theater, 253 West 125th Street, Manhattan, ☎ 212-749-5838. The historic Apollo Theater has been recognized as an African-American landmark since the 1930s. African-American actors and performers demonstrated their talents to audiences here when other outlets were unavailable to them. Music giants such as Duke Ellington, Count Basie, Charlie Parker, Bessie Smith, and Billie Holiday have all performed on the stage of the Apollo Theater. Legendary comedians such as Bill Cosby, Richard Pryor, Redd Foxx and many others have also entertained here. Apollo showcases a popular "Amateur Night" for promising African-American performers. Tours available Mon-Sat, by appointment only. Admission charge.

The Apollo Theater
© NYCVB

Claude McKay Former Home, 180 West 135th Street. Former home of African-American Harlem Renaissance writer. Not open to the public.

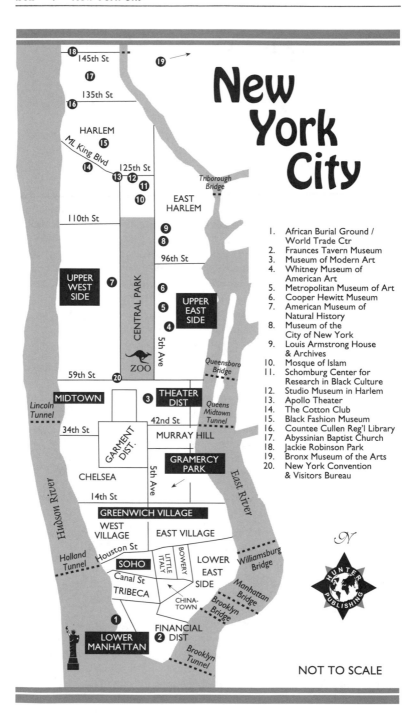

New York City

1. African Burial Ground / World Trade Ctr
2. Fraunces Tavern Museum
3. Museum of Modern Art
4. Whitney Museum of American Art
5. Metropolitan Museum of Art
6. Cooper Hewitt Museum
7. American Museum of Natural History
8. Museum of the City of New York
9. Louis Armstrong House & Archives
10. Mosque of Islam
11. Schomburg Center for Research in Black Culture
12. Studio Museum in Harlem
13. Apollo Theater
14. The Cotton Club
15. Black Fashion Museum
16. Countee Cullen Reg'l Library
17. Abyssinian Baptist Church
18. Jackie Robinson Park
19. Bronx Museum of the Arts
20. New York Convention & Visitors Bureau

NOT TO SCALE

Countee Cullen Regional Library, New York Public Library, 104 West 136th Street, ☎ 212-491-2070. Named in honor of prominent African-American poet Countee Cullen, from the Harlem Renaissance era of the 1920s and 1930s. The library houses the James Weldon Johnson Reference Collection for children. Mon-Tues, 10 am-4 pm; Wed, noon-8 pm; Thurs-Fri, noon-6 pm; Sat, 10 am-5 pm.

Dunbar Apartments, West 149th and 150th streets, Harlem, between Frederick Douglass Blvd and Adam Clayton Powell, Jr. Blvd. Among the famous African-Americans who have lived here are Bill "Bojangles" Robinson, Paul Robeson, W.E.B. DuBois, Countee Cullen, and Matthew A. Henson, who co-discovered the North Pole with Admiral Peary and A. Phillip Randolph. The complex was originally built for African-Americans and was financed by John D. Rockefeller, Jr.; it was named after African-American poet Paul Laurence Dunbar.

Harlem YMCA Theater Stage, 188 West 135th Street, ☎ 212-281-4100. James Earl Jones, Cicely Tyson, Ester Rolle, Isabel Sanford, Roscoe Lee Brown, Alvin Ailey, Glynn Turman, Calvin Lockhart and others have all performed on this stage at one time or another. YMCA hours, Mon-Fri, 6 am-10 pm; Sat, 6 am-6 pm.

Jackie Robinson Park, West 145th to 155th. Named in honor of the legendary baseball great, the park has a pool, basketball and volleyball courts, softball field, playground and recreational park.

James Weldon Johnson Home, 187 West 135th Street. Weldon was an African-American writer during the Harlem Renaissance era, professor at Fisk University and diplomat. He edited the *Book of Negro Spirituals* and wrote the popular poem, *God's Trombones*. He was honored with the Springarn Medal for Literature in 1925. Not open to the public.

Langston Hughes Home, 20 East 120th Street, Harlem. Known for his works, *The Weary Blues, The Ways of White Folks* and *Fine Clothes to the Jew*, African-American Harlem Renaissance writer Langston Hughes lived in this three-story Italian-style brownstone, which was built in 1869. Not open to the public.

Louis Armstrong House and Archives, 34-56 107th Street, ☎ 718-478-8274. Trumpeter and vocalist Louis "Satchmo" Armstrong and his wife, Lucille, purchased this modest house in the working-class neighborhood of Corona, Queens in 1943. They lived there together until Louis passed away in 1971; it remained Lucille's home until her death in 1983. The house was declared a National Historic Landmark in 1977 and a City of New York landmark in 1983. The archives include tapes, scrapbooks, photographs, music manuscripts, personal papers, trumpets and mouthpieces, books, journals and awards and plaques. Archives are located in the Rosenthal Library at Queens

College. Call for house tour hours. For information on the archives, ☎ 718-997-3670.

Malcolm Shabazz Masjid (Mosque of Islam), 116th and Lenox Ave. The East Coast headquarters for the Black Moslem Faith, named in honor of Malcolm X.

Marcus Garvey Memorial Park, 120th to 124th streets, between Mount Morris Park West and Madison Ave. Garvey was leader of the Universal Improvement Association (UNIA) during the early 1900s. The UNIA promoted African-American solidarity.

The Schomburg Center for Research in African-American Culture
Photo courtesy of the Schomburg Center

Schomburg Center for Research in African-American Culture, New York Public Library, 515 Malcolm X Blvd, ☎ 212-491-2200. Web site: www. nypl.org/research/sc/sc.html. The Schomberg Center provides access to research on the history and culture of people of African descent throughout the world. Its general reference collections range from literary masterworks by African-American authors to the US Federal Population Census (1790-1900). The Center won international acclaim in 1926 when the personal collection of distinguished African-American scholar and bibliophile Arthur A. Schomburg was added to the Division of Negro Literature, History and Prints of the 135th Street branch of the New York Public Library. Schomburg's collection includes over 5,000 volumes, 3,000 manuscripts, 2,000 etchings and paintings and several thousand pamphlets. He served as curator of the Negro Division from 1932 until his death in 1938.

Striver's Row at West 137th and 139th streets, between Adam Clayton Powell and Frederick Douglass. This district was once a popular neighborhood for such artists as W.C. Handy, Eubie Blake, Father Divine and others who were striving for recognition during the early 20th century. The townhouses along the street were once the homes of wealthy white families during the late 1800s until African-Americans moved in.

Sites Beyond New York City

Madame Walker Home, Villa Lewaro. Take US 9 north from Manhattan; the marker is on North Broadway in Irvington. The home of African-American millionaire and beauty-aid entrepreneur Madame Walker has been designated a National Historic Site. African-American architect Vertner Woodson Tandy designed the home. Not open to the public.

Harriet Tubman Home, 180 South Street, Auburn, ☎ 315-252-2081. This restored building was the home of Harriet Tubman during her numerous trips from Eastern Canada to the US East Coast. By appointment only.

Museums/Exhibits

Abyssinian Baptist Church, 132 West 138th Street, Harlem, ☎ 212-862-7474. In the early 1800s, Thomas Paul began establishing independent African-American Baptist churches throughout the US. Paul formed the Abyssinian Baptist Church in 1808. The church moved to its present location in 1921 and was built of New York bluestone in a Gothic design. The church has one of the largest African-American congregations in the US. Adam Clayton Powell, Jr. was once a prominent leader in this church. Artifacts and other memorabilia are contained in a small museum in the basement. Call for hours.

African Arts Cultural Center, 2191 Adam Clayton Powell, Jr. Blvd at 125th Street, Harlem, ☎ 212-996-3333. This African arts center houses more than 2,000 African artifacts and 1,000 paintings and sculptures. Open daily 9 am-5 pm. Free admission; charge for large groups.

African-American Museum, 110 North Franklin, Hempstead, ☎ 516-572-0730. The African-American Museum focuses on the historical contributions made by African-American Long Islanders. Displays include photos and special exhibits from the Smithsonian Institute. Thurs-Sat, 9 am-4:45 pm; Sun, 1 pm-4:45 pm; closed Mon-Wed.

The Abyssinian Baptist Church
Courtesy New York Convention & Visitors Bureau

American Museum of Natural History, Central Park West at 79th Street, Midtown Manhattan, ☎ 212-769-5000. Exhibits show various aspects of African family life, religion, music, culture and its diverse social systems. The museum's "Hall of African Peoples" exhibit features four distinct environments: desert, rainforest, grasslands and river valleys. Open daily, 10 am-5:45 pm; Wed, Fri-Sat, until 9 pm. Admission charge.

Black Fashion Museum, 157 West 126th Street, Harlem, ☎ 212-666-1320. The works of several African-American dress designers are displayed at this museum. Memorabilia, photographs and finished products from the late 19th century to the 20th century are presented. Mon-Fri, noon-8 pm by appointment. Tours available with 24-hour notice. Donation suggested.

Bronx Museum of the Arts, 1040 Grand Concourse, Bronx, ☎ 718-681-6000. Houses an extensive collection of works by noted African-American artist Romare Bearden. Sat-Thurs, 10 am-4:30 pm; Sun, 11 am-4:30 pm; closed Fri. Admission charge.

Cooper Hewitt Museum, 2 East 91st Street, ☎ 212-860-6868. This Smithsonian Institute National Museum of Design collection features African Kente cloth, raffia cloth, a Zulu basket and other samples from Africa. Tues, 10 am-9 pm; Wed-Sat, 10 am-5 pm; Sun, noon-5 pm.

Fraunces Tavern Museum, 54 Pearl Street, Lower Manhattan, ☎ 212-425-1778, Ext.3. This tavern was owned by Samuel Fraunces, a tavern-keeper of African-American and French descent. He purchased the property in 1762. It became one of the finest dining and drinking establishments in New York City and was a popular gathering spot for merchants and traders. It was frequented by General George Washington and other revolutionaries. Guided tours available. Mon-Fri, 10 am-4:45 pm; Sat-Sun, noon-4 pm. Admission charge.

Harlem African Wax Museum, 316 W 115th Street, Harlem, ☎ 212-678-7818. Web site: www.cato.ilt.columbia.edu/harlemlive/waxmuseum/. This unique wax museum features likenesses of prominent African-Americans, including Dr. Martin Luther King, Jr. Open by appointment only. Admission charge.

Metropolitan Museum of Art, 1000 Fifth Ave, ☎ 212-570-3930. Among the museum's collections of contemporary artists are works by 19th-century African-American artists such as Horace Pippin, Jacob Lawrence, Romare Bearden, Richmond Barthe and Gordon Parks. In the Mertens Gallery, the Crosby Brown Collection of Musical Instruments includes an extensive display of rare and unusual African musical instruments. Sun and Tues-Thurs, 9:30 am-5:15 pm; Fri-Sat, 9:30 am-8:45 pm. Admission charge.

Museum of the City of New York, 1220 Fifth Ave, ☎ 212-534-1672. Among its collection of New York City memorabilia are items of African-American performers, musicians and history. Tues-Sat, 10 am-5 pm; Sun, 1 pm-5 pm. Admission charge.

Museum of Modern Art, 11 West 53rd Street, ☎ 212-708-9400. Several art pieces by social-protest artist Jacob Lawrence are displayed here, as well as drawings, paintings, prints, photographs and sculptures by other African-American artists. Fri-Tues, 11 am-6 pm; Thurs, 11 am-9 pm; closed Wed. Admission charge.

Raven Chanticleer African-American Wax Museum of Harlem, 316 West 115th Street, Harlem, ☎ 212-678-7818. One of the most remarkable wax museums for African-Americans, the "Raven" was founded in 1989 and contains outstanding wax figures of Malcolm X, Dr. Martin Luther King, Jr. and many others. Tues-Sun, 1 pm-6 pm. Donation suggested.

Studio Museum in Harlem, 144 West 125th Street (between Lenox Ave and Adam Clayton Powell Jr. Blvd), ☎ 212-864-4500, fax 212-666-5753. This fine arts museum located in historic Harlem houses over 1,500 objects from 19th- and 20th-century African, African-American, and Caribbean artists. Works include paintings, artifacts and sculptures by artists such as Romare Bearden, Elizabeth Catlett, Robert Colescott, Melvin Edwards, Sam Gilliam, Jacob Lawrence, Alvin Loving, Howardena Pindell, Faith Ringgold, Betye Saar and others. Founded in 1967, the museum's mission is to collect, document, and interpret the art and artifacts of African-Americans and the African diaspora. Wed-Fri, 10 am-5 pm; Sat-Sun, 1 pm-6 pm. Admission charge.

Whitney Museum of American Art, 945 Madison Ave, ☎ 212-570-3600. Works by African-American artists Jacob Lawrence, Charles White and Richmond Barthe are part of the permanent collection here. Wed-Sat, 11 am-5 pm; Tues, 1 pm-8 pm; Sun, noon-5 pm. Admission charge.

Historic Colleges & Universities

City University of New York, Medgar Evers College, 1650 Bedford Ave, Brooklyn, NY 11225, ☎ 718-270-6024. Four-year state-supported college. Founded in 1969.

Shopping

Galleries & Specialty Shops

Adam Clayton Powell, Jr. Gallery, 163 West 125th Street, Second Floor of State Office Building, Harlem, ☎ 212-749-5298 or 212-873-5040. Minority artists, known and unknown, are represented at this gallery, which features paintings, sculptures and photography. Mon-Fri, noon-3 pm.

African Goods, Alemmasha Desta, 611 Vanderbilt, Brooklyn, ☎ 718-622-7989. African arts and crafts, carvings, masks, hats, beads, Kente cloth, jewelry, stickers, posters, canes, belts and other gift items. Mon-Thurs, 10:30 am-7 pm; Fri-Sat, 11 am-7:30 pm.

African Paradise, 27 West 125th Street, Manhattan, ☎ 212-410-5294, Mon-Sat, 10 am-7:30 pm; Sun, noon-6:30 pm.

Afriworks, 2035 Fifth Ave, National Black Theater Complex, Manhattan, ☎ 212-876-1447. This gallery houses numerous works representing African and African-American art and culture. Afriworks features original paintings, limited editions, sculptures, fine prints and posters. Mon-Tues, 11 am-6:30 pm; Wed-Fri, 11 am-7 pm; Sat, 10 am-7:30 pm; Sun, noon-6:30 pm.

Anita's Gift Emporium, 159-15 Jamaica Ave, Jamaica, ☎ 718-525-0811. Afrocentric products, accessories, favors, brooms, collages, unique cultural giftware, crafts. Mon-Sat, 9 am-5 pm.

Beads of Paradise, 16 East 17th Street, Manhattan, ☎ 212-620-0642. Specializing in ancient and modern beads, jewelry and African cloth. They also feature the Richard Meyer African Art Gallery. Mon-Sat, 11 am-7 pm; Sun, noon-6 pm.

Clinton Hill Simply Art and Framing Gallery, 583 Myrtle Ave, Brooklyn, ☎ 718-857-0074. Specializing in African-American, Caribbean, Southwestern and Latin-American fine art, reproductions and posters. Thurs-Sun, 10 am-7 pm.

Craft Caravan, Inc., 63 Greene Street, Manhattan, ☎ 212-431-6669. Specializes in traditional tribal objects, ethnic beads, furniture, textiles and utilitarian objects. Mon-Fri, 10 am-6 pm; Sat-Sun, 11 am-6 pm.

Doc's Antiques, 490 Atlantic Ave, Brooklyn, ☎ 718- 858-6903. This unusual antique store has something for everyone. It features a wide collection of Black memorabilia, photos of the Tuskegee Airmen and of Spelman College graduates from the 1800s. Call for store hours.

Elite Boutique, 2469 Adam Clayton Powell, Jr., Blvd, Manhattan, ☎ 212-234-1700. Specializing in Afrocentric artifacts, black figurines, collectibles, clothing, dolls, limited edition prints and posters, magnets, plaques and more. Mon-Sat, 11 am-7 pm.

Exotic Fragrances, Inc., 1490 Lexington Ave, Manhattan, ☎ 212-410-0600. Over 300 uncut fragrances, including oils, lotions, incense and bath fragrance items.

Family Store, 327 Atlantic Ave, Brooklyn, ☎ 718-488-9531. This Afrocentric store features black cameos, designer kente cloth fashions, gourds from Ghana, wooden sculptures and other high quality African items. The loft above the store regularly features poetry readings and jazz concerts. Tues-Sat, 11 am-7 pm; Sun, noon-6 pm; closed Mon.

Gallery M, 123 West 135th Street, Harlem, ☎ 212-234-4106. Features rotating exhibitions representing African-American artists. Call for current exhibition and schedule. Wed, noon-3 pm; Thurs & Fri, 1 pm-3 pm; Sat, 2 pm-4 pm.

Grinnell Gallery, 800 Riverside Drive, at 158th Street, #5E, Harlem, ☎ 212-927-7941. The Grinnell Gallery features works by African-American and Caribbean artists, photographers and sculptors. Open by appointment only.

New York City

Heritage Collection, 9 Fifth Ave, Manhattan, ☎ 800-969-5698. Afrocentric framed art, cards, gift wrapping, and "all occasion" novelties. Mon-Fri, 9 am-5:30 pm.

House of A Million Earrings, 169-17 Jamaica Ave, Queens, ☎ 718-297-7950. African earrings. Mon-Sat, 8 am-6 pm.

Isis & Associates, Mart 125, 260 West 125th Street, Harlem, ☎ 212-316-3680. Items of African culture, including books, greeting cards, gifts, dolls, videos and games. Mon-Tues, 10 am-6:30 pm; Wed-Sat, 10 am-7:30 pm; Sun, noon-5 pm.

Kenkelaba Gallery, 214 East Second Street, Manhattan, ☎ 212-674-3939. African and African-American art. Features sculptures, paintings and much more. Wed-Sat, 11 am-6 pm.

Korner Stop, 607 Fulton Ave, Hempstead, ☎ 516-485-4952.

Lady Alma's Card and Gift Boutique, 586 Nostrand Ave, Brooklyn, ☎ 718-789-1905.

Le Jardin Cultural, 225-09 Linden Blvd, Queens, ☎ 718-712-9377, fax 718-528-1799. Fine Haitian art. Representing Haitian artists, Le Jardin Cultural ("the cultural garden") specializes in works from the 1940s to the present. It includes original oils, acrylics and watercolor paintings, and arts and crafts. Mon-Fri, 10 am-7 pm; Sat, 10 am-6 pm; Sun by appointment.

Lewis Gallery, 525 Atlantic Ave, Brooklyn, ☎ 718-624-8372, fax 718-694-9865. Web site: www.blackarts.com. African-American fine art and custom framing. The Lewis Gallery represents original works by local and national artists. They also feature limited editions, mini prints, note cards and an extensive gift line. The gallery sponsors the Annual African-American Art Expo in New York City. Mon, Thurs & Sat, 10 am-8 pm; Sun, noon-5 pm.

Mehu Gallery, 21 West 100th Street, Harlem, ☎ 212-222-3334. Features a remarkable collection of Haitian, Caribbean and African-American artists, such as Dindga McCannon, Romare Bearden and Ademola. Tues-Fri, 11 am-3 pm and 4 pm-7 pm; Sat-Sun, noon-5 pm.

Original Peoples Culture Shop, 199-19 Murdock Ave, St. Albans, ☎ 718-464-6656. Afrocentric clothing, greeting cards and jewelry. Mon-Sat, 10 am-7 pm.

African Riches Treasures Gallery, 1211 Grand Ave, Baldwin, ☎ 516-481-5642. African and African-American art: prints, limited editions, artifacts, sculptures, masks and much more. Mon-Sat, 11 am-7 pm; Sun, noon-5 pm.

Savacou, 240 East 13th Street, Manhattan, ☎ 212-473-6904. African-American art and gift items. Tues-Sat, 10 am-6 pm.

Bookstores

A & B Bookstores, 149 Lauren Street, Brooklyn, ☎ 718-596-0872. African-American fiction and non-fiction books. Mon-Fri, 9:30 am-7 pm.

As-Suq Booksellers, 98 Smith Street, Brooklyn, ☎ 718-596-9390. Among their general interest collection, As-Suq sells African-American fiction and non-fiction books. Mon-Sat, 9 am-7 pm; Sun, noon-5 pm.

Afrikan Bookstreet, 177 Jamaica Ave, Queens, ☎ 718-206-1511. Afrocentric combination bookstore and specialty braids shop. Mon-Fri, 9 am-7 pm; Sat-Sun, 10 am-7 pm.

Awareness Communications Bookstores/MEC, 1150 Carroll Street, #208, Brooklyn, ☎ 718-270-6409. African-American literature. Mon-Sat, 9 am-6 pm.

Bestseller Bookstore, 43A Main Street, Hempstead, ☎ 516-564-5103. Mon-Sat, 10 am-6 pm.

Black Books Plus, Inc., 702 Amsterdam Ave (West 94th Street), Manhattan, ☎ 212-749-9632, fax 212-491-2234. African-American, books, greeting cards, cameos, gift items. Tues, Wed, Fri, 11 am-6 pm; Thurs, 11 am-7 pm; Sat, 11 am-5 pm.

Briscoe Brown Books, 3907 Dyre Ave, Bronx, ☎ 718-325-0543. African-American fiction and non-fiction books. Mon-Sat, 10 am-7 pm.

D & J Book Distributors, 229-21B Merrick Blvd, Queens, ☎ 718-949-5400. African-American books. Mon-Sat, 10 am-7 pm.

Dare Books, 33 Lafayette Ave, Brooklyn, ☎ 718-625-4651. African-American books. Mon-Fri, 9:30 am-6:30 pm; Sat, 10 am-6 pm.

Isis & Associates, Mart 125, 210 West 125th Street, Manhattan, ☎ 212-316-3680. African-American books. Mon-Tues, 10 am-6:30 pm; Wed-Thurs, 10 am-7:30 pm; Sun, noon-5 pm.

Maranatha Christian Bookstores, Inc., 11 Flatbush Ave, Brooklyn, ☎ 718-875-2083. Mon-Sat, 9 am-6 pm.

Nkiru Books, 76 St. Marks (Park Slopes), Brooklyn, ☎ 718-783-6306. Multicultural bookstore. African, African-American, Latin American, Native American, Caribbean and bilingual books. Mon, Tues, Wed & Sat, 11 am-7 pm; Thurs-Fri, 11 am-6 pm; Sun, noon-5 pm.

Fashions

4W Circle of Art & Enterprise, 704 Fulton Street, Brooklyn, ☎ 718-875-6500. This fine men's and women's clothing store features styles created by African-American designers Brenda Brunson-Bey, Mesura and Woza

Cephas, Shaka King and Bunn and Lipps. Mon-Sat, 11 am-9 pm; Sun noon-7 pm.

A & J Jackson Family Boutiques, 260 West 125th Street, Manhattan, ☎ 212-932-0354. African and African-American custom-designed clothing for men, women and children, and accessories. Mon-Sat, 10 am-6:30 pm.

Ashanti, 872 Lexington Ave, ☎ 212-535-0740. Contemporary women's clothing store that specializes in sizes 14 and up. Mon-Sat, 10 am-6 pm; Thurs, 10 am-8 pm.

Body Essentials, 2529 Adam Clayton Powell, Jr. Blvd, Manhattan, ☎ 212-926-8860. Women's lingerie. Mon-Sat, 11 am-8 pm; Sun, 9 am-1 pm.

Chris Creations, 645 Vanderbilt Ave, Brooklyn, ☎ 718-783-6420. African and African-American custom-designed clothing for men, women and children, and accessories. Tues-Sat, noon-7:30 pm.

Gourd Chips, 394 Atlantic Ave (near Bond Street), Brooklyn, ☎ 718-797-2739 or 718-797-5236. African-American women's clothing and accessories, wearable art, unique fashions, silver jewelry, girlfriend pins, ear robes and earrings, trunk shows. Tues-Sat, 1 pm-7 pm.

Spike's Joint West, 1 South Elliott Place, Brooklyn, ☎ 718-802-1000. Apparel related to Spike Lee films, as well as other caps, books, mugs, T-shirts, postcards and jackets. Mon-Fri, noon-7 pm; Sat, 10 am-7 pm.

Restaurants

◆ African

Demu Café, 773 Fulton, Brooklyn, ☎ 718-875-8484. Nigerian cuisine. Vegetarian and meat entrées. Mon-Fri, 11 am-midnight; Sat-Sun, 11 pm-midnight.

Joloff Restaurant, 930 Fulton Street, Brooklyn, ☎ 718-636-4011. West African cuisine. Vegetarian and meat dishes. Mon-Sat, noon-11 pm; Sun, noon-10 pm.

Koryoe Restaurant, 3143 Broadway, Harlem, ☎ 212-316-2950. Features foods from Ghana, the Ivory Coast, Nigeria, Senegal, Sierre-Leone and others. Open for breakfast, lunch and dinner. Mon-Thurs, 7 am-11 pm; Fri-Sat, 7 am-2 am; Sun, 11 am-6 pm.

Kuer N' Deye, 737 Fulton, Brooklyn, ☎ 718- 875-4937. Senegalese cuisine. Specialties include vegetarian and meat dishes. Tue-Sun, noon-10:30 pm.

Massawa Ethiopian and Eritrean Restaurant, 1239 Amsterdam Ave, Harlem, ☎ 212-663-0505 or 212-663-0545. Features hot and spicy meals from East Africa and specializes in delicious chicken, beef, lamb and vegetable entrées. Open daily, noon-midnight.

Zula Restaurant, 1260 Amsterdam Ave, ☎ 212-663-1670. Ethiopian cuisine. Features spicy traditional African entrées. Mon-Sun, noon-midnight.

◆ Barbeque

Rib Shack, 157-06 Linden Blvd, Queens, ☎ 718-659-7000. Soul food/Southern cuisine. Specializes in pork and beef entrées, sandwiches and trimmings. Sun-Thurs, 11 am-11:30 pm; Fri-Sat, 11 am-midnight.

◆ Caribbean

Bambou, 243 E 14th Street, New York, ☎ 212-358-0012. Caribbean cuisine. Their specialty is "bambou," which consists of shrimp and crab cakes. Mon-Sat, 6 pm-11 pm; closed Sun.

Brawta Caribbean Café, 347 Atlantic Ave, Brooklyn, ☎ 718-855-5515. Mon-Thurs, noon-11 pm. Fri-Sat, noon-11:30 pm. Sun, noon-10:30 pm. Featured in past issues of *The New York Times* and *New York Daily News*.

Caribe, 117 Perry Street, Manhattan, ☎ 212-255-9191. West Indian and Spanish cuisine. Sun-Thurs, 11 am-11 pm; Fri-Sat, 11 am-12:30 am.

Daphne's Caribbean Express, 233 E 14th Street, New York, ☎ 212-228-6144. Jamaican cuisine; specializes in a creative mixture of Eastern Caribbean and American soul food dishes. Open for lunch and dinner; Mon-Sat, 11 am-10 pm; closed Sun.

Day-O, 103 Greenwich Ave, Manhattan, ☎ 212-924-3161. Caribbean cuisine. Curried goat, drinks, Day-O punch. Sunday brunch buffet. Sun-Fri, 3 pm-3 am; Mon-Thurs, 3 pm-11 pm.

Foods For You, 3322 Church Ave, Brooklyn, ☎ 718-282-2261. Caribbean and Halal. Mon-Wed, 11 am-10 pm; Tues-Sat, 11 am-10:30 pm.

Island Spice, 402 W 44th Street, New York, ☎ 212-765-1737. Caribbean cuisine, featuring jerk chicken, oxtails, curried goat, Bajan kingfish, red snapper, and tropical drinks. Serves lunch and dinner. Mon-Fri, noon-11 pm; Sat, 4 pm-midnight.

Island Sunday Restaurant, 547 Malcolm X Blvd, Manhattan, ☎ 212-283-7575. Traditional Caribbean cuisine.

Jamaican Hot Pot, 2260 Adam Clayton Powell, Jr. Blvd, Harlem, ☎ 212-491-5270. This Caribbean-style restaurant features Jamaican fried fish, curried goat and oxtail and, of course, rice and peas. Sun-Thurs, noon-1 am; Fri-Sat, noon-2 am.

Jeans, 188-36 Linden Blvd, St. Albans, ☎ 718-525-3069. West Indian Cuisine. Mon-Sat, 7 am-11 pm.

Jenille's, 163-17 Archer Ave, Jamaica, ☎ 718-657-8640. West Indian, Chinese and American cuisine. Mon-Thurs, 11 am-11 pm; Fri-Sat, 11 am-2 am; Sun, noon-11 pm. Live Deejay Fri & Sat nights.

New York City

La Dentente, 23-04 94th Street, Jackson Heights, ☎ 800-540-8598 or 212-458-2172. Caribbean, Southern and continental cuisine. Open daily, live rhythm and blues entertainment nightly. Free parking two blocks south of LaGuardia Airport.

Mike's International Restaurant, 552 Flatbush Ave, Brooklyn, ☎ 718-856-7034. Specializes in Jamaican cuisine. Mon-Tues, 9 am-11 pm; Thurs-Sat, 9 am-midnight.

Negril's, 362 West 23rd Street, Manhattan, ☎ 212-807-6411. Caribbean cuisine. Sun-Thurs, 11 am-midnight; Fri-Sat, 11 am-4 am.

Oscar's Restaurant, 41 Remsen Ave, Brooklyn, ☎ 718-774-0500. Jamaican cuisine. Mon-Thurs, 10-10; Fri-Sat, 10 am-midnight; Sun, 10 am-9 pm.

Pepper's, 349 Broadway, ☎ 212-343-2824. Traditional West Indian cuisine. Mon, 10:30 am-8 pm; Tues-Wed, 10:30 am-11 pm; Thurs, 10:30 am-11 pm; Sat-Sun, 10:30 am-10 pm.

Planet One, 76 East 7th Street, Manhattan, ☎ 212-475-0112. Vegetarian Jamaican patties and soft coconut rice. Sun-Sat, noon-midnight.

Sprinkles, 466 Myrtle Ave, Brooklyn, ☎ 718-399-3085. Jamaican-American cuisine. Mon-Thurs, 11 am-11:30 pm; Fri-Sat, 11:30 am-midnight.

Tummy Paradise Caribbean Cuisine, 932 Utica Ave, Brooklyn, ☎ 718-282-5100. Caribbean cuisine, specializing in jerk chicken, jerk pork, seafood, West Indian entrées and tropical juices. Open all night Sat until Sun at 10 pm.

Vernon's Jerk Paradise, 252 West 29th Street, Manhattan, ☎ 212-268-7020. Caribbean cuisine. Specializes in jerk pork and chicken, curried goat and lunch specials. Mon-Sat, 11 am-11:30 pm.

◆ Soul Food

22 West, 22 West 135th Street, Harlem, ☎ 212-862-7770. Features traditional soul food items such as pig's feet, ham hocks, oxtails, chicken livers, fried chicken and more. Open for breakfast, lunch and dinner. Mon-Sun, 8 am-1 am.

Caroline Creek, 87 Utica, Brooklyn, ☎ 718-493-5907. Soul food cuisine. Specializes in fish and chips, fried shrimp, crab, ribs and chicken. Tues-Wed, 11 am-9 pm; Thurs, 11 am-10 pm; Fri-Sat, 11 am-midnight.

Copeland's Café and Restaurant, 547 West 145th Street, Harlem, ☎ 212-234-2357. Offers a wide variety of favorites at a popular chic spot, featuring Creole dishes, Southern oxtails, corn fritters and shrimp gumbo. Mon-Sun, 11:30 am-11 pm; Sun brunch, 11:30 am-3 pm.

Emily's, 1325 Fifth Ave, ☎ 212-996-1212. Southern/soul food. Mon-Thurs, 8 am-11 pm; Fri-Sat, 8 am-midnight; Sun, 8 am-9 pm.

Jezebel's, 630 9th Ave, Manhattan, ☎ 212-582-1045. Soul food/Southern cuisine. Specializes in Southern fried chicken, shrimp Creole and filet mignon.

Mon-Wed, 5:30 pm-10:30 pm; Thurs-Sat, 5:30-11:45 pm. Reservations required.

Kettle Pot, 446-A Dean Street, Brooklyn, ☎ 718-230-4047. Soul food to go.

Keur N' Deye, 737 Fulton Street, Brooklyn, ☎ 718-875-4937. Traditional soul food. Tues-Sun, noon-10:30 pm.

M & G Diner, 383 West 125th Street, Manhattan, ☎ 212-864-7326. Variety of soul food items, Southern fried chicken, collard greens. Quoted in *The New York Times* as having "Real Soul Food." Open 24 hours, seven days a week.

Mekka, 14 Ave A Street, Manhattan, ☎ 212-475-8500. Mon-Wed, 6 pm-1 am; Thurs, 6 pm-2 am; Fri- Sat, 6 pm-4 am.

Mityfine Restaurant, 24 West 125th Street, Manhattan, ☎ 212-348-4848. Traditional soul food. Mon-Sat, 8 am-8 pm.

Pink Tea Cup, 42 Grove, Manhattan, ☎ 212-807-6755. Soul food/Southern cuisine. Mon-Thurs, 8 am-midnight; Fri-Sat, 8 am-1 am.

Rencher's Crab Inn, 407 Myrtle Ave, Brooklyn, ☎ 718-403-0944. Traditional soul food. Sun-Wed, 1 pm-9 pm; Thurs, 1 pm-11 pm; Fri-Sat, noon-midnight.

Royston's Rhythm, 63 Lafayette Ave, Brooklyn, ☎ 718-243-0900. Cajun, Creole and Southern cuisine. Royston's is also a jazz club and showcases big-name acts at least once a month at their Friday after-work parties. Food service, Mon-Fri, 11:30-midnight; appetizers til 3 am; bar until 4 am.

Sapadillo Café, 412 Myrtle, Brooklyn, ☎ 718-797-1213. Soul food, Cajun and New Orleans cuisine. Tues-Thurs, noon-10 pm; Fri-Sat, noon-11 pm. Closed Mon.

Shirley's Soul Food, 2900 Frederick Douglass Blvd, Harlem, ☎ 212-283-8712. Open for breakfast, lunch and dinner, this friendly soul food establishment features turkey wings, chitterlings, black-eyed peas, collard greens and other favorites. Tues-Sat, 7:30 am-7:30 pm.

Soul Fixings, 371 West 34th Street, Manhattan, ☎ 212-736-1345. Specializing in fish and barbecue entrées, chicken and ribs. Mon-Fri, 11 am-10 pm; closed Sat-Sun.

Sugarhill's Supper Club, 609-615 Dekalb Ave, Brooklyn, ☎ 718-797-1727. Soul food/Southern cuisine. A great place for networking after hours. Live entertainment. Weekends open around the clock; Mon-Wed, 7 am-9 pm.

Sylvia's, 328 Malcolm X Blvd (Lenox Ave), Harlem, ☎ 212-996-0660. A very popular Harlem restaurant, Sylvia's has been serving traditional Southern home-cooked meals for more than 30 years. Open for breakfast, lunch and dinner. Mon-Sat, 7:30 am-10:30 pm; Sun, 1 pm-7 pm.

Table Top, 171 Einstein Loop, Bronx, ☎ 718-671-6290. Soul food/Southern cuisine. Tues-Sat, 8-9:30.

New York City

Two Steps Down, 240 Dekalb, Brooklyn, ☎ 718-399-2020. Soul food/Southern cuisine, featuring seafood entrées. Wed-Sun, 5 pm-11:30 pm; Sunday brunch, 11:30 am-3 pm.

Well's, 2247 Adam Clayton Powell Blvd, Harlem, ☎ 212-234-0700. Traditional soul food, barbecue ribs, ham, collard greens and other favorites, and their famous "Chicken and Waffles." Harlem's landmark jazz supper club. Sun-Thurs, 11 am-2 am; Fri-Sat, 11 am-4 am.

Entertainment

◆ Music

Café Wha, 115 Macdougal, ☎ 212-254-3706. Brazilian music.

◆ Dance Nightclubs

2 Potatoes, 143 Christopher Street, Manhattan, ☎ 212-255-0286. Live music. R&B, jazz.

Act III, 4415 White Plains Rd, the Bronx, ☎ 718-994-4510. Reggae, R&B, soul and calypso.

Bentley's, 25 East 40th Street, Manhattan, ☎ 212-684-2540. Dance nightclub. Reggae, hip-hop. Three levels of dance music, comedy and jazz. Dress code. Call for upcoming schedule.

Bowery Bar, 358 Bowery Street, Manhattan, ☎ 212-475-2220. Contemporary dance club and restaurant. Mon-Tues, groove; Thurs nights, a variety of music.

China Club, 2130 Broadway, Manhattan, ☎ 212-877-1166. Live contemporary R&B, hip-hop, reggae, jazz. 25-40 crowd. Monday nights are popular with local celebrities. Multiethnic crowd. Call for upcoming schedules.

Club Demarara, 215 West 28th Street, Manhattan, ☎ 212-643-1199. Reggae, R&B.

Club Vertigo, 27 West 20th Street, Manhattan, ☎ 212-366-4181. Reggae, R&B, hip-hop. House music on Saturdays.

Cotton Club, 656 West 125th Street, Manhattan, ☎ 212-663-7980. Popular dance nightclub.

Expo, 124 West 43rd Street, Manhattan, ☎ 212-819-0377. Reggae, hip-hop, house music and Latin. Call for upcoming schedules.

Nakisaki, 276 Fulton Ave, Hempstead, ☎ 516-292-9200. Reggae, hip-hop, calypso. Deejay.

The Cotton Club in Harlem
Courtesy New York Convention & Visitors Bureau

Shadows, 229 West 28th Street, Manhattan, ☎ 212-629-3331. Adults only. Strict dress code, and age requirements vary daily. Four rooms of jazz, dance, reggae, salsa, calypso and R&B classics. Thurs, 5 pm-1 am; Fri-Sat, 8 pm-1 am.

SOB's, 204 Varick Street, Manhattan, ☎ 212-242-4940. Jazz, dance, techno, reggae, hip-hop, alternative, R&B.

Soul Café, 444 West 42nd Street, Manhattan, ☎ 212-244-7685. R&B, hip-hop, jazz. Deejay.

System, 76 East 13th Street, Manhattan, ☎ 212-388-1060. Reggae, hip-hop. Wed-Sat. Sun nights, live Latin music.

Tunnel, 220 12th Ave, Manhattan, ☎ 212-695-4682. House music, hip-hop, techno, reggae.

Webster Hall, 145 East 11th Street, Manhattan, ☎ 212-353-1600. Four floors of dance music. Reggae, hip-hop, classics.

◆ Comedy Clubs

Apollo Theatre, 253 West 125th Street, Manhattan, ☎ 212-749-5838. Apollo showcases the popular "Amateur Night" for promising African-American performers.

◆ Jazz Clubs

Blue Note, 131 West 3rd Street, Manhattan, ☎ 212-475-8592. Jazz and other live acts.

Cotton Club, 656 West 125th Street, Manhattan, ☎ 800-640-7980. Jazz, blues and gospel nightclub. Historic landmark. Wed-Sat buffet dinners. Call for upcoming schedules.

Rooftop Café at B. Smith's, 771 8th Ave, Manhattan, ☎ 212-247-2222. Jazz.

Royston's Rhythm, 63 Lafayette Ave, Brooklyn, ☎ 718- 243-0900. Show-cases big-name acts at least once a month at their Friday after-work parties. See listing under *Soul Food* restaurants.

Showman's Café, 2321 8th Ave, Manhattan, ☎ 212-864-8941. Live contemporary and classic jazz. Restaurant. Call for upcoming schedule.

Sugarhill's Supper Club, 609-615 Dekalb Ave, Brooklyn, ☎ 718-797-1727. See their listing under *Soul Food* restaurants.

Tatou, 151 East 50th Street, Manhattan, ☎ 212-753-1144. Live jazz and dance nightclub. Call for upcoming schedule.

Lodging

Bed & Breakfasts

Akwaba Mansion, 347 McDonough Street, Brooklyn, NY 11218, ☎ 718-455-5958. This historic Tuscan villa was built in the 1860s and is located in the heart of the Stuyvesant Heights' landmark district of Bedford-Stuyvesant,

Brooklyn. The 18-room mansion has four distinctive guest bedrooms, a library, a TV and game room, and a glassed-in sun porch. A hearty Southern-style breakfast is served each morning on fine china, and guests are also treated with an afternoon tea. The Alwaaba Mansion has been featured in *The New York Times, Daily News* and *Black Enterprise Magazine*. Call for current rates and reservations.

White House Berries Inn, on Route 8, about 15 miles south of Utica in Bridgewater, NY 13313, ☎ 315-732-1963; restaurant, 315-822-6558. Built in a 19th-century Italian style, the Inn is a unique combination of Southern-style restaurant and charming Victorian-style bed and breakfast. The three guest rooms (open during weekends only) are decorated with 19th-century antiques, collectibles and Victorian-style furnishings. Weekend guests are served a full country-style breakfast. The restaurant is also open to the public on weekends. Local attractions include the beautiful Adirondack Mountains, Utica, Syracuse, many area colleges and universities and cultural events. Call for current rates and reservations.

Resorts

Hillside Inn, Rd 600, East Stroudsburg, 1½ hours from New York City. Off of Route 209, 1½ miles north of Marshalls Creek, Pennsylvania, ☎ 717-223-8238. Specializing in old-fashioned warmth, good food, personal service, Southern and Caribbean cuisine, family reunions, corporate retreats and weddings. Indoor heated pool, exercise room, hot spa, solarium, cocktail lounge, basketball, volleyball, softball, fishing, nine-hole par-3 golf course, tennis, nature trails, gift shop, game room, planned activities for children.

New York City

Travel Agents

Brown's Nationwide Travel, 89-40 164th Street, #2B, New York, NY 11432, ☎ 718-739-2255.

Budget Travel Bureau, 4243 White Plains Rd, New York, NY 10466, ☎ 718-994-9800. ITAS member.

CTC-VW Cruises & Tours, Inc., 135-47 225th Street, Laurelton, New York, NY 10034, ☎ 718-525-0173. Specializes in world cruises. ITAS member.

GiGi Travel, 799 Nostrand Ave, New York, NY 11225, ☎ 800-972-2351 or 718-778-8500. ITAS member.

Jamerica Travel and Tours, Inc., 2384 Adam Clayton Powell, Jr. Blvd, New York, NY 10030, ☎ 212-283-3366. Full service travel specialists, cruises, air, rail, hotels, packages, car rental, low fares.

Jem Travel/Gem Travel, 89-50 164th Street, #2B, New York, NY 11432, ☎ 718-723-8000.

Lakeview, USA, Inc., 419 Rose Ave, West Hempstead, NY 11552, ☎ 516-763-1800. ITAS member.

Leo Tours and Cruises, 1939 Third Ave, New York, NY 10029, ☎ 212-831-1169.

Our Gang Traveler, 1514 Fulton Street, Brooklyn, NY 11216, ☎ 888-5OURGANG, 201-763-3616, fax 201-763-3818. E-mail: argang@aol.com. Full-service travel agency. Ask for their newsletter.

Rainbow Travel, 377A Nassau Rd, Roosevelt, ☎ 516-378-9110. ITAS member.

Tradewinds Travel, 970 Wilson Blvd, Central Islip, ☎ 800-895-45552 or 516-234-4552. Cruise and tour specialists. African tours, group and individual cruises, family reunions, honeymoons.

Travel Clubs

Singles, Inc., c/o Corners of the World Travel, 117-02 Guy Brewer, Blvd, Second Floor, Jamaica, NY 11433, ☎ 718-978-4800, fax 718-978-1133. African-American singles travel organization.

Heritage Tours

African Burial Ground Project, Seneca Village, ☎ 212-432-5707. Call for tour information. For description, see listing under *Historic Sites & Landmarks.*

Harlem, Your Way, 129 West 130th Street, ☎ 212-906-1687. Go on a syncopated Champagne Safari to a Harlem cabaret, feast on a soulful breakfast at a Harlem church, clap hands to gospel music, and explore gorgeous brownstones on a customized tour planned by a Harlem-based organization that provides an insider's view of what it calls "the Black capital of the world." Call for tour rates and schedules.

Media

Radio

◆ Jazz

WAER 88.3 FM, 215 University Place, Syracuse, ☎ 315-443-4021. Public radio, jazz, news, sports.

◆ **Urban Contemporary**

WNJR 1430 AM, One Riverfront Plaza, #345, Newark, ☎ 201-642-8000. Ethnic format.

WRKS 98.7 FM, 1440 Broadway, ☎ 212-242-9870. Urban contemporary format.

Newspapers

New York Carib News, 15 West 39th Street, ☎ 212-944-1991. Tabloid newspaper with African-American orientation. Caribbean news and features. Distributed weekly on Wednesdays.

New York Voice, 75-43 Parsons Blvd, Flushing, ☎ 718-591-6600. African-American community newspaper. Distributed weekly on Fridays.

Publications

Big Black Book, Unlimited Creative Enterprises, Inc., PO 400476, Brooklyn, NY 11240-0476, ☎ 718-638-9675.

African-American Churches

AME

Allen Memorial AME, 944 Rogers Ave, Brooklyn, ☎ 718-282-7860.

Bethel AME, 52 West 132nd Street, Manhattan, ☎ 212-694-9420.

Bridge Street AME, 277 Stuyvesant Ave, Brooklyn, ☎ 718-452-3936.

Bright Temple AME, 812 Faile Street, Bronx, ☎ 718-542-7777.

Brown's Union AME, 384 East 155th Street, Bronx, ☎ 718-292-7480.

Brownsville AME Zion, 1593 East Manhattan Ave, Brooklyn, ☎ 718-385-4701.

Calvary AME, 790 Herkimer Street, Brooklyn, ☎ 718-467-0987.

Cosmopolitan AME, 39 West 190th Street, Bronx, ☎ 718-367-0612.

Ebenezer AME, 170 East 123rd Street, Manhattan, ☎ 212-348-8787.

Emanuel AME, 37 West 119th Street, Manhattan, ☎ 212-722-3969.

First AME Zion, 54 Macdonough Street, Brooklyn, ☎ 718-638-3343.

Greater Bethel AME, 32 West 123rd Street, Manhattan, ☎ 212-360-5004.

Greater St. James AME, 1158 Lenox Rd, Brooklyn, ☎ 718-495-9702.

Mother AME Zion, 140 West 137th Street, Manhattan, ☎ 212-234-1545.

Mother Walls AME Zion, 895 Home Street, Bronx, ☎ 718-542-9609.

MT Zion AME, 1765 Madison Ave, Manhattan, ☎ 212-289-9738.

Naomi AME Zion, 2502 Neptune Ave, Brooklyn, ☎ 718-266-1303.

St. James AME, 2010 5th Ave, Manhattan, ☎ 212-369-2020.

St. John AME, 132 West 134th Street, Manhattan, ☎ 212-281-2250.

St. Johns AME, 664 Halsey Street, Brooklyn, ☎ 718-574-8202.

St. Luke AME, 1872 153rd Amsterdam Ave, Manhattan, ☎ 212-283-9223.

St. Matthew's AME, 1788 Sedgwick Ave, Bronx, ☎ 718-583-7657.

St. Paul AME, 454 Essex Street, Brooklyn, ☎ 718-827-7277.

St. Peters AME Zion, 5 Greene Ave, Brooklyn, ☎ 718-855-0055.

St. Philips AME, 185 Ave B, Manhattan, ☎ 212-420-9351.

St. Stephen Community AME, 2139 8th Ave, Manhattan, ☎ 212-663-0693.

Trinity AME, 259 West 126th Street, Manhattan, ☎ 212-866-3303.

Turner Memorial AME, 104 West 131st Street, Manhattan, ☎ 212-283-7152.

Varick Memorial AME Zion, 806 Quincy Street, Brooklyn, ☎ 718-455-8907.

Williamsburg AME Zion, 40 Howard Ave, Brooklyn, ☎ 718-443-9157.

Woods Memorial AME Zion, 3124 Edson Ave, Bronx, ☎ 718-379-2109.

Baptist

Abyssinian Baptist Church, 132 West 132nd Street, Harlem, ☎ 212-862-7474.

Canaan Baptist Church, 132 West 116th Street, Harlem, ☎ 212-866-0301.

Metropolitan Baptist Church, 151 West 128th Street, Harlem, ☎ 212-663-8990.

Mount Olivet Baptist Church, 201 Malcolm X Blvd (Lenox Ave), ☎ 212-666-6899.

Mt. Calvary Baptist, 231-33 West 142nd Street, Manhattan, ☎ 212-234-1447.

Catholic

St. Charles Borremeo Roman Catholic, 211 West 41st Street, Manhattan, ☎ 212-281-0896.

COGIC

Church Of God In Christ, 15722 South Rd, Jamaica, ☎ 718-291-9281.

Beulah Church Of God In Christ, 956 Marcy Ave, Brooklyn, ☎ 718-783-9118.

Church Of God In Christ, 171 Reid Ave, Brooklyn, ☎ 718-453-8207.

Church Of God In Christ, 49 Kingston Ave, Brooklyn, ☎ 718-493-5723.

Church Of God In Christ Intl, 584 Myrtle Ave, Brooklyn, ☎ 718-622-2442.

Church Of God In Christ-Hill, 137 Buffalo Ave, Brooklyn, ☎ 718-773-3780.

First Church Of God In Christ, 210 Rogers Ave, Brooklyn, ☎ 718-756-8414.

First Church Of God In Christ, 15611 108th Ave, Brooklyn, ☎ 718-658-4176.

Episcopal

St. Andrew's Episcopal, 2067 5th Ave, Manhattan, ☎ 212-534-0896.

St. Martins Episcopal, 230 Malcolm X Blvd., ☎ 212-534-4531.

St. Phillips Episcopal, 204 134th Street, Manhattan, ☎ 212-862-4940.

Ethiopian

Commandment Keepers Ethiopian Hebrew Congregation, 420 West 145th Street, Manhattan, ☎ 212-234-6767.

Methodist

Salem United Methodist, 2190 Adam Clayton Powell, Jr. Blvd, Manhattan, ☎ 212-678-2700.

Reformed

Elmendorf Reformed Church, 171 East 121st Street, Manhattan, ☎ 212-534-5856.

Public Transportation

New York City Transit. Subway and bus information, ☎ 718-330-1234.

New York City

New York Area Resources

Boys Choir of Harlem, 127 West 127th Street, Manhattan, ☎ 212-749-1717.

Dance Theater of Harlem, 466 West 152nd Street, New York, NY 10031, ☎ 212-690-2880.

Harlem Dance Foundation, 144 West 121st Street, Manhattan, ☎ 212-662-2057.

Harlem Festival Orchestra, Church of the Intercession, 550 West 155th Street, Manhattan, ☎ 212-567-4643.

La Rocque Bey School of Dance, 180 West 135th Street, New York, NY 10030, ☎ 212-926-0188.

National Black Theater, 2031 5th Ave, Manhattan, ☎ 212-722-3800.

National Black Touring Circuit, 417 Convent Ave, Manhattan, ☎ 212-283-0974.

Opera Ebony, 2109 Broadway, #1418, Manhattan, ☎ 212-877-2110.

New York Convention & Visitors Bureau, Two Columbus Circle and 59th Street, New York, NY 10019, ☎ 800-NYC-VISIT or 212-397-8222. Mon-Fri, 9 am-6 pm; Sat-Sun & holidays, 10 am-6 pm.

New York Division of Tourism, One Commerce Plaza, Albany, NY 12245, ☎ 800-225-5697.

Philadelphia

Historic Sites & Landmarks

All Wars Memorial to Colored Soldiers and Sailors, at 20th Street & The Parkway across from the Franklin Institute Science Museum. This memorial was erected by Swiss sculptor Otto Schweiser and pays tribute to the African-American war heroes who fought in America's wars. The sculpture was commissioned in 1927 by the State of Pennsylvania through the efforts of African-American Legislator Samuel Beecher Hart.

Berean Institute, 1901 West Girard Ave, ☎ 215-763-4833. The Berean Institute was founded by Reverend Dr. Matthew Anderson in 1899. It provided training in the skilled trades to African-Americans who were denied access to other educational institutions because of racial discrimination. The institute was chartered in 1904 and has since expanded its curriculum to meet the changing needs of today's students. The Institute obtained its name from the Berean Presbyterian Church and the Berean Savings Association, both founded by Reverend Dr. Matthew Anderson.

Balch Institute for Ethnic Studies, 18 South Seventh Street, ☎ 215-925-8090. In addition to the institute's multicultural library, museum, archives and education center, there is an extensive collection of documents, manuscripts and artifacts relating to the history of African-Americans. Tues-Sat, 10 am-4 pm. Admission charge.

Charles L. Blockson Afro-American Collection, Temple University at Broad and Montgomery streets, ☎ 215-204-6632. This extensive collection contains more than 40,000 items relating to notable African-Americans, and includes books, slave narratives, letters, sheet music, photographs, and original recordings. Charles Blockson has written several books and has become a noted historian. Mon-Fri, 9 am-5 pm. Free admission.

Christian Street YMCA, 1724 Christian Street, ☎ 215-735-5800. Built in 1914, this was the first African-American YMCA in the country to have its own building. It remains an important legacy in Philadelphia's African-American community and provides educational and recreational opportunities for people of all ages. Mon-Fri, 7:15 am-8 pm; Sat, 9 am-3 pm.

Freedom Theater, 1346 North Broad Street, ☎ 215-765-2793. One of Pennsylvania's oldest and finest theaters, the Freedom Theater has become a landmark for thousands of aspiring African-American actors. The theater was founded in 1966 and has presented nearly 300 plays, including the classic *A*

Philadelphia Historic District

Vine St
Race St
Benjamin Franklin Bridge

Pier 24
Pier 19

❶

❷

Convention Center

Reading Terminal Market

Arch St

US Mint

⑪

Pier 5

95

Market St

Pier 3

Broad St
13th St
12th St
11th St
10th St
9th St
8th St
7th St
6th St
5th St
4th St
3rd St
2nd St
Front St

Independence Mall

⑩

Chestnut St

Walnut St

⑨

Locust St

⑧

Dock St

Christopher Columbus Blvd

Penn's Landing

❸

Spruce St

Pine St

Vietnam War Memorial

Lombard St

⑥

⑦

❺

South St

❹

NOT TO SCALE

1. All Wars Memorial to Colored Soldiers & Sailors
2. Philadelphia Convention & Visitors Bureau
3. Historical Society of Pennsylvania
4. Tindley Temple United Methodist Church
5. St. Peter Claver's Roman Catholic Church
6. Mother Bethel AME Church
7. James Forten House & Historical Marker
8. Washington Square
9. Liberty Bell & Independence Nat'l Historical Park
10. Balch Institute for Ethnic Studies
11. Afro-American Historical & Cultural Museum

Raisin In The Sun, by African-American writer Lorraine Hansberry. Open daily until sunset. Free admission.

Girard College, 2101 South Colgate Ave, ☎ 215-787-2600. Girard College was the focal point of a discrimination battle between the city of Philadelphia and the African-American community. Stephen Girard's 1831 will stipulated that the school be for "poor white boys." During the 1930s, noted African-American attorney and judge Raymond Pace Alexander charged the city with racial discrimination. Thirty years later, the case was finally won in the US Supreme Court by attorney Cecil B. Moore.

Historical Society of Pennsylvania, 1300 Locust Street, ☎ 215-732-6200. The society houses numerous documents relating to the antislavery movement and African-American history, as well as documents by writer, abolitionist and businessman William Still, who wrote *The Underground Railroad*, about fugitive slaves who traveled through Philadelphia. Tues, Thurs, Fri & Sat, 10 am-5 pm; Wed, 1 pm-9 pm. Admission charge.

James Forten Home & Historical Marker, 335 Lombard Street. James Forten was an abolitionist, sailmaker, businessman and civil rights activist. A marker has been placed here in remembrance of him. Forten founded the 18th-century Free African Society in 1787 and was a major organizer of Philadelphia's first African-American convention in 1830. His success in business derived from his invention of an apparatus for managing sails.

Joe Frazier's Gym, 2917 North Broad Street, ☎ 215-221-5303. Boxing center and gym owned by former heavyweight boxing champion Joe Frazier.

John W. Coltrane Home & Historical Marker, 1511 North 33rd Street, ☎ 215-763-1118. This is the former home of jazz saxophonist John Coltrane (1926-1967). Born on September 23, 1926 in Hamlet, North Carolina, Coltrane studied music at two Philadelphia music schools, played in military bands, and became famous when he joined the Miles Davis Quintet in 1955. He performed with jazz greats such as Thelonius Monk, McCoy Tyner, Dizzy Gillespie and many others. Coltrane died on July 17, 1967. A historical marker has been placed outside his former home. Open by appointment only during the summer. Free admission; donations accepted.

Johnson House, 6133 Germantown Ave, ☎ 215-843-0943. The attic and basement of this structure served as a hiding place for runaway slaves who traveled the Underground Railroad. The home was built in 1768 and was owned by Samuel and Jeanett Johnson, who were Quaker abolitionists. Meetings were held on the main floor; Harriet Tubman and other famous abolitionists attended. Today, the Germantown Mennonite Historic Trust owns and operates the home, using it as a resource and interpretive center. Tours by appointment only. Admission charge.

Philadelphia

Liberty Bell Independence National Historic Park, Sixth and Market streets, ☎ 215-597-8974 (voice or TDD). The name is derived from the "Friends of Freedom," an abolitionist literary group, who made reference to the Liberty Bell when calling for the freedom of slaves. Open daily, 9 am-5 pm. Free admission.

Mother Bethel African Methodist Episcopal Church, 419 Richard Allen Ave, Sixth and Lombard streets, ☎ 215-925- 0616. This church was purchased in 1791 by Bishop and Freemason Richard Allen and was the first AME church ever built. Preceded by three other buildings, the current structure was completed in 1889 and sits on the oldest piece of land owned continuously by African-Americans. Both religious and Masonic themes are featured in its stained glass windows, along with Allen's pulpit. Richard Allen and his wife, Sarah, along with Bishop Morris Brown, are entombed in the church's shrine. Tours: Tues-Sat, 10 am-2:30 pm; Sun, after worship service by appointment.

Mother Bethel Church
© Marc Daniels, Philadelphia CVB

Prince Hall Grand Lodge, 4301 North Broad Street, ☎ 215-324-3533. Established in 1797 under Worshipful Master Absolom Jones, Sr., Warden Richard Allen and First Treasurer James Forten, this was Philadelphia's first Masonic Lodge for African-Americans. Prince Hall was originally located in Old City on Lombard Street between Fifth and Sixth streets. Black Masonic lodges were formed as a result of discrimination by white Masons, who did not recognize African-Americans as legitimate Masons in their fraternity. Mon-Fri, 9 am-5 pm. Free admission.

St. Peter Claver's Roman Catholic Church, 1200 Lombard Street, ☎ 215-735-0799. This church was dedicated in 1892 for Black Catholics and was named in honor of an abolitionist and humanitarian whose efforts against slavery won him the honorary title of "Apostle of the Slave Trade." Call for tours.

Tindley Temple United Methodist Church, 762 South Broad Street, ☎ 215-735-0442. The church was named in honor of the Reverend Albert Charles Tindley. Born into slavery, Tindley studied for the ministry and moved to Philadelphia in 1870. Tindley helped migrants from the South and was a renowned composer of gospel songs. The church provides clothing and meals for Philadelphia's needy.

Washington Square, Sixth to Seventh & Walnut to Locust streets. Formerly known as "Congo Square," this area was the site of slave auctions during the Colonial days. American and British Revolutionary War soldiers were also buried here along with Black and white victims of the yellow fever epidemic in 1793. Washington Square, one of William Penn's five squares, later became a meeting place for freed African-Americans. Today it is lined with small businesses.

Sites Beyond Philadelphia

Arthur Ashe Tennis Center, 4015 Main Street, Manayunk, ☎ 215-487-9555. This complex was named in honor of African-American tennis great Arthur Ashe.

Father Divine Shrine, Woodmont Estate, 1622 Spring Mill Road, Gladwyne, ☎ 610-525-5598. This monument is located at the Woodmont Estate and is dedicated to Father Divine, who organized and founded one of the largest religious organizations, the Peace Mission Movement. He preached love and hope and attracted followers from diverse cultures. Divine also owned the Divine Tracy Hotel in West Philadelphia and the Divine Lorraine Hotel in North Philadelphia, which continues to be used as a hostel. Tours offered April-October on Sun, 1 pm-5 pm. Free admission.

James Bland Grave, Merion Memorial Park, Bryn Mawr Ave, Bryn Mawr, PA, ☎ 610-664-6699. Bland achieved his notoriety as a prolific songwriter and minstrel performer. Born in New York in 1854 as a free African-American, James Bland composed more than 600 songs. Bland died penniless in 1911 in Philadelphia. The American Society of Composers, Authors and Performers (ASCAP) discovered his grave and built a tombstone in his honor. Mon-Sat, 8:30 am-2:30 pm. Free admission.

Museums/Exhibits

Afro-American Historical and Cultural Museum, 701 Arch Street, ☎ 215-574-0380. Built in 1976, this fine museum is located in a historic African-American neighborhood. It contains four galleries for art exhibits and special presentations. Housing some of the finest African-American art collections in the nation, the museum's mission is to collect, preserve and highlight the contributions of African-Americans to the history of Pennsylvania and the Delaware Valley. Tues-Sat, 10 am-5 pm; Sun, noon-6 pm. Admission charge.

Philadelphia

Afro-American Historical and Cultural Museum
© Marc Daniels, Philadelphia CVB

Shopping

Galleries & Specialty Shops

Aya's Unique Boutique, 265 South 44th Street, ☎ 215-386-6707. Authentic African clothing, art, jewelry. Wed-Sat, noon-7 pm.

Amazulu on Eighth, 139 South Eighth Street, ☎ 215-923-8540. Authentic African clothing and jewelry. Mon-Fri, 10 am-6 pm; Sat, 10 am-5 pm.

Bird of Paradise, 62 North Third Street, ☎ 215-592-1029. African clothing, jewelry, books and art. Tues-Sat, 10 am-6 pm; Sun-Mon by appointment.

Chosen Image African-American Art Gallery, 6251 North Broad Street, ☎ 215-276-3200. African and African-American art, originals and lithographs, paintings, sculptures and much more. Wed-Sat, 11 am-7 pm; Sun, noon-5 pm.

Dizyners Gallery, 65 North Second Street, ☎ 215-627-8950. Contemporary African-American art. Wed-Fri, 11 am-5 pm; Sat, 1 pm-5 pm; other times by appointment.

Karavan of the Nile, Inc., 2045 Walnut Street, ☎ 215-557-0701. Authentic African artifacts, stone sculptures, paintings. Mon-Sat, 11:30 am-6 pm.

Lucien Crump Art Gallery, 6380 Germantown Ave, ☎ 215-843-8788. African-American art. Mon-Sat, 11 am-6 pm; Sun, 1 pm-5 pm.

Merchant of Alkebulan, 3744 Germantown Ave, ☎ 215-226-3240. African artifacts, Afrocentric carvings, books, jewelry and gifts. Mon-Sat, 10 am-6 pm.

Mocha Gallery, 5445 Germantown Ave, ☎ 215-844-3412. African-American art gallery and gift shop. African paintings, sculptures, masks and much more. Tues-Fri, noon-6 pm; Sat, 10 am-6 pm.

October Gallery, 68 North Second Street, ☎ 215-629-3939. African-American originals, serigraphs, lithographs and etchings. Tues-Fri, 11 am-6 pm; Wed, 11 am-8 pm; Sat, noon-5 pm.

Wilkerson Gallery, 2442 Christian Street, ☎ 215-985-9569. African and African-American art. Features oils, watercolors, limited editions, lithographs, serigraphs. By appointment only.

Bookstores

Afro Mission Bookstore, 104 South 13th Street, Philadelphia, ☎ 215-731-1680. Specializes in Afrocentric books and gifts. Mon-Fri, 9:30 am-6:30 pm; Sat, 10 am-6 pm.

Hakim's Bookstore, 210 South 52nd Street, ☎ 215-474-9495. African-American books. Mon-Sat, 9 am-7 pm.

Know Thyself Bookstore, two locations: 2045 Walnut Street, and 528 South 52nd Street, ☎ 215-748-2278. Afrocentric books. Tues-Fri, 11 am-7 pm; Sat, noon-5 pm.

Themes and Books, The Gallery at 9th and Market, ☎ 215-922-4417. Afrocentric books, games and dolls. Mon, Tues, Thurs, 10 am-7 pm; Wed, Fri, 10 am-8 pm; Sun 11:45 am-5 pm.

Truth Bookstore, 104 South 13th Street, ☎ 215-731-1680. African-American books and gifts. Mon-Fri, 9:30 am-6:30 pm; Sat, 10 am-6 pm.

Fashions

Babe, 110 South 52nd Street, ☎ 215-471-1727. Upscale women's clothing. Mon-Sat, 10 am-7 pm.

Bold Urge, 6365 Germantown Ave, ☎ 215-848-2112. Afrocentric clothing and accessories for voluptuous women. Tues-Sat, noon-7 pm.

Boyds, 1818 Chestnut Street, ☎ 215-564-9000. Designer men's and women's apparel, shoes, sportswear, big and tall department, in-store café. Considered a Philadelphia landmark. Mon-Sat, 9:30 am-6 pm.

Capathia's, 6601 Greene Street, ☎ 215-844-3215. Afrocentric clothing and gifts. Wed-Sat, 11 am-6 pm.

Philadelphia

Elegant Lady Boutique, 6045 Woodland Ave, ☎ 215-729-2935. Mon and Wed-Sat, 10 am-6 pm; closed Tues and Sun.

Fe-Male Fashions, 2949 North 22nd Street, ☎ 215-225-3075. Ladies contemporary under and outer wear. Mon, Wed, 10 am-5:30 pm; Tues, Thurs, Sat, 10 am-6 pm; Fri, 10 am-7 pm.

Gwen's Alcove, 19 Maplewood Mall, ☎ 215-438-3755. Women's clothing boutique. Features sports clothing, dresses and accessories. Mon-Sat, 10 am-6 pm; Sun, noon-5 pm.

House of Teo, 5443 Germantown Ave, ☎ 215-844-1550. High fashion and African fashion boutique. Tues-Sat, 11 am-7 pm.

The Hat Shop, 2843 Girard Ave, ☎ 215-236-5994. Afrocentric boutique and gifts. Tues-Sat, 10 am-6 pm.

Id's Hats, 5921 Woodcrest Ave, ☎ 215-473-5818. Mon-Fri, 5 pm-7 pm; Sat, 10 am-5 pm. Call first to confirm hours.

Jessie's Ladies Shoppe, 1537 South Street, ☎ 215-735-0458. Contemporary women's fashions and some African fashions. Tues-Fri, 10 am-6 pm; Sat, 10 am-5:30 pm.

Sandaga, 522 South Fifth Street, ☎ 215-829-1285. African art and clothing, as well as paintings, sculpture, musical instruments, jewelry and much more. Tues-Sat, 11 am-8 pm; Sun, 11 am-6 pm.

Uzoamaka, 2047 Walnut Street, ☎ 215-569-2400. Specializes in custom-made African and contemporary clothing, jewelry and accessories. Tues-Sat, noon-7 pm.

Golf Courses

Freeway Golf & Country Club, Sicklerville Road, off Route 42, Sicklerville, NJ, ☎ 609-227-1115. Open daily, 6 am-midnight. 18-hole public golf course owned by the city of Philadelphia. Restaurant and bar. Frequented by African-Americans.

Restaurants

◆ **African**

The Red Sea Ethiopian Restaurant, 229 South 45th Street, ☎ 215-387-2424. Ethiopian cuisine, lunch and dinner. Open daily, 10 am-midnight.

◆ Barbecue

Dwight's Southern Barbecue, 3734 Germantown Ave & 4345 Lancaster Ave, ☎ 215-879-2497. Pork, chicken and beef barbeque. Take-out only. Sun-Thurs, 11 pm-midnight; Fri-Sat, noon-3:15 am.

Grayes Bar B Que, 5017 Germantown Ave, ☎ 215-438-9847. Pork, beef and chicken. Mon-Thurs, 9 am-noon; Fri-Sat, 9 am-3 pm.

◆ Caribbean

Caribbean Café, 1811 North 54th Street, ☎ 215-473-0347. Traditional Jamaican cuisine. Open for lunch and dinner. Mon-Fri, 10 am-10 pm; Sat-Sun, 10 am-midnight.

Caribbean Delight, 1124 South Street, ☎ 215-829-1030. Authentic island cuisine. Open for lunch and dinner. Tues-Sun, noon-11 pm.

Ceslyn's Café, 3801 Market Street, 3rd Floor, ☎ 215-382-5005. Specializes in Caribbean and American cuisine. Lunch, Mon-Fri, 11:30 am-3:30 pm. Dinner, Thurs-Sat, 5 pm-1 am. Saturday night jazz sessions, 8 pm-2 am; Sunday brunch and dinner, 11 am-9 pm.

Garden of Bilal, 1616 Wadsworth Ave, ☎ 215-247-2300. Halaal cuisine, lunch and dinner. Mon-Thurs, 8:30 am-11 pm; Fri-Sat, 8:30 am-midnight; Sun, 8:30 am-10 pm.

Hummingbird Diner, 1530 Wadsworth, ☎ 215-247-1118. West Indian cuisine. Mon-Thurs, 10 am-10 pm; Fri-Sat, 10 am-11 pm.

Island Tropics, 813 East Chelten Ave, ☎ 215-848-7660. Specializes in Jamaican and American food. Mon-Sat, noon-10 pm.

Jamaica Jerk Hut, 1436 South Street, ☎ 215-545-8644. Specialty is Jamaican jerk and West Indian cuisine. Mon-Thurs, 11 am-10 pm; Fri-Sat, 11 am-11 pm.

◆ Soul Food

Big George's Stop-N-Dine, 285 South 52nd Street, ☎ 215-748-8200. Breakfast, lunch and dinner. Mon-Sat, 7 am-11 pm.

Delilah's, Reading Terminal Market, 12th & Filbert streets, ☎ 215-574-0929. Amtrak's 30th Street Station, 30th and Market streets, ☎ 215-243-2440. Lunch and dinner, Mon-Sat, 11 am-5 pm.

Holy Heaven Soul Food, 4109 Lancaster Ave, ☎ 215-382-9600. Mon-Sat, 11:30 am-7 pm.

Mama Rosa's, 5531 Germantown Ave, ☎ 215-848-3860 & 3838 North Broad Street, ☎ 215-225-2177. Southern cuisine. Tues-Thurs, 10:30 am-10 pm; Fri-Sat, 10:30 am-midnight; Sun, 11 am-9 pm.

Philadelphia

Mom's Soft Touch, 1314 South Street, ☎ 215-984-0497. Traditional soul food cuisine. Call for hours.

Prince's Total Experience, 1412 West Hunting Park Ave, ☎ 215-324-7562. Live entertainment. Soul food cuisine. Open daily, noon-11 pm. Jazz on Sunday, 4 pm-9 pm; Thurs-Sat, oldies.

Roxy's Soul Food Restaurant, Broad Street & Fairmont Ave, ☎ 215-232-2000. Call for hours.

Slim Cooper's, 6402 Stenton Ave, ☎ 215-224-0509. Soul food cuisine. Live jazz, Tues-Sat, 6 pm-2 am. Open for dinner only.

◆ **Vegetarian**

The Basic Four, Reading Terminal Market, 12th & Filbert streets, Aisle C. ☎ 215-440-0991. Vegetarian snack bar. Open daily, 10:30 am-4:30 pm.

Patterson Paradise, 538 North Fourth Street, ☎ 215-925-8355. Vegetarian and soul food cuisine. Call for hours.

Uhuru's Place, 4900 Chestnut Street, ☎ 215-476-5745. Vegetarian lunch and dinner. Live jazz. Tues-Sat, noon-8:30 pm; Sun, 2 pm-5 pm.

Entertainment

◆ **Jazz/Blues Clubs/Lounges**

Blue Moon Jazz Club & Restaurant, Fourth Street between Market & Chestnut streets, ☎ 215-413-2272. A premiere jazz spot to dine and dance. Club opens daily at 6 pm. Live jazz sets begins at 8 pm, 9 pm, & 11 pm. Earlier hours Thurs-Fri.

Chris' Jazz Café, 1421 Sansom Street, ☎ 215-568-3131. Jazz and fine dining. Mon-Sat, 9 pm-2 am.

Gloria's Café, 934 North 29th Street, near Girard Ave, ☎ 215-765-2934. Live jazz, comedy, blues and oldies two days a week; Fri-Sat, 9:30 pm-1:30 am.

J.J.'s Grotto Restaurant & Jazz Club, 27 South 21st Street, ☎ 215-988-9255. Live jazz, Italian cuisine, lunch/dinner. Music on Fri-Sat, 8 pm-midnight; Sun-Thurs, 7 pm-10 pm.

Meiji-En, Pier 19, Columbus Boulevard at Callowhill Street, ☎ 215-592-7100. Japanese/American cuisine, lunch and dinner. Live jazz on Fri-Sat, 7 pm-midnight.

Ortlieb's Jazzhaus, 847 North Third Street, ☎ 215-922-1035. Live jazz, lunch and dinner. Mon-Thurs, 8:30 pm-11:30 pm; Fri-Sat, 7 pm-midnight.

Prince's Total Experience, 1412 West Hunting Park Ave, ☎ 215-324-7562. See listing under *Soul Food* restaurants.

Slim Cooper's, 6402 Stenton Ave, ☎ 215-224-0509. Live jazz, soul food. See listing under *Soul Food* restaurants.

Warmdaddy's, Six South Front Street, ☎ 215-627-8400. Southern cuisine. Live blues nightly. Tues-Sat, 8:30 pm-2 am.

Zanzibar Blue, Park Hyatt Hotel at the Bellevue, ☎ 215-893-1776. Live jazz. African and Caribbean cuisine and music. Dinner served daily. Jazz sets Mon-Wed, 8:30, 10, and 11:30 pm; Fri-Sat at 9 and 11 pm. ☆ *Specially recommended.*

◆ **Dance Nightclubs**

Egypt on the Waterfront, 520 North Columbus Boulevard, ☎ 215-922-6500. Adult disco. Open weekends, 9 pm-2 am.

Travel Agents

Addison Tours & Travel, 4712 Baltimore Ave, Philadelphia, PA 19143, ☎ 215-729-1116. ITAS member.

Au Re Voir Travel, 6373 Germantown Ave, Philadelphia, PA 19144, ☎ 215-848-2220. ITAS member.

Cobbs Creek International, 6235 Chestnut Street, Philadelphia, PA 19139, ☎ 215-747-0880. ITAS member.

Community Travel, 3601 Lancaster Ave, Philadelphia, PA 19104, ☎ 215-222-9000. ITAS member.

Departure Travel, Four Penn Centre Plaza, 16th and JFK Boulevard, Philadelphia, PA 19102, ☎ 315-496-9333. ITAS member.

E-Jay Travel Agency, 1500 Market Street, Philadelphia, PA 19102, ☎ 215-564-6380. ITAS member.

Espri Travel, 4950 Parkside Ave, Philadelphia, PA 19131, ☎ 215-877-7000. ITAS member.

Olivine's Travel Agency, 4145 Lancaster Ave, Philadelphia, PA 19104, ☎ 215-382-6333. ITAS member.

Palace Travel, 5301 Chestnut Street, Philadelphia, PA 19139, ☎ 215-471-8555. ITAS member.

R & A Tours & Travel, 1624 Wadsworth Ave, Philadelphia, PA 19119, ☎ 215-753-1300. ITAS member.

Rodgers Travel, 4518 City Ave, #300, Philadelphia, PA 19131, ☎ 215-473-1775. ITAS member.

Philadelphia

Heritage Tours

Afro-American Historical and Cultural Museum, 701 Arch Street, ☎ 215-574-0380. The museum offers an African-American heritage tour of 22 Philadelphia sites.

African-American Historical Tours, 4601 Market, ☎ 215-748-3222. Learn about Philadelphia's rich African-American history by visiting some of the city's historical landmarks. Call for reservations and more information on specific sites visited.

Tour of Possibilities, ☎ 215-877-7004. See the first African Methodist Episcopal Church in the world. Marvel at the first museum in the nation to maintain a collection that speaks to and exhibits the African-American culture, and stroll the streets where African-American merchants used to sell their wares. Tour of Possibilities (TOP) provides visitors with a birds-eye view of these sites and others in the city. TOP also provides historical tours for girls' clubs, museum curators/staff and travel agent societies. By appointment only.

Media

Radio

◆ Jazz
WRTI 90.1 FM, ☎ 215-204-5277.

◆ Adult Urban/Classic Soul
WDAS 105.3 FM, ☎ 215-581-2100.

◆ Urban Contemporary
WUSL 98.9 FM, ☎ 215-483-8900.

◆ Gospel
WDAS 1480 AM, ☎ 215-581-2100. 24-hour talk radio.

WHAT 1340 AM, ☎ 215-574-9064.

Newspapers

Philadelphia New Observer, 1930 Chestnut, ☎ 215-665-8400. African-American community newspaper. Distributed weekly on Wednesdays.

Philadelphia Sunday Sun, 628 West Rittenhouse Street, ☎ 215-848-7864. African-American community newspaper. Distributed weekly on Sundays.

Philadelphia Tribune, 522 South 16th, ☎ 215-893-4050. African-American community newspaper. Distributed bi-weekly on Tuesdays and Fridays.

Publications

Greater Philadelphia Black Pages, 350 East Willow Grove, M716, Philadelphia, PA 19118, ☎ 215-247-6500.

Share The Heritage; African-American Historical and Cultural Guide, Philadelphia Convention & Visitors Center, 1515 Market Street, #2020, Philadelphia, PA 19102, ☎ 215-636-3300.

Sojourner; An African-American Visitor's Guide to Philadelphia, Philadelphia Tribune, 520 South 16th Street, Philadelphia, PA 19146, ☎ 215-893-4050.

African-American Churches

AME

AME Union Church, 1614 Jefferson Street, ☎ 215-765-5868.

Emanuel AME Church, 5917 Chestnut Street, ☎ 215-747-9422.

Metropolitan AME Church, 20th and Fitzwater streets, ☎ 215-545-3840.

Mother Bethel AME Church, 419 Richard Allen Ave, ☎ 215-925-0616.

St. Paul's AME Church, 86th Street and Bartram Ave, ☎ 215-365-6710.

Wesley AME Zion Church, 1500 Lombard Street, ☎ 215-735-8961.

Baptist

Bright Hope Baptist Church, 12th Street and Cecil B. Moore Ave, ☎ 215-232-6004.

Christian Faith Baptist Church, 6012 Market Street, ☎ 215-476-1484.

First Baptist Church of Paschall, 1208 South 71st Street, ☎ 215-724-3294.

Greater White Rock Baptist Church, 5335 Market Street, ☎ 215-748-6983.

Mount Zion Baptist Church, 8101 Endrick Street, ☎ 215-624-8869.

White Rock Baptist Church, 5240 Chestnut Street, ☎ 215-474-1738.

Zion Baptist Church, 3600 N Broad Street, ☎ 215-223-5460.

COGIC

Canaan Church of God in Christ, 2001 Spring Garden Street, ☎ 215-972-7080.

Faith Temple Church of God in Christ, 3213 West Cumberland Street, ☎ 215-226-2128.

Philadelphia

Prayer Chapel Church of God in Christ, 1914 North 54th Street, ☎ 215-477-3434.

Zion Hill Church of God In Christ, 529 East Washington Lane, ☎ 215-438-6300.

Episcopal

African Episcopal Church of St. Thomas, 6361 Lancaster Ave, ☎ 215-473-3065.

Calvary Episcopal Church, 814 North 41st Street, ☎ 215-222-2070.

Church of the Advocates, 18th and Diamond streets, ☎ 215-236-0568.

St. Thomas Episcopal Church, 401 North 52nd Street, ☎ 215-473-3065.

Presbyterian

First African Presbyterian Church, 42nd and Girard streets, ☎ 215-477-3100.

Olivet Covenant Presbyterian Church, 22nd and Mount Vernon streets, ☎ 215-232-2019.

United Methodist

Camphor Memorial United Methodist Church, 5620 Wyalusing, ☎ 215-747-2600.

Calendar of Annual Events

◆ January

Martin Luther King, Jr. Birthday Annual Concert, Philadelphia Orchestra, ☎ 215-893-1955.

Martin Luther King, Jr. Birthday Annual Luncheon, Martin Luther King, Jr. Nonviolence Association, ☎ 215-751-9300.

Annual Ecumenical Service, PUSH Philadelphia, ☎ 215-223-5460.

◆ February

Black Family Reunion Center Annual African-American History Month Celebration, Community College of Philadelphia, ☎ 215-438-6441.

Black History Month Activities, citywide, Philadelphia Convention & Visitors Bureau, ☎ 215-636-3300.

◆ June

Father's Day Rally Committee Annual Picnic, Memorial Hall, Fairmount Park, ☎ 215-978-1411.

Odunde African New Year Festival, Philadelphia Convention & Visitors Bureau, ☎ 215-636-3300.

◆ July

African-American Heritage Festival, Black Family Reunion Cultural Center, ☎ 215-438-6441.

Essence of Entertainment Concert Series, ☎ 215-686-0844. Rhythm and blues and jazz concerts.

◆ August

Caribbean Festival, Philadelphia Convention & Visitors Bureau, ☎ 215-636-3300. Features ethnic foods, clothing and entertainment.

African-American Extravaganza, Philadelphia Convention & Visitors Bureau, ☎ 215-636-3300. Features ethnic food, clothing and entertainment.

Leon H. Sullivan Charitable Golf Tournament, Ashbourne Country Club, Cheltenham, ☎ 215-223-8141.

Days of Unity Celebration, WDAS-FM, ☎ 610-617-8500.

◆ September

Yo! Philadelphia Festival, Philadelphia Convention & Visitors Bureau, ☎ 215-636-3300. Celebration of Philadelphia's neighborhoods and cultural diversity.

Super Sunday Celebration, Philadelphia Convention & Visitors Bureau, ☎ 215-636-3300. Celebration by Philadelphia's educational and cultural institutions.

◆ December

Annual Afro-American Art Expo, October Gallery, Pennsylvania Convention Center, ☎ 215-629-3939.

Amazulu'z Annual Craft Marketplace, Int'l House, ☎ 215-627-8667.

Kwanzaa Celebration, Black Family Reunion Cultural Center, call for location, ☎ 215-684-1008.

Philadelphia

Public Transportation

Philadelphia International Airport, ☎ 215-937-6800.

Port Authority Transit Corporation (PATCO). Call for local bus routes and schedules, ☎ 215-922-4600.

Southeastern Pennsylvania Transportation Authority (SEPTA). Call for commuter train routes and schedules, ☎ 215-580-7800.

Taxi Services

Olde City Taxi Coach Association, ☎ 215-AIR-PORT.

Quaker City Cab, ☎ 215-728-8000.

United Cab Association, ☎ 215-238-9500.

Philadelphia Area Resources

Africamericans for Cultural Development, 3701 Chestnut Street, ☎ 215-772-0807.

African-American Chamber of Commerce of Philadelphia, 12 South 12th Street, Philadelphia, PA 19107, ☎ 215-925-8510.

Black Family Reunion Cultural Center, PO Box 5-8118, Philadelphia, PA 19102, ☎ 215-438-6441.

Coalition of African-American Cultural Organizations, 2253 North Broad Street, ☎ 215-765-5055.

Minority Arts Resource Council, 1421 West Girard Ave, ☎ 215-236-2688.

Mill Creek Jazz & Cultural Society, 4624 Lancaster Ave, ☎ 215-473-4273.

Odunde, 2308 Grays Ferry Ave, ☎ 215-732-8508.

Philadelphia Convention & Visitors Center, 1515 Market Street, #2020, Philadelphia, PA 19102, ☎ 215-636-3300. Web site: www.libertynet. org/phila-visitor.

Philadelphia Visitors Center, 1525 JFK Boulevard, Philadelphia, PA 19102, ☎ 215-636-1666. Mon-Fri, 8 am-4 pm.

West Philadelphia Cultural Alliance, 3500 Lancaster Ave, ☎ 215-387-1712.

San Francisco Bay Area

Historic Sites & Landmarks

African-American Center and **Collections of the San Francisco Public Library,** 108 Larkin, Civic Center, ☎ 415-557-4400. The African-American Center, located on the third floor of the Main San Francisco Public Library, houses materials about African-American history, education, and the arts, with special emphasis on the history and cultures of the African diaspora. The African-American Collection of the library in its Bayview-Waden and Western Addition branch libraries also have items of interest about African-Americans. Mon, 10 am-6 pm; Tues-Thurs, 9 am-8 pm; Fri, 11 am-5 pm; Sat, 9 am-5 pm; Sun, noon-5 pm.

Black Panther Party Former Home, 5624 Martin Luther King, Jr. Way, Oakland. This is the former home of the Black Panther Party, which became popular in the 1960s during the Civil Rights Movement. The organization was founded by Huey Newton and Bobby Seale.

Brownie McGhee Home, 688 43rd Street, Oakland, ☎ 510-655-7363. This historical site, considered "the home of the Blues," is maintained by the Blues is Truth Foundation. It is the former home of legendary Blues artist Brownie McGhee, who died in 1996. Call for hours. Free admission.

DeFremery Park, 26th and Myrtle streets, West Oakland. This beautiful park was the site of many Black Panther Party meetings and events.

Institute for the Advanced Studies of Black Family Life & Culture, 175 Filbert, ☎ 510-836-3245.

Northern California Center for Afro-Americans History and Life, 5606 San Pablo Ave, Oakland, ☎ 415-658-3158. History center and museum of East Bay African-Americans. Artifacts, photographs and research materials. Tues-Sat, 12:30 pm-5 pm. Free admission.

Oakland Tribune **Tower Building,** 1200 Broadway. This is the home of the first African-American-owned major metropolitan newspaper. The late Robert Maynard was editor-in-chief. The *Oakland Tribune* Tower adds sparkle to Oakland's night skyscape. The *Oakland Tribune* is currently located at 66 Jack London Square, ☎ 510-208-6300.

San Francisco African-American Historical Society, 762 Fulton Street, ☎ 415-292-6172. The Society preserves and promotes the history and culture of San Francisco's African-Americans, and maintains an extensive collection of African-American books and pamphlets, ephemera, manuscripts, peri-

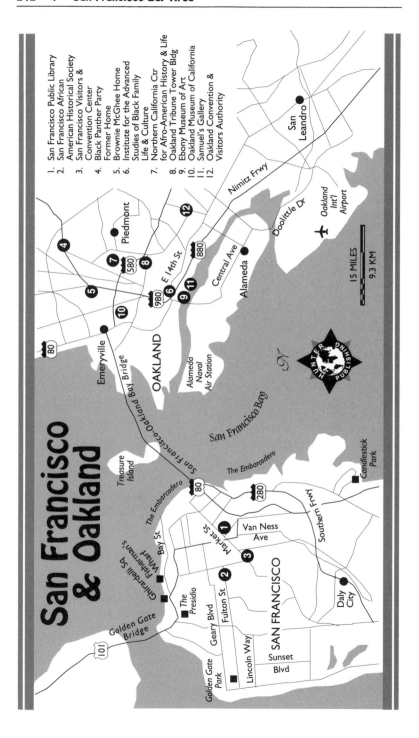

1. San Francisco Public Library
2. San Francisco African American Historical Society
3. San Francisco Visitors & Convention Center
4. Black Panther Party Former Home
5. Brownie McGhee Home
6. Institute for the Advanced Studies of Black Family Life & Culture
7. Northern California Ctr for Afro-American History & Life
8. Oakland Tribune Tower Bldg
9. Ebony Museum of Art
10. Oakland Museum of California
11. Samuel's Gallery
12. Oakland Convention & Visitors Authority

odicals, posters, paintings, exhibits, and maps relating to San Francisco's African-American population. Wed-Fri, noon-8 pm; Sat, 10 am-5 pm. Free admission.

St. Andrews African-American Episcopal Church, 2131 Eighth Street, Sacramento, ☎ 916-448-1428. This was the first African-American church and also the first California public school for African-Americans, Chinese and Native American children on the West Coast. By appointment only.

Museums/Exhibits

Ebony Museum of Art, 30 Jack London Square, Oakland, ☎ 415-763-0745. This museum by the bay has an extensive representation of authentic African art pieces – statues, masks, furniture and memorabilia, including art by East Bay area African-Americans. Tues-Sat, 11 am-6 pm.

Jack London Village, location of the Ebony Museum and Samuel's Gallery.
Courtesy Oakland Convention and Visitors Authority

Egyptian Museum, 1342 Naglee Ave, San Jose, ☎ 408-947-3600. Over 4,000 Egyptian artifacts. Open daily 9 am-5 pm. Admission charge.

Oakland Museum of California, 1000 Oak, Oakland, ☎ 510-238-2200, fax 510-238-2258. This city museum houses a collection of works by African-Americans, 1960s memorabilia, and Black Panther exhibits. Wed-Sat, 10 am-5 pm; Sun, noon-7 pm (free from 4 pm-7 pm); closed Mon-Tues. Admission charge.

San Francisco

Shopping

Galleries & Specialty Shops

African Heritage Gallery, 2230 Hilltop Mall Rd, Hilltop Mall, Richmond, ☎ 510-223-2296. Mon-Sat, 10 am-9 pm; Sun, 11 am-6 pm.

African Outlet, 524 Octavia Street, ☎ 800-89-AFRICA or 415-864-3576. African crafts, garments, rare jewelry items. Mon-Sat, 10 am-7 pm.

Bomani Gallery, 251 Post Street, #600, ☎ 415-296-8677. African-American art gallery established by motion picture actor Danny Glover and his wife, Asake Bomani. Includes a fine selection of artwork by African-American artists such as Romare Bearden, Jacob Lawrence, John Outterbridge, Elizabeth Cathlett and others. Tues-Sat, 10 am-5 pm.

Butterflies & Critters, Jack London Village, Oakland, ☎ 510-839-6794. Animal figures and ethnic memorabilia. African-American figurines, statues, "All God's Children" collectibles and much more. Mon-Sat, 11 am-6 pm; Sun, noon-6 pm.

Cynthia's Educational Toys, 501 14th Street, Oakland, ☎ 510-452-4099. Afrocentric gifts, toys. Emphasis on education. Mon-Fri, 10 am-6 pm; Sat, noon-4 pm.

Dolls of Color, 1500 Geneva Ave, ☎ 415-586-2073. African-American figurines and collectibles, greeting cards, books, Black Santa and ornaments. Closed Sun-Tues. Wed-Fri, 2 pm-6 pm; Sat, 10 am-5 pm.

Do For Self Enterprise, 5908 Foothill Blvd, Oakland, ☎ 510-633-2042. African art pieces, Kwanzaa sets, ethnic greeting cards, bath and body oils, jewelry and T-shirts. Mon-Sat, noon-8 pm; Sun, noon-6 pm.

Essentials Body Care, 3223 Grand Ave, Oakland, ☎ 510-893-5757. Afrocentric bath and body shop. Mon-Wed & Sat, 11 am-6 pm; Thurs-Fri, 11 am-7:30 pm; Sun, noon-4 pm.

Ibota USA (cross-culture), 3227 Lakeshore Ave, Oakland, ☎ 510-834-2035. West African fabrics, furniture, jewelry, crafts and African audio tapes. Mon-Sat, 10 am-6 pm; Sun, noon-5 pm.

Images of Culture, 340 California Ave, Palo Alto, ☎ 415-326-2090. Fine African art. Mon-Fri, 10 am-6 pm; Sat, 10:30 am-6 pm.

Karibu, 30 Jack London Square, Oakland, ☎ 510-444-6906. Ethnic gifts and accessories, stone carvings, ethnic dolls, arts and crafts, jewelry. Mon-Sat, 11 am-5 pm; Sun, noon-6 pm.

Markstyle Bookstore, 828 Willow Rd, Menlo Park, ☎ 415-325-5257. Tues-Sat, 10 am-6 pm; closed Sun-Mon.

Post Street Gallery, 1064 The Alameda, San Jose, ☎ 408-297-6245. Imported African and African-American arts featuring abstracts, originals, lithographs, imported vases and sculptures from Nigeria, Ghana and other African countries. Mon-Sat, 10:30 am-7 pm; Sun, noon-5 pm.

Private Reserve Ethnic Art and Jewelry, 4500 Barrett, Richmond, ☎ 510-234-1553. Tues-Sat, 12:30 pm-7 pm; closed Sun-Mon.

Samuel's Gallery, 30 Jack London Square, Oakland, ☎ 510-452-2059. Exclusive African-American art gallery specializing in African-American imagery. Samuel's Gallery houses one of the most extensive and finest collections of African-American art throughout the country. Prints and posters, original artwork and custom framing. Mon, noon-5 pm. Tues-Sat, 11 am-6 pm; Sun, noon-6 pm. ☆ *Specially recommended.*

Something of Value, 3817 San Pablo Ave, Emeryville, ☎ 510-654-3304. Antiques, collectibles.

Ujama African Arts and Crafts, 411 Divisadero Street, San Francisco, ☎ 415-252-0119. African clothing, cards and jewelry. Mon-Sat, 11 am-6 pm.

Vickie's Black Art Pictures, 1404 Alameda Street, Vallejo, ☎ 707-648-0336. Call for hours.

Victorian Dreams Gifts, 10970 East 14th Street, #V-4, Oakland, ☎ 510-638-2710. African-American collectibles and ceramics. Mon, Wed-Sat, 11 am-7 pm. Closed Sun and Tues.

West Afrique International, 22795 Watkins Street, Hayward, ☎ 510-581-2820. Traditional and contemporary African fabrics, custom designed wedding clothes, ethnic cards and gifts.

Bookstores

African Book Mart, 244 Durant Ave, Berkeley, ☎ 510-843-3088. African and African-American fiction and history books. Mon-Sat, 11 am-6:30 pm.

African and European Imports, 1611 Telegraph Ave, Oakland, ☎ 510-763-6993.

Culture Plus Books, 273 Southland Mall, Hayward, ☎ 510-783-6071. Afrocentric books, cards, games, dolls, prints and more. Mon-Fri, 10 am-9 pm; Sat, 10 am-8 pm; Sun, 11 am-6 pm.

Marcus Book Stores (two locations), 3900 Martin Luther King, Jr., Oakland, ☎ 510-652-2344. Mon-Sat, 10 am-6 pm; Sat & Sun, noon-5 pm; 1712 Fillmore Street, San Francisco, ☎ 415-346-4222. Mon-Sat, 10 am-7 pm; Sun, noon-5 pm. Extensive collection of books by and about African-American people, ethnic greeting cards, posters, maps, flags, art prints, newspapers, magazines, games and more.

Torchlight Books, 353 Grand Ave (use Perkins Street entrance), Oakland, ☎ 510-272-0737. Mon-Fri, 9 am-6 pm. Sat, 9 am-5 pm.

San Francisco

Fashions

Africa by the Bay (two locations), 3303 Lake Shore Ave, Oakland, and 2504 Telegraph Ave, Oakland, ☎ 501-763-1493. Custom-designed African clothing. Traditional and contemporary styles. African fabrics and accessories.

African Rainbow Fashions, 787 55th Street, Oakland, ☎ 510-653-2188. Custom tailored fine fabrics, carvings, gift baskets and jewelry. Mon-Fri, 11 am-6 pm. Sat, noon-4 pm.

Albo African Gift Shop, 6421 Telegraph Ave, Oakland, ☎ 510-428-2526. Custom-designed men's and women's fashions. Mon-Fri, 11 am-7 pm; Sat, 10 am-6 pm; Sun, noon-5 pm.

Panache, 333 Hegenberger Rd, #805, Wells Fargo Bank Building, Oakland, ☎ 510-632-4400. Women's and men's apparel. Evening dresses and suits, casual and business attire to size 26, shirts, ties and men's pants. Tues-Fri, 11 am-5 pm; Sat, 10 am-4 pm.

Restaurants

◆ African

Nyala, 39A Grove Street, ☎ 415-861-0788. Ethiopian restaurant/café. Vegetarian buffet. Mon-Fri, 11 am-10 pm; Sat, 4 pm-11 pm. Live Ethiopian music on Sat.

◆ Barbeque

Big Nate's Barbeque, 1665 Folsom, ☎ 415-861-4242. Popular neighborhood barbeque restaurant. Ribs, chicken, and sausage dinner plates with all the trimmings. Mon-Sat, 11 am-9:45 pm; Sun, noon-9:45 pm.

Brother-in-Law's Barbeque, 705 Divisadero Street, ☎ 415-931-7427. Barbeque ribs, baby ribs, chicken and sausage link sandwiches and dinners. Tues-Thurs, 11 am-midnight; Fri-Sat, 11 am-2 am; Sun, noon-8 pm.

Doug's Barbeque, 3600 San Pablo, Emeryville, ☎ 510-655-9048. Chicken, sausage, goat, lamb, turkey barbeque sandwiches and dinners with all the trimmings. Mon-Thurs, 11 am-9 pm; Fri-Sat, 11 am-midnight; Sun, noon-9 pm.

Everett & Jones Barbeque, three locations: 3411 Telegraph, ☎ 510-601-9377; 1955 San Pablo Ave, Berkeley, ☎ 510-548-8261; 2676 Fruitvale Ave, Oakland, ☎ 510-533-0900. Call for hours.

Leon's Barbeque, 1911 Fillmore Street, ☎ 415-922-2436. Open daily 11 am-9 pm.

◆ **Caribbean**

Geva's, 428A Hayes Street, ☎ 415-863-1220. Caribbean cuisine. Tues-Thurs, 5:30 pm-9:30 pm; Fri-Sat, 5:30 pm-10:30 pm.

Miss Pearl's Jam House, 601 Eddy Street, ☎ 415-775-5267. Wed, 6 pm-10 pm; Fri-Sat, 6 pm-11 pm; Sunday brunch.

◆ **Creole**

Café Dumas, 903 B. Street, Hayward, ☎ 510-247-9370. Soul food/creole cuisine. Jazz Fri and Sat nights. Sun-Thurs, 5 pm-9:30 pm; Fri-Sat, 7:30 pm-10 pm; Sundays, buffet only.

◆ **Soul Food**

Gingerbread House, 741 5th Street, Oakland, ☎ 510-444-7373. Very popular Bay Area Louisiana-style restaurant. Reservations highly recommended.

Powell's Place, 511 Hayes Street, ☎ 415-863-1401. Fried chicken, home-made pies. Open daily, 9 am-11 pm.

Roscoe's House of Chicken and Waffles, 210 Broadway, ☎ 510-444-5705. Mon-Wed, 11 am-3 am; Thurs, 9:30 am-3 am; Fri-Sat, 9 am-1:30 am; Sun, 9 am-8 pm.

Soul Brothers Kitchen, 5239 Telegraph Ave, Oakland, ☎ 510-655-9367.

Southern Café, 5327 East 14th Street, Oakland, ☎ 510-261-1404. Tues-Thurs, noon-8:45 pm; Fri-Sun, noon-9:45 pm.

Entertainment

◆ **Jazz/Blues Nightclubs/Lounges**

Eli's Mile High Club, 3629 Martin Luther King, Jr. Way, Oakland, ☎ 510-655-6661.

Jazz at Pearl's, 256 Columbus Ave, ☎ 415-291-8255. Live jazz, big band every Mon night, 9 pm-12:30 am. Minors welcome. Free admission.

Johnny Love's, 1500 Broadway, ☎ 415-931-8021.

Slim's, 333 11th Street, ☎ 415-522-0333. Hours vary depending on shows. Call for schedule of upcoming events.

Lodging

Bed & Breakfasts

Bedside Manor Bed & Breakfast, Valle Vista Ave, Oakland, ☎ 510-452-4550.

San Francisco

Travel Agents

A & T Travel, 9859 MacArthur Blvd, Oakland, CA 94605, ☎ 510-430-8606. ITAS member.

A-Phi International Travel, 944 Market Street, San Francisco, CA 94102, ☎ 415-398-5227. ITAS member.

Blue World Travel, 50 1ˢᵗ Street, San Francisco, CA 94105, ☎ 415-882-9444. This full-service travel agency plans African-American theme cruises to the Caribbean. Cruises feature African-American music and activities. Call for more information and reservations.

College Avenue Travel, 5391 College Ave, Oakland, CA 94618, ☎ 510-652-6990.

Heritage Tours

Oakland/Eastbay Water Tours, Jack London Square, Oakland, CA 94607, ☎ 510-835-1306. Offers a variety of standard packages, including harbor tours.

Midnight Reggae Cruises, Pier 33 on the Embarcadero, ☎ 800-267-8900 or 415-788-8866. Seasonal cruise ship tours from June through September, midnight until 3 am. Live reggae music and buffet. Admission charge.

African-American Churches

Baptist

Corner Stone Baptist Church, 3535 38ᵗʰ Street, Oakland, ☎ 510-530-9166.

Episcopal

First African Episcopal, 530 37ᵗʰ Street, Oakland, ☎ 510-655-1527.

Media

Radio

◆ Jazz

KCSM 91.1 FM, 1700 Hillsdale Blvd, ☎ 415-574-6586. Traditional jazz.

KKSF 103.7 FM, 455 Market Street, ☎ 415-975-5555. Contemporary jazz.

◆ Urban Contemporary

KBLX 102.9 FM, request line ☎ 800-683-5259. Adult urban contemporary.

KDIA 1230AM, 384 Embarcadero West, 3rd Floor, Oakland, ☎ 510-251-1400. Urban contemporary/soul.

KSOL 98.9 FM, 642 Harrison Street, ☎ 415-989-5765. Urban contemporary; gospel on Sundays.

Newspapers

Berkeley Metro Reporter, 1366 Turk Street, ☎ 415-931-5778. African-American community newspaper. Distributed weekly on Tuesdays.

Berkeley Tri-City Post, 630 20th Street, Oakland, ☎ 510-703-1120.

Black Business Listings, 436 14th Street, Oakland, ☎ 510-839-0690, fax 510-839-0565. Listing of Oakland area African-American businesses. Distributed weekly.

California Voice, 1366 Turk Street, ☎ 415-931-5778. Distributed weekly on Thursdays.

New Bayview, 1624 Oakdale Ave, ☎ 415-826-1484. African-American community newspaper. Distributed weekly on Thursdays.

Oakland Post, PO Box 1350, Oakland, ☎ 510-763-1120. African-American community newspaper. Distributed on Wednesdays and Sundays.

Richmond Post, 630 20th Street, Oakland, ☎ 510-763-1120. African-American community newspaper.

San Francisco Post, PO Box 1350, Oakland, ☎ 510-763-1120. African-American community newspaper. Distributed on Wednesdays and Sundays.

Publications

A Walking Tour of the Black Presence in San Francisco During the 19th Century, San Francisco African-American Historical & Cultural Society, 762 Fulton Ave, San Francisco, CA 94102, ☎ 415-292-6172. This publication guides visitors on a walking tour through some of San Francisco's historical African-American neighborhoods, homes and buildings.

Minority Business & Professional Directory, 2101 Webster Street, #1500, Oakland, CA 94612, ☎ 510-874-7740. Directory of predominantly African-American-owned businesses in the Bay Area.

San Francisco

Calendar of Annual Events

◆ **January**

Martin Luther King, Jr. March & Rally, City of Oakland, ☎ 510-635-0138.

◆ **February**

Bay Area Urban League Annual Anniversary Dinner, ☎ 510-271-1846.

Bob Marley Day Concert, ☎ 510-238-7765 or 510-762-2277.

◆ **June**

Juneteenth Celebrations, citywide celebrations. City of Oakland, ☎ 510-238-2136. Oakland Zoo, ☎ 510-632-9525. Oak Public Library, ☎ 510-238-6713.

◆ **August**

Annual Eddie Moore Jazz Festival, ☎ 510-601-7715.

◆ **September**

Annual Blues and Jazz at Dunsmuir, Patrons of the Arts & Humanities, ☎ 510-615-5555.

Annual Carijama "Carnival" Festival, Memorial Day Weekend, ☎ 510-597-5038.

Annual Oakland Blues Heritage Festival, Bay Area Blues Society, ☎ 510-836-2227.

Monterey Jazz Festival, PO Box Jazz, Monterey, CA 93942, ☎ 408-313-3366. Annual jazz festival featuring national and international performers. Call for lineup of artists and events.

◆ **October**

Annual Black Cowboy & Heritage Festival, Black Cowboy Association, ☎ 510-531-7583.

Annual Festival at the Lake, First District Agricultural Association of Oakland, ☎ 510-286-1061.

◆ **December**

Black Nativity, Allen Temple Cantateers, ☎ 510-444-8575 or 510-762-BASS.

Public Transportation

Bay Area Rapid Transit (BART), ☎ 415-992-2278.

Oakland International Airport, ☎ 510-577-4000.

San Francisco International Airport, ☎ 415-876-2377.

San Francisco Bay Area Resources

African-American Chamber of Commerce/East Bay, Jack London Village, #206, Oakland, CA 94607-3715, ☎ 510-835-1306.

African-American Museum and Library, 5606 San Pablo Ave, Oakland, CA 92260, ☎ 510-597-5053.

Black Business Listings, 436 14th Street, Oakland, CA 94612, ☎ 510-839-0690, fax 510-839-0565.

Black Repertory Group, Inc., 3201 Adeline, Berkeley, ☎ 415-652-2120.

Caribee Dance Center, 1408 Webster, Oakland, CA 94612, ☎ 501-835-4006.

Center for African-American Art and Culture, 762 Fulton Street, ☎ 415-292-6172.

Citicentre Dance Theater, The Alice Arts Center, 1428 Alice Street, Oakland, CA 94612, ☎ 510-451-1230. Oakland's oldest multi-ethnic dance organization.

Cultural Arts Division, City of Oakland, ☎ 510-238-2106.

Lorraine Hansberry Theater, 620 Sutter, San Francisco, CA 95982, ☎ 415-474-8800.

Oakland Ensemble Theater, 1428 Alice, Oakland, CA 94612, ☎ 510-763-7774.

Oakland Convention & Visitors Authority, Oakland Convention Center, 550 10th Street, Oakland, CA 94607, ☎ 510-839-9000.

Panache Black Singles Network, 5337 College Ave, #708, Oakland, CA 94618, ☎ 415-874-4767.

Paramount Theatre of the Arts, 2025 Broadway, Oakland, ☎ 510-465-6400.

Santa Clara County Black Chamber of Commerce, 325 South First, #4B, San Jose, ☎ 408-294-6583.

San Francisco

San Francisco African-American Historical and Cultural Society, 762 Fulton Street, San Francisco, CA 94102, ☎ 415-292-6172.

San Francisco Black Chamber of Commerce, 330 Townsend, #208, San Francisco, CA 94107, ☎ 415-536-1890.

San Francisco Convention and Visitors Bureau, 900 Market Street, San Francisco, CA 94133, ☎ 415-391-2000.

Washington, DC

Historic Sites & Landmarks

African-American Civil War Memorial, 10th and U streets NW. Metro: U Street-Cardozo. This special memorial honors the over 180,000 African-Americans, known as the US Colored Soldiers, who served with the Union Forces during the Civil War. The memorial is appropriately located in the Shaw neighborhood, named after Colonel Robert Gould Shaw, the white commander of the first Black regiment in the Union Army, which was featured in the movie *Glory*.

African-American Resource Center, 2400 Sixth Street NW, Howard University, ☎ 202-806-7242. Metro: Shaw-Howard University. This part of the Department of Howard University African-American Studies maintains a rare collection of African-American books and other materials that are no longer in print or available to the public. Mon-Fri, 9 am-5 pm.

Anthony Bowen YMCA, 1816 12th Street NW. Metro: Shaw-Howard University. Founded in 1853 by Anthony Bowen, a former slave, this YMCA was the first in the world for African-Americans. Prior to being at this location, Washington's Colored YMCA had many addresses, but this final site united Washington's African-American community in an unprecedented fundraising effort. The five-story facility was designed by one of the nation's early African-American architects and contained 72 rooms and a swimming pool. The branch was renamed after the prominent educator, religious leader and clerk at the US Patent Office, Anthony Bowen, in 1972.

A. Philip Randolph Statue, Union Station, 50 Massachusetts Ave NE. Metro: Union Station. The bronze statue is a memorial to the founder of the Sleeping Car Porters Union, A. Philip Randolph. Randolph also orchestrated the famous 1963 March on Washington.

Association for the Study of Afro-American Life and History, 1407 14th Street NW. Metro: U Street-Cardozo. Originally located in the home of its founder, Carter G. Woodson, this association was founded in 1915 to promote and encourage African-American historical research. The association's publication, *Journal of Negro History*, was also one of Woodson's efforts to inform the world of the important roles African-American people played in America's history and civilization. Not open to the public.

Barry's Farm, Southeast Washington. Now a public housing project, Barry's Farm was originally created in 1865 by the Freedman's Bureau. In response to the influx of Civil War freedmen and African-American refugees into

Washington, DC

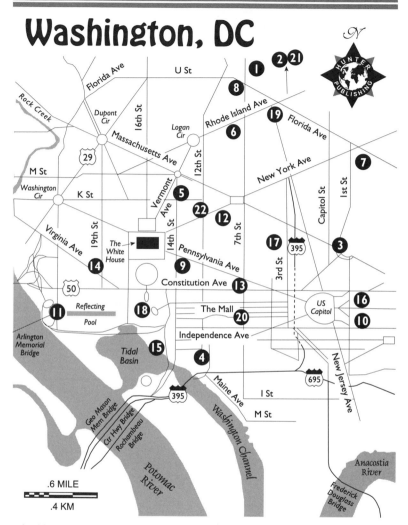

1. African-American Civil War Memorial
2. African-American Resource Center
3. A. Philip Randolph Statue
4. Benjamin Banneker Memorial Circle and Fountain
5. Bethune Museum & Archives
6. Carter G. Woodson Residence
7. Dunbar High School
8. Family Heritage Center
9. Freedom Plaza
10. Library of Congress / Emancipation Proclamation
11. Lincoln Memorial
12. Martin Luther King, Jr Memorial Library
13. National Archives
14. Negro Mother & Child sculpture
15. Tidal Basin Bridge & Seawall
16. US Supreme Court
17. Washington Jail site
18. Washington Monument
19. Africare House
20. National Museum of African Art
21. Howard University
22. Washington Visitors & Conv. Ctr

Washington, General Oliver O. Howard (Howard University) used government and private charitable funding to purchase the Talbert, Barry and Stanton Farms. Barry's was one of the farms reserved for African-American freedmen; the self-help community was also built by dedicated freedmen.

Benjamin Banneker Memorial Circle and Fountain, Mall end of L'Enfant Promenade & Maine Ave SW. Metro: L'Enfant Plaza. This memorial commemorates the contributions and accomplishments of Benjamin Banneker, the self-taught African-American astronomer, surveyor and mathematician. Banneker made the first wooden striking clock in America, and in 1792 published the *Banneker Almanac*, which was available throughout the 13 colonies. He was a major contributor in the surveying and planning for the creation of the nation's capital.

Blanche Kelso Bruce Residence, 909 M Street NW. Metro: Mt. Vernon Square. Located along a row of Victorian houses, the last remnants of a once elegant and lavish neighborhood, is the former home of the first African-American to serve a full term in the US Senate. Bruce began his term in 1875. The former escaped slave is noted for being one of the most recognized and successful men of his time. He also held the position Registrar of the US Treasury Department and was appointed Recorder of Deeds of the District of Columbia. Not open to the public.

Cardozo High School, 13th and Clifton streets NW. Metro: U Street-Cardozo. This high school is named after Francis Cardozo, Sr., an outstanding Washington educator. Cardozo moved to Washington in 1877, where he worked as a clerk in the Treasury Department and taught Latin at Howard University. As the first principal at the M Street High School, he more than doubled the enrollment and expanded the rigorous classical curriculum to a full four-year program. He also served as principal at several other high schools within the District and organized the first business department in a Washington high school. The Cardozo Business School was thus named in his honor and has since become a neighborhood school, located in the Old Central High School building.

Carter G. Woodson Residence, 1538 Ninth Street NW. Metro: Shaw-Howard University. This former home of the famed African-American historian was also the original location of the Association for the Study of Negro Life and History. Woodson founded the association to encourage African-American historical research. His lifelong efforts to inform the world about the accomplishments and contributions of African-Americans in American history resulted in the successful establishment of Black History Week, which was later expanded to encompass the month of February during the 1976 Bicentennial celebration. Not open to the public.

Charles Drew Building (Howard University's Men's Dormitory), Fifth & Gresham streets NW. Metro: Shaw-Howard University. This building was named in 1960 in honor of Dr. Charles Drew, a Washington native who is world-renowned for developing the method of preserving blood by the use of blood plasma, a technique which saved thousands of lives during World War II. Dr. Drew was also chief surgeon at Freedman's Hospital (now the site of Howard University's School of Communications). In 1976, a painting of Dr. Drew became the first portrait of an African-American man ever to be displayed in the National Institute of Health.

Dr. Anna J. Cooper Residence, 201 T Street NW. Metro: Shaw-Howard University. This quaint Victorian home is the former residence of Dr. Anna J. Cooper, who opened her home to allow Frelinghuysen University (The Bible Educational Association) to be housed there as well. Cooper, who had been born into slavery, became one of the first African-American female graduates of Oberlin College in 1884. She was a member of the distinguished M Street-Dunbar High School faculty, and was principal there from 1901 to 1906. She fought aggressively to gain equal educational opportunities for African-Americans. Dr. Cooper is remembered for her undying devotion to education and instilling promoting the ideals of self-improvement, racial pride and scholarship. Not open to the public.

Duke Ellington Residence, 1212 T Street NW. Metro: U Street-Cardozo. Within the once stately rowhouses of T Street is the former home of one of America's greatest composers, Edward "Duke" Ellington. T Street was Shaw neighborhood's main residential street for the respectable and hard-working middle class in the early 1900s. The community watched Ellington, famously known as "The Duke," grow from a young child selling ice cream during the summer to the legendary musician who made the 20th century swing. Not open to the public.

Duke Ellington School of the Arts, 35th & R streets, NW, ☎ 202-282-0123. Keeping alive the spirit and memory of Washington native Duke Ellington, one of the nation's most widely acclaimed composers, is the Duke Ellington School of the Arts. The DC public high school, a four year pre-professional institution, educates the most artistically gifted of the city's youth in academics and the arts. Entrance into this distinguished school is gained through a rigorous audition process. Tours available once a month.

Dunbar High School, West side of First Street, between N and O streets. Metro: Mount Vernon Square-UDC. Remembered as being one of the country's premier African-American high schools in the early 1900s, Dunbar maintained a distinguished faculty whose academic credentials compared favorably with professors at many US universities. The school had such a distinguished reputation that its students could enter major northern colleges and universities without a special entrance examination. Dunbar traces its roots back to the 1870s when the Preparatory High School for Negro Youth was the first public high school for African-American students in the US.

Enduring name changes and site relocations, that school eventually became the famous M Street High School, which directly preceded Dunbar.

Emancipation Memorial, Lincoln Park, East Capitol Street, between 11th and 13th streets NE. Metro: Eastern Market. Found at the west end of Lincoln Park, this was the primary tribute to President Lincoln from its dedication in 1876 until the Lincoln Memorial was dedicated in 1922. The Emancipation Memorial was financed solely by freed slaves and African-American soldiers who fought in the Union Army during the Civil War. It shows a liberated slave made in the likeness of Archer Alexander, the last man captured under the Fugitive Slave Law. Alexander's figure is depicted as physically breaking the chains of slavery as President Lincoln extends the Emancipation Proclamation.

Emancipation Proclamation, 101 Independence Ave SE, Library of Congress, ☎ 202-707-5000. Metro: Capitol South. The original draft of the Emancipation Proclamation is located here in the Library of Congress. Considered the world's largest library, the Library of Congress has more than 100 million items in three buildings.

Family Heritage Center, Garnett Patteron Middle School, 10th & U streets NW, ☎ 202-673-7329. Metro: U Street-Cardozo. This historical and educational supplement to the African-American Civil War Memorial was created to educate the public about this significant segment of history. Visitors at the center can research the genealogy of soldiers commemorated by the memorial and locate millions of descendants of the Civil War Colored Soldiers.

Family Tree of Life Statue, 16th Street & Colorado Ave NW, in Rock Creek Park, adjacent to the Carter Barron Amphitheater. The 15-foot totem of red oak by Dennis Stroy, Jr. represents an African-American family.

Frederick Douglass Home, 1411 West Street SE. Metro: Anacostia. Frederick Douglass, who has been called the father of the Civil Rights Movement, was an influential Black spokesman in national affairs long before he arrived in Washington in 1872. Born a slave in Maryland, Douglass fled to New York in 1838 and then to Massachusetts, where he joined the abolitionist movement. Entirely self-educated, he became an eloquent speaker, author and journalist for the abolition cause. During the Civil War, he counseled President Abraham Lincoln and urged African-Americans, including his sons, to join the Union Army. After the war, he supported the constitutional amendments that granted African-Americans citizenship and the right to vote. Also known as Cedar Hill, the beautiful Victorian building overlooking historic Anacostia is Douglass' former home. It was purchased in 1877 for $6,700. The Visitor Center here features exhibits and a documentary film of Douglass' life. The house, with original furnishings, reflects his many interests and his concern for civil rights for African-Americans and for women. Open daily 9 am-4 pm. Closed Thanksgiving, Christmas and New Year's Eve.

Frederick Douglass National Historical Site
Photo courtesy of the Washington DC Convention and Visitors Association

Freedmen's Savings Bank Site, northeast corner of Pennsylvania Ave and Madison Place NW. Organized in 1865, this bank was a showcase of African-American economic achievement for almost 10 years, until unfortunate mismanagement and fraud resulted in its collapse. Congress chartered the bank in New York City during the Civil War in an effort to establish banking facilities on army posts to protect the paychecks of African-American soldiers and employees from swindlers. They named General Oliver O. Howard (Howard University's namesake) as president. In 1874, Frederick Douglass was elected bank president.

Freedom Plaza, Pennsylvania Ave between 13th and 14th streets NW. Metro: Federal Triangle. This site holds the Martin Luther King, Jr. time capsule, which was buried on January 15, 1988. It contains the bible, robe, and other memorabilia of the slain civil rights leader. The capsule is scheduled to be opened on January 15, 2008.

Howard Theatre, 624 T Street NW. Metro: Shaw-Howard University. This historic site was built in 1910 and was part of the "Chitlin Circuit" that featured such artists as Marvin Gaye, Duke Ellington and Pearl Bailey.

Howard University, 2400 Sixth Street NW. Metro: Shaw-Howard University. Founded in 1867 in response to the Missionary Society for the First Congregational Church for Washington and recognizing the need for higher education for freed African-Americans after the Civil War, General Oliver Otis Howard, a former Union Civil War general, commissioned Freedmen's Bureau. He was a staunch supporter of the proposed school and founded the university through an act of Congress. The university bears his name and the name of the original campus. Only the Oliver Howard House, overlooking Georgia Ave, remains and is now a National Historic Landmark. Today, Howard is one of the most prestigious, historically African-American universities in the country. The campus contains the Mooreland-Spingarn Research Center, as well as many buildings named in honor of significant leaders throughout the university's history.

Lincoln Memorial, West Potomac Park at 23rd Street NW, ☎ 202-426-6841. Metro: Foggy Bottom. This grand memorial overlooking the reflecting pool has a 19-foot-tall marble statue of the 16th President, with inscriptions of the Gettysburg Address and Lincoln's second inaugural address. Famous African-Americans connected with this site include Dr. Robert Morten, president of Tuskegee University, who in 1922 delivered one of the dedicating speeches; contralto Marian Anderson, who gave her famous Easter morning concert here in 1939; and Dr. Martin Luther King, Jr., who delivered his famous "I Have a Dream" speech here in 1963.

Lincoln Park, East Capitol S, between 11th and 13th streets NW. Metro: Eastern Market. Still retaining the ambiance of the late 19th century, this historic park is situated exactly one mile east from the center of the US Capitol. It celebrates the abolition of slavery in the District of Columbia. During the Civil War this area quartered a campground full of Union soldiers and housed the temporary war facility, Lincoln Hospital. The park is currently the site of the Emancipation Memorial and the Mary McLeod Bethune Memorial.

M.W. Prince Hall Grand Lodge, Free and Accepted Masons, U Street, at Vermont Ave NW. Metro: U-Street-Cardozo. Built in 1922, this marble-and-concrete building (named after Prince Hall, the first freemason of color) housed the first Black Masonic Order chartered below the Mason-Dixie Line. The Grand Masonic Lodge of DC was founded in 1825 by 10 free African-American men. Prince Hall, an influential member of society who lobbied for the abolition of slavery and equal education, founded African Lodge No. 459 in 1775 after being rejected from membership in a white Masonic lodge. Not open to the public.

Malcolm X and Marcus Garvey Statue, 1440 Belmont Street NW. Metro: U Street-Cardozo. A 12-foot-tall steel and stained-glass statue honors the two famous African-American nationalist leaders. The statue was inspired by ancestral art work from Gabon by sculptor A. Uzikee Nelson.

Malcolm X Park, 16th Street, between Florida Ave and Euclid Street NW. Metro: U Street-Cardozo. A beautifully terraced park containing 13 fountains that were randomly developed until the 1880s. It once had a farmhouse that was used as a hospital during the Civil War. It took many years before the 12-acre park, originally called Meridian Hill Park, was completed. Because it was frequently used as a rallying place for civil rights groups in the 1960s, the park was unofficially designated as Malcolm X Park, in honor of the assassinated African-American nationalist leader.

Martin Luther King, Jr. Memorial Library, 901 G Street NW, ☎ 202-727-1111. Metro: Gallery Place-Chinatown or Metro Center. The main branch of the city's public library system is a memorial to the slain civil rights leader. Of special interest are the Washingtoniana Division, with a vast assortment of clippings and photos depicting the history of the nation's capital, and the Black Studies division of the Oral History Research Center. The library also hosts rotating gallery exhibits and free film and concert programs. Also housed at the library is the King Mural by Don Miller, a pictorial documentation of the life and legacy of Dr. Martin Luther King, Jr. Mon-Thurs, 9 am-9 pm; Fri-Sat, 9 am-5:30 pm; Sun, 1 pm-5 pm. Summer hours vary. Call first. Tours offered Mon-Thurs, 9 am-4 pm.

Mary Church Terrell Residence, 326 T Street NW. Mary Church Terrell's spent her life fighting for racial equality, from the time of the Emancipation Proclamation in 1863 to the 1954 Supreme Court decision desegregating the nation's public schools. She was the first African-American woman to be appointed to the District of Columbia School Board in 1895; founder and the first president of the National Association of Colored Women; and she served on the committee that laid the foundation for the NAACP. Ms. Terrell also assisted in the formation of the Delta Sigma Theta Sorority at Howard University in 1914, and wrote the Delta Creed. Her home has been designated as a historic landmark. Not open to the public.

Mary McLeod Bethune Statue, Lincoln Park. East Capitol Street, between 11th and 13th streets NE. Metro: Eastern Market. Erected in 1974 by the National Council of Negro Women, this memorial is the first memorial honoring an African-American in the nation's capital and also the first memorial dedicated to a woman in a public park. The statue depicts Bethune resting on the cane presented to her by President Franklin D. Roosevelt and passing on her legacy to two African-American children. It is symbolic of the final words directed towards America's African-American youth in her will. Recognized as a national leader, Mrs. Bethune was elected president of the National Association of Colored Women in 1924 and later became the founder and president of the National Council of Negro Women. She became Special Advisor for Minority Affairs to President Franklin D. Roosevelt in 1934 and was instrumental in establishing the "Black Cabinet." In 1936, she was appointed Director of Negro Affairs in the National Youth Administration, making her the first African-American woman to head a federal office.

Mary McLeod Bethune Statue
Photo courtesy of the Washington DC Convention and Visitors Association

Mooreland-Spingarn Research Center, located in the Founder's Library on the Howard University Campus, 2400 Sixth Street NW, ☎ 202-806-7266. Metro: Shaw-Howard University. The Center contains one of the world's largest collections of material relating to the history and culture of African-Americans in Africa, the US, the Caribbean and Latin America. It is named in honor of Dr. Jesse E. Mooreland, who donated his extraordinary private library of books on African-Americans in America and Africa, and in honor of Arthur B. Spingarn, who assembled an exceptional collection of books in 20 languages by African-American authors.

Mt. Zion Cemetery and Female Union Band Cemetery, 2700 Block of Q Street NW. Found in historic Georgetown, where the African-American community lived in large numbers until the 1940s, these two neighboring cemeteries constitute the oldest predominantly African-American burial grounds in Washington. Interred there are some of the major African-American leaders from the city's past. The cemetery sites were at one time about to suffer a fate of urban renewal but, due to protests of the planners of the 1976 US Bicentennial celebration, were subsequently declared historic landmarks.

National Archives and Record Administration, Seventh Street and Pennsylvania Ave NW, ☎ 202-501-5205. TTY, 202-501-5044. Metro: Archives-Navy Memorial. This building houses more than three billion records and documents, including the Emancipation Proclamation. It was here that author Alex Haley conducted part of his research for his best-selling book, *ROOTS: An American Saga,* which traced his African-American heritage back to

Africa. Mon-Sun, 10 am-5:30 pm. Spring and summer, 10 am-9 pm. Guided tours available.

Negro Mother and Child Sculpture, Department of the Interior, C Street, between 18th and 19th streets NW. Metro: Farragut North. Sculpted by Maurice Glickman, this bronze piece is found within the inner courtyard of the Department of the Interior. It was produced with the support of the Public Works of Art Project in 1934. Founder's Library at Howard University houses the original plaster model.

Paul Lawrence Dunbar Residence, 321 U Street NW. Metro: U Street-Cardozo. This is the former residence of Paul Lawrence Dunbar, one of the first African-American poets to achieve international acclaim. Dunbar was taught to read as a toddler by his uneducated mother. After graduating from high school, he published his first book of poetry in 1892. His writing efforts earned rave reviews and national recognition. Dunbar's LeDroit Park home was once considered to be the African-American community's cultural and intellectual core. Not open to the public.

Ralph J. Bunche Residence, 1510 Jackson Street NE. This is the former residence of Ralph J. Bunche. In 1944, Bunche was the first African-American desk officer at the State Department. His assertive peacemaking efforts and remarkable work in the United Nations earned him the 1950 Nobel Peace Prize, making him the first African-American to receive this award. Not open to the public.

Robert Weaver Residence, 3519 14th Street NE. This is the former home of Robert Weaver, a native Washingtonian and Dunbar High School graduate. Weaver became the first African-American to head a cabinet department in the federal government when President Johnson appointed him as Secretary of the Department of Housing and Urban development (HUD) in 1965. Prior to this appointment, Weaver held such notable positions as Advisor on Minorities to the Secretary of the Interior, leader of President F. Roosevelt's informal "Black Cabinet," Rent Commissioner for New York State, and Director of Housing and the Home Finance Agency during the Kennedy Administration. Not open to the public.

Scurlock Photography Studio Site, 900 U Street NW. Metro: U Street-Cardozo. The studio opened in 1911 under the direction of photographer Addison N. Scurlock. Scurlock's reputation drew noted African-Americans from across the country to have their portrait taken by him. Among Mr. Scurlock's photographs are images of the great leaders of his day, including Booker T. Washington, Mary McCleod Bethune, W.E.B. Dubois, Charles Drew, Madame Evanti, and Paul Lawrence Dunbar. Scurlock's career spanned 64 years; the family businesses continued under the direction of Addison's son, Robert Scurlock. Not open to the public.

Senator Edward Brook Residence, 1938 Third Street NW. In the historic LeDroit Park area is the former home of Senator Edward Brook, who in 1966 became the first African-American elected by popular vote to the US Senate. Brook received the Bronze Star in World War II for his outstanding and dedicated military service. He was also the first African-American to win a statewide office in 1962 when he was elected Attorney General of Massachusetts. As a US Senator, he was the first to call for President Nixon's resignation during the Watergate scandal. Not open to the public.

Shaw Junior High School (original location; now Asbury Dwellings, a housing facility for the elderly), southeast corner of Seventh Street and Rhode Island Ave NW. Metro: Mount Vernon Square. The grand brick-and-limestone Romanesque building is the former Shaw Junior High School. Transferred to the Black system by the school board in 1928 due to its fallen condition as a technical high school for whites, the already 75-year-old school was renamed Shaw and used until 1977, at which time the new Shaw opened. The old Shaw underwent a rehabilitation project sponsored by Asbury United Methodist Church and, to date, is the largest adaptive reuse of a district school building.

Sterling Brown Residence, 1222 Kearney Street NE. Metro: Brookland-CUA. Sterling Brown was a prominent literary figure during the Harlem Renaissance years. Until the time of his death in 1989 he was considered to be the dean of African-American poets in the US. Brown taught English at Howard University and served as editor of Negro Affairs for the Federal Writer's Project, part of the Washington Performing Arts Program. Not open to the public.

St. Martin De Porres Statue, 1602 Morris Rd SE. Metro: Anacostia. This statue of an African-American saint is located in the first inlet of Our Lady of Perpetual Help.

Tidal Basin Bridge and Seawall, south end of 15th Street SW. Metro: Smithsonian. Located in West Potomac Park, which is best known for its famous and beautiful cherry blossoms, the bridge and seawall were designed in 1942 by African-American engineer and bridge builder Archie Alexander.

US Capitol, National Mall. Metro: Capitol South or Union Station, ☎ 202-224-3121; tours 202-225-6827. In 1863, during the Civil War, African-American labor helped place the great dome atop the Capitol. Located in the great rotunda hall of the Capitol is a memorial statue of Dr. Martin Luther King, Jr. Open daily 9 am-4:30 pm; tours, 9 am-3:45 pm.

US Supreme Court, One First Street NE, ☎ 202-479-3030. Metro: Capitol South or Union Station. The nation's highest court. In 1947, Justice Thurgood Marshall became the first African-American to be appointed here. Historic case decisions affecting African-Americans include the Dred Scott Decision of 1857, which deemed slaves as property instead of citizens, and Brown vs. the Board of Education in 1954, which outlawed school segregation. Visitors can attend court sessions and view exhibits and a film. Mon-Fri, 9 am-4:30 pm. Closed on federal holidays.

Washington Jail Site, Judiciary Square and southwest corner of G & Fourth streets NW. Metro: Judiciary Square. Serving as storehouses for the District's slave traders, Washington's first two jails were designated for any African-American person who defied the city's Black Codes. The second jail, on G and Fourth Street, was built in 1839 to alleviate the overcrowded conditions of the first jail on Judiciary Square. By 1874 both jails had been destroyed, but during their existence they housed, under terrible conditions, thousands of slaves and free African-Americans arrested as runaways.

Washington Monument, National Mall at 15th Street NW, ☎ 202-426-6841. Metro: Smithsonian. One of the tallest masonry structures in the world, this majestic obelisk, patterned after the African pyramid, was dedicated in 1885 to the memory of the first US President. The Honorable Frederick Douglass was an invited dignitary at the dedication ceremony. Open daily, 9 am-5 pm; from April-Labor Day, until midnight. Closed Christmas.

Whitelaw Hotel Site, 1839 13th Street NW. Metro: U Street-Cardozo. Built after World War I, this was the only large hotel for African-Americans in Washington prior to the Dunbar Hotel. This popular facility was named after the African-American businessman, John Whitelaw Lewis, who was responsible for building it. Popular legend, however, says that it was named for the "white laws" that segregated all public accommodation facilities in the city. The building has been beautifully renovated and now serves as a residential apartment dwelling.

Museums/Exhibits

Africare House, Museum of African Art, 440 R Street NW, ☎ 202-462-3614, fax 202-387-1034. E-mail: Africare@africare.org. Metro: Shaw-Howard University. This headquarters building contains authentic African art and artifacts from various African countries. Africare is a non-profit organization that assists African families in the areas of agriculture, water, environmental management, health and emergency humanitarian aid. Tours and art viewing by appointment only.

Anacostia Museum, 1901 Fort Place SE, ☎ 202-287-3369. Metro: Anacostia. Since its beginning in 1967, the Anacostia Museum has evolved from a neighborhood museum without formal themes or elaborate exhibits to a cultural facility that researches, designs and produces its own exhibitions on the art, history, culture and contributions of African-Americans. The museum focuses on history and urban issues in the upper South: South Carolina, North

Carolina, Georgia, Maryland, Virginia and the District of Columbia. The museum has a collection of more than 5,000 items, including photographs, documents, books and artifacts. Open daily, 10 am-5 pm.

Bethune Museum and Archives, 1318 Vermont Ave NW, ☎ 202-332-1233. Metro: McPherson Square. Born to slaves on the McLeod Plantation in Mayesville, SC, Mary McLeod Bethune was the 15th of 17 children. Recognizing the need for freedom and equality, she became a powerful force in the struggle for civil rights as a counselor to four presidents, director of a government agency, founder of the National Council of Negro Women and an umbrella group for organizations of African-American women. Her home served as headquarters for this organization from 1943 to 1966. Today, it is a center for emphasizing the contributions of African-American women to American life through exhibits and programs. Mon-Fri, 10 am-4 pm.

Black Fashion Museum, 2007 Vermont Ave NW, ☎ 202-667-0744. Metro: U Street-Cardozo. An affiliate of the Harlem Institute of Fashion, the museum is a non-profit cultural institution that serves as a repository for both antique and modern-day garments that have been designed, made and/or worn by African-American people. It also educates and informs the community about the contributions of African-Americans throughout history in the world of fashion. By appointment only.

Blackburn Gallery, 2400 Sixth Street NW, Howard University, ☎ 202-806-5978. Metro: Shaw-Howard University. Features unique paintings, sculptures and exhibitions from African and African American artists. Mon-Fri, 10 am-9 pm.

Charles E. Sumner School Museum Archives, 17th and M Street NW. Metro: Farragut North. Named in honor of US Senator Charles Sumner, because of his outspoken advocacy an African-American primary school and public high school. Housed in the museum today as part of its permanent collection is the African-American history map of the US, the Reverend Martin Luther King, Jr. Memorial, and the diploma from the first high school graduation of African-American students, held at the Sumner School in 1877. Mon-Fri, 10 am-5 pm; the Archival Library is open Mon-Fri, 10 am-4 pm.

Historic Colleges & Universities

Howard University, 2400 Sixth Street NW, Washington DC 20059, ☎ 202-806-2750. Private university. Founded 1867.

University of the District of Columbia, 4200 Connecticut Ave NW, Washington, DC 20008, ☎ 202-282-7300. State-supported university. Founded 1976.

Shopping

Galleries & Specialty Shops

African Eye, 2134 Wisconsin Ave, Georgetown, ☎ 202-625-2552. African and African-American fine arts and crafts. Gift shop, jewelry, home furnishings and bridal boutique. Tues-Fri, noon-8 pm; Sat, 10 am-8 am; Sun, 11 am-4 pm.

Boutique Mikuba, 1359 U Street NW, ☎ 202-483-6877. West African art and woodcrafts. Mon-Sat. 11 am-8 pm.

Miya Gallery & Wonderful Things, 629 East Street NW, ☎ 202-347-6330. African art sculptures, paintings and African-American gift items and prints. Mon-Fri, noon-6 pm.

Gallery Exact, 739 Eighth Street SE, ☎ 202-546-7186. African and African-American art, paintings, sculptures, prints and much more. Tues-Thurs, 11 am-7 pm; Sun, 11 am-5 pm.

Ramee Art Gallery, ☎ 202-291-0067. African-American art, reproductions and bronze sculptures. Tues-Fri, noon-6 pm; Sat, 11 am-5 pm.

Yawa Books & Gifts, 2206 18th Street, ☎ 202-483-6805. Books, gifts, fragrance oils, greeting cards and art prints. Mon-Sat, 11 am-9 pm; Sun, noon-6 pm. Free storytelling on Saturdays for children, 2 pm-3 pm.

Zawadi, 1524 U Street NW, ☎ 202-232-2214. Authentic African art, home furnishings, fabrics and gifts. Mon-Sat, 11:30 am-7 pm.

Bookstores

NIA's Books-N-Things, 9053 Liberia Ave, Manassas, VA, ☎ 703-369-1412. African clothing, books, and jewelry.

Pyramid Books, 2849 Georgia Ave NW, Ledroit, ☎ 202-328-0190. Afrocentric books, posters, cards and maps. Mon-Sat, 11 am-7 pm; Sat, noon-5 pm.

Reprint Book Shop, 455 L'Efant Plaza SW, ☎ 202-554-5070.

Renaissance Books and Collectibles, 644 Massachusetts Ave NE, ☎ 202-543-5833.

Sisterspace and Books, 1354 U Street NW, ☎ 202-332-3433. Tues-Fri, 10 am-7 pm; Sat, 10 am-6 pm; Sun, noon-5 pm.

Vertigo Books, 1337 Connecticut Ave NW, ☎ 202-429-9272. African and African-American books. Mon-Sat, 10 am-8 pm; Sun, 11 am-6 pm.

Yawa Books & Gifts, 2206 18th Street, ☎ 202-483-6805. Books, gifts, fragrance oils, greeting cards and art prints. Mon-Sat, 11 am-9 pm; Sun, noon-6 pm. Free storytelling on Saturdays for children, 2 pm-3 pm.

Fashions

African Heritage Gift Shop, 2113 Rhode Island Ave, ☎ 202- 269-3113. African fabrics, clothing and books. Mon-Sat, 10 am-6 pm.

Gihgi, 6218 Georgia Ave NW, ☎ 202-723-2994. African prints and woven batiks, Nigerian wedding gowns. Mon-Sat, 11 am-6 pm.

Mood Indigo, 1214 U Street NW, ☎ 202-265-6366. Tasteful collection of vintage garments from the 1920s through the 1960s. Mon-Sat, noon-8 pm; Sun, noon-6 pm.

Seven Powers of Africa, 2906 Georgia Ave, Ledroit Park, ☎ 202-667-0681. African fabrics and clothing. Mon-Sat, 11 am-7 pm.

Restaurants

◆ African

Addis Adaba, 2106 18th Street NW, ☎ 202-232-6092. Ethiopian cuisine. Specialties are spicy chicken and lamb entrées. Sun-Thurs, 11 am-2 am. Fri-Sat, 11 am-3 am. Another location in Toronto, Ontario.

Bukom, 2442 18th Street NW, ☎ 202-265-4600. Nigerian cuisine. Live reggae and West African music. Sun-Thurs, 4 pm-2 am; Fri-Sat, 4 pm-3 am.

Fasika's, 2447 18th Street NW, ☎ 202-797-7673. Ethiopian cuisine; lamb and vegetarian dishes are their specialty. Sun-Thurs, 11:30 am-2 am. Fri-Sat, 11:30 am-3 am.

Meskerem, 2434 18th Street NW, ☎ 202-462-4100. Popular Ethiopian restaurant. Reservations recommended. Sun-Thurs, noon-midnight; Fri-Sat, noon-2 am.

Red Sea, 2463 18th Street NW, ☎ 202-483-5000. Ethiopian cuisine. Open daily, 11:30 am-11:30 pm.

Zed's Ethiopian, 3318 M Street NW, Georgetown, ☎ 202-333-7140. Among the 100 best restaurants in DC, 1989-94. Open daily, 11 am-11 pm.

◆ Barbecue

Blaze Bar-B-Que, 1110 U Street NW, ☎ 202-234-0361. Hickory pit ribs, chicken and sandwiches. Mon-Thurs, 11 am-10 pm; Fri-Sat, 11 am-midnight.

◆ Caribbean

Hibiscus, 3401 K Street, NW, Georgetown, ☎ 202-965-7170. Features fish and "wings and tings." Caribbean Sunday brunch. Tues-Sat, 6 pm-10 pm; Sun 5 pm-10 pm; Closed Mons.

The Islander, 1762 Columbia Rd, upstairs, ☎ 202-234-4955. Tropical beverages. Tues-Thurs, noon-10 pm; Fri-Sat, noon-11 pm.

◆ Creole

Blues Alley, 1073 Wisconsin Ave NW, Georgetown, ☎ 202-337-4141. Popular DC jazz club. Sun-Thurs shows, 8 pm and 10 pm; Fri-Sat, 8 pm, 10 pm and noon.

Foxtrappe, 700 Water Street SW, ☎ 202-554-2600. Waterfront jazz club/restaurant. Features live jazz or blues Tues-Fri, 7 pm-11 pm, urban contemporary music and dancing Tues-Sat evenings.

◆ Cafés

Café Nema, 1334 U Street NW, ☎ 202-667-3215. Sandwich shop. Live jazz and Somali music on weekends. Open daily, 9 am until ?

Mangos, 2017 14th Street NW, ☎ 202-332-2104. Dinner served, 6 pm-10 pm; Fri-Sat, 6 pm-noon. Open mike poetry on Tues, 8 pm-10 pm.

Morgan's Coffee Café, 1352 U Street NW, ☎ 202-265-4032. 25 flavors of coffees, including Southern pecan and toasted almond. Tues-Thurs, 7 am-2 am; Fri-Sat, 5 am until ?; Sun, 9 am-9 pm.

◆ Soul Food

B Smith's, Union Station, Massachusetts Ave NE, ☎ 202-289-6188. Elegant soul food establishment. Mon-Sat, 8 am-9 pm; Sun, 8 am-6 pm.

Ben's Chili Bowl, 1213 U Street NW, ☎ 202-667-0909. Popular diner known for its chili. Mon-Thurs, 11 am-10 pm; Fri-Sat, 11 am-midnight; Sun, 11 am-6 pm.

French's, 1365 H Street NE, ☎ 202-396-0991. Homestyle breakfast, lunch and dinner entrées. Mon-Thurs, 8 am-8 pm; Fri-Sat, 8 am-9 pm; Sun, 8 am-6 pm.

Georgia Brown, 950 15th Street, ☎ 202-393-4499. Fine Southern/soul cuisine. Mon-Fri, 11:30 am-11 pm; Sat, 6 pm-midnight; Sun, 11:30 am-3 pm and 5 pm-11 pm.

Imani, 1918 Martin Luther King, Jr. Ave SE, ☎ 202-678-2864. Open for breakfast and lunch. Mon-Fri, 8 am-4 pm; Sat-Sun, 9 am-5 pm.

Heart & Soul Café, 424 Eighth Street SE, ☎ 202-547-1892.

Jimmy French's Southwestern and Southern, 1940 11th Street, ☎ 202-234-8790. Southern/soul cuisine. Features meatloaf and chitterlings. Tues-Thurs, 11 am-10 pm; Fri-Sat, 11 am-midnight. Sun, 11 am-6 pm.

Webb's Southern Fish & Ribs, 1361 U Street NW, ☎ 202-462-3474. Features crabcakes, bone croaker, shrimp platters and ribs. Mon-Thurs, 11 am-9 pm; Fri-Sat, 11 am-midnight; Sun, noon-7 pm.

◆ American

Black Entertainment Network (BET) Sound Stage, 9640 Lottsford Court, Largo, MD, ☎ 301-883-9500. Located about 25 miles south of downtown Baltimore next to the Washington Bullets' US Air Arena, take Rt. 95 south. This unique music video theme restaurant serves up classic American entrées with a Southern flair, including steaks, seafood, Caribbean jerk chicken, New Orleans Creole gumbo and homemade desserts. Dress code is smart informal. Sunday brunch (11 am-3 pm) features BET Network Bobby Jones Gospel sounds. Mon-Thurs, 11:30 am-1 am; Fri-Sat, 11:30 am-2 am; Sun, 11 am-midnight.

Mr. Henry's, 1836 Columbia Rd NW, ☎ 202-797-8882.

Florida Avenue Grill, 1100 Florida Ave NW, ☎ 202-265-1586.

Entertainment

◆ Jazz Nightclubs/Lounges

Blues Alley, 1073 Wisconsin Ave NW, Georgetown, ☎ 202-337-4141. Popular DC jazz club. Sun-Thurs shows, 8 pm & 10 pm; Fri-Sat, 8 pm, 10 pm and midnight. Creole cuisine.

Café Nema, 1334 U Street NW, ☎ 202-667-3215. Live jazz and Somali music on weekends. Sandwich shop. Open daily, 9 am until ?

Foxtrappe, 700 Water Street SW, ☎ 202-554-2600. See listing under *Creole* restaurants.

One Step Down, 2517 Pennsylvania Ave, ☎ 202-331-8863. Features live traditional jazz and jazz fusion Thurs-Mon nights. Open Mon-Fri, 10 am-2 am; Sat-Sun, noon-2 am.

Takoma Station, 6914 Fourth Street NW, ☎ 202-829-1937. Popular jazz spot for 12 years. Mon-Thurs, 4 pm-2 am; Fri-Sun, 4 pm-3 am. Live music begins at 8 pm.

◆ Reggae

Erico, 1334 U Street NW, ☎ 202-265-1911. West African establishment featuring Caribbean music. Sun, reggae; Tues, open mike poetry; Wed, 1970s-1980s dancing; Thurs, Caribbean; Fri-Sat, Calypso, reggae and zouk. Call for hours.

◆ Dance Nightclubs

Solar Eclipse, 2820 Bladenburg Rd, ☎ 202-526-3533. Popular R&B dance club. Tues & Thurs-Sat, 6 pm-midnight.

Republic Gardens, 1355 U Street NW, ☎ 202-232-3356. Contemporary upscale dance nightclub. Attracts adult patrons. Sun-Thurs, 5 pm-1 am. Fri-Sat, 5 pm-3 am.

The Ritz, 919 East Street SW, ☎ 202-638-2582. Open nightly from 9 pm-until. Cover charge.

◆ **Theatre**

Pinpoints Theatre, 1001 African-American inventions, ☎ 301-582-0002.

Lodging

Bed & Breakfasts

Rockland Farm Retreat, 3609 Lewiston Rd, Bumpass, VA 23024, ☎ 540-895-5098 or 301-384-4583. Rockland is much more than a bed and breakfast, it's a 75-acre country estate that caters to both large and small groups. This establishment is in an isolated area in Spotsylvania County on beautiful Lake Anna, surrounded by majestic trees, quiet pastures and wildlife. Rockland is about 75 miles south of Washington, DC and features gourmet dinners, antique furnishings, magnificent views and a rich African-American history. Call for current rates and reservations.

Travel Agents

Allen Travel, 1134 11th Street NW, Washington, DC 20001, ☎ 800-221-3197 or 202-371-8740.

Eldorado Travel, 1444 Eye Street NW, #212, Washington, DC 20024, ☎ 202-289-0226.

Lawton's Travel, 1006 North Settlers Landing Rd, Hampton, VA 23669, ☎ 804-723-0701 or 804-727-5773 (Hampton). ITAS member.

Peacock World Travel, Inc., 1809 Riggs Place, NW #3, Washington, DC 20009, ☎ 202-388-5049.

Thaxton's Travel Agency, Inc., 6400 Georgia Ave NW #11, Washington, DC 20012, ☎ 202-829-6400.

Heritage Tours

Site Seeing Tours, African-American focus, ☎ 301-445-3821.

Capitol Entertainment Services, 3629 18th Street NE, Washington, DC 20018, ☎ 202-636-9203, fax 202-529-3402. Capitol features educational tours of the Washington, DC area and offer everything from US Government tours to African-American history tours, which include visits to the Frederick Douglass National Historic Site, National Museum of African Art, "From the Fields to the Factory" exhibit at the National Museum of American History and the Dr. Martin Luther King, Jr. Memorial. Call for more for information and reservations.

Media

Radio

◆ Jazz

WDCU 90.1 FM, 4200 Connecticut Ave NW, ☎ 202-282-7588.

WJZE 105.9, 5321 First Place NE, ☎ 202-722-1000.

WPFW 89.3 FM, 202 H Street NW ☎ 202-283-3100.

◆ Urban Contemporary

WHUR 96.3 FM, 529 Bryant Street NW, ☎ 202-806-3500.

WKYS 93.9 FM, 4001 Nebraska Ave NW, ☎ 202-686-9300.

WMMJ 102.3 FM, 400 H Street NE, ☎ 202-675-4800.

WOL 1450 AM, 400 H Street NE, ☎ 202-675-4800.

◆ Gospel

WVST 1120 AM, 815 V Street NW, ☎ 202-462-0011.

WYCB 1340 AM, 529 14th Street NE, ☎ 202-737-6400. Gospel format.

Newspapers

Washington Afro-American Newspaper, 1612 14th Street NW, ☎ 202-332-0080. E-mail: www.afroam.org

Publications

African American Historical Attractions Guide, Washington DC Convention and Visitors Association, 1212 New York Ave NW #500, Washington, DC 20005-3992, ☎ 202-789-7000, fax 202-789-7037.

African and African American Resources at the Smithsonian, Smithsonian Institute, 1000 Jefferson Drive, Washington DC 20560.

Washington DC Black History National Recreation Trail Brochure, Parks and History Association, Washington DC National Park Service, Department of the Interior.

Washington Visitors Guide, Washington DC Convention and Visitors Association, 1212 New York Ave NW #500, Washington, DC 20005-3992, ☎ 202-789-7000, fax 202-789-7037.

African-American Churches

AME

Brown Memorial AME, 130 14th Street NE, ☎ 202-543-0473.

Campbell AME Church, 2562 Martin Luther King, Jr. Ave SE, ☎ 202-889-3006.

John Wesley AME Zion, 1615 14th Street, ☎ 202-667-3824.

Metropolitan AME Church, 1518 M Street NW, ☎ 202-331-1426.

Pilgrim AME, 612 17th St NE, ☎ 202-396-8582.

St. Paul AME Church, 4901 14th Street NW, ☎ 202-882-7088.

Ward Memorial AME, 241 42nd Street NE, ☎ 202-898-3899.

AME Zion Full Gospel AME Zion, 4207 Norcross Street, Temple Hills, ☎ 301-899-9411.

Baptist

19th Street Baptist, Eighth & H streets NW, ☎ 202-347-8355.

Greater New Hope Baptist, 816 Eighth Street NW, ☎ 202-789-9419.

Gethsemane Baptist, 5119 Fourth Street NW, ☎ 202-723-9723.

Metropolitan Baptist, 1225 R Street NW, ☎ 202-483-1540.

Mount Airy Baptist, 1100 North Capitol Street, ☎ 202-842-3698.

Mount Bethel Baptist, First & Rhode Island Ave NW, ☎ 202-667-4448.

Mount Carmel Baptist, 901 Third St NW, ☎ 202 842-3411.

Nineteenth Street Baptist, 4606 16th Street, NW, ☎ 202-829-2773.

Shiloh Baptist, 1510 Ninth Street NW, ☎ 202-232-4200.

Union Temple Baptist, 1225 West Street SE, ☎ 202-678-8822.

Catholic

St. Augustine Catholic, 1425 V Street NW, ☎ 202-265-1470.

COGIC

Emmanuel Church of God in Christ, 2815 Stanton Rd SE, ☎ 202-678-7193.

Friendship Church of God in Christ, 3900 Kansas Ave NW, ☎ 202-723-9702.

Kirkland Church of God in Christ, 624 Eighth Street NE, ☎ 202-543-9651.

Second Church of God in Christ, 624 Eighth Street NE, ☎ 202-546-2899.

Star of Bethlehem Church of God in Christ, 5331 Colorado Ave NW, ☎ 202-462-5016.

CME

St. John CME Church, 2801 Stanton Rd. SE, ☎ 202-678-7788.

Methodist

Ebenezer United Methodist Church, corner of 4th and D streets, SE, ☎ 202-544-9539.

Calendar of Annual Events

◆ January

Martin Luther King, Jr. Birthday Celebration, citywide activities, ☎ 202-619-7222.

◆ February

Black History Month, citywide activities. Smithsonian Institute, ☎ 202-357-2700; Martin Luther King, Jr. Memorial Library, ☎ 202-727-0321; National Park Service, ☎ 202-619-7222; Ford's Theater, ☎ 202-347-4833.

Black History Month Salute to Black Artists, ☎ 202-332-2879. African-American arts festival.

◆ March

The Taste of Soul, ☎ 202-562-5239. Annual festival showcases the cuisines of local African-American restaurateurs and caterers.

◆ April

Duke Ellington Birthday Celebration, ☎ 202-331-9404. Celebrates this native Washingtonian's contributions to American music.

Marvin Gaye/Save the Children Festival, African-American Music Foundation, ☎ 202-678-0503. Street festival features performances by local and national entertainers. Proceeds benefit Marvin P. Gaye, Jr. Memorial Scholarship Fund.

◆ **May**

Malcolm X Day, ☎ 202-724-4093. Celebrations honoring the life of the slain civil rights leader and orator.

Worldfest, ☎ 202-724-5430. Features the cuisine of Washington, Maryland and Virginia area restaurateurs. Entertainment, food booths and other special attractions.

◆ **June**

Unifest, ☎ 202-678-8833.

Public Transportation

Baltimore-Washington International Airport, ☎ 410-859-7111. Outside Baltimore, ☎ 800-I-FLY-BWI. TDD ☎ 410-859-7227.

Baltimore Metro and Light Rail, ☎ 410-539-5000.

MARC Trains, ☎ 800-325-RAIL.

Metropolitan Area Transit Authority (Metrobus), ☎ 202-637-7000.

Washington Dulles International Airport, ☎ 703-661-2700.

Washington Metro, ☎ 202-637-7000.

Washington National Airport, ☎ 703-419-8000.

Taxi Services

Potomac Pedicabs, ☎ 202-332-1732.

Red Top Executive Sedan Company, ☎ 800-296-3300 or 703-525-0900.

Washington Flyer/Arlington Blue Cab, ☎ 703-243-8575.

Washington, DC Area Resources

Washington DC Convention and Visitors Association, 1212 New York Ave NW, #500, Washington, DC 20005-3992, ☎ 202-789-7000; fax 202-789-7037. Web site: www.washington.org.

Nova Scotia

Historic Sites & Landmarks

African Nova Scotian Training Centre (ANSTC), 2178 Gottingen Street, Halifax, ☎ 902-492-0633. Established in 1995 as a response to the growing needs to prepare Blacks in Nova Scotia for the job market, the ANSTC trains Black men and women to develop marketable job skills, offers job placement assistance, academic upgrading and helps them obtain a better understanding of African Canadian history.

Africville (Seaview Memorial Park), along the Bedford Basin under the McKay Bridge. Once a small community of Blacks, Africville was settled in the late 1830s and early 1840s by Blacks from Preston and Hammons Plains. Because of economic depression in these areas, residents moved to Halifax for better opportunities. Separated from the white community due to racial discrimination, they built their own school and church. The site is located on the northern arm of the city along Bedford Basin. In 1967, urban renewal plans destroyed the community, moving its residents to the Gottingen and Barrington streets area of Halifax to government-subsidized housing. A memorial cairn is located within the park. Former residents of Africville hold an annual reunion and picnic each July.

Amherst, Hwy 104, Exit 15 West along the Nova Scotia Sunrise Trail. During the early 1900s, Bermudian and West Indian immigrants worked in the coal mines of Amherst. Many of the residents in the Sandhill section of Amherst are descendants of those immigrants.

Annapolis Royal, Hwy 101 to Hwy 8 along the Nova Scotian Evangeline Trail. Blacks have settled here since prior to the Loyalist period. The town is famous as the home of Rose Fortune, who owned a successful baggage handling business that operated until 1970. Few Blacks live in Annapolis Royal today. View the watercolor and tapestry in Fort Anne.

Beechville, Hwy 103 and Rt 3, along the Nova Scotian Evangeline Trail just south of Liverpool. The Beechville United Baptist Church (est. 1848) is located in this town. The community center was formerly an African school.

Birchtown, Hwy 103, along the Nova Scotian Evangeline Trail. Birchtown is the home to Black Loyalists who landed there in 1783. Once the first and largest free African-American settlement in North America, Birchtown is located in Shelburne County on the Northwest arm of Shelburne Harbour. The town was named after General Samuel Birch, who signed the papers to free Black refugees from slavery at the conclusion of the Revolutionary War. The

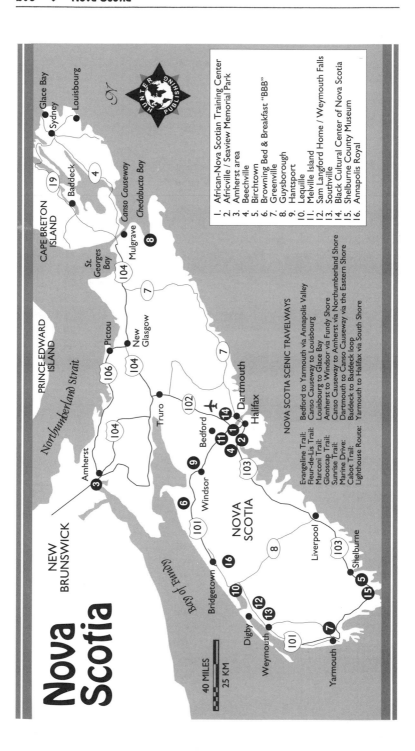

Nova Scotia

NEW BRUNSWICK

PRINCE EDWARD ISLAND

CAPE BRETON ISLAND

Northumberland Strait

Bay of Fundy

St. Georges Bay

Chedabucto Bay

Canso Causeway

NOVA SCOTIA

40 MILES
25 KM

Glace Bay
Sydney
Louisbourg
Baddeck
Mulgrave
Pictou
New Glasgow
Truro
Amherst
Dartmouth
Halifax
Bedford
Windsor
Bridgetown
Liverpool
Shelburne
Digby
Weymouth
Yarmouth

19
4
8
104
7
106
104
104
102
103
101
8
103
101
7

1. African-Nova Scotian Training Center
2. Africville / Seaview Memorial Park
3. Amherst area
4. Beechville
5. Birchtown
6. Browning Bed & Breakfast "BBB"
7. Greenville
8. Guysborough
9. Hantsport
10. Lequille
11. Melville Island
12. Sam Langford Home / Weymouth Falls
13. Southville
14. Black Cultural Center of Nova Scotia
15. Shelburne County Museum
16. Annapolis Royal

NOVA SCOTIA SCENIC TRAVELWAYS

Evangeline Trail: Bedford to Yarmouth via Annapolis Valley
Fleur-de-Lis Trail: Canso Causeway to Louisbourg
Marconi Trail: Louisbourg to Glace Bay
Glooscap Trail: Amherst to Windsor via Fundy Shore
Sunrise Trail: Canso Causeway to Amherst via Northumberland Shore
Marine Drive: Dartmouth to Canso Causeway via the Eastern Shore
Cabot Trail: Baddeck to Baddeck loop
Lighthouse Route: Yarmouth to Halifax via South Shore

Shelburne County Museum (Charlotte Lane, ☎ 902-875-3219) has artifacts from an archeological dig in Birchtown among its collection. Summer hours: daily, 9:30 am-5:30 pm; winter hours: Mon-Sat, 9:30 am-noon and 2 pm-5 pm. Admission charge.

Bridgetown, Hwy 101, Exit 19 along the Nova Scotian Evangeline Trail. Located on Bay St in the town of Bridgetown is a small settlement of African-Canadians. The Inglewood United Baptist Church (est. 1874) here was erected in 1889. A plaque in front of the church commemorates the formation of the African United Baptist Association. The Inglewood Community Centre was probably a former Black school prior to the end of segregation in the 1960s.

Cape Breton Island, along the Nova Scotian Marconi-Fleur De Lis Trail. This area in northern Nova Scotia is populated by immigrants from the state of Alabama and the Caribbean Islands, who came here to work in the steel plants of Cape Breton Island. St. Phillip's African Orthodox Church, the only one of its kind, was established in 1921 by Whitney Pier. In 1984, the church was recognized as a heritage site. In 1967, Isaac Phillips (1896-1985) of Sydney, Nova Scotia, was the first Black in Canada to receive the prestigious Order of Canada.

Dartmouth area, (East Preston, North Preston, Cherry Brooks), on Hwy 7, north Halifax Harbour along the Nova Scotian Marine Drive Trail. Dartmouth is the largest of the four towns and has the largest population of African-Canadians. North Preston and East Preston have small settlements of African Nova Scotians. The Nova Scotia Home for Coloured Children, the East Preston United Baptist Church and the Black Cultural Centre are located in these areas. The George Washington Carver Credit Union (☎ 902-462-3737) is in North Preston, Hwy 7, near Lake Major. It is the only Black banking institution of its kind the Nova Scotia. North Preston is also the home of the famous African-Canadian basket weaver, Edith Clayton (1920-1989).

Digby Area (Jordantown, Acaciaville and Conway) off Hwy 101 along the Nova Scotian Evangeline Trail. This area has small settlements of African-Canadians who have lived here since the late 1800s. Jordantown has a few homes scattered in the community and an African burial ground. Acaciaville is the focal point of the area and the location of the Acaciaville United Baptist Church (est. 1853), formerly the Digby Baptist Church. The Acaciaville-Conway Community Centre used to be a Black school. The African Burial Ground is located at 411 Hwy 303 North in the town of Digby, next to the Sunset Beverage Room and Grill.

Gibson Woods, off Hwy 101, near the town of Centreville, along the Nova Scotian Evangeline Trail. The Gibson Woods Community Centre and the Gibson Woods United Baptist Church are located in this small settlement of African-Canadians. Stay at the Browning "BBB" Bed and Breakfast (see the

Lodging section) and take in some interesting history on African-Canadians who live in the area.

Greenville, near Yarmouth on Hwy 101 to Dayton, along the Nova Scotian Evangeline Trail. The Greenville United Baptist Church (est. 1853) is on Greenville Road and was formerly the Salmon River Church. A mid-19th century graveyard is found on the former site of the African Bethel Church (est. 1949) in Greenville.

Guysborough, Hwy 104, Exit 16 along the Nova Scotian Sunrise Trail. There are African-Canadians residing in the nearby towns of Upper Big Tracadie, Monastery, Lincolnville and Sunnyville. The St. Monique Catholic Mission, a Black church in Tracadie, was established in 1956 with the help of The Sisters of St. Martha's and Father Henry Anthony of the Augustine Order.

Halifax. Halifax has always had one of the largest African-Canadian populations in the country. Since the mid-1800s, many slaves and Black Loyalists emigrated from the United States into Nova Scotia. Most African-Canadians in Halifax live in the north end of the city in the vicinity of Creighton, Maynard and Gottingen streets. Many are former residents and descendants of Africville (see *Africville*). The United Baptist Church, the mother church of the African United Baptist Association, is located on Cornwallis Street, and the African Nova Scotian Training Centre is on Gottingen Street.

Hansport, Hwy 101 along the Nova Scotia Evangeline Trail. See the commemoration for William Nelson Hall (1829-1904) at the Hansport United Baptist Church. Hall was the first Canadian sailor and first Nova Scotian to win the Victoria Cross for valor. Additional African-Canadian settlements include nearby Falmouth, Mount Denson and Five-Mile Plains (also called Windsor Plains), where the Windsor Plains United Baptist Church (est. 1812) is found. It is reportedly the oldest African Baptist church in Nova Scotia. The community hall nearby was formerly a school for Blacks and was built in 1914.

Lequille, along the Nova Scotian Evangeline Trail on Route 8, south of Hwy 101. This small town is located within the Annapolis region of Nova Scotia, where many Blacks have settled since the late 1800s. On West Dalhousie Rd. is the Major Ritchie Community Centre and School and the Lequille Baptist Church. The community centre and school educates Black children during the morning hours and adults during the afternoon hours. The building was constructed by Blacks who financed the project and included residents from Lequille, Cornwallis and Greenwood. The Baptist church was moved from another location in 1912 and the congregation has been established since 1896.

Melville Island, located on the northwest arm of Halifax Harbour. In 1815, this was the immigration depot for 100-200 Southern Black refugees of the War of 1812. The Armdale Yacht Club located on the island was once used to shelter these Black refugees. They were given food and clothing until they later settled in surrounding areas. A stone marker commemorates the history of Melville Island.

New Glasgow, Hwy 104, along the Nova Scotian Sunrise Trail. A few African Canadians reside in this town. The Second United Baptist Church is located on Washington St and was founded by Rev. Dr. W.A. White (1874-1936) who was the first Black captain in the British Empire and a chaplain of the #2 Construction Battalion, Canada's only segregated Black unit during World War I (see *Pictou,* below).

Pictou, Hwy 104 along the Nova Scotian Sunrise Trail, Exit 20 to West River Rd. Black slaves arrived in what was called "New Scotland" in the late 1700s, and many settled in Pictou County. The #2 Construction Battalion headquarters was located at Marker Wharf in Pictou. Organized in 1916, the battalion (1916-1920) was Canada's only segregated Black Unit during World War I and in Canada's military history. The unit was used to support the front lines, provide first aid for wounded soldiers, build roads and diffuse enemy land mines. Many of the #2 Construction Battalion were either killed or wounded in action.

Childhood home of Sam "Boston Tarbaby" Langford
Photo by author

Sam Langford Home, Hwy 340 along the Nova Scotian Evangeline Trail, Weymouth Falls. Sam Langford, also know as the "Boston Tarbaby," lived in this home during his childhood. At the age of 14, Langford ran away from home and ended up in Boston, where he worked as a cleaner for a short time and eventually became a boxer. Although Langford was qualified to fight in all weight classes other than heavyweight, champions would risk their title to fight against him. He was defeated by heavyweight champion Jack Johnson in a 15-round bout. However, for fear of losing his own title, Johnson would not give Langford a rematch. Langford won the heavyweight championship in Mexico in 1923. He fought over 300 bouts in his 21-year career and lost only 25. Langford has been proclaimed as one of the all time greatest ring warriors of recorded history. He died in Cambridge, Massachusetts in 1956. The Langford home (a bright yellow house) is located on the only street in Weymouth Falls and is now a private residence. Relatives of Langford still live in the area. Just ask around.

Sam Langford Community Centre, Weymouth Falls, Hwy 340 along the Nova Scotian Evangeline Trail, ☎ 902-837-4004. The community centre is named after boxing champion Sam "Boston Tarbaby" Langford, who was born in Weymouth Falls. The centre is an outreach and job placement and employment counseling institution and has a multicultural library with a remarkable collection of books by people of African descent. The centre also provides day camp and other programs for Weymouth Falls youth. Memorabilia of the late Sam Langford are on display. There is also a memorial plaque in front of the centre by the Canadian flag, recognizing Sam Langford and his achievements.

Southville (Danvers), on Route 340 off Hwy 101 along the Nova Scotian Evangeline Trail. About 250-300 African-Canadians live in this community and its surrounding areas of Danvers and Hasset. Visit St. Theresa's Roman Catholic Church and view the statue of the Black Saint (St. Martin du Porret) inside the church. A similar statue is located in Washington, DC. Church doors are usually open for visitors.

Truro, along the Nova Scotian Glooscap Trail. There is a small community of African Canadians who reside in the areas of Upper/Lower Ford St (Marsh), Young St (Hill) and West Prince Street. The Zion United Baptist Church on West Prince Street was established n 1869. Truro is the birthplace of world renowned contralto singer Portia White (1910-1968).

Yarmouth, off Hwy 101 along the Nova Scotian Evangeline Trail. African-Canadian residents are located in the south end of the town of Yarmouth. The Sharon Assembly Church (est. 1877), formerly the Disney African Methodist Episcopal Church, is located at East and Albert streets and is the only original AME building in Nova Scotia.

Weymouth Falls, on Hwy 340 off Hwy 101, along Nova Scotia's Evangeline Trail near the town of Weymouth. This village has a settlement of African-Canadians who have lived here since the late 1700s. It is the home town of boxer Sam "Tar Baby" Langford (see Sam Langford) and has two prominent religious denominations: St. Matthew Anglican (est. 1914) and the Mount Beulah Baptist Church (est. 1853).

Museums/Exhibits

Black Cultural Centre for Nova Scotia, 149 Main Street, Dartmouth, ☎ 902-434-6223. The Black Cultural Centre for Nova Scotia is a museum and a cultural and educational complex. It is the nucleus for historical information and cultural events for people of African descent in Nova Scotia. Contained within the centre are artifacts depicting the history and culture of Black people here and throughout the world. Its library has books, audio-visual and archival materials. There is also a gift shop and bookstore. Mon-Fri, 9 am-5 pm; Sat, 10 am-4 pm. Admission charge. ☆ *Specially recommended.*

David Nairn House, Shelburne County Museum
(Photo by Norman Burke, courtesy of the museum)

Shelburne County Museum, Charlotte Lane, Shelburne, ☎ 902-875-3219. This county museum has among its collection artifacts from an archaeological dig from the Black Loyalist town of Birchtown. Summer hours: daily, 9:30 am-5:30 pm. Winter hours: Mon-Sat, 9:30 am-noon and 2 pm-5 pm. Admission charge.

Shopping

Black Star Books, Black Cultural Centre for Nova Scotia, 1149 Main Street, Dartmouth, ☎ 902-434-6223. A variety of history and cultural books by and about African Canadian. Mon-Fri, 9 am-5 pm; Sat, 10 am-4 pm.

Restaurants

◆ Caribbean

Lyn D's Caribbean Café, 1520 Queen Street, near Springhill in downtown Halifax, ☎ 902-492-8100. West Indian cuisine. Features jerk, curried and ginger chicken, beef and chicken roti, jerk and calypso pork, honey-smoked pork ribs, pastas, seafood and a variety of rice dishes and tropical drinks. Cozy atmosphere. Mon-Sat, 11:30 am-9 pm. ☆ *Specially recommended.*

Lodging

Bed & Breakfasts

Browning's Bed & Breakfast ("BBB"), 8358 Hwy 221, Gibson Woods, 1.3 miles east of Centreville, Route 359 from Kentville, ☎ 902-582-7062. BBB is set in a rural community on 22 acres of beautiful farmland, and features a duck pond, picnic tables, paddleboats and a nicely landscaped yard with a view of North Mountain. The home has three private rooms with shared baths, each with a sitting room and large living area; all are smartly decorated with antique furnishings and accessories. A full breakfast is served to guests each morning in the well-appointed dining area. BBB is about an hour from Halifax and is just 10 minutes from trout fishing and many local historic attractions. If traveling along the Nova Scotia Evangeline Trail to view various African-Canadian sites, BBB is a convenient place to stay. Call for current rates and reservations. ☆ *Specially recommended.*

Churches

Baptist

Cornwallis Street Baptist Church (African United Baptist Church), 5457 Cornwallis Street, Halifax, ☎ 902-429-5573.

East Preston United Baptist Church, 224 Brooks Drive, Hwy 7 to East Preston, ☎ 902-435-1565.

Second United Baptist Church, 330 Washington Street, New Glasgow, ☎ 902-752-1360.

Zion United Baptist Church, Prince Street, Truro, ☎ 902-895-6744.

Media

Radio

CKDU FM95.7, 6136 University Ave, Dalhousie University, Halifax, NS B3H 452, ☎ 902-494-2487. This station is the only radio station in Nova Scotia that airs Black programs. In addition to music, their lineup features programs dealing with African-Canadian issues.

Magazines

Black Focus, PO Box 46016, RPO, Halifax, NS B3K 5VB. This quarterly publication profiles African-Nova Scotians. Subjects include finance, religion, education, employment, history and art.

Black in Business, 1575 Brunswick Street, Halifax, NS B3J 2G1, ☎ 902-426-2224. This quarterly publication is published by the Black Business Initiative and is targeted towards the African-Canadian business community of Nova Scotia.

Calendar of Annual Events

For the following events, contact the Black Cultural Centre, ☎ 902-434-6223.

◆ February

African Heritage Month Activities. Food, entertainment throughout Nova Scotia.

◆ May

Terry Symonds Invitational Basketball Tournament, Halifax. Victoria Day weekend.

◆ June

Multicultural Festival, food, arts and crafts, music and fun.

◆ July

Africville Picnic and Reunion, Seaview Memorial Park, Halifax. Food, music, entertainment, arts and crafts.

Atlantic Jazz Festival, second weekend in July. International artists perform at this annual event.

◆ **August**

African Baptist Association Convention, third week of August.

◆ **September**

Black Cultural Centre Anniversary, second week of September. Guest speakers, banquet and achievement awards.

Nova Scotia Resources

Black Business Initiative, PO Box 1575, Brunswick Street, NS B3J 2G1, Canada, ☎ 902-426-2224.

Black Cultural Centre for Nova Scotia, 1149 Main Street, Westphal, ☎ 902-434-6223, fax 902-434-2306. E-mail: blackcct@fox.nstn.ca, Web site: www.nstn.ca/bccns/bcc.html

Dalhousie University Black Student Centre, 6136 University Ave, NS B3H 452, ☎ 902-494-6648.

Evangeline Trail Tourism Association, 5518 Prospect, New Minas, NS, B4N 3K8, ☎ 800-565-ETTA, 902-681-1645, fax 902-681-2747. E-mail: etta@fox.nstn.ca; Web site: www.valleryweb.com/evangelinetrail.

Nova Scotia International Visitor Centre, 1595 Barrington Street, Halifax, NS Canada B3J 1Z7, ☎ 902-490-5946, TDD 902-492-4833, fax 902-490-5973. Web site: http://ttg.sba.dal.ca/nstour/halifax.

Nova Scotia Visitor Information Centre, 1596 Barrington Street, Halifax, NS Canada B3J 1Z7, ☎ 800-565-0000 or 902-425-5781.

Shelburne County Cultural Awareness Society, PO Box 832, Shelburne, NS BOT 1WO, ☎ 902-875-2114.

Ontario

Historic Sites & Landmarks

Anthony Burns Grave Site and Victorian Lawn Cemetery, Queenston Street, west of Homer Bridge, St. Catharines. The Reverend Anthony Burns was the last person tried under the Fugitive Slave Act in Massachusetts. Riots broke out in Boston when a verdict returned him to slavery. Boston area abolitionists bought Burns' freedom and educated him. He eventually settled in St. Catharines.

BME Church, Nathaniel Dett Memorial Chapel & Norva Johnson Heritage Library, British Methodist Episcopal Church, 5674 Peer Street, Niagara Falls, ☎ 416-358-9957. The current congregation of this historic church includes descendants of the original African-American settlers.

BME Church, Salem Chapel, 92 Geneva, St. Catharines. Harriet Tubman attended this church while living in St. Catharines. The Ontario Heritage Foundation dedicated a plaque here in her honor.

Bertie Hall, 657 Niagara Parkway, Fort Erie. Escaped slaves used this house as a haven after crossing the Niagara River. A Niagara Freedom Trail plaque at the site explains the history of the home. Today, Bertie Hall houses the Mildred M. Mahoney Silver Jubilee Doll's House Gallery.

Colored Corps Plaque, Queenston Heights Park, Queenston/Niagara-on-the-Lake. The plaque explains the role of the first Colored Corps during Ontario's formative years.

Fort Malden National Historic Park, Amherstburg. Site of the War of 1812 battle involving African-Canadian Josiah Henson.

Harriet Tubman Plaque, British Methodist Episcopal Church of St. Catharines, Salem Chapel, 92 Geneva Street, St. Catharines. A plaque on this site commemorates Harriet Tubman.

Lakeside Park, Port Dalhousie, St. Catharines. This park was a popular site for thousands of African-Americans who gathered here annually from the 1920s to the 1960s to celebrate Emancipation Day.

Little Africa/Miller's Bay at Fort Erie. Now a marine and part of the Niagara Freedom Trail, this site was once an export point for lumber coming from the settlement, "Little Africa." Many African-Americans made their living working at this marina during the 1840s.

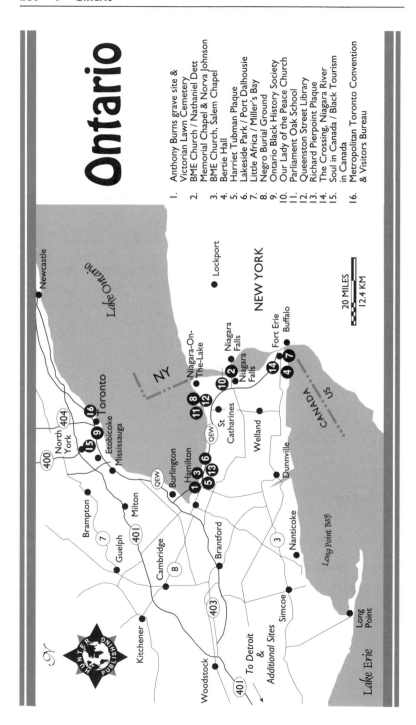

Ontario

1. Anthony Burns grave site & Victorian Lawn Cemetery
2. BME Church / Nathaniel Dett Memorial Chapel & Norva Johnson
3. BME Church, Salem Chapel
4. Bertie Hall
5. Harriet Tubman Plaque
6. Lakeside Park / Port Dalhousie
7. Little Africa / Miller's Bay
8. Negro Burial Ground
9. Ontario Black History Society
10. Our Lady of the Peace Church
11. Parliament Oak School
12. Queenston Street Library
13. Richard Pierpoint Plaque
14. The Crossing, Niagara River
15. Soul in Canada / Black Tourism in Canada
16. Metropolitan Toronto Convention & Visitors Bureau

Negro Burial Ground, 494 Mississauga Street, Queenston/Niagara-on-the-Lake. This site, now a burial ground, was once home to an African-American Baptist church.

Ontario Black History Society, 10 Adelaide Street E, Toronto, ☎ 416-867-9420. The Ontario Black History Society is dedicated to the study and promotion of African-Canadian history. The Society houses a small collection of exhibits which focus on the contributions made by Afro-Canadians during a 400-year period and includes a reference library of books by and about African-Canadians. Historic motorcoach tours and presentations are offered by the Ontario Black History Society.

Our Lady of Peace Church, 6989 Stanley Ave, Niagara Falls. This Roman Catholic church was once a Pilgrimage sanctuary for escaped slaves. The church at the time (1861) was under the leadership of Pope Pius IX.

Parliament Oak School, 325 King Street, Queenston/Niagara-on-the-Lake. An antislavery act passed in 1793 was signed into law in Niagara-on-the-Lake. A wall sculpture symbolizes this historic event.

Queenston Street Library, Queenston/Niagara-on-the-Lake. This historic building was built between 1842 and 1845 and was once the Queenston Baptist church, where African-Canadians made up half of the congregation.

Ontario

Sandwich Baptist Church
Photo courtesy of the Windsor, Essex County & Pelee Island CVB

Richard Pierpoint Plaque, Oakdale Ave, behind St. Catharines General Hospital, St. Catharines. A plaque donated by the Ontario Heritage Foundation commemorates Richard Pierpoint in recognition of his outstanding military service to the Crown during the American Revolutionary War.

Sandwich Baptist Church, 3852 Peter Street, Olde Sandwich Towne section of Windsor, ☎ 519-252-4917. This church was built by fugitive slaves who resided in the Windsor area. After a day's work, the slaves gathered materials from the Detroit River to make bricks, from which they built this house of worship.

Sheffield Park, Collingwood, ☎ 705-445-0201 or 705-444-1287. Site of historic Great Black Mariners plaque. Open for camping May to October.

The Crossing, Niagara River, by Fort Erie. Many African-Americans escaped slavery by crossing this river. A Niagara Freedom Trail plaque explains the ferry system and its significance during that time (1895).

Uncle Tom's Cabin Historic Site, Park Street, Dresden, located on Kent County Road 40, 0.6 miles southwest of Dresden, ☎ 519-683-2978. The story of Josiah Henson comes to life when visitors explore African-Canadian heritage at this historic site. Henson was the character in Harriet Beecher Stowe's novel *Uncle Tom's Cabin* and is recognized for his courageous achievements. After 41 years of slavery, Henson and his family escaped to Upper Canada in 1830. The site includes the newly restored Henson Home, the James Harris House – a place where fugitive slaves may have resided – and a church representative of that era where Henson could have preached. There's also an interpretive center, gift shop and museum. Open late May through October. Mon-Sat, 10 am-4 pm; Sun, noon-4 pm. Call for upcoming schedule.

Museums/Exhibits

John Freeman Walls Historic Site and Underground Railroad Museum, 8 miles east of the Windsor/Detroit border in Maidstone. From Township Road 401, take Exit 28 at Puce Rd, then go north one mile. ☎ 519-258-6253 or 519-971-7790. This attraction chronicles the route taken by many enslaved African-Americans on the Underground Railroad. The journey begins in Africa, then crosses the Atlantic Ocean. It continues through the slave states to freedom in Canada and concludes at the attraction's log cabin, which was built in 1896 as a terminal of the Underground Railroad. Open daily, July 1 through Labor Day, 10 am-5 pm. Admission charge.

John Freemen Walls Historic Site
Photo courtesy of the Windsor, Essex County & Pelee Island CVB

North American Black Historical Museum and Cultural Centre, 277 King Street in Amherstburg, east on Ontario Hwy approximately a 30-minute drive from the Detroit/Windsor border, ☎ 519-736-5433. Depicting a dream of freedom, this museum and cultural center is set in the midst of the original African-American settlement in Amherstburg. It maintains a collection of historical artifacts, art displays, photographs, sculptures and materials donated by descendants of the early settlers of the Underground Railroad. Within this two-story complex are the 1848 Nazery AME Church, a log cabin of the same period, a gift shop, books and souvenirs. Open April through November, Wed-Fri, 10 am-5 pm; Sat-Sun, 1 pm-5 pm. Admission charge.

Raleigh Township Centennial Museum, North Buxton. Take Hwy 401 to Bloomfield Rd, head south on Bloomfield Road, turn west on Eighth Concession, then south on County Road 6. ☎ 519-352-4799 or 519-354-8693. This museum is a memorial to the Elgin Settlement, once a haven for fugitive slaves in the pre-Civil War years. The Elgin Settlement was for many years the last stop of the Underground Railroad and later became a self-sufficient community of some 1,200 to 2,000 persons. The museum site includes a research library, video presentations, an old school building and cemetery, farm implements and tools, household goods, furnishings, jewelry and personal belongings of the original settlers. Open May through September, Wed-Sat, 1 pm-4:30 pm. Other times by appointment. Admission charge.

Shopping

Galleries & Specialty Shops

Ashanti Room, 28 Lennox Street, Toronto, ☎ 416-588-3934. Africa-inspired home furnishings. African fabrics for clothing, decorator-accents or upholstery. Tues-Sat, 11 am-6 pm; Sun, noon-5 pm.

Burke's Greeting & Gifts, 1032 St. Clair Ave W, Toronto, ☎ 416-656-5366. Afrocentric cards, dolls, figurines, prints, posters, books and African-Canadian calendars. Mon-Sat, 10 am-6 pm.

Eman Fine Arts, 867 Main St E, Hamilton, ☎ 905-544-2244. Afrocentric art prints and gift items. By appointment only.

Mirror Images, 15 Courleigh Square, Hamilton, ☎ 905-846-4914.

Tribal, 250 Carlton Street, Toronto, ☎ 416-975-5566. African arts and crafts south of the Sahara and the Diaspora. Large selection of Afrocentric postcards and greeting cards. Mon-Sat, 10 am-6 pm.

World Art Deco, 803 Queen St W, Toronto, ☎ 416-363-6340. African and Caribbean masks, statues, paintings, prints, jewelry and music items. Tues-Sat, 10 am-6 pm.

Bookstores

Bailey's Christian Book Supplies, 3064 Dundas St W, Toronto, ☎ 416-767-7796. Christian and African books. Mon-Fri, 9:30 am-8 pm; Sat, 9:30-6 pm.

Spas

Jean Pierre Esthetics and Spa, One Charles Street, Toronto, ☎ 416-964-2505. African-Canadian-owned professional spa. Advanced hair and skin care specialists. Face and body treatments, hair removal, professional manicures and pedicures, and much more. Call for an appointment. Mon, Tues, Thurs & Fri, 10 am-8 pm; Sat, 10 am-4 pm; closed Sun and Wed.

Restaurants

◆ African

Kingdom of Ethiopia Restaurant, 10 Young Street, Hamilton, ☎ 905-527-1099. Mon-Thurs, 11 am-10 pm; Fri-Sat, 11 am-midnight. Sun, 4 pm-midnight.

◆ Caribbean

Albert's Real Jamaican Foods, 542 St. Clair Ave W, Toronto, ☎ 416-658-9445.

Bachus Roti Shop, 216 Close Ave, Toronto, ☎ 416-532-8191, fax 416-538-7684. Meat and vegetarian rotis.

Barb's Roti Shop, 1181 Lake Shore Rd E, Mississauga, ☎ 905-278-4713. Specializes in Guyanese and Caribbean cuisine. Tues-Sat, 1:30 am-9 pm; Sun, 11:30 am-9 pm.

Canadian Caribbean Restaurant, 1598 Queen St W, Toronto, ☎ 416-538-6292.

Caribbean Delite, 8 George St N, Brampton, ☎ 905-455-6699. Traditional West Indian cuisine: oxtail, roti, beef and chicken patties, curried chicken and goat. Mon-Thurs, 11 am-9:30 pm; Fri, 11 am-10:30 pm; Sat, 11 am-9 pm.

Circle B Restaurant, 726 St. Clair Ave W, Toronto, ☎ 416-656-5680. Jamaican and Canadian cuisine. Features traditional West Indian cuisine and jerk and fried chicken, oxtail, curried goat and chicken. Open daily, 10 am-2:30 am.

Club Epiphany Restaurant & Lounge, 11 Arrow Rd, North York, ☎ 416-740-9389. Classy Jamaican and Canadian restaurant. Breakfast, lunch and dinner. Sunday brunch includes saltfish, mackerel, dumplings, callaloo, curried goat, oxtail, rice and peas. Open daily, 7 am-1 am. Reggae and dance music at night. See listing under *Entertainment.*

Club Paradise, 220 Attwell Drive, Etobicoke, ☎ 416-213-1999 or 416-213-1993. Caribbean-style restaurant/nightclub. Caribbean and Cajun cuisine. Live entertainment. Restaurant hours vary; call first. See listing under *Entertainment.*

Don's West Indian Restaurant, 1748 St. Clair W, Toronto, ☎ 416-658-7365.

Genei's Restaurant, 4699 Keele Street, Toronto, ☎ 416-661-7820. Classy authentic Caribbean and international cuisine, vegetarian dishes. Dress code (semi-formal). Mon-Fri, 11 am-3 pm and 5 pm-8 pm; Sat buffet, 7 am-3 pm and 5 pm-8 pm; Sunday brunch, 11 am-3 pm.

New Taste of Jamaica Restaurant, 1822 Jane Street, Toronto, ☎ 416-243-2053. Traditional West Indian cuisine: oxtail, curried chicken and goat, roti, beef and chicken patties, tropical drinks. Mon-Thurs, 11 am-9 pm; Fri-Sat, 11 am-11 pm.

Island Foods, two Toronto locations: 1182 King St W, ☎ 416-532-6298 and 900 Dufferin St (Dufferin Mall), ☎ 416-532-5338. Traditional West Indian cuisine: chicken, beef, goat and vegetable roti entrées, beef patties, bean cake, seafood and a selection of tropical drinks. Casual, informal setting. Mon-Sat, 11:30 am-9:30 pm. ☆ *Specially recommended.*

Ontario

Islandville Restaurant, 1876 Finch Ave W, Weston, ☎ 416-635-2811. Jamaican and Canadian cuisine. Specialty is jerk pork and jerk chicken.

Jamaica House, 2531 Finch Ave W, Weston, ☎ 416-744-2913. Jamaican cuisine and features oxtail, curried goat and chicken, stew beef and fish. Open daily, noon-11 pm.

Jerklicious Caribbean & Canadian Restaurant, 22 The Esplanade, Toronto, ☎ 416-368-2904. Mon-Fri, 11:30 am-9:45 pm; Sat, noon-9:45 pm; Sun, 11:30 am-4 pm.

Mobay Caribbean Cuisine, 200 Carlton Street, Toronto, ☎ 416-925-7950. Mon-Thurs, 11:30 am-11 pm; Fri, 11:30 am-1 am. Sat, 11:30 am-noon.

Mr. Jerk Restaurant (several locations), 3050 Don Mills, Toronto, ☎ 416-491-3593. Jamaican cuisine. Specialty is Boston-style jerk pork and jerk chicken.

Palamino West Indian Restaurant & Catering, 83 Kennedy Road, Brampton, #24, ☎ 905-459-2244. Canadian and island cuisine. Features curried meats such as goat, chicken, and shrimp, spicy fried chicken, jerk chicken and cow foot, as well as soup and Irish moss. Mon-Sat, 7 am-9 pm; call first.

Ralph's Take-out, 6650 Finch Ave W, Etobicoke, ☎ 416-674-7765. Specialty is curried goat, oxtail, patties, yams and bananas.

Real Jerk, 709 Queen St E, Toronto, ☎ 416-463-6906. Popular Caribbean restaurant.

Shanty's Restaurant, 1806 Eglinton Ave W, Toronto, ☎ 416-785-1205. Jamaican cuisine. Curried goat, oxtail, beef patties, jerk chicken. Mon-Sat, 10 am-midnight. Sun, noon-10 pm.

Tipper Fast Food, Ltd., 1341 Weston Road, Toronto, ☎ 416-240-8335. Caribbean/Canadian cuisine. International flavor. Mon-Thurs, 10 am-10 pm; Fri, 10 am-11 pm; Sat, 10 am-10 pm.

Willy's Jerk, 2351 A Finch Ave W, Weston, ☎ 416-740-5893. West Indian cuisine. Mon-Sat, 10 am-10 pm; Sun, noon-8 pm.

◆ Cajun/Creole

N'awlins, 299 King St W, Toronto, ☎ 416-595-1958. Popular Cajun-Italian restaurant which features Cajun-spiced chicken breast, sausage-chicken gumbo, coconut shrimp and much more. Smart casual dress. Reservations recommended. Live jazz nightly. Also listed under *Entertainment.* Open daily for dinner, 5 pm-2 am and for lunch, Mon-Fri.

Sammy's New Orleans Creole, 3409 Lake Shore Boulevard W, Toronto, ☎ 416-251-2036. Cajun/creole cuisine which features alligator, monkfish creole, steak, blackened fish, coconut beer shrimp and New Orleans bread pudding. Smart casual dress. Reservations recommended. Tropical indoor patio. Lunch Mon-Fri. Live jazz.

Southern Accent, 595 Markham Street, ☎ 416-536-3211. Cajun and Creole cuisine, featuring catfish filet, piquant shrimp and Louisiana bread pudding. Reservations recommended. Open daily, 5:30 pm-10:30 pm. Bar open until 1 am.

Entertainment

◆ Jazz Nightclubs/Lounges

N'awlins, 299 King St W, Toronto, ☎ 416-595-1958. Live jazz nightly. Mon-Thurs, 8 pm-11:30 pm; Fri-Sat, 9 pm-1 am. Sun, 7 pm-11 pm. See listing under *Cajun/Creole* restaurants.

Trattoria Spinello, 53-55 Colborne Street, Toronto, ☎ 416-955-0306. Monday night jazz.

◆ Dance Nightclubs

Club Paradise, 220 Attwell Drive, Etobicoke, ☎ 416-213-1999 or 416-213-1993. Caribbean-style restaurant/nightclub. Caribbean and Cajun cuisine. Reggae, R&B, soul, hip-hop. Live entertainment. Tues-Sun, 6 pm-3 am.

Cutty's Hideaway Restaurant & Nightclub, 538 Danforth Ave, Toronto, ☎ 416-463-5380. Caribbean-style music and food. Live bands & DJ. Fri-Sat, 8 pm-3 am.

Club Epiphany Restaurant & Lounge, 11 Arrow Road, North York, ☎ 416-740-9329. Dining and dancing establishment with Jamaican flavor. Restaurant and lounge specials daily. Reggae and dance music throughout the week. Call for schedule.

Tempo Toronto, 488 Dupont, Toronto, ☎ 416-588-4726, fax 416-534-3521. Popular contemporary 24-hour nightclub.

◆ Comedy Clubs

Yuk Yuk International Stand-Up Comedy, 2335 Yonge Street, Toronto, ☎ 416-967-6425. All Black comedy shows monthly, featuring the Nubian Disciples of Pryor. Nubian Disciples Hotline, ☎ 416-588-9239. Call for upcoming shows.

◆ Dinner Theaters

Clifford E. Walls Dinner, ☎ 519-258-6253 or 519-971-7790.

Lodging

Bonnevue Cottages, Prince Edward Country, Quinte's Ilse Picton, Ontario, ☎ 416-533-2644. Small, quiet, private cottages two hours from Toronto,

Ontario

overlooking the scenic sand dunes. Sheba's island community on the shores of Westlake, Bay of Quinte Region, offers you a quiet and restful vacation. Nearby is a provincial park drawing thousands of visitors. Fishing, camping, sailing, trails. Large lakefront lots; spacious two-bedroom, comfortably furnished cottages. Call for current rates.

Bed & Breakfasts

Bonnevue Manor, 33 Beaty Ave, Toronto, ☎ 416-536-1455. Bonnevue Manor is a fully restored heritage mansion built in 1891. This Victorian-style private home is located on a lovely tree-lined residential boulevard in Toronto's oldest historic village. Nestled on the shores of Lake Ontario, near beautiful parks, within easy walking distance of public transportation, and only minutes to major downtown attractions. Single and double rooms and private suites, private and semiprivate baths; complimentary breakfast; free parking. Very personalized service and a warm and friendly atmosphere. Call for current rates. ☆ *Specially recommended.*

Media

Radio

◆ R&B

WBLK 93.7 FM, 1867 Yonge Street, Toronto, ☎ 416-932-2207. Progressive.

CHRY 105.5 FM, 4700 Keele Street, Toronto, ☎ 416-736-5293. Caribbean-style music.

◆ Jazz

CIUT 89.5 FM, 91 St. George Street, Toronto, ☎ 416-595-5063. Jazz, reggae, Caribbean and a variety of other music styles. 24 hours.

◆ African

CKLN 88.1 FM, 380 Victoria Street, Toronto, ☎ 416-595-1477.

Newspapers

Caribbean Camera, 2390 Eglinton Ave E, #211 Scarborough, Ontario M1K 2P5, ☎ 416-750-1402. Canada's largest Caribbean newspaper.

Dawn; The Multicultural Newspaper, 7 Wingreen Court, #7, Don Mills, Ontario M3B 1B8, ☎ 416-447-8451. African-Canadian community newspaper.

Pride, 2250 Modland Ave, Scarborough, Ontario M1P 4R9, ☎ 416-609-0058. Canada's national Caribbean and African culture voice. Weekly. Free.

Magazines

Business Connections, 347 Bay Street, #1201, Toronto, Ontario M5H 2R7, ☎ 416-364-1900. Web site: www.blackpages.net. Magazine for African-Canadian entrepreneurs. Seasonal publication.

Jump Magazine, 347 Bay Street, #1201, Toronto, Ontario M5H 2R7, ☎ 416-364-1900. Toronto's carnival magazine. Annual in the summer.

Mic Check, 30 Duncan Street, Toronto, Ontario M5V 2C3, ☎ 416-205-9754. African-Canadian urban contemporary entertainment magazine. Monthly. Free.

The Black Link, 25 Peel Centre Drive, Bramalea, Ontario L6T 5M2, ☎ 905-457-6089, fax 905-457-5346. African-Canadian business directory for metro Toronto and vicinity.

Word, 77 Mowat Ave, #312, Toronto, Ontario M6K 3E3, ☎ 416-588-9673. Toronto's urban culture magazine. E-mail: metword@io.org. Monthly. Free.

Publications

Black Pages, 347 Bay Street, #1201, Toronto, Ontario M5H 2R7, ☎ 416-364-1900. Annual directory of Toronto area African-Canadian businesses.

The Link (Black Business Listing), 25 Peel Centre Drive, Unit 51016-111, Bramalea, Ontario L6T 5M2, ☎ 905-457-6089.

Toronto's Official Visitors Guide, Metropolitan Toronto Convention & Visitors Association, Queen's Quay Terminal at the Harbourfront Centre, 207 Queen's Quay West, Toronto, Ontario M5J 1A7, ☎ 416-203-2600, fax 416-203-6753.

Heritage Tours

African-Canadian Heritage Tour, Chatham-Kent Tourist Bureau, PO Box 944, Chatham, Ontario, Canada N7M 5L3, ☎ 800-561-6125 or 519-354-6125. A self-guided tour that explores African-Canadian heritage sites, including the North American Black Historical Museum and Cultural Centre, historic Sandwich Baptist Church, historic First Baptist Church-John Brown Meeting House, Uncle Tom's Cabin Historic Site, and the Raleigh Township Centennial Museum. Call or write for free brochure guide.

Discover Black History in Toronto Tour, Ontario Black History Society, 10 Adelaide St E, #202, Toronto, Ontario M5C 1J3, ☎ 416-867-9420. The Society's three-hour tour explores the presence of African-Canadians since the 1700s. Visitors will enjoy over 15 sites throughout Toronto and shopping at African-Canadian-owned establishments. Call for more information.

Ontario

Great Adventure Tour Guides, 1702 County Road 27, South Woodslee, Ontario, Canada N0R 1V0, ☎ 800-638-3945 or 519-728-2679, fax 519-728-1018. Great Adventure features group tours to African-American and African-Canadian sites and landmarks in Windsor, Ontario, and Detroit, Michigan. Packages feature visits to Uncle Tom's Cabin, Raleigh Centennial Museum, John Freeman Walls Underground Railroad Museum, Motown Museum and much more. Call or write for more information.

Niagara's Freedom Trail Tour, Region Niagara Tourist Council, 2201 St. Davids Road, Box Thorold, Ontario, Canada L2V 4T7, ☎ 800-263-2988 or 905-984-3626. This self-guided tour travels the Niagara Region's freedom trail sites: Fort Erie, Little Africa/Miller's Bay, Niagara Falls, Negro Burial Ground, Harriet Tubman home and many more. Call or write for free brochure and more information.

Soul in Canada/Black Tourism in Canada, 773 The Queensway, #312, Toronto, Ontario M8Z 6E9, ☎ 416-763-8350. Soul in Canada provides a variety of services to those interested in African-Canadian sites, sounds and foods in the Ontario area. Call Clarence N. Haynes for a personalized tour of Ontario's African-Canadian history and culture.

Underground Railroad Heritage Tours, Inc., 33 Beaty Ave, Toronto, Ontario, Canada M6H 3B3, ☎ 416-536-1455, fax 416-533-2644. This company specializes in a variety of tour packages from one-day tours of the Ontario area to two-day tours of Ontario and Detroit. Tours offered include the Harriet Tubman Tour, the Josiah Henson Tour, the Black Heritage Tour, the Frederick Douglass Tour, the Mary Ann Shadd Tour and the popular Carabana Carnival Tour. Call or write for more information.

Calendar of Annual Events

◆ February

African Canadian Achievement Awards, *Pride* Newspaper, ☎ 416-609-0058. African-Canadian achievement of excellence.

Celebration of Black History Month, Metropolitan Toronto Convention & Visitors Association, ☎ 416-203-2600.

◆ June

DuMaurier Downtown Jazz Festival, Toronto Jazz Society, ☎ 416-363-8717.

Metro International Caravan, International Festival Caravan, ☎ 416-977-0466. Toronto's annual around-the-world party at 40 international pavilions across metro Toronto. Concerts, foods, arts and crafts.

Windsor's Ethnocultural Festival, Multicultural Council of Windsor & Essex County, ☎ 519-255-1127. Food, entertainment, cultural displays. Free admission.

◆ **July**

Carnival, Antigua & Barbuda Department of Tourism & Trade, ☎ 416-961-3085. Annual Caribbean celebration. Calypso music, food.

◆ **August**

Caribana Parade and Festival, Caribbean Cultural Committee, ☎ 416-465-3811, or call the Metropolitan Toronto Convention & Visitors Association, ☎ 416-203-2600. Toronto's world-famous African-Caribbean parade, music and arts festival.

Public Transportation

Toronto Transit Commission (TTC), ☎ 416-393-4636. Local bus schedule and information.

Taxi Services

Diamond Taxicab, ☎ 416-366-6868.

Ontario Area Resources

Caribbean Cultural Committee, 138 Hamilton Street, Toronto, Ontario M4M 2E1, ☎ 416-465-3811.

Creativity Cave Theatre Company, ☎ 416-742-8370. Call for upcoming events. African-Canadian theatre company.

First Friday's, Inc., Box 114, 123 Queen Street, Toronto M5H 2MB, ☎ 416-441-0792. African-Canadian after-work networking and socializing organization. Call for upcoming events.

Metropolitan Toronto Convention & Visitors Association, Queen's Quay Terminal at the Harbourfront Centre, 207 Queen's Quay West, Toronto, Ontario M5J 1A7, ☎ 416-203-2600, fax 416-203-6753.

Multicultural Council of Windsor & Essex County, ☎ 519-255-1127.

Soul in Canada/Black Tourism in Canada, 773 The Queensway, #312, Toronto, Ontario M8Z 6E9, ☎ 416-763-8350.

Toronto Jazz Society, ☎ 416-363-8717.

Ontario

We Are One Theatre Productions, ☎ 416-516-8419. Black Caribbean theater company. Call for upcoming events.

Windsor Essex County & Pelee Island Convention & Visitors Bureau, 333 Riverside Drive W, City Centre #103, Windsor, Ontario N9A 5K4, ☎ 800-265-3633 or 519-255-6530, fax 519-255-6192. Call for upcoming events.

Appendix

We are pleased to list a selection of bed & breakfasts, resorts, beaches and cruises that are popular with African-American travelers. The businesses profiled here are generally owned or operated by African-Americans.

Bed and Breakfasts

◆ Alabama

Cottonwood Mineral Hot Springs and Motel, 600 Hot Springs Rd., Cottonwood, AL 36320, ☎ 800-526-7727 or 334-691-4101. A subsidiary of *Upscale* magazine and Bronner Bros. Cosmetics Mfg., this "Rolls Royce" of spas has lodging, delicious meals, therapeutic massages and other rejuvenating packages that include access to the mineral waters. RV hookups, massages, bicycle rental and much more. View their Web site at www. wiregrassarea.com/classifieds/hotsprings.html.

◆ California

Terrace Manor, 1353 Alvarado Terrace, Los Angeles, CA 90006. See *Los Angeles* listing.

◆ Georgia

Weekender, Sapelow, GA 31327. ☎ 912-485-2277. See listing in the *Atlanta* chapter for more information.

Wise House, in the Nickey Lake area of Atlanta, GA. ☎ 404-691-WISE (691-9473); e-mail: wisehouse@juno.com. Call for directions. See their listing in the *Atlanta* chapter for additional information.

◆ Indiana

Le Chateau Delaware Bed & Breakfast Inn, 1456 North Delaware St, Indianapolis, IN 46202. ☎ 317-636-9156. See the *Indianapolis* chapter for more information.

◆ Louisiana

Lagniappe, 1925 Peniston St, New Orleans, LA 70115. ☎ 800-317-2120 or ☎ 504-899-2120. See *New Orleans* listing.

La Maison á L'Avenue Jackson, 1740 Jackson Avenue, New Orleans, LA 70113. ☎ 504-522-1785, fax 504-566-0405. E-Mail: aaa@I-way.net. See the *New Orleans* chapter for additional information.

Wisteria Inn Bed & Breakfast, 2127 Esplanade Ave, New Orleans, LA 70119. ☎ 504-558-0181 or 504-943-8418.

◆ Massachusetts

Shearer Cottage, Rose Avenue, Oak Bluffs, MA 62557. ☎ 508-693-2364. See *Boston* chapter for details.

Twin Oaks Inn, Eight Edgartown Road, PO Box 1767, Vineyard Haven, MA 02568. ☎ 508-693-8633, fax ☎ 508-522-1122. See *Boston* chapter for additional information.

◆ Mississippi

Fort-Daniel Hall LLC Bed & Breakfast, 184 S. Memphis, Holly Springs, MS 38635, ☎ 601-252-6807. Located 35 miles south of Memphis, TN. Built in 1850 for the Hugh Craft family, this home is among 61 antebellum homes in the Holly Springs area. Its three spacious guest rooms are uniquely decorated in early American, European and Asian style. Some rooms have private bath, some shared. A full Southern-style breakfast is served each morning. Call for rates and reservations.

◆ Missouri

Somewhere Bed & Breakfast, 2049 Sidney St, St. Louis, MO 63104. ☎ 800-730-2PAM or 314-664-4PAM, fax 314-773-0PAM. E-mail: somewherep@aol.com. This "nowhere from somewhere" bed and breakfast pampers guests with candlelight dinners, full breakfasts, therapeutic massages, manicures and pedicures. Located one block west of historic Benton Park, Somewhere Bed & Breakfast was built in 1881 and is a three-story, second-empire, Victorian brick-and-stone house. It features a large parlor on the second floor, Italian marble fireplaces, a Victorian garden, two luxurious guest suites, and a spa. Call for current rates and reservations.

◆ New Mexico

Apache Canyon Ranch, #4 Canyon Drive, Canoncito, NM 87026. ☎ 800-808-8310 or 505-836-7220. This bed and breakfast is just 20 miles outside Albuquerque, and was part of the Herrera Ranch, an historic home for Native Americans dating back 500 years. Surrounded by several hundred acres of rolling hills, distant views and rich Native American culture, visitors can explore the area or just relax and enjoy the tranquil setting. Breakfasts are a combination of Southern and Southwestern cooking, and guests are spoiled with afternoon teas and evening sherry. Accommodates small and large groups. Call for current rates and reservations.

La Tienda Inn, 445-447 West San Francisco St, Sante Fe, NM 87501. ☎ 800-889-7611 or 505-989-8259. Just four blocks from the Santa Fe Plaza, La Tienda Inn was built in the 1930s and is an historic adobe compound. All seven guest rooms are individually furnished with antiques and furniture designed and built in northern New Mexico. The charming inn has a romantic fountain, garden and courtyard. Guests will enjoy fresh flowers, bottled water, tasteful artwork and a generous breakfast served in one of the private rooms or in the garden during the summer. Call for reservations and current rates.

◆ North Carolina

Morehead Manor Bed & Breakfast, 914 Vickers Ave, Durham, NC 27701, ☎ 888-437-6333 or 919-687-4366, fax 919-687-4245. Originally built in 1910 for the CEO of Liggett & Meyers Tobacco Company, the two-story Colonial-style home has four guest rooms. Rooms have queen- or king-size beds and private baths. Guests have access to five common rooms, with piano, game table, fireplace and books. A full breakfast is served each morning. Morehead Manor is conveniently located just two blocks from the new Durham Bulls Athletic Park and is close to shopping, downtown Durham, Duke University, and North Carolina Central University, and just minutes from Raleigh-Durham International Airport. Call for current rates and reservations.

◆ New York

Akwaba Mansion, 347 McDonough St, Brooklyn, NY 11218, ☎ 718-455-5958. See *New York City* chapter.

White House Berries, Inc., Route 8, Bridgewater, NY 13313, ☎ 315-732-1963. See *New York City* chapter.

◆ Ohio

Henderson House, 1544 Atcheson St, Columbus, OH 43202, ☎ 614-258-3463. Once the home of President Rutherford B. Hayes, this 19th-century farm house has accommodated guests the likes of Paul Robeson, Willie Mayes, Duke Ellington and a number of other celebrities and dignitaries. The Georgian-style home is in the heart of Columbus and is minutes away from Columbus' area attractions and shopping centers. Call for current rates and reservations.

◆ Oregon

Woods House, 333 North Main St, Ashland, OR 97520, ☎ 541-488-1598, fax 541-482-8027. E-mail: Woodshse@mind.net. Web site: www.mind. net/woodshouse. This 1908 craftsman-style bed and breakfast inn is within minutes of downtown Ashland. Accommodations include six sunny rooms with in-room private baths, amenities, reading material and fresh flowers. Breakfast is served in the dining room or in the garden on warm summer mornings. Woods House has been listed in *Best Places to Stay in the Pacific Northwest, Northwest Best Places* and *America's Wonderful Little Hotels & Inns,* among other travel guides. Call for rates and reservations.

◆ Virginia

Rockland Farm Retreat, 3609 Lewiston Rd, Bumpass, VA 23024, ☎ 540-895-5098 or 301-384-4583. Located about 75 miles south of Washington, DC. See their listing in the Washington, DC chapter for more information. Rockland features gourmet dinners, antique furnishings, magnificent views and a rich African-American history. Call for current rates and reservations.

Appendix

B.D. Williams House, Seattle, Washington
Photo courtesy of Williams House

◆ Washington

B.D. Williams House, 1505 Fourth Ave N, Seattle, WA 98109-2909, ☎ 800-880-0810 or 206-285-0810, fax 206-285-8526. Located in the historic Queen Ann Hill area and minutes from downtown Seattle, this Edwardian-style bed and breakfast was built in 1905 and has commanding views of the Cascade Mountains, the Seattle skyline and Puget Sound. Each of five guest rooms have down comforters and king- or queen-sized beds with both private and shared bath arrangements. Guests are greeted each morning with a variety of breakfast choices. Call for current rates and reservations.

Blue Rose, 1811 Ninth St, Anacortes, WA 98221, ☎ 360-293-5175.

Resorts

Hillside Inn, Rd 600, East Stroudsburg, 1½ hours from New York City. Off of Route 209, 1½ miles north of Marshalls Creek, PA, ☎ 717-223-8238. See the *New York City* chapter for more information.

Popular Beaches

American Beach, Amelia Island, Florida, about 40 miles northeast of Jacksonville, ☎ 800-733-2668.

Atlantic Beach, Horry County, South Carolina, off US 17 near the junction with Route 9, near the North Carolina border. ☎ 803-446-7166. Chamber of Commerce, ☎ 800-356-3016.

Ink Well Beach, Oak's Bluff, Martha's Vineyard, Massachusetts.

Cruises

Jamaica Jam, Annual African-American cruise package featuring a variety of African-American entertainment, private African-American movie theater visiting various Caribbean ports of call. See the *Los Angeles* chapter under *Travel Agents* for additional information.

African-American Mega-Churches

Listed below are popular Black churches throughout the United States that have sizeable congregations and may be of interest to travelers. Call for dates and times of services and special events.

◆ Atlanta

New Birth Missionary Baptist Church, 2778 Snapfinger Rd, Decatur, ☎ 770-981-5594.

World Changers Ministries (non-denominational), PO Box 490124, College Park, ☎ 770-907-9490.

◆ Chicago

Salem Baptist Church, 11800 South Indiana Ave, Chicago, ☎ 773-821-4300.

United Church of Christ, 400 West 95th St, Chicago, ☎ 773-962-5650.

◆ Dallas

St. Luke "Com munity" United Methodist Church, 5710 East R. L. Thornton Frwy, ☎ 214-821-2970.

◆ Detroit

Hartford Memorial Baptist Church, 18900 James Couzens Hwy, Detroit, ☎ 313-861-1300.

Hope United Methodist Church, 26275 Northwestern Hwy, Southfield, ☎ 810-356-1020.

Word of Faith International Christian Center (non-denominational), 23800 W. Chicago, Redford Township, ☎ 313-255-7000.

Appendix

◆ **Indianapolis**

Light of the World Christian Church, 5640 East 38ᵗʰ St, Indianapolis, ☎ 317-543-2266.

◆ **Los Angeles**

Crenshaw Christian Center (non-denominational), 7901 S. Vermont Ave, Los Angeles, ☎ 213-758-3777.

West Angeles Church of God in Christ, 3045 S. Crenshaw Blvd, Los Angeles, ☎ 213-733-8300.

◆ **Memphis**

Mississippi Blvd. Christian Church (non-denominational), 70 N. Bellevue, Memphis, ☎ 901-729-6222.

◆ **New Orleans**

Greater St. Stephen Full Gospel Baptist Church, 3030 Canal St, ☎ 504-895-6800.

◆ **New York City**

Allen AME Church, 111-54 Merrick Blvd, Jamaica, ☎ 718-526-3511.

St. Paul Community Baptist Church, 859 Hendrix St, Brooklyn, ☎ 718-257-1300.

Christian Life Center (non-denominational), 1400 Linden Blvd, Brooklyn, ☎ 718-272-0303.

Riverside Church (non-denominational), 490 Riverside Dr, ☎ 212-870-6700.

◆ **San Francisco/Oakland**

Allen Baptist Church, 8500 A. St, Oakland, ☎ 510-569-9418.

◆ **Washington, DC**

Jericho Baptist Church, 4419 Douglas St, NE, ☎ 202-398-1155.

Greater Mount Calvary Holy Church (non-denominational), 610 Rhode Island Ave, NE, ☎ 202-529-4547.

St. Augustine Catholic Church, 1419 V. St, NW, ☎ 202-265-1470.

Index